LOST PARADISE

ELIZABETH DRAYSON is Emeritus Fellow in Spanish
at Murray Edwards College, University of Cambridge;
she is a specialist in medieval and early modern Spanish
literature and cultural history. The author of *The Moor's
Last Stand*, *The Lead Books of Granada* and *The King
and the Whore*, Drayson has also produced the first
translation and edition of Juan Ruiz's *Libro de buen
amor* to appear in England. She lives in Cambridge.

LOST PARADISE

THE STORY OF GRANADA

ELIZABETH DRAYSON

An Apollo Book

First published in the UK in 2021 by Head of Zeus Ltd
This paperback edition published in the UK in 2022 by Head of Zeus Ltd,
part of Bloomsbury Plc

9 7 5 3 1 2 4 6 8

A catalogue record for this book is available from
the British Library.

ISBN (PB): 9781788547437
ISBN (E): 9781788547444

Maps: Jamie Whyte
Front cover painting: *Hall of the Embassadors*, Alhambra, Granada, 1909 (oil on
canvas) by Joaquín Sorolla y Bastida (1863–1923), © Bridgeman Images.
Back cover image © Shutterstock

Printed and bound in Great Britain by
CPI Group (UK) Ltd, Croydon CR0 4YY

MIX
Paper from
responsible sources
FSC® C171272
FSC
www.fsc.org

Head of Zeus Ltd
5–8 Hardwick Street
London EC1R 4RG
WWW.HEADOFZEUS.COM

For the people of Granada,
past and present.

CONTENTS

'The true paradises are the paradises we have lost.'

Marcel Proust

'To live in the present does not mean that we should be ignorant of the past, when knowledge of it is sought as a means of liberation from the prejudices and misconceptions of today, and as a way of understanding the human mystery, which is the goal of all wisdom.'

Miguel Ángel Ladero Quesada

'Look at the map of Iberia. It is like a taut bull's skin, crisscrossed by the paths left by men and women whose voices and faces we in Spanish America dimly perceive. The message is clear: the identity of Spain is multiple.'

Carlos Fuentes

ACKNOWLEDGEMENTS

◆◆◆◆◆◆◆◆◆◆◆◆◆◆◆◆◆◆

Sincere gratitude is due to the many colleagues and friends both in the United Kingdom and in Spain who have helped and encouraged me in the years taken to research and write this book. I would also like to express my appreciation to the President and Fellows of Murray Edwards College, University of Cambridge, for their practical and moral support for my project. In Granada, very special thanks are due to José María Pérez Lledó of the Ayuntamiento de Granada, who went beyond the call of duty under COVID restrictions to provide me with many beautiful images and reference books, as well as a wealth of useful information. Sincere thanks also to Estrella Corro Delgado, Secretary to the Most Illustrious Mayor of Granada, for her cheerful assistance. I have visited many libraries, archives and museums to conduct research on the history of Granada, and in particular would like to mention Bárbara Jiménez Serrano at the archive of the Alhambra, who welcomed me and made some fascinating material available, as did the archivists and staff of the municipal archives, in particular Eulalia Beltrán García whom I thank for her patience and kindness, Silvia Maroto Romero at the Museo Arqueológico de Granada, the Centro Federico García Lorca, the Centro Europeo de las Mujeres Mariana Pineda, the Palacio de los Olvidados, the Museo Sefardí, the Museo Cuevas del Sacromonte, the Museo de la Mujer Gitana and the Casa-Museo Manuel de Falla; I am immensely grateful to them all for their indispensable help. I have received great support and encouragement from my colleagues Professor José María Pérez Fernández and Dra. Mercedes Castillo Ferreira in Granada, and from the students and colleagues at Cambridge and elsewhere who have shown such interest in my project. I must also acknowledge with thanks the help of Syracuse University Press, who kindly granted permission to reprint a poem from the collection *The Adam of Two Edens* by Mahmoud Darwish.

It has been an enormous pleasure to work with my inimitable agent at A. M. Heath, Bill Hamilton, whose faultless guidance, advice and perceptive understanding of the project have been deeply appreciated. Warmest thanks are due also to my editor, Richard Milbank, ever courteous and thoughtful, who made numerous improvements to the manuscript, and also to Matilda Singer, copy-editor Dan Smith, Jessie Price, Anna Nightingale, Clémence Jacquinet, Anthony Cheetham and the marvellous production team at Head of Zeus who have made this book a reality. Above all, heartfelt gratitude as always to my husband Kiernan Ryan, who is my inspiration, and to my daughter Fiona for her good-humoured encouragement and enthusiasm.

TIMELINE

⋅ ◆ ⋅ ◆ ⋅ ◆ ⋅ ◆ ⋅ ◆ ⋅ ◆ ⋅ ◆ ⋅ ◆ ⋅ ◆ ⋅ ◆ ⋅ ◆ ⋅

PREHISTORY TO AD 711

3450 BC	Diadem found in the Cave of Bats dates from this time.
2600–2100 BC	Earliest art in the region.
2000 BC	First bell-shaped ceramic vessels used in the region of Granada.
1900–1200 BC	Rise of the culture of El Argar, in the future province of Granada.
800 BC	First Phoenician trading posts on the coast of Granada.
700 BC	The alabaster sculpture known as the Lady of Galera dates from this era.
650 BC	Founding of the ancient oppidum of Ilturir, later named Iliberis, by the Iberian Bastetani tribe.
600–400 BC	The statue of the bull of Arjona dates from this era.
400 BC	Lady of Baza, Iberian sculpture found at Cerro del Santuario, dates from this time.
218 BC	Roman Senate designates Hispania as a Roman province.

44 BC	Iliberis becomes a Roman colony.
27 BC	Iliberis becomes a Roman municipality known as Florentia.
AD 300–2	Christian Council of Elvira held in Iliberis.
415	Visigoths enter Hispania.
552	Justinian I, Eastern Roman Emperor, founded the Byzantine province of Spania, which included Iliberis.
570	Visigothic King Liuvigild I conquers Baza and the surrounding area.
624	Visigoths reclaim the southern province of Spania from the Romans.
711	Muslim invasion of Spain and defeat of the Visigoths.

711–1492

711–14	Capture of Granada by Muslim forces under governor Abd al-Aziz, and the building of the first mosque begun.
756	Founding of the Umayyad caliphate in Cordoba.
1016	Zirid dynasty of Muslim sultans rule in Granada, led by Zawi b. Ziri.
1031	Collapse of the Umayyad caliphate.
1085	Fall of Toledo to Christian armies led by King Alfonso VI of Castile.
1090	Almoravids invade Granada, led by Yusuf ibn Tashufin.
1107	Granada becomes the capital of al-Andalus (Muslim Spain).
1156	Granada conquered by Almohad leader Abu Sa'id Uthman.

1237	Founding of Granada as capital of the Nasrid dynasty of Muslim rulers by Sultan Muhammad I.
1248	Surrender of Muslim Seville to the Christian King Fernando III el Santo.
1425	First documentary evidence of the presence of gypsies in Spain, in the form of King Alfonso V of Aragon's royal permit allowing Juan of Egypt to travel in his dominions.
1459–60	Birth of Muhammad XI, Boabdil, last Muslim sultan of Granada.
1492	Surrender of Nasrid Granada to Catholic Monarchs Ferdinand II of Aragon and Isabella I of Castile on 2 January.

1492–1600

1492	Alhambra Decree ordering the conversion or expulsion of all Jews in Spain.
1493	Muhammad XI, Boabdil, sails into exile in north Africa.
1499	First Decree on the assimilation of the gypsy population issued by Ferdinand II of Aragon and Isabella I of Castile, which threatened them with expulsion unless they ceased to wander, and took up acceptable occupations.
1499–1500	Albaicín revolt of Moriscos against the Catholic authorities.
1501	Cardinal Cisneros orders burning of Arabic books and manuscripts in the Plaza Bib-Rambla.
1502	Royal Decree compelling all Muslims in Spain to convert to Christianity.

1504	Death of Isabella I of Castile.
1516	Death of Ferdinand II of Aragon.
1518	Birth of Juan Latino, poet, humanist and first black professor at the University of Granada.
1531	Founding of the University of Granada by King Charles V, Holy Roman Emperor (Charles I of Spain).
1568–70	Morisco uprising or rebellion of the Alpujarras.
1588	Spanish Armada defeated in battle against the English fleet led by Sir Francis Drake. Discovery of the Torre Turpiana parchment and relics on the site of the old Mosque of Granada.
1595	Discovery of the first Lead Books of the Sacromonte.

1600–1900

1609–16	Expulsion of the Moriscos from Spain.
1610	Founding of the Abbey of the Sacromonte by Archbishop Pedro de Castro to house the Torre Turpiana relics and the Lead Books. Edict of Expulsion of all Andalusian Moriscos.
1619	Law obliging all gypsies to settle in towns with a population of 1,000 or more inhabitants or to leave Spain within six months.
1749	The Great Raid, when 9,000 gypsies were arrested by the government.
1768	Building of Granada's first bullring.
1808	Start of the War of Independence between Napoleon and Spain.
1810	Napoleon's troops enter Granada under the command of General Sebastiani.

1812	Spanish Constitution of Cadiz, the founding document of Spanish liberalism.
1831	Execution of Mariana Pineda in Granada.
1833	First cholera epidemic in the province of Granada.
1853	Second cholera epidemic in Granada.
1884	Severe earthquake in Andalusia.
1885	Third cholera epidemic in Granada.
1892	First electric lights installed in the city of Granada and the founding of the General Electricity Company.
1895	Start of the construction of the Gran Vía de Colón.
1898	Birth of the poet Federico García Lorca on 5 June.

1900–2000s

1906	Death of the gypsy Chorrojumo.
1909	The guitarist Andrés Segovia's first concert, aged sixteen, in Granada.
1920	The composer Manuel de Falla moves to Granada.
1921	Defeat of Spanish troops in the campaign to gain control of Morocco.
1922	*Cante jondo* competition in the Alhambra, organized by Federico García Lorca and Manuel de Falla.
1929	Granada is designated an 'artistic city' by royal decree.
1931	Fall of the Spanish monarchy and establishment of the Second Republic.
1936–9	Spanish Civil War.

1936	Granada comes under the control of fascist rebels on 20 July.
	Assassination of Federico García Lorca outside Granada in August.
1939	First visit of General Franco to Granada on 20 April.
1947	Eva Perón, Argentina's First Lady, visits Granada.
1949	The first flamenco club in Franco's Spain, Peña la Platería, opens in the Albaicín.
1955	Spain joins the United Nations.
1970	Construction workers' strike in Granada.
1971	First world conference of the International Romany Union.
1975	Death of General Francisco Franco in Madrid on 20 November.
1978	New Spanish Constitution sanctioned by the King on 27 December.
1982	A new socialist government is elected.
1986	Spain joins the European Union.
1989	Islam is fully recognized by the Spanish state.
2017	New light railway or metro opens in Granada.

INTRODUCTION

◆◆◆◆◆◆◆◆◆◆◆◆◆◆◆◆◆◆

Granada casts a spell on you. As long ago as the ninth century, the Muslim sage Abd al-Malik described it as an idyllic place of enchantment, a view echoed by the fourteenth-century poet and vizier Ibn Zamrak, whose verse graces the walls of the Alhambra. There he sings of Granada as the city that wears a crown upon its forehead, bejewelled with diamond stars, clustered round the ruby that represents the Moorish palace itself. From the German physician Hieronymus Münzer's grand tour of Spain in the late fifteenth century to the English novelist George Borrow's trip to Andalusia in the 1820s, early foreign travellers to the city were bewitched by its splendour. In more recent times, Granada has become Spain's top tourist attraction, where countless visitors flock each year, including film stars, artists, musicians and political figures such as the former American president Bill Clinton and recent First Lady Michelle Obama. The seductive allure of Granada runs deep in the European psyche, so deep that the name of the city even became a brand name for British cinemas, service stations, a model of Ford car and a well-known TV and radio station, while Spain's own Granada chain of theatres was designed using Moorish décor. The name of its most familiar landmark, the Alhambra, meaning 'the Red One', has become a fashionable symbol of luxury, glamour and exoticism used for ranges of wall tiles, fabrics, yarns, men's jeans, cars and beer. It is even the name of a city in Los Angeles County. Romantic and exotic, tragic and nostalgic, the city has resonated with travellers worldwide as a place of peerless beauty which captures the imagination, a place that lives as potently in the mind as in reality. It is the stuff of story and legend, with an unforgettable history to match.

Granada speaks to us through the senses, and perhaps nowhere more so than through its architecture. Looking down on the city from high on the sacred hill of the Sacromonte, what first catches the eye from afar is the great Moorish fortress of the Alhambra, and beneath it, in the old city, the Spanish Renaissance Catholic cathedral. These two sites of cultural and religious power are visible symbols of the meeting of Muslim and Christian civilizations in this place. Perhaps the most striking and familiar aspect of Granada's history is its Moorish past, as capital city of the Nasrid dynasty of Muslim rulers from 1237 to 1492. That past lives on all around, in the winding narrow streets of the old Moorish quarter of the Albaicín, in the old silk market near the cathedral, in ancient walls, fountains, gardens, and most prominently in the Alhambra itself. As the Reconquest of Muslim Spanish territory by Christian armies in the Middle Ages pushed the Muslim border ever southwards, Granada had the distinction of being the final bastion of Islamic rule in Europe, surviving until 2 January 1492, when Boabdil, the last sultan in Spain, relinquished the city to the Christian rulers Ferdinand and Isabella. That day of surrender marked a watershed in Spanish and European history. Over seven centuries of Muslim rule in the Iberian Peninsula came to an end and Spain was unified by religion, language and politics under the Catholic Monarchs. The cathedral of Granada represents the conversion of Islamic Granada to the Christian city it has remained ever since, and where Catholicism is still central to the life of its people.

Because of that great moment of historical and cultural change alone, Granada has a unique importance in the history of Spain and Europe. Less familiar but also vitally significant is its other cultural heritage, which has left covert physical traces in many areas of the city. We can appreciate this heritage in visual form if we visit the Albaicín district, opposite the Alhambra hill, where hundreds of metres of monumental city walls still stand, built in the time of the Zirid dynasty of Muslims in the eleventh century. Recent restoration works have revealed how the Zirids actually laid their walls on top of Roman ramparts, which were in turn built on an already existing defence wall made by the Iberians, the first people to populate the place in the sixth century before Christ. Not far away, in the Realejo district, are reminders of Granada's ancient Jewish population, whose medieval messages and signs carved into the walls of the buildings are still visible, while the popular Sacromonte district boasts a honeycomb of caves which were, and still are, the dwellings of the Granadan gypsies. The importance of Granada's past as a multicultural and multiracial society is central to the debate over the way Spaniards see themselves and define their identity. Equally crucial to this debate is Granada's recent cultural evolution, in which the Islamic past remains vividly alive and has been reinvigorated by the opening in 2003 of the first mosque in the city for five hundred years, and by the creation of a number of small museums, such as the Sephardic and gypsy museums, that celebrate the city's varied cultural legacy.

Granada is not only important because of its historical and material reality. Granada is an idea, an image, a utopian dream that has beguiled many people worldwide. Its intense beauty and the sensuous, sophisticated lifestyle of its Islamic rulers lent it the charms of an earthly paradise for its inhabitants as well as for the writers, travellers, artists and musicians it inspired, from the ninth century to the twenty-first. After the Christian conquest in 1492, it became, and continues to be, a symbol of great nostalgia and longing for many Arab and Muslim people, as well as one of rebellion against repression, and of the desire to recreate an idealized past there.

This is a book about a unique and pivotal European city. While there are a number of interesting biographies of major cities such as London, Rome, Istanbul, Jerusalem and Barcelona, this is the first narrative history of the city of Granada for English-speaking readers, which celebrates and explores the distinctive, evolving identity of the place. It is an account which brings to the fore the image of the city as a lost paradise, reveals it as a place of perpetual contradiction, of beauty and violence, and links it to the great dilemma over Spain's true identity as a nation.

My aim is to paint a compelling portrait of the city of Granada from its origins to the present day, taking the reader on a vibrant historical voyage of discovery that uncovers its many-layered past and establishes it as Spain's most important city. This is the story of a vanished Eden, of a place that questions and probes Spain's deep obsession with forgetting, and with erasing historical and cultural memory. The rich heritage of this smouldering city at the heart of Spanish history and culture is the epitome of Spain's true identity. This is a book for general readers, whatever their religious and political beliefs, and is structured broadly chronologically, allowing the often dramatic and at times momentous events and lives of the Granadan people to be set in their historical context, acknowledging their distance from our own lives and diminishing the risk of unduly imposing our present preoccupations on them. It is not meant to be a comprehensive reference book for all aspects of Granada, nor is it a guidebook that examines every nook and cranny exhaustively. This is the story of Granada as the key to Spanish history and identity. It is not a history of religion in Granada, although religion is of prime importance to the past and present life of the city. Its exceptional story unfolds through the lives of individuals – among them sultans and kings, soldiers and poets, nuns and dancers – who have shaped the character of the city over many centuries.

Such a panorama demands the subtle shifting of a kaleidoscope of varied sources. The voices and opinions of contemporary

Granadans are vital fragments of the overall picture, those immigrants, gypsies, artists, museum-keepers, tradesmen and many others who make the city what it is today. There are also many written materials which uncover the patterns of Granadan history, including historical documents themselves, mostly in Spanish. From the Middle Ages to the present, Spanish historians have written and rewritten their accounts of the city, at times fabricating their materials to create an image of Granada which suited their religious or political purposes. Alongside these, and often contradicting them, are more factual materials, many lodged among the rich documentation carefully guarded in Granada's municipal archives, cathedral archives and the archive of the Alhambra itself among others. In these archives we find legal documents, sales and purchases of property, architectural records and the records of the Inquisition to name just a few. To take a couple of instances, we can read copies of the documents signed by King Ferdinand II of Aragon, Queen Isabella I of Castile and Sultan Muhammad XI, Boabdil, outlining the fateful terms of surrender of the city in 1492. Another document, a deed of property transfer, shows us that the Sultana Aixa, Boabdil's mother, owned and sold land and houses in the city and its outskirts in the late fifteenth century. In later times, national and local journalistic records give us eyewitness accounts of the terrible violence the city suffered during the Civil War of 1936, while biographical writing, such as Ian Gibson's life of the poet Federico García Lorca, gives insights into the personal lives of many eminent Granadans. Not all written sources are strictly factual or purport to be accurate. The ever-growing body of prose fiction and poetry that retells the history of the city or meditates upon its fate is at times truer and more poignant than a conventional chronicle. The bestselling 2009 novel *The Hand of Fatima* by Barcelona lawyer Ildefonso Falcones makes real the terrible plight of the Moriscos of Granada in the years just before their expulsion, experienced through the eyes of a young mule-driver torn between two religions and the love of two women. Falcones gives us a powerful image of a city and province pervaded by tension and conflict, by secrecy and deceit, using individual characters to express the anguish of many. The tale of Granada as it has evolved in all manner of literature over the last thousand years has moulded an image of the city which is recognized internationally.

Visual art and culture also play their part in the kaleidoscope of sources. In early modern drawings of Granadan Moriscos in traditional costume, in great historical paintings of the nineteenth century that depict the surrender of the city in 1492 from a political angle, in contemporary Arab painting and sculpture, Granada has been celebrated and its image refashioned by art. Early nineteenth-century photography and prints allow us to relish the ethereal qualities of the Alhambra palace or, in extreme contrast, to shudder at the series of illustrations depicting the horrors of an outbreak of cholera in the city. Music and dance are there too – the traditional Morisco *zambra* danced barefoot, gypsy flamenco, the plangent strains of the Granadan guitar, Arab song and rhythms, all convey the vivacious yet soulful cultural hybridity of the city and its unique musical flavour.

Perhaps the most easily accessible sources for this book are those that form the city itself, tangible sources, archaeological remains, extraordinary architecture, sculpture and monuments. The latest archaeological digs give physical substance to the most up-to-date theories, as the skeleton of the city is gradually revealed, uncovering over two thousand years of Granada's past and baring its ancient Iberian, Roman and Visigothic bones. Muslim and Christian architecture vie with or overlay each other where former mosques have been converted to churches, and minarets to bell-towers. They tell the story of Christian conquest in stone, while sculptures of Christopher Columbus bowing to Queen Isabella I of Castile, of Boabdil, last sultan of Granada, accepting the rose of reconciliation, and a statue of the Jewish translator and poet Yehuda ibn Tibbon silently represent the multicultural history of the city.

There are other sources of inspiration too, which engage us because of their perspectives. There are maps, including an early drawing of the city limits of Islamic Granada, showing the flexible boundaries of the medieval city. In the present, a casual glance at a modern street map immediately shows the named districts of the city – the old Moorish quarter of the Albaicín, the even older Jewish district of Realejo, Cartuja with its exuberant Baroque monastery and site of the university, the gypsy district on the sacred hill, the Sacromonte, all with their narrow streets of twists and turns, clustered round the old town centre of Bib-Rambla, with the Alhambra on the hill above. On the outskirts, the streets form a modern grid of apartment blocks and offices, shops and department stores. But if we climb to the top of the Saint Nicholas viewing point or *mirador*, or up the steep slopes towards the Alhambra, the impression is quite different. We see a white city inlaid with conifers so dark they are almost black, red-tiled roofs amid a patchwork of greenery against which the lofty walls of the reddish Alhambra and the yellow stone of the cathedral and old city are arresting. In the distance lie the snow-capped peaks of the Sierra Nevada mountain range. It is a breath-taking prospect. Watching the sun go down over the mountains, we might well understand why so many have spoken of Granada as a paradise on earth.

But perspective is crucial. If our lens zooms out further and we take in an aerial view, Granada, girdled by mountains and watered by four rivers, stretches out to meet the great fertile plain of the *vega* to the west of the city, once a vital frontier between the Muslim state and Christian territory, dotted with small villages often perched in dramatic and precarious locations on rocky crags and hillsides. These different standpoints, these visual sources, expose fundamental features of the character of the city. The street map speaks of its cultural hybridity, the *mirador* of Saint Nicholas its natural beauty and the aerial view charts the vital features of its geographical terrain which have been so important to Granada's history.

This book does not have a conventional chronological structure because Granada does not have a single, linear history. It is a place of many histories, made up of too many lives and interlinked fates to conform to a one-dimensional narrative sequence. The span of time from prehistory up until 1492 bears the indelible scars of countless conflicts, of many invasions, that left a land deeply fractured by racial, religious and political discord. Despite the rhetoric of political and religious unity that prevailed after 1492, difference was not eliminated but repressed. The seeds of future disharmony sown in Granada's early history grew into religious rifts and unreconciled oppositions that rose to the surface and were played out over the next five centuries. The fragmented yet exceptionally diverse history of Granada is in many ways unique, and demands a narrative structure that reflects its unusual trajectory. This book responds to that demand in having two separate yet intersecting axes, one that explores the city and province as a place through time, and another that dwells upon those people of Granada who were never its rulers, but whose lives had a profound influence on its society and culture. Traditional chronological narration is punctuated by chapters that step outside that narrative to consider these specific groups of people, the Jews, the gypsies, and the women of Granada, all marginalized, persecuted or oppressed, but fundamental to the history of the city. Their stories begin in the distant past, and unfold over the centuries up to the present, encompassing themes of great interest to us today – anti-Semitism, racial oppression and women in society – and providing an opportunity for deeper reflection on the vital role they played in the evolution of their city.

I have also focused on motifs, ideas and themes that have repeated themselves throughout the history of the city, weaving a pattern not so much of difference and rupture as one of continuity and coherence. These motifs and themes stitch the narrative together and roughly correspond to aspects of what I describe as cityscape, landscape and mindscape. Important motifs of the cityscape include gardens, from the romantic Generalife of the Alhambra to the modest domestic gardens of Granada's many *cármenes* or Moorish houses; local customs and *fiestas*, such as the annual festival of Saint Cecilius, which takes the form of a mass pilgrimage every year in February to the Sacromonte hillside, where a huge picnic takes place; the subterranean world beneath the city and its outskirts; sites of power in the form of key buildings and monuments, such as the Alhambra, the cathedral and the Abbey of the Sacromonte. The motifs of landscape relate to water, running and still, and in particular to the advanced system of water management introduced by the Arabs; to mountains as protectors and as holy places; caves as forges, dwellings and sites of holy relics; to snow, ice and heat and its relationship to the natural history of the Granadan environment, and how they have played a role in its warfare and conflict. Some of the motifs of mindscape relate to the idea of paradise, lost and regained, to many forms of fakery and forgery, to war, conflict and violence, and to the city of Granada as it has been imagined.

This book is about Granada, but it is also about Spain's relationship with the city. There is a longstanding, ongoing debate among Spanish scholars, intellectuals and writers about the true nature of the nation's identity. It tends to polarize into two groups, those often right-wing polemicists who insist on a strictly European, Christian heritage in which Catholicism is the defining aspect, and those often left-wing liberals who acknowledge the need to embrace Spain's multicultural past in the form of its Islamic and Jewish legacy, and who at times put forward the idea that Spain's unique history might serve as a model or inspiration for the future relationships of European countries with non-Europeans. Often the argument between the two sides is virulent. I hope that this book may respond to some of the issues raised by this polemic, and that it may give Granada the importance and status it deserves in the history of the Spanish people.

GRANADA
THE PLACE I

Prehistory to 1492

PARADISE AND POMEGRANATES

◆·◆·◆·◆·◆·◆·◆·◆·◆·◆·◆·◆·◆·◆·◆·◆

THE EARTHLY PARADISE

On decorative tiles and tourist mementos, in guidebooks and on postcards, the verses addressed to a blind beggar by the nineteenth-century Mexican poet Francisco Icaza have become well known for the touching feelings they express:

> Give him alms, good woman, for there is no greater sadness in life
> Than being a blind man in Granada.[1]

These lines that convey the anguish of being unable to see the physical environment of the city highlight its potent visual appeal. Granada is a place of powerful and elemental natural beauty. Capital city of the province of Granada, it lies at the foot of the great Sierra Nevada mountain range, whose Mount Mulhacén, the legendary resting place of one of the last sultans of Granada, towers above the city at a height of 3,478 metres, making it the highest peak in the Iberian Peninsula. The snows that cap these mountains melt in spring and summer, swelling the four rivers, the Beiro, the Darro, the Genil and the Monachil, which flow down and meet where the city spreads out below. Yet at its highest points, Granada is 738 metres above sea level, rising on three hills or plateaux of the Sierra

Nevada, the Sabika, the Albaicín, and the Sacromonte. Below these hills lies the celebrated *vega*, the richest part of the province, upon whose fertile plain irrigated by ice-cold mountain springs grow trees, flowers, fruits, vegetables and grains in abundance, tended by the folk who live in the scattered white-washed villages of its forty-seven districts. It is a place of strong natural contrasts, fiery summer heat and frosty winters, brilliant sunlight and dramatic shade, mountain heights and deep valleys. It is small wonder that Granada has become an image of paradise on earth.

This vision of an earthly paradise has an ancient history. The Greeks and Romans linked happiness with gardens, and their literature is rich in descriptions of utopian natural surroundings. In his work *The Statesman,* Plato recalls happy times when Chronos reigned in a land of plentiful fruits, trees and plants, with a temperate climate, and Virgil and Ovid evoke a Golden Age that echoes the Elysian fields of the *Aeneid.* But mostly we think of the Bible story in the book of Genesis[2] describing a place called Eden in the east, watered by four rivers, blessed with trees for shade and food, and strewn with gold and precious stones. This paradise is first and foremost a garden, based on the Old Persian word *apiri-daeza* meaning an orchard surrounded by a wall. In ancient Hebrew, this word was taken over as *pardès,* which had become *paradeisos* by the time the Septuagint, the earliest Greek translation of the scriptures from Hebrew, was written in the last two or three centuries before Christ. Paradise was believed to represent natural bounty, reflected in its abundant water flowing from four rivers, perpetual springtime, sweet fragrances and plentiful fruits such as pomegranates, apples, figs, olives and vines, and it was often located on a high mountain. This was certainly the image of Eden created in his work *Cathemerinon* by the Roman poet Prudentius (*c.*AD 328–410), who was born in Spain; two centuries later, the great polymath Saint Isidore of Seville (AD 560–636) referred to paradise as the Happy Isles and believed it was a real place as well as an imaginative concept. His conviction that paradise still existed was part of a tradition older than Christianity. In the ancient Jewish Book of Jubilees, we read how Noah divided the earth among his three sons, giving the Garden of Eden, bounded to the north by the River Don and to the south by the Nile, to Shem. Much later, Christopher Columbus also believed firmly in the existence of an earthly paradise, which he located at a high altitude, in a region of pleasant climate and endless supply of clean water.

The ideal paradise garden of the medieval West was initially an enclosed area, a *hortus conclusus*, of the kind monks cultivated in monasteries for medicinal plants, and also for meditation, as a retreat for the spirit. This image was echoed in the Muslim idea of paradise too. The gardens and palaces of Islam reflected the traditions of Persian paradises whose enclosures offered protection from the desert winds, and shelter for animals. For the dwellers in the desert, the idea of such an oasis was envisioned in the after-life. In the Koran[3] paradise is a garden of delight, flowing water, fruit, gold and precious stones, and the seventh heaven in the Prophet Muhammad's nocturnal journey, recorded in the *Book of the Ladder of Mohammad*, is an orchard, enclosed by walls, with fountains and fruit trees.[4]

In past times, remoteness and isolation amid a magnificent geo-graphical setting that echoed images of paradise in its mountain fastnesses, four rivers, cornucopia of trees, fruit and grain, and beguiling climate all combined to give Granada a special cachet which set it apart from other Spanish cities, and in particular from its Andalusian rivals Seville and Cordoba. Muslim writers, both native and foreign, were the first to sing the city's praises, beginning in the ninth century with Abd al-Malik, the Muslim doctor of law and native of Granada who wrote of the mountains 'smoothly varnished in milk-white and pink', whose melting snow provides 'crystalline waters'. Here Nature unfurls 'as if it had been touched by a magic wand'. He described the people who inhabited the banks of the two gold-bearing rivers of Granada, the Genil and the Darro, as 'carefree folk who lived under the light of the same sun which gives us life today'.

The eleventh-century sultan of the Zirid dynasty, Abd Allah ibn Buluqqin, who we will meet again in Chapter 3, recalls how his men realized that Granada had become the main city of the region: '… they contemplated a beautiful plain, full of streams and groves, watered by the river Genil… They looked upon the mount where today Granada stands, and understood that it was the centre of the entire region… ' Both descriptions draw attention to the natural beauty and running water which later became such a fundamental feature of the gardens in the medieval urban spaces of Nasrid Granada.

The account of the city of Granada written by the Damascene prince and warrior Abulfeda in his early fourteenth-century geography of Spain develops these ideas further. He states: 'In Granada there are various places to relax and it resembles Damascus, surpassing the latter because it rises on an eminence which dominates its fertile valley which is open to the north.' Perhaps it was natural for Abulfeda to compare Granada with his native city but this alignment with Damascus, which he claims is actually outdone by its Andalusian counterpart, became a constant refrain in Arab literature. Over a hundred years later, the Egyptian traveller and writer Abd al-Basit visited Spain between December 1465 and February 1466, during the reign of Abu l-Hasan, father of the last Muslim sultan of Granada, Boabdil. Abd al-Basit, who knew Syria well, describes his first impressions of the Nasrid capital:

> Granada strikes me as a pleasant, extensive country, one of the largest in al-Andalus. It is the capital of the Muslim king of al-Andalus and his royal residence, and has a marvellous position, splendid buildings, it is lovely, agreeable, and in an admirable location. I saw many kinds of craftsmanship there, and it resembles Damascus in Syria.

He too emphasizes the presence of running waters, orchards, gardens and vines, then points out that Granada was a place where all manner of culture thrived amid the abundance of nature: 'It is a meeting place of illustrious people, of poets, scientists, artists; the best men of our time are there, amid grand monuments and pleasant spots. Its boundaries have the same size as those of Damascus, but the population is much denser, and its inhabitants are among the best and most valiant of men.'

Abd al-Basit praises Granada's marvellous technical expertise, literary culture and religious community, making it, he asserts, 'one of the best and most beautiful cities of the West'. This fifteenth-century Egyptian paints a picture of a bustling city with excellent defences, rich in architectural and natural beauty, where science, art and religion thrived, on a par with one of the most beautiful and important cities of the Arab world.

There can be no better testament to the paradise image of Granada than the verses of the fourteenth-century mural poet and vizier of Muhammad V, Ibn Zamrak, born in 1333, around the time al-Basit was writing his geography. His evocation of the Koranic conception of the garden as paradise in his poetry is inscribed on the walls of the Alhambra as follows:

> This house is a garden of immortality, permanent
>   happiness and good fortune,
> where all manner of moist shade and fresh waters
>   meet in search of bliss.

He continues his evocation of the city itself using similar, idealized images:

> Granada is a bride whose tiara,
> jewels and garments are the flowers,
> her tunic is the Generalife,
> her mirror the peace of strangers, her pendant earrings pearls of dew.

The travellers and scholars who expressed these views were all Arab

Muslims, whose admiration and respect for Granada is perhaps unsurprising. But we can hear a Christian opinion from the late medieval traveller Hieronymus Münzer, a physician who practised in Nuremberg and visited Spain for five months from September 1494 to February 1495. He arrived in Granada in October 1494, nearly three years after the fall of the city to the Christians. The governor of the Alhambra, the Count of Tendilla, took Münzer on a tour of the palace, which the German declared to be unlike anything else in Europe, 'all so magnificent, so majestic, so exquisitely fashioned, that the onlooker cannot be sure that he is not in a kind of paradise'.

But Granada is not only an earthly paradise – it is also a paradise of the mind. These favourable impressions of the city endured in many works of literature and history after the end of the Middle Ages and continue today in the nostalgic writing of contemporary Arab authors, who see the city as a site of irreparable loss which must be reclaimed by Islam. Yet inherent in that perception of longing and loss is a darker aspect which sits uneasily alongside the rhapsodized image of the Nasrid capital. The idealized myth of a site of unsurpassed beauty clashes with the harsh realities of life in a city too often torn apart by violence and death, not only in its medieval and early modern history, but also in modern times, during the bloody events of the Spanish Civil War in the twentieth century. There is the modern Granada of flamenco, of gypsies, of Romantic travellers in the nineteenth century, but there is also the ambiguous Granada of the Inquisition, of Morisco persecution in the Counter-Reformation, of intolerance and cruelty, as religions and politics collide and tear the city apart. Granada is a city of illusions, or *engaños* to use the Spanish word, where things are not as they seem, where architectural magnificence expressed in the solidity of stones, bricks and mortar hides a conflicted past and alludes covertly to the multicultural history of the city.

Approaching Granada at a distance, we are struck by the rugged silhouette of the Alhambra outlined against the dramatic, mountainous skyline, our first impression of a building which has become a metonym of Granada and its Muslim heritage – yet that silhouette presents a paradox. The powerful allure of the Alhambra's running and still water, its gardens, its identity as a three-dimensional book, its extraordinary colours and architecture and its moonlit magic still endures. *The Hitchhiker's Guide to the Galaxy: Earth Edition* describes it like this:[5]

> Set on the point of a ridge overlooking the city of Granada and the plains beyond, the Alhambra is the most stunning building in Spain and probably in the whole of Europe. This may sound subjective, but it is not. Nearly 800 years after its conception by the Moors, much of the architecture remains pristine, somehow appearing delicate, grand and humble simultaneously. Its ramparts climb hundreds of vertiginous feet above the river below. Its halls echo with folklore; tales of passion, violence and piety were all played out within its walls. The Moors also set out to recreate paradise in their gardens, and it is difficult to argue that they did not succeed.[6]

Even so, the monument's fairy-tale glamour has not been created by Granada's tourist office and the Ministry of Culture alone, as its status as a UNESCO World Heritage site shows. At the same time, this romantic aura belies its nature as a military stronghold, a citadel as well as a pleasure palace, whose mighty walls loom threateningly if we view them from the outside. Impenetrable and unscalable, they send a message of military strength and unassailability to the outside world.

The opposing aspects of the Alhambra – the monolithic majesty that inspires awe and fear and contrasts with its interior grace, elegance and beauty – encapsulate the essential contradiction between beauty and violence that characterizes Granada, and which is due in large part to its singular history. Spain is almost alone in Europe, with the exception perhaps of Russia, in having been invaded and settled by so many peoples, a singular circumstance that is reflected in the history of Andalusia. Granada's identity has been forged by many hands, those of Iberians, Phoenicians, Romans and Goths, Arabs, Jews and gypsies. But it is equally clear that Muslims from Arab and Berber tribes, and the Islamic faith they brought with them, remained on the Hispanic peninsula for eight hundred years, longer than any other people who settled in the land, and the fact is that Arab culture has played a vital part in shaping what is often described as Western civilization. Granada is one of the few places in Europe today where you can still see and touch that history, where you can grasp in a tangible way the fact that the history and culture of Spanish Islam was and still is a crucial part of European history and culture.

To grasp how this came about, we must revisit those historical events that followed the Muslim invasion of 711 and the defeat of Visigothic Spain, when the Muslims, who were nomadic tribal warriors, adeptly transformed themselves into urban rulers and built their cities as a result of the speedy growth of a monetary economy founded on the commercial value of produce. At the zenith of Muslim rule in Spain between 711 and 1010, Cordoba was the supreme Islamic city in Spain, ruled by the Umayyad caliphs from Damascus. In the mid-eighth century, Umayyad power in the emerging Islamic world had been crushed by the Abbasid dynasty, who moved the capital of the caliphate from Damascus to the newly founded city of Baghdad. The sole survivor of the Umayyad dynasty, Abd al-Rahman I, fled to Spain, where he united political and religious power in proclaiming Cordoba an independent emirate, not governed by Baghdad, and establishing what was effectively an independent al-Andalus. A glittering civilization was created there in the tenth century, as Cordoba grew into a sophisticated city with over seventy well-stocked libraries, public baths, paved streets and street lighting at a time when Londoners walked on roads made of mud and lit the dark by candlelight. In the tenth century Cordoba was praised by the learned German nun Hrotswitha of Gandersheim, who wrote a glowing account of the Muslim city, describing it as 'the brilliant ornament of the world'.[7] In Cordoba the three great religions of Moses, Jesus and Muhammad began their long, vexed, yet often tolerant and fertile relationship. Another prodigious structure, the Great Mosque, was built here. Its forest of red and white arches reminded its founder, Abd al-Rahman I, of the palm trees of his beloved native Syria, and this marvel of Islamic architecture brought together every Mediterranean style that had touched the Hispanic peninsula – Carthaginian, Roman and Byzantine. For a while, Cordoba was the epitome of luxury and beauty, enriched by books, jewels, dancers and musicians from the East, slaves, gold and cereals from north Africa, and wood for arms and ship-building from Europe.

Yet its glory was fleeting – the power of the Umayyad caliphate became too centralized, and suddenly collapsed in 1031. Muslim Toledo fell to the Christians in 1085, and in 1090 the Almoravids, fierce and fanatical Berber tribespeople from north Africa, invaded southern Spain, bringing a strange combination of puritanical Islamic mysticism and military expertise. By 1106 they had occupied all the important cities of al-Andalus. In a bizarre twist, despite their professed asceticism, they quickly succumbed to the wealth and glitter of court life, and to the steadily growing strength of Spain's Christian armies, and were finally ousted in 1145. Then came the Almohads, anti-secular Muslim extremists who had captured most of the cities of al-Andalus by 1145 and made Seville their capital, the natural heir to Cordoba as the cultural centre of the peninsula. There the Almohads oversaw one hundred years of artistic and intellectual expansion, during which they laid the foundations for the imposing Alcazar, built the city walls and founded a great mosque, raising its renowned minaret, the Giralda, which is now the bell-tower of Seville cathedral. But Muslim power was starting to wane, as the Christian armies consolidated their first great victory over Toledo and swept southwards. Seville surrendered to the Castilian King Ferdinand III, the Saint, in November 1248.

The Christian conquest of Seville marked the start of the third epoch of Muslim rule in Spain, and if the first and second eras had been epitomized respectively by Cordoba and Seville, the third and final period belonged to Granada. The two hundred and fifty-year rule of the Nasrid dynasty of emirs gave the city an unsurpassed historical legacy that remains vividly alive in Spanish politics and culture today. This, together with the beauty of its geographical location and architecture, set it apart, not just from its Andalusian neighbours, but from all other Spanish cities.

THE SYMBOL OF THE POMEGRANATE

Granada speaks through its cityscape, through its architecture. It also whispers to us casually through the ornamentation and embellishment of its streets, exterior walls and even its municipal ironworks. It is not just the Alhambra that is an open book written in stone. To the observant passer-by, the fountains, paving stones, bollards and even manhole covers silently reveal the city's past, for many of these places, and these objects, are adorned with the image of the pomegranate. You have to look closely but then suddenly you see them everywhere – on the street sign for Calle Cárcel Baja (Lower Prison Street), one of the leading thoroughfares of the old city; on the fountain of Charles V's palace in the Alhambra; on the elaborately designed mosaics underfoot in the tiny but shady Plaza de la Trinidad (Trinity Square). These are not mere artistic reflections of the living pomegranate trees and bushes with their dark green leaves, red flowers and voluptuous fruits that flourish in the parks, squares and roadsides of the city. They evoke for us not only the diverse history of the place but also its name and essence, for the word 'Granada' means 'pomegranate' in Spanish.

It is an ancient fruit, whose scientific name *Punica granatum* comes from the Latin words for an apple, *pomum*, and *granatum* which means 'seeded'. It originates from a region stretching from modern-day Iran to India, and it is thought humans cultivated it as long ago as 5000 BC. Beloved of the ancient Egyptians, for whom it was a symbol of prosperity and ambition, pomegranates were even entombed with the dead. A large, dry pomegranate was found in the tomb of Queen Hatshepsut's butler to take with him to the afterlife. In ancient Greek mythology, it was also known as the fruit of the dead, believed to have sprung from the blood of Adonis. It sustained the goddess Persephone, daughter of Zeus and the corn goddess Demeter, although the six seeds she ate condemned her to spend half the year as queen of the underworld with her husband Hades, while the earth lay dormant until her return to her mother brought the arrival of spring. A symbol of fecundity in both Eastern and Western cultures because of its profusion of jewel-like seeds, the pomegranate is said to have arrived in Rome from the Phoenician city of Carthage, a provenance which gave rise to its Roman name *mala punica*, the Punic or Carthaginian apple. We might imagine that it was familiar to those Romans who lived in the city that would later become Granada after they had defeated the Carthaginians of the peninsula during the Second Punic War, since there is a story that the traders from Carthage originally introduced the pomegranate to the south of Spain.

For the Jews, a people who were among the earliest inhabitants of the province and city of Granada, the pomegranate has intense symbolic meaning. In the biblical Old Testament book of Deuteronomy,[8] when Moses has brought down the Ten Commandments from Mount Sinai, his reward is the Promised Land:

> For the Lord thy God bringeth thee into a good land, a land of brooks, of water, of fountains and depths that spring out of the valleys and hills; a land of wheat, and barley, and vines, and fig trees, and pomegranates; a land of olive oil and honey; a land wherein thou shalt eat bread without any scarceness, thou shalt not lack any thing in it; a land whose stones are iron, and out of whose hills thou mayest dig brass.

The Granadan Jews might well have thought they had found this promised land when they first arrived in a province where pomegranates abounded. The pervasive presence of these fruit in Judaic art and craft, from clothing and jewellery to cooking utensils, underlines their significance. The Book of Exodus[9] describes the blue, purple and scarlet pomegranates that decorated the hem of Aaron the high priest's robe, while the stirring account of the master smith Hiram's inspired creation of the great pillars of the Temple of Solomon in the Book of Kings[10] dwells upon the two hundred brass pomegranates that adorned them.

Some Jewish scholars believe that the pomegranate was the forbidden fruit of the garden of Eden, and in Jewish tradition they symbolized righteousness, knowledge and wisdom, their alleged six hundred and thirteen seeds representing the same number of commandments in the Torah. In the mystical experience of the Kabbalah, the adept enters the 'garden of pomegranates' or *pardes rimonim*, a phrase the sixteenth-century mystic Moses ben Jacob Cordovero, whose family came from Cordoba, used for the title of his book on the subject. The crown-shaped calyx of the fruit inspired the Jews to paint the original, traditional design of the celestial crown or saintly halo. The modern state of Israel still uses the motif of the fruit on coins and stamps, and it is the symbol of the Jewish New Year, Rosh Hashana.

It seems that the Muslims of Granada first called the city *Garnata* in the ninth century, a name whose true meaning has caused a good deal of argument. We know that they used the name *Hizn Garnata*, meaning 'castle or fortress of the pomegranate tree', to describe the ancient Roman site at the top of the Albaicín hill. The Arab chronicler Al-Maqqari concluded that *Garnata* was derived from the Latin variant word for pomegranate, *granata*. Some say it means 'hill of pilgrims' and has nothing to do with the pomegranate, while other more imaginative interpretations of the word attribute the name and foundation of the city to a daughter of Noah called Grana, of whom no record exists, or set its origins back in the time of the

Visigothic King Roderic and the Arab invasion of 711. In this last version of the etymology of *Granada*, it was said to be a translation of the name *Cave of Nata* (*Cueva de Nata*), Nata supposedly being the name of the daughter of Roderic's general Count Julian of Ceuta, with whom the king had a love affair that was later blamed for the fall of Christian Visigothic Spain to the Muslims.

Whatever the case, the Arabs were the first to use the name, and the city became identified with a fruit that was greatly revered in Islamic tradition, according to which eating a pomegranate cleanses the heart and fills it with light, keeping you free from sin and temptation for forty days. It is considered one of the golden fruits of the trees of the Islamic Paradise. There is a Hadith in which Muhammad told his companions that each fruit contains a seed from paradise itself, imbuing it with a seductive power that perhaps accounts for the Muslim belief that pomegranates have a dangerous side to them too. Their beauty, mystery and female dimension made them a favourite image in the ornamentation of Islamic manuscripts and pottery. The Granadan Muslims were the first to grow real pomegranates on a large scale in the orchards surrounding the city, where their bittersweet taste lent a perfume to drinks and their garnet-coloured seeds flavoured savoury dishes of chicken and lamb. Today, Spain is still the world's largest exporter of these fruits.

Christianity also embraced the pomegranate in its symbolism and iconography, as an image of its own church in its multiple structure inside a single fruit, representing the unity of belief of many peoples, and as a visual emblem of the shedding of Christ's blood and of his resurrection. Fray Luis de Granada (Brother Louis of Granada), a Dominican friar born in the city in 1504, lived like a saint in a poor monastic cell, where he spent thirty-five years writing spiritual and theological works. In 1584 he published his book *Introduction to the symbol of the Faith* (*Introducción al símbolo de la fe*) in which he enthuses over the beauty and ingenious design of the pomegranate:

The Creator seems to have wished to show that it is the queen of fruits. None can surpass it at least in the colour of its seeds, as vivid as corals, nor in the flavour and health-giving qualities of this fruit. Because it is cheerful to look at, sweet on the palate, tasty to the healthy and curative to the sick.[11]

The healing qualities of the pomegranate had already been praised by Saint John of God, a Portuguese traveller who settled in Granada in 1538, establishing a hospital and devoting his life to caring for the sick and the poor. He was later canonized and became one of Granada's patron saints. The Basilica of Saint John of God was built in his memory, in the street in Granada that bears his name, and statues of the saint depict him holding a pomegranate with a cross emerging from its crown-like calyx.[12]

Nearly one hundred years before Fray Luis's book appeared, the pomegranate had taken on an indelible meaning for the kingdom of Granada, when King Ferdinand II of Aragon and Queen Isabella I of Castile incorporated the fruit into the shield of the city after they captured it in 1492. How closely the pomegranate was linked to Granada, both city and province, in the imagination as well as reality, is apparent in a local tradition in which Queen Isabella is said to have stood with one of the fruits in her hand and proclaimed: 'I will take over Granada just like the pomegranate, seed by seed.' It is a remarkable thought that, from 1492 until now, the Granadan pomegranate and the arms of the kingdom of Granada have formed part of the Spanish coat of arms, and of the coats of arms of all Spain's monarchs and of all its regimes, Trastámara, Habsburg, Bourbon, Bonaparte and Savoy, as well as two Republics, and it adorned the ensigns and emblems of opposing parties in the four civil wars since 1833.[13] Sculpted or embroidered, the heraldic pomegranate is lifelike, with realistic red stripes, or entirely red, with two green leaves. Interestingly, these colours, red and green, were transferred to the city flag in 1980, in memory of the standard of Sultan Muhammad I, founder of the Nasrid dynasty of Muslim rulers in 1237, thereby aligning the great symbol of the Catholic Monarchs with their arch-antagonists, the Nasrid sultans.

The pomegranate is not only a political symbol of the uneasy association between Christians and Muslims in Granada itself. In 2017 a newspaper article by writer and journalist César Girón lamented the absence of this representative image of the historically most important part of Andalusian territory from the political or cultural sphere of Andalusia as a region,[14] an absence that he felt effectively erased all memory of a noble past. Yet if it does not appear on the flag of Andalusia, the Granadan pomegranate remains permanently on the shield of Spain as one of the loftiest symbols of the nation, which Girón points out is a testament to the enduring symbolic value of the kingdom of Granada past and present in the history, politics and territorial organization of Spain.

The symbolic importance of the pomegranate resurfaced in a blog on Andalusian recipes[15] that published an anecdote in January 2019 about the smart new restaurant called *Ruta del Veleta*, the Route of the Weathervane, on the Sierra Nevada road on the city outskirts. In 2013 the Pedraza brothers, who own the place, acquired an old table from a location in the Albaicín to furnish the bar, and were astonished when a sharp tap on the table revealed a secret compartment hidden behind the central drawer of the piece of furniture. Inside was an ancient manuscript dating from Nasrid times containing contemporary recipes, which the restaurant has made public. The first recipe was called 'the dish of the three religions', and consists of couscous with raisins and pomegranate seeds, ingredients commonly available to and consumed by the Christians, Muslims and Jews of Andalusia. This couscous of coexistence, made with locally grown grains, grapes and pomegranates, suggests the fundamental interconnection of the multi-religious society of al-Andalus through the food its people ate, an idea revived by the *Ruta Veleta* restaurant in the twenty-first century.

In the course of its history Granada has been a city of multiple names and identities – Iliberis, Florentia, Garnata al-Yahud – whose diversity and fundamental unity are best expressed in its most familiar name, Granada, Pomegranate, the fruit whose image has lasting importance for the diverse ethnic and religious peoples who have populated the city throughout its history. To begin to understand that history, we need to go back to a time before records were kept and chronicles written, before the city as such came into being, and listen to the ancient voices of the peoples who inhabited the southern land and mountains of Hispania.

2

THE MISTS OF TIME

*From prehistory to the
reign of the Visigoths*

❖❖❖❖❖❖❖❖❖❖❖❖❖❖❖❖❖

FIRE, ICE AND METAL

Long ago, in the place where Granada now stands, there was
nothing except the rivers, valleys and the mountains named after
their icy peaks capped with snow that melted in the fiery sun and
flowed downhill to water the land beneath. Then, as now, a place
of searing summer heat and cold winters, of rocky heights and
verdant depths, of arid desert and lush, fecund plains, highland
tundra and subtropical coasts, extreme contrasts would form an
essential part of the character of its landscapes and peoples. Rain
fell abundantly on the uplands of the Sierra Nevada and gave
life to the native forest trees: holm oak, elm, pine and palmetto.
In prehistoric times, these dense, rainy forest landscapes were
roamed freely by bears and wild boar, oxen, deer, goats, hares,
quails and bustards. Then the humans came, the very first settlers
who crossed the straits of Gibraltar from the deserts of north
Africa and lived in the open air or inside deep caves camouflaged
by boulders and rocky crags.

The first human presence on the European continent is documented as dating from 1,400,000 years ago in the territory of Granada, in a place called Lion Ravine (Barranco León) in Orce, where, along with primitive stone workings and the remains of extinct animals from the first age of man, a molar belonging to *Homo sapiens* was discovered. It can now be seen in Granada's archaeological museum, which re-opened in the spring of 2018 after many years of closure. These earliest people used hand-carved stone tools and weapons to hunt and gather food, settling in areas well supplied with shelter, water, fuel and stones suitable for their needs. Hunters of the Paleolithic age and later, gatherers in the Mesolithic era, they were defined by their skill in stone, until in the Neolithic age, 6000 to 3100 years BC, their lives were revolutionized as they evolved from a predatory culture to become farmers. The late Stone Age people of Granada grew crops including cereals, olives and grapes for wine, domesticated animals such as pigs, horses, cattle, goats and sheep, and made ceramic pots to cook and preserve their food, relinquishing their nomadic life and settling into a sedentary one. Perhaps the most moving item still existing from that time is a pair of esparto sandals found in the evocatively named Cave of Bats in Albuñol in the Alpujarras, not far from the city of Granada, beautifully woven, uncannily modern in appearance, and unbelievably preserved for over six thousand years.

One of the simplest and yet most powerful exhibits in Granada's archaeological museum is a plain band of beaten gold, a diadem, also discovered in the Cave of Bats, and believed to date from 3450 BC. It has a remarkable story. In 1831 a local man discovered the cave, noticed traces of lead, and some years later assembled a team of miners to prospect for the metal. What they discovered was reported by the archaeologist and historian Manuel de Góngora in his book of 1868. Upon unblocking the entrance, they found 'three skeletons, one of which was certainly male, and wore a simple diadem of pure gold… Beside them, each skeleton had a basket made of esparto, two full of what seemed to be sandy, black soil…

and other small baskets with strands of hair or flowers, and a large number of poppy seeds and single-valve shells. In another area the miners found twelve cadavers placed in a semi-circle around the skeleton of a woman, remarkably preserved, dressed in a tunic of animal skin... wearing an esparto grass necklace, hung with sea-shells, with a wild boar's tusk carved at one end in the centre ring.'[16] Beside the skeletons were clay vessels, knives and chisels made of bone and wooden spoons, fashioned from stone and fire. In other parts of the cave the explorers found around fifty more skeletons, all wearing esparto grass clothing in the style of chain-mail, all accompanied by stone or bone weapons.

While we cannot know the circumstances of this spectral gathering, which was perhaps a ritual sacrifice or a death cult, these corpses speak through the craftsmanship they left behind. They reveal not only their astonishing skill in weaving esparto, but also their mastery of metal. The era in which they lived, known as the Copper Age, was exceptional in the south-east area of Spain which would become the province of Granada. Their society was unequalled and complex, with a degree of civilization ahead of the rest of Europe, and the crafting of metal artefacts raised their culture to another level. Its specialist coppersmiths and stonemasons wielded advanced tools such as hole-punches, awls for pricking, palette knives for mixing pigments, and instruments for polishing. By the Bronze Age (2500–1800 BC), a time when men found out that adding tin to copper made bronze, the societies of south-east Spain began to acquire materials such as ivory or ostrich egg shell, and the first bell-shaped ceramic vessels were used in Granada before 2000 BC. These luxury items, probably from north Africa, tell us that these early Andalusians were no longer isolated but were now trading with the peoples just across the short stretch of sea that separated the Iberian Peninsula from the African continent. The earliest art of the region, associated with burial rites and the protection of the dead, was created between 2600 and 2100 BC, carved in varied geometric designs on slate floors and on the stone dolmens of Fonelas close to present-day Granada. One celebrated carving displays human arms, hands, sexual organs, legs and feet, and sports a short skirt and headdress, and the small community of Fonelas adorns its municipal flag with an image of that ancient human figure today.

The lands of Granada are rich in subterranean minerals; its mountains contain copper sulphides, lead and silver ore, and the waters of the Darro and Genil rivers sparkle with gold. In the western highlands and valleys of the region, the culture known as El Argar arose sometime between 1900 and 1200 BC, formed by a people whose expert craftsmen fully exploited the local resources to forge the weapons and tomb ornaments, the latter often bronze and silver earrings, that highlight the sophistication of their society. Specialist metallurgists were needed to create these products, as well as a whole network of prospectors, miners, smelters, casters and metal tradesmen. In these times before history was written, the Argar people left traces of their society in the remains of strategically positioned fortifications, vestiges of rectangular huts with wooden roofs, wattle-and-daub walls and stone foundations on artificially terraced hillsides, and in their megalithic burial sites. Here ancestors were laid to rest in close proximity to the living, in earthen tombs or sometimes in large jars where the corpse lay in a foetal position, accompanied by ceramic vessels, food, arms and tools to take into the afterlife. The Argar were united by ties of local identity but divided by social hierarchy rather than lineage in a society that appears to have been sufficiently egalitarian to maintain a harmonious lifestyle for many hundreds of years.

Around a thousand years before Christ, that harmony was ruffled but not shattered by the arrival of outsiders. Different peoples from the eastern Mediterranean, first the Phoenicians, then the Carthaginians, settled on Spain's southern coasts. At the start of the eighth century BC the first Phoenician trading posts sprang up on the shorelines of the regions of Malaga and Granada. The traders built houses whose rectangular rooms opened onto spacious streets organized into a distinct urban plan that would later be assimilated into early Iberian architecture. These seafaring merchants came from Tyre, in what is now Lebanon, and brought wine, oil and other luxuries from Egypt, Etruria and Greece, which they sold to the local aristocrats. One such exotic item on display today in Granada is the funeral urn of the Pharaoh Takelot II (c.850–825 BC), bearing a cartouche with his royal seal, and the inscription: 'Your eyes glow within you. Your word is the breath of life, that makes throats inhale.'[17] In exchange the Phoenicians bought iron, silver, lead and tin from the interior, and founded trading and agricultural towns like Adra, Salobreña and Almuñecar, where production of the notorious fermented fish sauce and their famous purple dye flourished. They also brought the skills of iron metallurgy, the potter's wheel, the mint, and improved cultivation of olives and grapes.

In the ninth century BC the Phoenicians had founded the colony of Carthage in north Africa, which became a wealthy commercial centre in its own right. Carthaginian sea traders maintained the Phoenician settlements in Iberia from the sixth century BC onwards. After that time, the exchange of goods and techniques between the colonists and the native communities made it more difficult to differentiate between the two, so that the southern regions round Granada became a real Iberian melting pot. The people of the region adopted certain Eastern gods and goddesses, such as Melqart and Astarte, tutelary god of Tyre and fertility goddess respectively. They used Eastern funeral rites and absorbed oriental symbols, mythological winged monsters, griffins or sphinxes, while foreign-style items marked the wealth and status of their owners. Yet they still kept their local character with their ancient burial barrows and indigenous styles of buckles and knives. By the seventh century BC, the people of the Granadan *vega* had left behind their prehistoric way of life and developed their thriving industries and trade in wine and oil. Urban life was free from conflict, and peace reigned in southern Iberia.

The genesis of Iberian culture in the peninsula, and with it, the birth of the settlement that would become Granada, came at this time. The three ancient pre-Roman Iberian tribes of the south-eastern regions, who are believed to have spoken the Iberian language, were the Oretani, who dwelt in Linares, the Turduli, whose capital was at Porcuna, and the Bastetani, whose biggest town was on the site of modern-day Baza. They shaped Iberian civilization for five hundred years, until the second century BC. Much of the province of Granada was Bastetani territory and in 650 BC, on the upper part of hill that is the current Albaicín of Granada city, where the Arab Alcazaba Cadima or old fortress would be built, they founded the ancient oppidum or fortified settlement of Iliberis or Iliberri, which housed two magnificent necropolises. The city's antique pedigree first came to light in the late nineteenth century when two reddish ceramic urns painted with wavy lines in Iberian style and containing bones and ashes were found on the Mauror hill of the Albaicín. A second burial site, discovered in the twentieth century on the slope where the modern Faculty of Theology, Philosophy and Letters of Granada University lies, revealed Iberian swords or falcatas with curved blades, and bronze and ceramic artefacts.

The Bastetani of ancient Andalusia built fortified cities in strategic areas, with streets and houses arranged in an orderly way, and their society had a clear hierarchy. They were shepherds and farmers as well as miners, but they stand out for their creative and artisan skills, manifested in their striking black and red ceramics, iron lances and swords with unique curved blades. Expert sculptors, they shaped bas-reliefs and an outstanding body of statues for religious and burial rites. But it was the funerary rituals and sculptures of the Iberians that enshrined motifs and places that would mould the psyche of both the Granadan and the Spanish people.

The bull of Arjona was carved from limestone sometime between 600 and 400 BC. He was found on a farm near Arjona in Jaén province in the 1920s, and now sits on two plinths in pride of place in the archaeological museum of Granada. Over four and a half feet long (142 cm) and nearly two feet high (53 cm), this venerable Iberian sculpture could easily be mistaken for the work of an artist like Henry Moore or Brâncuşi, but it also has a timeless quality that suggests it might belong to any age. The bull's wrinkled skin is like a lion's mane, his eyes are bold, his nostrils flaring. Sacred, cultic and iconic, the bull is a symbol of power and life, of wild strength and fertility. Worshipped in the religious cults of the pre-Roman Iberians, he guarded their cattle trails and in later times was sacrificed in that greatest of Spanish ritual murders, the bullfight. The bull would be reincarnated in Picasso's *Guernica* as a symbol of tragedy and untrammelled energy, and the great, black *toro bravo* or fighting bull lives on today, watching over major roadways as a giant advertisement for Spanish brandy. The imposing bull of Arjona betokens the adaptation by the local Iberians of a symbol of Greek and Eastern origin for use in their own spiritual and mythological universe, one which would become commonplace in the cultural mythology of Spain.

Caves were also sacred to the Iberians, and may have been part of a cult, since terracotta grave goods representing a cave have been found elsewhere in Spain. Usually situated in hidden locations, the generally damp conditions of the cave regenerated life and growth, and the spirits of the dead could rest at ease. Unchanging, dark and occult, they were believed to be places where a spirit or divine power presided, and where rituals were performed inside, usually involving fire or water, the latter essential in healing rituals, and thought to be part of the divine presence. It is telling that caves have held unceasing significance for Granada, from its earliest pre-historic troglodytes, to the later Iberian cave-worshippers, to the gypsies who have lived on the Granadan hillside, to the present-day chic apartments and boutique hotels in the caves of the Sacromonte. They have given shelter, acted as holy places and also as sources of buried treasure and relics. They are a crucial part of the landscape and mindscape of both city and province. In the wild desolate country with its dense covering of evergreen bushes near what is today Jaén, a hundred miles north of Granada, two Iberian mountain sanctuaries in the Sierra Morena, or Dark Mountains, were used by worshippers, who gathered in the external sacred areas outside caves and brought with them the precious bronze statuettes that were specially fashioned for these sanctuaries for at least three hundred years, from the fifth to the third centuries BC. The little statues represented warriors, riders and worshippers in reverent attitudes, and some are of women offering small gifts of bread or bowls of food to the deities. Animals were also brought into these holy places – bulls, rams, birds and horses, valued possessions and beneficial symbols. The local Granadans worshipped horse gods in these locations as emblems of abundance and fecundity, and plentiful carved horse images have been recovered from the holy hills in the Granada basin near Pinos Puente, and from the valley of the River Genil. Like caves, mountain sanctuaries are something very ancient in human culture. The hills and surrounding mountains and caves where Granada is built have abiding significance in the cultural memory of the city.

The fruitful mix of Iberian and Phoenician cultures existing in pre-Roman times was enriched even more by the arrival of another group of settlers from the east. Between 600 and 570 BC, Greek adventurers had sailed to Spain and founded a new Greek settlement on the north-east coast of Catalonia. It was named Emporion, meaning 'trading place', and gradually a trickle of Greek imports began to flow south, as traders from the new settlement undertook commercial voyages to the Mediterranean coastline of the peninsula. By the sixth century BC the Iberians of Granada had extended their oppidum to include the area which is now the lower Albaicín, with improved outer walls. The settlement was originally called Ilturir, later latinized as Iliberri. In the next two hundred years, the Iberians of Ilturir and the south-east enjoyed an abundant supply of Greek pottery, much of it from Athens, in the form of Attic jars and pots decorated with characteristic black and red figures. Most of these containers for liquid or perfume were used by the local people for libations in honour of the dead, or at sacred banquets, so they had a ritual function. Although this Greek pottery was important, there was only a relatively small proportion of it in comparison with locally produced goods. What makes it important is the unmistakeable influence it exerted on Iberian sculpture. Take the case of the celebrated Lady of Baza, found in the north-east of the province of Granada and considered a masterwork of European art of its time (400–350 BC). The Lady was recovered from a warrior's tomb dating from 400 BC at Cerro del Santuario in 1971, majestically enthroned and life-size, which was very rare in Iberian sculpture. She is unidealized, her figure dumpy and her face sad, painted to show rouge on her cheeks and two little curls on her forehead, the picture of maternal authority. She is holding a dove in her ringed hands, presiding over the life and death of her soldiers as a funerary goddess. The polychromed surface also shows the texture and colours of her linen and wool clothes and her throne of dark brown wood, and reveals the detail of her heavy jewellery.[18] Despite her Iberian origins, she has the distinct look of Greek or Etruscan sculpted figures. At the same time, these Iberian artists also maintained their own unique tradition and way of seeing. Their painted ceramic items ran roughshod over the elegant proportions of classical Greek vase painting, and their taste was inventive and fantastical. Their pottery bristles with irregular lines and shapes, and sports dynamic motifs such as swastikas, stars, rosettes, crosses, floral spirals, wheels and zigzags. Sometimes a sun sign or a flower morphs playfully into an animal or a fish. The choice of decoration opens a window onto their world, through which we can glimpse what was important, interesting or beautiful to them.

We can know a people through their art, and the Andalusian Iberians also depicted their everyday life on their ceramic creations. From it we learn of their pursuits, typically bullfighting, horse taming, hunting, dancing and magic rituals, harvesting and

funeral ceremonies. The artworks found in their cemeteries disclose important information about the type of society that had
evolved by the fourth and third centuries BC. At the large Iberian
burial chamber in Galera, in the province of Granada, a venerable
religious statue was unearthed, known as the Lady or Goddess of
Galera. Carved in alabaster as early as the seventh century BC, she
sits between two sphinxes and holds a bowl for liquid that pours
from two holes in her breasts. Her hair, costume, sturdy shape and
the presence of the sphinxes suggest Egyptian or Mesopotamian
sculpture, and she no doubt came from a Phoenician trader. Possibly
once a sacred object, the Lady of Galera was buried as grave goods
in the prestigious tomb of a wealthy individual, showing that this
society was ranked by hierarchy and had an aristocracy.

The Iberians had created the first documented political and
cultural entity in Spain, and the first advanced, independent civilization west of Italy. Their lands were described by the most ancient
writers as the location of the legendary kingdom of Tartessos,
reputed to have a boundless supply of gold, silver, lead and tin.
The Greek Stesichorus, the first great lyric poet of the west, gives
us the earliest textual reference to a specifically Spanish location for
Tartessos, dating from around 620 BC. He mentions the boundless,
silver-rooted springs of the River Tartessos, now taken to refer to
the mighty River Baetis, later named Guadalquivir (meaning 'great
river') by the Arabs. Early geographers such as Strabo, writing
in the first century BC at the time of the later Roman Republic,
echoed its mythical identity as Tartessus. Strabo notes that the
folk of this golden region were allegedly the wisest of the Iberians,
complementing the abundant nature of their land, for whose
territories 'there is no worthy word of praise left to him who wishes
to praise their excellence…'.[19] If we are to believe their accounts
of this area that comprised Turdetania and also Bastetania, which
nowadays lie within the boundaries of Granada province, we
would have to conclude that in pre-Roman times this place was
a paradise, whose resources and prosperity surpassed those of any

other region. It was also a place of cultural and ethnic wealth – rich seams of Phoenician, Greek and north African civilization were inlaid in the bedrock of Andalusian Iberian culture, paving the way for the next great colonizers, the Romans.

STONES, STATUES AND LAWS

Granada is a city of hidden things, a place of surface veneers and occult strata, of history that is both in plain view and subterranean. A case in point is El Zaidín, which means 'land between rivers' in Arabic, the most heavily populated modern area of the city of Granada, famed for its tapas, and home of the new football stadium, the Science Park and the Andalusian Astrophysics Unit. El Zaidín grew quickly in the 1960s, and its urban cityscape on the ground is a familiar one of purpose-built blocks of flats and futuristic office buildings. But viewed from the air, we might discern the distinct outline of something infinitely older. By chance, while workmen were digging up the ground to lay new pipework in Calle Primavera (Spring Street) some thirty years ago, they unearthed a series of Roman mosaics, some with images of dolphins, in what is now Plaza Ilíberis, which became a public archaeological park in 2019. These mosaics, hidden beneath the ground for two thousand years, mark the site of a luxury Roman villa from the first century AD, with its patio and columns, baths, its own necropolis and surrounding agricultural area. This acute juxtaposition of modernity and antiquity draws us back into the unfamiliar Roman past of the city, veiled by time and overlaid by later civilizations.

The Romans first came to the region of Granada not to colonize it but because it was an area of passage and contact. The existence of the urban nucleus specifically named Iliberis coincided with a time of major confrontation between Rome and Carthage in the first Punic War, mainly fought in Sicily but spreading to Cerdeña

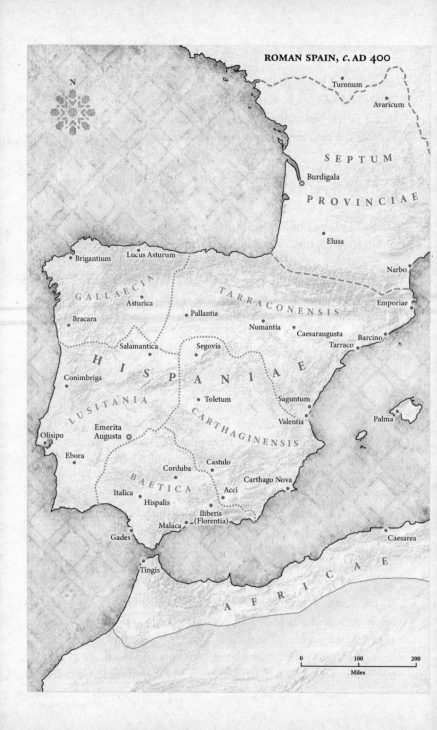

ROMAN SPAIN, *c.* AD 400

N

Turonum
Avaricum

SEPTUM

Burdigala

PROVINCIAE

Elusa

Brigantium   Lucus Asturum

Narbo

GALLAECIA   TARRACONENSIS   Emporiae

Asturica   Pallantia
Bracara   Numantia   Caesaraugusta   Barcino
Salamantica   Segovia   Tarraco

HISPANIAE

Conimbriga   Toletum   Saguntum

LUSITANIA   CARTHAGINENSIS   Valentia   Palma

Olisipo   Emerita
Augusta

Ebora   Corduba   Castulo
Italica   BAETICA   Acci   Carthago Nova
Hispalis
Iliberis
Malaca   (Florentia)   Caesarea
Gades

Tingis   AFRICAE

0   100   200
Miles

in northern Spain, where the Carthaginians were expelled by the Romans in 241 BC. Soon after, in 237 BC, the Carthaginian leader Hamilcar Barca, whose surname means 'thunderbolt', was sent to the Iberian Peninsula with his young son Hannibal, where he gained a foothold in southern Spain for nine years and brought Turdetania under his control, before dying in battle in 228 BC. His general Hasdrubal, who was said to have married the daughter of an Iberian king, was regarded by the southern Iberians as their military leader, and is credited with creating the last Carthaginian colony in Cartagena on the south coast. He died in 221 BC, ignominiously murdered by a slave. Hamilcar's great son Hannibal also married an Iberian princess from Castulo, a powerful Iberian city allied with Carthage, taking over from Hasdrubal after his death and ruling the south of Spain as commander of the Carthaginian army before he left for Italy, leading his war elephants over the Pyrenees and Alps to take Rome by surprise with fire and steel in 218 BC.

In that same year, 218 BC, the Roman Senate first designated the Iberian Peninsula, which they called Hispania, as a province. This meant that they could send an army there to exercise military control – there was no sense that there was a political claim to the region. They were merely interested in Hispania, and in the south in particular, because of the presence there of the Carthaginians; their struggle against the great north Africans would be the most desperate they ever undertook in their long history of almost continuous warfare. Inevitably, the region around Iliberis became involved in the last great conflict between them, the Second Punic War, and the Roman objective was to liberate the native Iberians from Carthaginian domination. There was a degree of collaboration between the Roman troops and the indigenous people but, in fear of jumping from the frying pan into the fire, there was at the same time a lot of local resistance to Roman control too.

The Greek mathematician and philosopher Ptolemy (AD 100–70), who was a Roman citizen, mentions the city of Iliberis as the furthest east of the twenty-eight cities he knew in the region, and

Pliny (AD 23–79), Roman author and naturalist, wrote that it was among the most famous cities of the interior between the River Guadalquivir and the ocean coasts. Although the Romans first knew Granada as Iliberis, Pliny called it Iliberri Florentinum. The city enters written history via its coinage. The very first coins from the time of the Roman conquest were struck there in the first half of the second century BC and they provide the oldest genuine testament to the name of the city, which appears in Iberian characters. One hundred years later, these Iberian characters were replaced by the Latin alphabet, as Iliber, signalling the rise of Latin and the waning of the Iberian tongue, though the Iberians held on to the fascinating imagery that embellished their money – crude, spontaneous fantasy figures such as the human head with three legs running after each other that symbolized the moon on its path over the horizon, or winged spirits bearing a shield and lance, a whole sidereal pantheon inspired by the natural world.

As the Iberians slowly adopted Roman ways of life, the city became an autonomous administrative body under Roman Imperial rule, but the laws promulgated by the emperor organized the community, and in 44 BC it became a Roman colony, ruled by magistrates and the Senate. It gained the status of a municipality around 27 BC, which gave its citizens legal privileges akin to those enjoyed by its rulers. On the basis of this, Granada took on another name, Municipium Florentinum Iliberritanum, known in Roman sources as Florentia. The city was allowed to evolve freely, peacefully and in line with Roman Republican rules. At this time, the Emperor Augustus divided the former province of Hispania Ulterior, of which Florentia was a part, into two regions. North of the River Guadiana became Lusitania, and south of the river, where the Roman city lay, became Baetica. Crucially, a new modification to the borders of Baetica (in the last decade before Christ) turned Florentia into a frontier town, a feature it would retain and which would play a key role in its future incarnations.

Granada tends not to be associated with its Roman past, still largely buried and forgotten. The sparse written references to it mean we must turn to coins and archaeology as vital resources in bringing that past alive. Since the sixteenth century, its ancient stones, statues and other treasures have been rescued bit by bit from oblivion, and show us without doubt that the Ibero-Roman city known to the Iberians as Iliberri, and as Florentia to the Romans, spread out over the hill of the Albaicín.[20] Recent research shows that the forum was in the centre of the upper part of today's city, near Calle María de la Miel. There are epigraphs and inscriptions, white marble sculptures, tombs, skeletons, Republican and Imperial Roman coins (including bronze coins from Nero's reign), gold and glass jewellery, bronze arrow-heads, and the mosaic paving of the kind in El Zaidín which marks the sites of villas.

Before taking a closer look at some of these witnesses to Roman civilization in Granada, we first need to consider the bigger picture, the urban scale. The father of European urban planning is considered to be the architect Hippodamus (498–408 BC), who came from the ancient Greek city of Miletus. His Hippodamian system structured an urban centre in the form of a grid, based on the idea that a town plan might embody and clarify rational social order. The order and regularity of his urban plans contrasted with the intricate confusion of the layouts of cities such as Athens. Urban roads were set at right angles, with a central area for public buildings and leisure areas on the outskirts, a plan also adopted in cities such as Damascus and Alexandria. The equally rational, orderly Romans knew his system and added new elements, using vertical arteries to divide urban areas into districts. They transformed the Iberian Iliberi by using right angles and creating a typical Roman urban layout with two main axes marking a main street running east to west. In the modern city, these axes are Calle San Juan de los Reyes (Saint John of the Kings Street) and Zacatín Street (Clothes Market Street). An intersecting street ran north to south, today's Calle Elvira (Elvira Street) and Calle Molinos (Mill Street). We know that the urban area stretched beyond the

VISIGOTHIC SPAIN, 586–711

N

B a y   o f   B i s c a y

Lucus

GALLAECIA

ASTURA

CANTABRIA

Auca

Pallantia

SEPTIMANIA

Narbo

Bracara

Caesaraugusta

Barcino

Tarraco

Secovica

TARRACONENSIS

Salamantica

CARTHAGINENSIS

Viseum

LUSITANIA

Toletum

Valentia

Palma

Emerita

Castulum

BAETICA

Cartagonova

Corduba

Acci

Hispalis

Basti

Iliberis

Malaca

M e d i t e r r a n e a n   S e a

0   100   200

Miles

Albaicín hill, as the remains in Calle San Juan de los Reyes include tombs, always extramural, which probably belonged to ancient villas or leisure lodges, and the current area of Cartuja reveals the ruins of a ceramics industry, legally obliged to be situated outside the city limits. Pottery items, woven fabrics and metalwork made in such potteries were disseminated across the empire via its flourishing trade networks.

The ancient urban traditions influenced by the Phoenicians and still present in the topography of the city were made uniform where possible. Red and white marble fragments of cornices, columns, capitals and base stones brought to light in the eighteenth century hint strongly that Florentia encompassed the main traditional Roman structures; one of the unearthed fragments bore a second-century inscription 'FORI ET BASILICAE ...', words which relate to the central market place or Roman forum, and the basilica, used for legal, public or private business. The city is likely to have had a main temple, usually dedicated to Jupiter Optimus Maximus; a semi-circular theatre; a circular or oval amphitheatre for games and gladiator fights; a gymnasium for general education and sports training; and hot, warm and cold steam baths for public use. There were no doubt typical Roman houses, with a central patio and entrance hall. The late Roman ruins of a fortress, known by the name Hizn Román, can still be seen near the church of Saint Nicholas in Callejón de San Nicolás (Saint Nicholas Alley). The old door in the castle fortress – blocked up in later times by the Zirid emir Badis ibn Habus – may have allowed access to the inner city, a vital entrance for the peasants who frequently came to the city to do business or take part in its everyday life. They sold their merchandise, mainly corn, oil, wine and salted fish, went to games and the baths, and took part in religious festivals.

In this way, the city had close economic and commercial ties with the surrounding countryside, which produced abundant crops of wheat, olives and grapes. Viticulture was authorized by the soldier-emperor Severus Alexander (r. AD 222–35), who encouraged the planting of vines for the production of wine, prohibited since the end of the first century AD by a decree by the emperor Domitian in an attempt to protect Italian vineyards. Outside the city walls, the largest agricultural and livestock farmsteads, known as *villae*, housed their owners in beautiful buildings decorated with mosaics and stucco, some of whose remains still lie in the villages of Salar and Los Vergeles on the outskirts of the urban area. Their crops were irrigated by the abundant waters of the rivers Darro and Genil via a Roman-era conduction system, long since forgotten and destroyed, which sprang from a fountain in the town of Deifontes, a Roman word meaning 'fountain of the Gods'.[21] The system carried water by aqueduct some 30 kilometres along what is now the road from Granada to Jaén; the arches that belonged to this aqueduct have sadly crumbled or disappeared entirely in places. In later times, the Arabs would perfect this irrigation of the *vega*, often improving on old Roman structures.

Iliberis was a crossroads from which four highways followed the points of the compass: one along the River Genil as far as the town of Loja and on to Anticaria, now Antequera; one to Castulo, now Linares; another to Sexi, now Almuñecar on the Mediterranean coast; and the fourth to Acci, now Guadix. The present bridge over the River Genil, known as the Roman bridge (*puente romano*), was constructed in its current form by the Arabs, who replaced the older Roman one built to ease road communication. An educated guess would put the area of the urban precinct in Roman times at about 20–25 hectares, with a population of maybe 6,000–7,000 people; if those who lived outside the city limits are included, it might have comprised a community of 150,000 people, many of them country dwellers. At this stage in its evolution, the city proper was perhaps similar in size to a small market town.

As the Iberians of Iliberis gradually adopted Roman ways of life, absorbed the Latin language and consolidated their city, their society also took on the formal structure of the Romans, with its patricians or aristocrats, plebeians or common folk, and slaves.

There was no middle class. In Roman Granada, agriculture was the main economic activity and nine-tenths of the population lived in rural areas and made a living from it. As a result, the upper echelons of society were not formed by businessmen, merchants and bankers but by landholders, who formed the urban elite. This circumstance would have an enduring influence on the history of the city and its commercial and social development. All estates and strata of Roman society are documented in the town of Iliberis, with members of the town aristocracy mainly represented.

It seems that religion was also important in Iliberis, as one-third of the forty or so existing Roman inscriptions are religious in nature, or refer to priestly duties. The religion of the native Iberians was a nature cult with Phoenician influences. Coins minted in Iliberis provide evidence that the cult of the moon as an astral divinity flourished here; they bear a triquetra or three interlaced arcs on a circle on one side, the symbol for the three dimensions of female divinity that symbolizes life, death and reincarnation. This lunar goddess worship was akin to the worship of the Eastern goddess Astarte, and the Roman goddess Juno. Although the Romans were tolerant of indigenous religions provided that they posed no threat to their political aims, Roman beliefs infiltrated the Iberian mind and native cults and divinities slowly merged with similar Roman gods and rituals.

From the broad panorama of life in Roman Iliberis emerge unique insights into the lives of certain individuals, who come to life through stone and statues. In 1982 a bronze statue 1.6 metres (5 ft 2 in.) high of a Roman man wearing a masterfully sculpted toga, whose elegant folds of fabric belie the centuries-old metal it is made from, was found on a farm in Periate, near Granada. Cast using the Lost Wax method[22] and missing its right arm, this life-size sculpture of a mature man, whose short hair and beard, elevated absent gaze, and pupils and irises drawn in by incision all disclose its late Roman style, dates from the last third of the third century AD. The statue is thought to be a likeness of Emperor

Claudius II the Goth (AD 268–70), who won several victories in Hispania and regained control of the territory temporarily ruled by a pretender.[23] Its solidity betokens the tangible presence of Roman imperial power in Granada's ancient past.

Roman stones name some of the cast of elite inhabitants of Iliberis, raising an unexpected curtain on their lives. Members of the wealthy equestrian order, or *equites*, were granted the dignity of a knight or gentleman by the emperor. They enjoyed the right to a military horse funded by the state, which also paid for its food for life. Only one member of the *equites* is documented in Iliberis: one of Granada's Roman inscriptions identifies him as Quintus Cornelius Marcus, son of Valerianus, who lived at the end of the first century AD. After a long military career, in which he won many decorations, he rose to become a judge in Rome. Another inscription tells us that his son definitely lived and was honoured in Iliberis.[24]

Iliberis also had a group of senatorial families, very distinguished and famous men, who are documented there throughout the High Roman Empire until at least the third century AD. Quintus Valerius was the first senator of the Valerii family[25] in the reign of Vespasian. His family had lived a long time in Iliberis, as his lineage is recorded there as early as AD 26, and they held the highest social rank in Baetica. Quintus Valerius had an important political career, in which he was honoured as a consul, as were his son and grandson after him, and he was later obliged to live in Rome, where he built a house in the Quirinal. When its ruins were excavated, it was found to have been built using a technique common in Hispania but rare in Rome, called *tapial*, in which the walls are built of compacted clay inside a wooden framework, showing that Quintus clearly took with him the building skills of his native land. His family probably married into another illustrious Iliberian family, the Cornelii. The senator Publius Cornelius Anullinus was one of the most influential men of the second half of the second century AD, enjoying a long military career and holding a number of high public offices, including governor of Hispania Baetica, as well as of Narbonne, of Africa and prefect of Rome, spanning the reigns of Marcus Aurelius, Commodus and Septimius Severus, of whom he was a personal friend.[26] An equally brilliant senator of this era in Iliberis was Gnaeus Papirius Aelianus, who was governor of Britannia in AD 146.[27]

The Roman town of Iliberis reached its zenith in the second century AD. Not only could it boast important senators with connections in high places, but it also had a significant number of *liberti*, rich freemen who had acquired their wealth not from agriculture but from business, manufacture or banking. Commerce was flourishing, with a roaring trade in metals, and gold in particular; on the outskirts of the city, gold-seekers panned in the iron-rich red riverbeds of the Darro and Genil. High-quality marble was excavated from quarries near Iliberis and transported to Rome to adorn the buildings of the imperial capital. Another prized Iliberan export was a lustrous, dark green marble, worked unpolished. Granada's biggest Roman archaeological treasure is the ancient Roman pottery at Cartuja, on the site of the university campus. Here the porous yellow clay from the banks of the River Beiro was transformed into tiles, bricks and everyday ceramic items thrown and fired in the local style known as *granatensis*. Shards and fragments of fine red pottery, decorated with characteristic concentric circles and wavy lines, reveal that the potters of ancient Iliberis endowed the Roman technique of *terra sigillata* with a uniquely Iberian flavour.

Iliberis embodies the lasting influence of Rome on Spanish culture. The Romans established the city, as they had the other great cities of the interior of the peninsula, creating a government and public institutions where there were none, and forging an idea of unity and human allegiance precisely through urban life. Three emperors, Trajan, Hadrian and Theodosius, were born in Hispania, along with four great writers: Seneca, Lucan, Quintilian and Martial. Small wonder that there was an enduring Roman influence on Granadan and Spanish civilization, through the Latin language, law, philosophy and the recording of history. But the Romans remained sympathetic to the Granadan Iberians' attachment to their urban locality and customs, to the villages of the *vega*, to their hereditary landscape and mythologies. That individualism, so deeply ingrained in the Spanish soul, perhaps had its origins in tribal pride and native creativity, and it entwined itself in a unique marriage with Roman culture. Under the Romans, Iliberis, or – aptly – Florentia, flourished, but a new order was beginning, bringing with it an unquiet and changing world.

Monks and monarchy: the coming of the Goths

As the mighty empire of Rome began to crumble in the third century AD, Iliberis became a society in transition. Roman culture remained strong there until two new outside forces began to transform the physical, social and religious landscape of the city. The collapse of Roman power in Hispania was certainly not the result of internal tensions. Spain was probably the wealthiest province of the empire, the breadbasket of Rome, so loyally Roman that only one legion remained symbolically stationed there. But the disappearance of a Roman order that had lasted for over a thousand years in the ancient world left a vacuum in Hispania that was filled by invasion and a new religion, in the form of barbarian conquerors known as the Visigoths, and the faith of Christianity.

The turning point came in the autumn of the year 409, when northern invaders braved the high mountain passes of the Pyrenees and marched into Spain. They comprised three ethnic groups, the Alans (who may have originally been Iranian but more recently had migrated to the western steppe), Sueves and Vandals (whom the Romans believed to be Germanic). These events are vividly described to us by the priest Orosius, born in Roman Iberia and writing at this time. He claims that the soldiers of the rebel emperor Constantine III (407–11) deliberately turned a blind eye to the Vandals crossing the mountain passes to cover up their own looting of the civilian population. It was at this point that the legitimate emperor Honorius (395–423) lost control of the Spanish provinces. Orosius laments that the arrival of the Balkan invaders led to a time of famine, starvation and even cannibalism. Seven years later, in 416, the Roman general Constantius attempted to regain control of the peninsula. He subdued the Visigoths and made a pact with his new ally, the Visigothic King Wallia (415–19), to destroy the marauding Vandals, Alans and Sueves, although Wallia's troops were withdrawn from Spain in 419. For their military assistance, Honorius rewarded the Visigoths by granting them land in Gallia Aquitania, in the south-west of modern France.

The Visigoths had originally arrived in Hispania in 415 after a long journey through the Roman Empire, with the aim of crossing the Straits of Gibraltar and reaching Africa, but destiny in the form of a violent storm prevented them. The southern region of Spain was not their destination as a permanent settlement but a place of passage on the way to the African continent. Their arrival here bore similarities to that of the Romans, who had come not to conquer Baetica but to fight off the Carthaginians.

Wallia ruled the tribe who would become the masters of Spain in the fifth century. The historian Roger Collins tells us that confusion reigns over their ultimate origins.[28] In essence they were a mercenary army consisting of different ethnic groups from the Balkans, and their name, the Visigoths, is thought to mean 'Goths from the west'. After Theodoric II (453–66), a later Visigothic king, took his army into Spain in 456 and defeated the Sueves near the northern town of Astorga, the Visigoths went on to take control of most of the country. As a group, they followed a ruling family, a small aristocratic elite whose success depended on an aura of success in military matters and a commanding economic position. They brought with them a royal treasure, which some believe contained priceless jewels, gold and silver artefacts including the Jewish Menorah, which had been taken from the temple of Jerusalem by Emperor Titus in AD 70. The story goes that Alaric, first king of the Visigoths (395–410), plundered this treasure when he sacked Rome in AD 410. It was later brought secretly to Spain as a mark of their triumphs, as material evidence of a shared history and common identity. Legend has it that the last Visigothic king of Spain, Roderic, buried this treasure somewhere in the vicinity of Granada in the early eighth century, but it has never come to light despite the many treasure seekers who have looked for it over the centuries.

We have only shadowy, confused pictures of life in Iliberis in the time of the Visigoths. Like the Romans, their covert but unmistakeable presence abides in the inscriptions, ceramics and necropolises exposed by archaeology in the underground world that lies inside and outside the city limits. In the fifth century, Iliberis kept its status as a capital city, along with its legal adminis-tration and religious functions, but its city walls crumbled, its forums became quarries, its public services were abandoned and its spacious Roman houses were divided up for the use of several families. Roman grandeur made way for squalor and decay, and as the city deteriorated, much of its population moved out into the surrounding countryside. As city life declined, the great farming estates or *villae* became agricultural production centres of vital economic importance. Society was organized less around the city and citizens and more around territorial possession by a minority of owners, upon whom the peasants depended.

From the early sixth to seventh centuries, a new element enlivened the potent mix of Iberian, Phoenician, Roman and Visigothic cultures that constituted Iliberis. From 552, when the Eastern Roman emperor Justinian I founded the province of Granada, to 624, the Byzantine province of Spania stretched along the southern coast of the peninsula, created under the aegis of Justinian I in an attempt to restore the western provinces of the empire. In the mid-sixth century, the Byzantines became embroiled in a struggle between two rival Visigothic kings, Agila and Athanagild, who disputed the territory of Baetica. Athanagild asked Justinian for help and the emperor sent his army to the south of Spain, where they fought for two years until Agila was defeated and murdered, and Athanagild became king. But he couldn't get rid of the Byzantines so easily. They had settled comfortably in several coastal towns and cities of the south, and Spania remained a Byzantine province for the next seventy years, until the Visigoths eventually reclaimed it in 624. During that time, Iliberis again became a frontier location, this time between the Visigoths and the Byzantines, a topographical and psychological element that would continue to be a crucial part of its identity throughout the history of the city and province.

The Visigothic kings were the first to create a monarchy that was solely Spanish in its geographical area and which in principle ruled the entire peninsula, Iliberis included. In future times, medieval Castilian kings would hark back to this absolute monarchy as an ideal they could evoke and aspire to, but which they could never seem to fulfil. The Visigoths believed in firm government and produced notable law books, whose crowning glory was the twelve-volume *Law of the Visigoths* (*Lex Visigothorum*), larger than any early collection of laws other than Roman law, on which it was based almost entirely. It replaced all earlier legal systems on the peninsula and made all inhabitants of the Visigothic kingdom subject to the same laws. The *Lex Visigothorum* remained in force until the fourteenth century. Through their laws and style of government, the Visigoths aimed to increase the central power of their state, and also of their religion, which was Christianity. And in this, Iliberis played a central role.

We must go back in time, before the coming of the Visigoths, to find the first documented historical evidence of primitive Christianity in the Hispanic peninsula. The arrival of the very first Christians in Spain is the stuff of legend. According to one enduring myth, Saint James the Apostle, brother of Saint John and son of Zebedee, was ordered by Jesus to preach in Spain, where he had a vision of the Virgin Mary standing on a pillar, surrounded by angels, in which she exhorted him to build a chapel there. James became Spain's patron saint, and the great cathedral at Santiago de Compostela in Galicia in north-western Spain – which is the goal of the famous pilgrimage to that city – is dedicated to him. But there is no evidence in any early sources for Saint James's presence in Spain, not even among the first Spanish Christian writers. Another important story sets the origins of Christianity in Granada. In the legend of the Seven Worthy Apostles, Torcuatus, Tesiphon, Segundus, Indalecius, Euphrasius, Hesiquius and Cecilius were consecrated as bishops of Rome, probably by Saints Peter and Paul, and were sent to evangelize Hispania. They pitched up in Roman Acci, which became Guadix, near Granada, in the first or second century AD and began to preach in the province of Granada. As we will see, this legend would later take on great significance for the Granadans, and Cecilius became the patron saint of the city.

These Christian myths first come into written existence in medieval manuscripts of the ninth and twelfth centuries, although Hispanic Christianity is brought into sharp focus in a document written many centuries earlier. In AD 254, Cyprian, Bishop of Carthage, wrote a letter supported by thirty-seven other African bishops, concerning a problem with the bishops of two Spanish churches in the north-west of the peninsula. Just fifty years later, at the start of the fourth century (in AD 300 or 302), a land-mark Christian council meeting, the Council of Elvira, was held in Iliberis.[29] Its Acts, which are the earliest of any disciplinary council of the Christian Church, provide us with a list of bishops, presbyters and deacons in attendance from at least thirty-seven Christian congregations in the peninsula, most of them from Baetica. They also give us a sense of the persisting vitality of the religion in this area even around the time of the great persecution of Christians in the Roman Empire by the emperors Diocletian and Galerius in 303. We also know that the Bishop of Iliberis at this time, Flavianus, attended the council meeting, which sheds fascinating light on life in cities like Iliberis, and on the nature of Christianity there.

The Acts of the Council reveal a strong Christian community in Iliberis, drawn from different urban classes such as magistrates, landowners, farmers, slaves and their owners, merchants and free men. Paganism still rubbed shoulders with the Cross, and the problems addressed at the Council of Elvira were sparked by this uneasy coexistence. Those church members who were leading a double existence as *flamines*, priests of the imperial cult, were barred by the Council from taking communion – even at their death – if they were still performing sacrifices or funding gladiatorial games and theatrical events. The wealthy Christians of Iliberis could not accept rent from their tenant farmers if it constituted an offering of first fruits to a pagan god. Idols representing pagan household gods were permitted provided they were the idols of slaves and their master kept well away from them. The use of magic, the lighting of candles in cemeteries and gambling for money were also banned. Such happenings were clearly part of the everyday life of fourth-century Iliberis.

The other big problem for the Council of Elvira was sex. The majority of the council decrees – or canons – deal with sexual morality and marriage problems: consecrated virgins who committed adultery could not take communion, nor could Christian parents who prostituted their daughters. Priests were not allowed to have sexual relations with their wives or beget children, and Christian women were prohibited from marrying non-Christian men. Particularly interesting are the decrees constraining relationships between Christians and the Jews of Iliberis, whose history will unfold in a later chapter. But it is clear that from the very beginning, the Spanish Catholic Church flinched at sexual transgression, wracked by the tensions of a saintliness shielding erotic longings.

Even at this early stage in the life of the city, Iliberis shone as a cultural centre, lit up by the intellectual and religious prowess of its learned men. Two of them – one a priest and poet, the other a bishop – stand out in particularly sharp relief. One of the best-known Christian writers of late antiquity was the Roman Spanish poet Juvencus, a priest from an illustrious family who lived about AD 330 during the reign of Constantine the Great. A marginal note in the copy of Saint Jerome's collection of short biographies of famous men, *On Illustrious Men* (*De viris illustribus*), in Leon cathedral in northern Spain refers to Juvencus as '*elliberitanus*', meaning 'from Iliberis'. This brief reference is all we have to go on but it appears to confirm the poet as a native of the city. Juvencus was a pioneer – his *History of the Gospels* (*Libri evangeliorum*) is a re-creation mainly of Saint Matthew's gospel in simple, clear verse, the first attempt at the epic form in Christian writing and a vital step in blending Christianity with Latin poetry and ousting pagan mythology.

The other great Granadan writer from this time appears in the list of bishops of Granada in the *Codex Emilianensis* kept in the Spanish royal palace of El Escorial. Bishop Gregory of Iliberis (or of Elvira) was ordained after Bishop Flavianus, and was probably born around AD 320. Saint Jerome tells us he lived to a great age and was still writing in AD 392. Gregory was praised by two fellow priests in a letter to the Emperor Theodosius as the 'holy and very constant Bishop of Iliberis, defender of the pure faith'.[30] The pure faith was little less than an obsession for Gregory, who became involved in the contemporary battles over the dogma of the Holy Trinity. In his treatise *On Faith* (*De fide*), he explains the orthodox conception of the Trinity as one God in three divine forms, the Father, Son and Holy Ghost. This view clashed with that held by the advocates of Arianism, whose perceived heresy, taught by the Libyan priest Arius of Alexandria, was to consider Christ to be similar to God but not the same as God; Christ was divine and born of God but distinct from and subordinate to him. This difference of opinion caused such a ruckus that Emperor Constantius II had to intervene in favour of the Arians. Gregory, however, remained intransigent and when the emperor died, the orthodox position that had been defined by the Council of Nicaea in AD 325 was reinstated. The Granadan bishop's rigorous, hard-line attitude informed his life and writing, which was not limited to *On Faith* but also included twenty sermons on Old Testament themes, which attacked Jewish observances in his See of Iliberis, plus a short treatise on the Church, *Noah's Ark* (*De arca Noe*) and five books on the Song of Songs, which were the first Latin commentaries on that unique Old Testament celebration of sexual and spiritual love. Gregory of Granada is esteemed as a Father of the Church, severe, orthodox, honoured by posterity, praised by Isidore of Seville and included in medieval calendars and martyrologies. His festival on 24 April was celebrated in Granada from the fifth century until 1601, when he was replaced by Saint Cecilius as the city's patron saint.

The history of Granada in the fourth century AD is defined by religion, framed by the Church Council held there at its start and by the great figure of Bishop Gregory at its end. The Visigoths who first came to the region in the next century followed the Arian creed that Gregory had condemned, until in 589, at the third Council of Toledo, the Visigothic King Reccared converted to Catholicism in order to unify his people, an act witnessed by Isidore of Seville, and two bishops from Iliberis, Esteban and Pedro. Now part of a land of hermits and monks, the city, which had previously been Roman in its urban landscape, demonstrated the Christianization of urban topography. Temples were replaced by churches, bishop's houses, church schools and religious cells for men and women, remoulding the cityscape of Iliberis in terms of its Catholicism. Even the dead bear witness to this transformation. The Visigothic burial site at Black Poplar Farm in Colomera near Granada yields its secrets – fifty corpses buried in dug graves or stone coffins, with the head facing east according to Christian ritual. Despite the ravages of tomb raiders in the 1980s, there remain ceramic, bronze and silver dishes, according to the social status of the dead, along with rings, necklaces, earrings and brooches, sometimes of gold, to ease their transition into the afterlife.

Smiths par excellence, the Visigoths worked metal and precious stones not just for religious ceremonies but also for commerce and for royal adornment, of which striking examples still exist in the magnificent votive crowns worn by their kings. Artisan crafts featured prominently in the economy of places like Iliberis in the sixth and seventh centuries, and this was reflected in the areas of the city devoted to workshops for metallurgy, textile production, ceramics and minting of coins. Iliberis had an important mint which created gold coins, miniature works of art in their own right, bearing the head of Reccared I (586–601) and of the eleven succeeding Visigothic monarchs up to the eighth century. On the reverse were the words '*Eliberri Pius*' ('Holy Iliberis'). Locally made bricks, ceramic vessels decorated with geometric moulding, with Chi-Rhos, peacocks and bunches of grapes, along with cups and lamp-holders of delicate, greenish glass, were sold to north Africa, Italy, to Mediterranean neighbours and to the country dwellers who lived close by. All betoken the cultural attainments of the civilization that produced them, a civilization which still remains tantalizingly beyond our grasp.

But we can briefly glimpse everyday life in Iliberis at the time of the Visigoths as it appears in the nineteen miniatures of a controversial seventh-century manuscript known as the *Ashburnham Pentateuch*. This exquisite work of art, kept in the National Library of Paris, is believed to come from Visigothic Spain, possibly Seville. If it does not, it was certainly created by a Spanish monk in Visigothic times, and though it depicts the first five books of the Bible, those depictions take us into a Visigothic world of buildings with masonry walls and domes, and of four-wheeled carts drawn by pairs of horses. We see how horses were caparisoned, what rural farmsteads looked like, how bricks were made. It is also a world of exotic influences, of palm trees and camels, of heat and light, all framed by its Christian religious message.

At this time Iliberis took on one of its characteristic features – it became a fortress, part of a frontier system created by the Visigothic armies to defend their territory against the Byzantines. The frontier defence consisted of a series of fortifications called *castra*, manned by peasant-soldiers who carried out a military role alongside their agricultural work. The second line was made up of fortified cities, of which Iliberis was one, where regular troops who fought in military campaigns were garrisoned. This double defence of frontier and city would play a vital role in the life of Granada in later eras.

By the seventh century, Iliberis was a Visigothic city with clear military, political, economic and religious dimensions. It was also a place of learning and culture, enriched by the influence of African books brought to Spain by the monk Donatus, who arrived from Africa with seventy monks, armed with a very large collection of written works for use in trade, as gifts and in religious instruction. Poetry, liturgy, grammar and anti-Arian treatises contributed to the creation of a cultural environment of lasting influence. The Visigothic liturgy in Spain, nowadays usually referred to as the Mozarabic rite, and treasured for its literary and theological qualities, is still performed in Toledo to this day.

The warlike Gothic invaders had given Iliberis strength and stability, with excellent defences and a thriving artisan and agricultural economy. These perceived barbarians also left a legacy of learned literature, finely wrought works of art and craft, a longstanding legal system, and a strongly embedded tradition of Catholic Christianity. The endless coups, feuding and massacres that devastated the Visigothic monarchy allowed the Christian Church to gain decisive power, forging a mainly Catholic community of believers in Iliberis and throughout the peninsula. At this early time another constant of Spanish, and later of Spanish American, politics was established: the almost continuous presence of the Church in public affairs.

No one knew that in a few short years, this Visigothic Catholic city, site of tradition, transition and renovation, would be shaken to its foundations by conquerors from a foreign land, a people both familiar and strange, alluring yet fearsome.

3

CITY OF
THE MUSLIMS

❖❖❖❖❖❖❖❖❖❖❖❖❖❖❖❖❖❖

FRONTIERS AND FAITHS:
THE MAKING OF MUSLIM GRANADA

In a corner of wild Andalusia there is a wide plain girdled by picturesque, rugged mountains to the north and west, and bordered to the east by fertile hills and sheltered valleys. In the east a mountain range with the highest peaks in the land forms a canopy. At the first signs of winter's harshness the immense cordillera becomes a desert, from which fowls and wild beasts flee. Reptiles lie dormant and rocks are buried beneath a blanket of ice. There, the rain is snow, the mists and dewdrops form icicles and frost. The bright white surface reflects the daylight and like a splendid beacon lights up the amphitheatre of the nearby lands with double intensity. In the evening when shadows have invaded the plains and deep valleys, the sun still bathes the highest peaks, ceaselessly renewing the rainbow clouds of sunset or creating a view of the mountain gently glazed with milk and rose-pink.

Then, when spring arrives, the snow turns liquid, the ice melts and the echo of waterfalls booms in the valleys. Crystalline waters expand to form lakes and pools, and the buds that were tightly closed unfold with a marvellous speed, as if they had been touched by a magic wand. Almond, strawberry and wild apple trees flower, and roses, violets, pinks, honeysuckle, marshmallows and a thousand aromatic and medicinal plants tint the valleys. Fowls reclaim their old nests, precipices and caverns are filled with wild beasts and vermin. In the midsummer heat of August, shepherds take their flocks up to flowery pastures, on whose slopes rivers form, the most famous known to the Romans as Singlis and now called Genil. It rises in a gloomy cleft called the Valley of Hell and runs down to the plains, at the bottom of which, almost on the banks of the Genil and the Darro, which bears gold in its sands, Abd al-Aziz occupied a settlement under clear skies, lit by the same sun that revitalizes us today.

This vignette of the enchanted arcadia of Granada was penned not by a nineteenth-century Romantic but in the early ninth century by Abd al-Malik ibn Habib (790–853). A native of the village of Huétor Vega less than 10 kilometres from the city itself, he speaks to us from personal experience. His poetic account focuses on abundance, water, light, on the mountains and on violent contrasts in climate, motifs that have defined the place as an ideal abode, isolated and protected by its rocky peaks which create a natural frontier, a border area where peoples from different tribes and faiths have met in peace and in war.

Abd al-Malik's father was a spice trader who owned an oil press in the *vega*, but his son rose from these humble beginnings to become one of the most important Muslim scholars of his time, the first writer on medicine in al-Andalus and an eminent expert on law. As a youth he travelled to the east to complete his education and make a pilgrimage to Mecca, the *hajj*. In Medina – home of the sacred Islamic site of the Ka'aba and tomb of the Prophet Muhammad – he learned about Malikism in Sunni Islam and played a vital role in establishing Malikite Law in Spain, which relies on the Koran and the Hadiths or words of Muhammad. When he returned home from Arabia he was summoned to the sultan's court at Cordoba, where he was named *mufti* of the city and became known as the 'wise man of al-Andalus'. It is thought that Abd al-Malik wrote over a thousand works, the most famous being his *World Chronicle* telling the story of Spain, as well as his medical treatises and poetry. He owned lands and olive groves near Granada but died of bladder stones in Cordoba in 853, where he was buried.

How was it, then, that this first son of Granada to win literary fame was a Muslim, and who was the Abd al-Aziz referred to in his portrait of the region above? In the second decade of the eighth century, less than eighty years before Abd al-Malik was born, the Visigothic city was conquered by invaders from the south. North African traders had been making expeditions to Spain for many years, but this time it was different. On 29 April 711, a Berber chieftain and governor of Tangiers who was once a slave sailed at the orders of the governor of north Africa, Musa ibn Nusayr, on a surprise raid to the southern shores of Spain with several thousand troops. There is a story that he burnt all his boats on landing, and climbed to the top of a towering cliff to survey the fertile plains and wide blue bay beneath. This man was Tarik ibn Ziyad, and his name lives on in the place where he landed, Jebel al-Tarik, or Gibraltar, meaning the Rock of Tarik. The Berber commander liked what he saw and promptly led his men north to cross swords with the last Visigothic king of Spain, Roderic, who suffered an astounding defeat by the Berber and Arab troops at the Battle of Guadalete in western Andalusia on 19 July, after a week of fighting. Roderic had come to the throne only a year before, in 710, amid rumours that he was a usurper who had enjoyed an illicit love affair with the daughter of his general in Ceuta, Count Julian.[31] The new king had been flexing his military muscle against the Basques of the north when news arrived of Tarik's landing. In a panic, Roderic hastened south, allegedly encumbered by a heavy robe, archaic crown and jewellery, and riding in an ivory carriage drawn by white mules. Betrayed by the nobles and by Count Julian, who is said to have colluded with Tarik and Musá in revenge for Roderic's violation of his daughter, the king vanished after the battle and the circumstances of his death remain shrouded in mystery. It was a battle that ended Roderic's reign and the rule of the Visigoths with it. That sudden demise of Visigothic Spain heralded the dawn of a Muslim presence in the peninsula that would last nearly eight hundred years, during which Granada came to play the key role.

Spurred on by his unexpected success, Tarik quickly captured the Visigothic capital of Toledo, and his victories encouraged Musa to follow his lead in 712 and capture Seville. In the name of the Umayyad caliphate, the Muslims wasted no time in vanquishing all of Spain except the north-western kingdom of Asturias. They pressed on further, crossing the harsh, snowy Pyrenees to enter what is now southern France in pursuit of the *jihad* or holy war, but their defeat in 732 by Charlemagne's grandfather Charles Martel at Poitiers put an end to their expansion north, and to the prospect of what would have been a very different Europe under Islamic rule.

On his way to Toledo, Tarik had sent some of his men to ravage the area around Granada, which was eventually captured after a violent struggle sometime between 711 and 713, under the aegis of the newly appointed governor of the country Abd al-Aziz, son of Musa, to whom Ibn Habib referred as the first Muslim overlord of the city. All later sources describe Jewish collaboration with the Muslim forces, the city's Jewish inhabitants being left in charge of its garrison. Between 716 and 756, al-Andalus, including Granada, was ruled by a rapid succession of Arab and Berber governors appointed by the governor of the Umayyad province of Ifriqiya. These men came from two tribal groups, one from Yemen and the other from Syria, and intermarried with the local population. The local Visigoths and Hispano-Romans were given the choice of conversion to Islam or of pursuing their own religion, provided they paid a special tax and adhered to certain rules, which prohibited them from building new churches or synagogues, displaying crosses or ringing bells.

In 756, a dramatic and far-reaching event sparked nearly two centuries of brilliant cultural and social development in southern Iberia which left the rest of Europe far behind. A member of the ruling Umayyad family in Damascus, Abd-al Rahman I (r. 756–88), fled to Spain to escape the massacre of his family by the rival Abbasid dynasty, and proclaimed himself emir or temporal Muslim ruler, with his capital at Cordoba, which later became the centre of the new Umayyad caliphate. His enforced exile led to an era of unprecedented growth and abundance, with a firm Islamic orientation in every facet of life. Schools were built, the construction of the Great Mosque was begun, literature flourished and a famous law school was established. It was at this great court that Abd al-Malik was honoured by the second emir, the learned and pious Abd al-Rahman II (r. 822–52).

In the eighth century, the city of Granada, still known as Iliberis, was only a *cora*, a province of the state headed by Cordoba. A hundred years later, the Latin *Calendar of Cordoba* for the year 961 compiled by Recemundus, the Mozarabic bishop of the nearby town of Elvira, gives us written proof that the city had assumed its famous name for the first time in its long history. An entry states that the festival of Saint Gregory took place 'in civitate Granata', 'in the city of Granada'. Muslim chronicles concerned specifically with Granadan territory in the years from 711 to 1000 have nearly all been lost, and although what remains is a patchwork of impressions and events, these still reveal a striking feature of this era, which is the fascinating mosaic of ethnicities and religious faiths forming the population of Granada. Tarik's Berbers, along with Arabs from Yemen and the Maghreb, and those from Syria who arrived in 741, diversified the composition and beliefs of the Granadans in the eighth century. Islam was the dominant religion, though its progress was slow to start with – the main mosque of the city was begun in 714 and only finished in 864. These peoples were a rich mix of tribes who merged with the existing inhabitants, many of whom were *muladíes*, the name for those Christians attracted by Islamic culture, who converted to Islam and lived among Muslims. The latter staged a substantial revolt in the province in the late ninth century so we know their numbers were large. There was also a dense population of *mozárabes*, Christians living in Granada who practised their faith and paid tribute under Islamic law, and we have a complete if questionable list of their bishops, from Saint Cecilius to Recemundus. Finally, there were the Jews, whose history in Granada is the subject of Chapter 5. Gradually over these centuries Granada took on its markedly oriental, Muslim character, and the behaviour of the previously nomadic, diverse tribes changed as they became more anchored in one place, the city, with its emerging civilization, state government and military conquests. But the power of the clan in these Islamic societies was tenacious and would, in time, spawn a culture of internal divisions and conflicts that would ultimately weaken the Muslim dynasties of al-Andalus fatally.

It was at this time that Granada became a multi-ethnic, multi-religious dwelling place. In 2017, a stretch of city wall was uncovered high up in the Albaicín district as part of the Spanish Cultural Heritage Institute's restoration project. It has an important story to tell, because the walls were built by the Berber dynasty of Zirids in the eleventh century on the foundations of a pre-existing Roman wall, built in turn on walls constructed as a defence by the earliest inhabitants of the city, the Iberians. These massive structures stand as stone metaphors for the rich cultural substrata of Granada, a visual manifestation of the abundant diversity of its history. Zawi ibn Ziri, a Berber chief of the Sinhaya tribe who governed north Africa on behalf of the Fatimid caliphs of Egypt, led the Zirid dynasty. Zawi was very wealthy but his riches did not refine him, as he wore simple clothing and was known to have a rough nature, predisposed to fighting. Zawi was a born leader, cunning, proud and daring, and he arrived in southern Spain around 1002–3 at the time when the Caliphate of Cordoba was on its last legs, before its final collapse in 1031. Chaos and disunity reigned as the land split into tiny kingdoms known as *taifas*, ruled by opportunist emirs, and the last *taifa* king of Granada, Abd Allah, would soon finish his days in exile in Africa in the lands of his ancestors. Zawi brought his nephews with him across the straits and quickly alighted upon Granada as the ideal place to create the new capital of the Sinhaya Berbers, creating a Berber emirate in the *taifa* kingdom, of which he was the first ruler. Around 1016, he persuaded the inhabitants of the nearby city of Elvira, which until then had been capital of the province, to transfer to Granada. For Zawi ibn Ziri, as a military leader, the city had outstanding strategic advantages as a defensive location; it was high up, was situated in the centre of the region, and had abundant supplies of food and water, making attack unlikely. Without further ado, his men demolished the city of Elvira and both Andalusians and Berbers built their houses afresh in Granada. During Zawi's time in the city, work was begun on a new main mosque – which would be completed in 1055 – and the area inside the Old Fortress or Alcazaba Vieja was developed as the citadel.

But around 1025 the Zirid leader made a fatal mistake: he returned to north Africa, where his enemies murdered him with a poisoned drink. At this point his nephew, Habus ibn Maksan (r. about 1025–38) entered the city in a coup d'état and took command of the citadel as the first effective monarch of the Zirid kingdom of Granada, adopting the honorific title 'Sword of the State'. Habus turned out to be a very good thing for Granada, reigning in peace, safety and prosperity as a friend to its diverse inhabitants. He strove to create a literary culture, in order to vie with the cultivated, Hispanicized sovereigns who ruled other parts of al-Andalus, such as al-Mutamid of Seville. One famous figure from Habus's court was Ibn al-Samh (979–1035), an Arab mathematician and astronomer famous for his treatises on the construction and use of the astrolabe.[32]

With the great Jewish vizier Samuel ibn Nagrela at his side,

Habus became a shrewd politician and diplomat. But the eighteen-year peace of his reign was broken when he died in Granada during Ramadan in 1038 without safeguarding a successor. The issue of legitimate succession bedevilled the Muslim rulers of Spain throughout their history, mainly because clan loyalties clashed and collided in the bid for power. Habus had favoured his nephew Yaddyr over his first-born son Badis, but with the help of the cunning schemes of his vizier ibn Nagrela, the legitimate heir took the throne and enjoyed a long reign as Badis ibn Habus (1038–c.1073). Although he had a good grasp of politics and withstood adversity with stoicism, Badis had a very different personality and political aims from his father. At times he could be ruthless and was also ambitious in his policy of expanding Granadan territory. Zirid political and military might reached its zenith in his reign, mainly due to the political and financial contributions of Samuel ibn Nagrela, who continued to serve as vizier, and who raised Granada into a major power. The other Berber *taifa* kings did not like the fact that a Jew wielded such authority and were reluctant to accept Granada's ascendancy, but when Samuel died in 1056, he was succeeded as vizier by his equally powerful son Yusuf.

Remnants of Badis's palace, which had a mosque inside it, can still be seen inside the present-day church of Saint Peter in the Carrera del Darro. The palace, whose foundations lie in the Corral de la Lona and in the Dar al-Horra palace in the Albaicín, must have been finished by the time of Nagrela's death in 1056 and was celebrated by the historian Ibn al-Jatib as without equal in Muslim or infidel lands. The Arab al-Zuhri, writing in the twelfth century, reveals that the most striking novelty of the palace was a tower topped by a brass talisman weighing over 100lbs, in the form of a weathervane. It had a horse's body but the head and tail of a cockerel, with a mail-clad rider wearing a cockscomb on his head,[33] and was an imitation of a famous armed rider on top of the eighth-century palace of al-Mansur in Baghdad. The weathervane on Badis's palace, a poignant echo of the remote imperial capital of early Islamic times, reinvented by an upstart Berber dynasty, bore a tragic prophecy that predicted the ruin of both master and palace.

Instrumental in that ruin foretold was the intertwining of Zirid and Jewish lives which, paradoxically, had brought such glory to the Muslims of Granada in the first half of the eleventh century. Badis's death in 1073 caused another succession crisis. The emir had planned to name his elder son Buluqqin as heir, a young man with no experience of government or military affairs, with a gentle, understanding character which endeared him to the Granadan people. Badis's vizier Yusuf ibn Nagrela sought to further his own political interests in cultivating Buluqqin, whom he later poisoned in 1064, when the young Zirid was twenty-five. The untimely death of the popular Buluqqin caused widespread disquiet, and hatred began to grow for the wealthy Jew in his fortified residence on the site where the Alhambra would stand, which overshadowed the sultan's own palace. Yusuf's scheming led to his own murder and the massacre of most of Granada's Jewish population on New Year's Eve 1066 (the full story of which tragedy will be told in Chapter 5). In the meantime, Badis lapsed into drunken idleness and fell prey to the curse of the Spanish Muslims, the inability to choose a clear successor. In the absence of the murdered Buluqqin, he felt obliged to name his younger son Maksan, whom he loathed, as heir. Badis, the first independent Zirid sultan of Granada, died on 30 June 1073 and was buried in the mosque of his palace. His name was inscribed on a foundation stone now on display in the Hall of Kings in the Alhambra.

But the unpopular Maksan was not to be sultan. The elders of the Sinhaya Berbers acted quickly and elected Abd Allah ibn Buluqqin (r. 1073–90), Badis's younger grandson, as the new sovereign in 1073 when he was only eighteen. Abd Allah, as he was known, left a remarkable legacy in the form of his *Memorias*, a personal memoir and history of the Zirids consisting of eighty folios found in a walled-up room in the Great Mosque of Fez sometime between 1931 and 1947. For the first time, we hear in the *Memorias* the voice of one of the sultans of Muslim Spain, and it is often the voice of wisdom, diplomacy and reconciliation. In the eyes of Arab historians, Abd Allah's preference for poetry, calligraphy and the sciences, at which he excelled, over battles and bloodshed made him a weak, incompetent ruler. But he was not by nature a violent man and, despite his youth, he viewed himself as well prepared to rule. He describes his personal schooling in politics and monarchy by his grandfather Badis:

> From the very first I strove to show him the utmost respect and give him no cause to think that I wished to hasten along my accession to the throne… I never decided any matter without consulting him, and without insisting on the help of his oldest and most experienced viziers, whose opinion I listened to with filial attention. My attitude created such a favourable impression on these dignitaries that they welcomed the idea that I should succeed the king…'[34]

Abd Allah inherited an extensive town of 75 hectares,[35] with nearly 4,500 houses belonging to Jews, Berbers and Arabs, clustered on the sloping hills of the Alcazaba and the Alhambra, whose appearance was already similar to the building the Christians would marvel at in 1492, together with a province that included the areas around Almeria and Malaga. Sultan Abd Allah cared about the welfare of his subjects and curbed the authority of the viziers so he could have more direct contact with his people. For about ten years relative peace reigned, hard won, since the sultan had to contend with the twin pressures of Christian aggression from the north and the intense rivalry between Berber Granada and Arab Seville. No sooner had Abd Allah risen to the Granadan throne than he was threatened by Al-Mutamid, the Arab ruler of Seville. At around the same time, the Catholic monarch Alfonso VI of León was eyeing Granada and sent his ambassador to Abd Allah to demand a tribute of 20,000 dinars, which was refused. Alfonso's plan was to keep extracting money from Granada and leave it weak and impoverished, so that he could capture it for himself. After a lot of wheeler-dealing between Seville and Granada, Abd Allah negotiated a peace treaty with his rival, as both men understood the need to unite against the threat of 'the foreign sword' of the Christians. In 1085, a small Berber army of 300 horsemen from Granada won an important victory over the Christians at Nivar, 12 perilously close kilometres north of the city. Even so, the pact between Granada and Seville was not enough to stem the Christian tide – in the same year, May 1085, the former Visigothic capital of Toledo fell to Alfonso VI, who was bent on pushing further south. The Christian victory sent shock waves through al-Andalus. It was a time for desperate measures and Granada looked across the water to north Africa and the Almoravids for help.

The Almoravids were political and religious reformers from the north African coast with a zealously puritanical mindset. Asking for their help was not merely a royal initiative but a popular aspiration supported by the *qadis* who represented the Muslim community. When the Almoravid leader Yusuf ibn Tashufin gathered his army at Ceuta, Abd Allah feared the worst. He was right to do so, for Yusuf's secret intention was to take Granada. Arriving in Algeciras in June 1090, Yusuf ordered Abd Allah to meet him in person at the castle of Belillos, just 20 kilometres outside Granada, and surrender the city; at the same time, he assured Abd Allah of his safety. Knowing the Granadans were against him and consoling himself with the thought that the city would at least be inherited by Muslims, without violence or destruction, he went to surrender on 8 September 1090, 'like someone led to his execution, without knowing what awaited me, like an automaton, with my trust in Providence'.[36]

Abd Allah describes in his own words the deep humiliation he suffered at the hands of the Almoravids:

The emir's General Garur said to my mother and me: 'Take your clothes off in front of me, because the sultan knows you are hiding the choicest pearls in your clothing.' Despite protesting our innocence, I had to undress before him. He also pulled all the wool out of the cushions, turned the chests upside down, and unfolded all the clothes in an unprecedented ransacking, and even dug up the floor our tent stood on, in case we'd buried something.[37]

Garur also confiscated the ten necklaces of precious pearls, gold worth 16.000 dinars and some rings that Abd Allah had secreted with him. The Zirid sultan was forced to depart from Algeciras for exile in north Africa. He and his family were given 300 dinars, three servants and five mules for their belongings, and were told to embark for Ceuta, sailing in a violent storm which left them tired and frightened. Abd Allah lived out the rest of his life in Aghmat, a Berber city in the south of Morocco, where Yusuf had made a small palace available for him and his family, and where the deposed and exiled sultan would father two sons and a daughter. He ended his days on a date unknown, his passing unnoticed and unmarked by his contemporaries.

The Zirid dynasty came to an end upon the death of Abd Allah, a sultan ironically denigrated for his bookishness, diplomacy, tolerance and desire for reconciliation at all costs. These qualities enabled him to prolong the political and geographical independence of Granada, a city riddled with intrigue and all too vulnerable to conquest. His aim was peace above all, and his shrewd diplomatic handling of two powerful enemies, Alfonso VI and al-Mutamid, ensured a long period of tranquillity for the city at a time of intensifying conflict that pitted Christians against Muslims, and Muslims against each other. Abd Allah's reign represented the high point of a dynasty that effectively created the impregnable fortress that was Granada in the new millennium. The Zirids had forged a permanent home for their families and subjects, and a monument to their military might. Most of all, they fostered a diverse society of Berbers, Jews and Arabs who overcame the complexities of racial and religious difference, and lived mostly in harmony and cooperation; an astonishing feat in the unquiet world of eleventh-century al-Andalus.

But now the Almoravids swept through the land and by 1106 they occupied all the important cities of al-Andalus. On 15 September 1090, Yusuf ibn Tashufin entered the fortress and royal palace in Granada at the start of his short reign. He discovered treasure inside the like of which had never been found before by any ruler of the peninsula. There was a rosary set with 400 precious stones, each worth a hundred gold pieces. There were also pearls, rubies, emeralds beyond price, as well as two million gold coins. Despite this colossal wealth, his warrior temperament may have contributed to Yusuf's inability to maintain peace, made more difficult because of attacks from the Christian kingdoms of the north, combined with popular demonstrations against the Mozarabic community of Christians living under Muslim rule. The Almoravids lacked the religious tolerance of the Zirids, and in May 1099, Yusuf ordered the destruction of a beautiful and much-loved church close to the gate of Elvira. It was not until a quarter of a century later, in 1125–6, that Alfonso I of Aragon (known as the Battler), launched a bold attempt to rescue the Christians of Granada, reportedly with an army of 50,000 men, who secretly arrived close to the city at Nivar. Foiled by bad weather and lack of food, they failed to overcome the Muslims, who retaliated by flogging, torturing and killing the remaining Mozarabs in Granada. The lucky ones were deported to Africa.

A greater threat to the Almoravids came from the heart of Islam. In 1130, Muhammad Ibn Tumart, the Mahdi or Allah's envoy, died. He was the founder of a new and puritanical religious movement among the Moroccan Berbers centred on unity and austerity; upon his death this movement took on a military and political dimension, headed by the Mahdi's successor Abd al-Mu'aim, the first caliph of the Almohads (1130–63). This name comes from the Arabic word for 'unitarians' – those who shared their beliefs were 'peoples of Paradise' and those who did not were 'peoples of Hell'. The new Mahdi scorned the Almoravids as pagans and began to wage war on them in a series of guerrilla attacks from their mountain hideouts in north Africa. The Moroccan Almoravids were undermined by these conflicts and soon relinquished power to the Almohad enemy.

In al-Andalus, confusion reigned after the Almoravid collapse, and both Andalusians and Almoravids favoured the Almohads over the Christians when the former turned their attention to the southern regions of Spain. In November 1148, Cordoba and Jaén surrendered to the Almohads, although Granada proved an island of resistance to their attacks until 1156–7, when it was conquered by the *sayyid*[38] Abu Sa'id 'Uthman. The new ruler was an intriguing character, who loved literature, especially poetry, and gathered a group of notable poets around him, thereby inspiring an important literary élite in the city. He also fell in love with a famous Granadan woman poet, Hafsa bint al-Hayy, whom we will meet again in Chapter 11. Abu Sa'id's personal secretary, Ibn Tufayl, who became his vizier in 1163, was one of the great figures of Spanish Aristotelianism. Ibn Tufayl (*c.*1105–85) was born in Guadix in the province of Granada and was educated by the Arab polymath Avempace (Ibn Bājja). A physician and personal doctor to Abu Sa'id's son, Avempace wrote many books on medicine, in which he was one of the first to support the use of dissection and autopsy. In this era of eminent Andalusian scholars who built on the discoveries of earlier Muslim science and breathed new life into philosophy, Ibn Tufayl was an intellectual giant. The main theme of Arab philosophy was the rational interpretation of the Koran under the influence of the works of Aristotle, which had been known to Arab scholars since the eighth century. Ibn Tufayl's most remarkable achievement was to write the first philosophical novel, *Hayy ibn Yazqan* (*Alive, son of Awake*, also known as *Philosophus Autodidactus* in Latin), the story of a feral child who lives alone on a desert island and is raised by a gazelle. Despite his lack of contact with other humans, he discovers ultimate truth through reasoned inquiry. The novel was to have a significant impact on Arab and European writers – it was a bestseller in western Europe in the seventeenth and eighteenth centuries, and moulded the views of Thomas Hobbes, John Locke, Isaac Newton and Immanuel Kant.[39] It first appeared in English in 1708 and may have inspired Daniel Defoe's *Robinson Crusoe,* as well as attracting the attention of other European writers such as Leibniz, Robert Barclay and Voltaire. Ibn Tufayl retired from political life in 1182 and died in Morocco in 1185.

Granada had become the capital of Muslim Spain in 1107, under the lengthy governorship of the Almoravid general Abu l'Tahir Tamim ibn Yusuf, who served from 1106 until 1143. It was during this time that Arab writers began to sing the praises of the city. The Almerian geographer al-Zuhri, who described the notorious weathervane, visited the city in 1137–8 and extolled Granada's beauty as well as its imposing defences, in particular the city gates, strengthened with iron plates on top of their wooden panels, and fitted with two small doors to bring in water during wartime.[40] Ibn Galib, a geographer and historian born in the city in the twelfth century, reiterated that it was one of the most extensive, beautiful and well-fortified cities of al-Andalus, and he described the River Darro as shining with gold. He wrote of a time of plenty, of abundant cereals, olives, figs, pomegranates, oranges and lemons, bananas, sweet, musky apples and sugar cane. Vineyards flourished, and although wine-drinking is prohibited by the Koran, young Granadans met outside the mosque to drink wine and have fun. The imbibing of wine must have been a common occurrence; in the eleventh century Abd Allah's vizier Simaya had ordained the death penalty for any drunkard who refused to pay a hefty fine for his excesses.

Mulberry trees had been feeding silkworms since the early tenth century and high-quality silk from the *vega* was sold throughout the country as well as exported. Andalusian flax, used for making linen, was superior to that grown in the Nile delta, and was sent to distant Muslim countries. The Arabs introduced cotton, locally grown and exported, as well as saffron and cumin. Everything that grew here was watered by the rivers of the plain using a hydraulic irrigation system operated by the Romans and the Visigoths, but perfected by the Muslims, whose *norias* or waterwheels harnessed the waters of the Darro to power the grain mills and irrigate the land. The profusion of plant life, flowers, medicinal and aromatic herbs was matched by the age-old profusion of minerals mined from deep in the rocks: gold, silver, iron, copper, lead, mercury and antimony, as well as pure white marble used to fashion glasses, plates, cups and trays.

This natural Eden was again profaned by human violence as the stage was set for the next dramatic act in Granada's Muslim history. A man named Ibn Hamusk, the Andalusi governor of the hilltop town of Carmona near Seville, until it was captured by the Almohads, conceived a daring and foolhardy plan to rebel against the invaders. One night early in 1162, in governor Abu Sa'id's absence, Ibn Hamusk connived with the former Jewish treasurer of Granada, Ibn Dahri, who opened the city gate to the suburbs and let him in. The Andalusi then took over what is described as the red fortress on the Sabika hill,[41] later to be the Alhambra, and alerted Ibn Mardanis, lord of Murcia, who also opposed the spread of the Almohad caliphate. The Almohads were holed up in their fortress on the other side of the River Darro, in the Albaicín, and stoutly resisted the hail of stones catapulted over from the Sabika hill. Forced to retreat to Malaga, the ousted Abu Sa'id made plans to regain his city, bolstered by the support of the Moroccan caliph in Rabat, Abd al-Mu'min, who sent 20,000 cavalry and infantry to aid him. But Ibn Hamusk's forces were also boosted by reinforcements in the form of 8,000 troops sent by the Christian Count of Urgel, and by a similar number who arrived from Murcia with Ibn Mardanis. All of these men were stationed above the Almohad army in the Albaicín.

There was bright moonlight on the night of 12 July 1162, as Abu Sa'id's Almohads silently approached Granada. The next day a ghastly battle took place in which thousands of Almohads were disembowelled by the Christian troops. Clouds of dust obscured the fighting, such that disembodied sounds of mortal sword blows, heads chopped off and terrible cries rent the air. When it seemed as if the rebel offensive was gaining the upper hand, the troops of Ibn Mardanis and the Christians became blinded and disorientated by the dust, and suddenly fell to their deaths down the precipitous slopes of the River Darro, where their bodies lay in pieces on the riverside. On contemplating this dreadful spectacle, the Murcian leader turned and fled, along with Ibn Hamusk.

Abu Sa'id liberated his followers before midday, and set about reconstructing the city's defences with the help of the caliph. But there was no respite. No sooner had the rebellion been quashed than the Christians to the north renewed their offensive, spurred on by Pope Innocent III's call for united action against Islam. Although Alfonso VIII of Castile suffered a heavy defeat against the Almohads at Alarcos in 1195, he won a great victory against the Almohad caliph Muhammad an-Nasir on 16 July 1212 at las Navas de Tolosa near Jaén, where his army of soldiers from Castile, Navarre, Aragon and the Pyrenees inflicted heavy casualties on the Muslims. No Christian army had penetrated so far south and it signalled the eventual demise of the Almohads. With the momentum of victory behind them, the Castilians and Aragonese swept southwards and by 1248 al-Andalus had lost almost all its major cities, including Cordoba and Seville, to the Christians.

Spain's history had reached a crossroads. Muslim power was waning and the progress of the Christian Reconquest seemed inexorable. When the learned Cordoban Abu Walid al-Saqundi (d. 1232) wrote his *Eulogy of Andalusian Islam* (*Risala fi fadl al-Andalus*), his purpose was to show the superiority of al-Andalus to Berber north Africa, with Granada as the jewel in the crown: 'Granada is the Damascus of al-Andalus,' he wrote, 'nourishment to the eyes, elevation of the soul… where the silver ingots of its streams branch among the emerald of its trees and its delightful walks enchant the eyes and heart and refine the soul.'[42] But the clash of faiths on its frontiers which had established the city in the first place now threatened to destroy this abode of beauty and cultural diversity founded by the Muslims.

THE ISLAMIC STATE OF GRANADA: THE REIGN OF THE NASRIDS

Just as Islamic culture in the Iberian Peninsula was about to founder, a remarkable thing happened. Against all odds, a new Muslim dynasty arose in the small town of Arjona, in the rolling hills near Jaén. On 18 April 1232, as he left the mosque after Friday prayers, a local chief named Muhammad ibn Yusuf ibn Nasr ibn al-Ahmar, 'the Red', boldly proclaimed himself ruler of a small area that included Baeza to the east, Guadix to the south and the city of Jaén itself. Just five years later, in 1237, the city of Granada became his capital, and the Nasrid dynasty was born, its identity taken from the new chief's resonant name of Nasr, meaning Victory. His tribe or clan was known as the Banu Nasr, or Banu l-Ahmar, and this daring fighter proclaimed himself emir of the Muslims, taking the title of Muhammad I and creating a dynastic line that would rule Granada for more than two hundred and fifty years.

Ibn al-Ahmar, a farm labourer who became a sultan, was a figure of paramount importance for Granada. Chivalrous, daring and charismatic, a warrior who could wield a mace weighing ten kilos in battle as if it weighed nothing, he was the man for the moment. His military prowess was a vital asset at a time when the Christians were pushing ever further south. The fourteenth-century Andalusian historian Ibn al-Jatib describes him as:

... a valiant warrior, a hero, a tough man, of great strength, who disdained a life of calm and leisure and preferred simplicity and poverty. He ate soberly, had no affectations, simple in arms, of great energy, fierce, very intrepid; he scorned presumption, was a good friend to his relatives, did good to his people, and was jealous in the reclaiming of his rights.[43]

Muhammad I's kingdom succeeded against all expectations and it secured the presence of Islam in Spain for another quarter of a millennium, at a time when its future seemed doomed.

What do we know of the province of Granada when Muhammad I ruled, and why did he choose to make the city of Granada his capital? The kingdom coincided closely with today's Andalusian provinces of Granada, Malaga and Almeria, and like Zawi b. Ziri before him, geographical location was unquestionably the most significant factor in Muhammad's choice of capital city. Its position on the edge of the mountain range of the Sierra Nevada gave it a strong defensive advantage and its urban confines met the Granadan *vega,* watered by the latest Arab technology, which supplied a bounty of fruit, nuts, vegetables and grain crops to inhabitants of the city, as well as acting as a defensive barrier. The Nasrid kingdom was bordered by the abundant coast along the Mediterranean Sea from Gibraltar to Almeria, and by mountain ranges interspersed with fertile valleys and plains, giving it an alpine dimension. The only way to reach small towns and populations was often by narrow mountain passes frequented by mule trains. Its climate had violent contrasts, hot and arid near the sea, dry and cold in the mountain reaches, with rich, varied soils and climatic nuances which made it good agricultural land. With its natural mountain defences and its capacity to supply plentiful food, both to the kingdom and the city, plus its magnificent location dominating the borders of Muslim lands, it seemed an ideal location for the emerging Islamic state.

Granada was already ancient, with its old citadel or *alcazaba* at the heart of the fortified city built on the hill on the right bank of the River Darro. The Zirids had reinforced the old ramparts, taking them to the edge of steep natural slopes that made potential attacks very difficult. By the early thirteenth century, Granada had developed into a large urban centre, with its *medina*, the traditional Arab walled city centred on a castle or citadel, divided in two by the river. One thousand years later, that vital centre of the city remains in the same place, confirming the clever urban planning of the Zirids in adapting their needs to the topography of their environment.

If we walk around the city today, we can see some of the fundamental features of the Muslim city that were put in place during the eleventh century. The church of San José was super-imposed on the site of a mosque built in that era, whose minaret is now used as the bell-tower. The Muslim *hammam* or public baths in today's San Pedro area were built at the same time. By the beginning of the twelfth century if not before, the main mosque of Granada stood in what is now the Calle de los Oficios in the city centre, and the parish church of the Sacrarium (*iglesia del Sagrario*), attached to the cathedral, occupies the same plot of land. We know that the main mosque was very beautiful, with marble columns and pillar heads and doors brought specially from Cordoba; it was still in use up to 1492 and began to be converted into the church and cathedral site in 1501.

Such was the setting for the first Nasrid emir's entrance into the city. One Friday during Ramadan he came to the outskirts of Granada at dusk, soberly clothed, with the intention of arriving the following morning, but he changed his mind and carried on through the city gates at sunset. The early fourteenth-century Moroccan historian Ibn Idhari describes the moment, with eye-witness details from Abu Muhammad al-Basti: 'I saw the day of his entry into Granada with my own eyes. He wore a tunic of striped cloth, torn at the shoulders. When he stopped at the gate of the Aljama mosque in the Alcazaba, the muezzin was calling the faithful to evening prayer… Then he reached Badis's palace,

his way lit by candles.' Ibn Idhari adds that he had girded his
sword, and with torches burning at the gate of the Zirid palace,
he entered with his chief ministers like a bridegroom hastening
to meet his bride.[44]

In 1238–9 Muhammad I embarked on an undertaking which
became the symbolic and representative hallmark of the Nasrid
era, and an iconic and defining feature of the history of Granada:
the city's new fortress, the Alhambra, meaning 'the red one'. For
a while the emir stayed in the old fortress, with the idea that he
could live alongside some of his subjects, but he decided that this
did not befit a sultan, who should instead live apart from his people.
He thoroughly inspected the site of the Alhambra and marked the
foundations of the building, organized the excavations, and in less
than a year, tall defensive structures had been raised, supplied
with water from the Darro carried there by a specially created
irrigation channel. There were stores for food and arms, and a
public treasury in this place that had served as a refuge for rebels
and leaders since the earliest times of al-Andalus. The walled city
of the Alhambra with its flowing water and lofty fastness had
come into being.

The historian Ibn al-Jatib gives us a glimpse of how the newly
enthroned sultan spent his time. He records that Muhammad I
held general audiences for his people twice a week, which
began with religious readings, and during which injustices were
denounced to him, poets recited, and he received ambassadors and
consulted advisers. These meetings were attended by the cream
of the royal court, including qadis, who were magistrates, senior
officials and the royal family, and ended with a prayer from the
Koran, after which the emir went to a private chamber to work
on administrative affairs. In the afternoon, he ate lunch with his
closest family and the qadis he was most fond of.[45] He adopted
the honorary title 'al-Galib bi-Llah' ('Only God is conqueror'),
the future motto of the Nasrid dynasty previously borne on the
battle standards of the Almohads in their victory at Alarcos in 1195.

The title reflected the pious yet dominant character of the first Nasrid emir, aligning him with the ethos of the Almohads and matching both the role his dynasty assumed and the time in which they lived – fraught with violence, subjection and domination.

By the time Muhammad I made the city the capital of his new Islamic state in 1238, Granada both looked like and functioned as a city in Muslim north Africa rather than in Christian Spain. The status of the city led to two different categories of Muslims in the Iberian Peninsula at this time: first, the numerous Muslims who lived as subjects of the Christian kingdoms of Castile, Aragon and Navarre, and second, those who lived in the small, crowded independent Muslim kingdom of Granada, who spoke Arabic and were rightly felt to form part of the Islamic world. From the earliest years of Islamic Spain, Muslims had a remarkably strong sense of their essential religious and cultural unity, and were proud of what they called *jazīrat al-Andalus*, the peninsula of al-Andalus. It seemed to provide a guarantee that Muslims everywhere in Spain would be respected. Although most of the Iberian Peninsula was under Christian rule by 1248, from Muhammad I's time onwards, there is no record of native Christians anywhere in Muslim Andalusia. Those who do get mentioned are slaves, merchants, refugees or resident foreigners. As a result, Nasrid Granada tended towards a culture that was purely Arabic in its expression. The quality known as *convivencia* – the living side by side of three different religious communities – which had been such an important feature of Islamic Spain in earlier centuries, was entirely absent from Granada from this time until 1492.

The Nasrid dynasty was prey to a series of repeating political and dynastic patterns arising from a history beset by intense disorder, conflict, betrayal and murder. In 1232, Muhammad I took the title of emir and leader of believers. That title implied an absolute dominion over his subjects, though he was held partly in check by the traditions of Islamic government in which some power is vested in theologians and thinkers; it was also tempered by the power of the leaders of clan-based social groups or lineages. One aspect which became a critical complication by the late fifteenth century was the absolute power of the emir to designate his successor. Although there was no written law on the subject, it was logical in Muslim political tradition for the father to be succeeded by his eldest son. As we will see, this right was dramatically disputed on occasions. The visual reinforcement of Muhammad I's power, the heraldic emblem of the Nasrids, was a shield with a band across it bearing the Nasrid motto, said to have been granted to the emir by the Christian king Ferdinand III. The colour of the standard, and the sealing wax, seals and paper of documents from his chancellery were red, in recognition of his name as founder of the dynasty, al-Ahmar, the Red. It was a fearful omen of the bloody future of his line.

The first Nasrid emir's takeover of Granada in 1237 came at a vital moment, as a testimony of Muslim power. In their crusading zeal against the Muslims, the Christians of Castile had conquered Cordoba in 1236, and the Aragonese had won Valencia in 1238. Soon Muhammad I found himself in direct conflict with the Castilians, though how the conflict started is not clear, as Christian and Muslim accounts blame each other. He agreed a peace settlement with the Castilian king Ferdinand III, in which the emir accepted Ferdinand as his overlord and was obliged to pay him large amounts of money as tribute.[46] Two aspects of this agreement with the Castilians are very important. The first is the decision of Muhammad I to become Ferdinand III's vassal, because it set a pattern that would be repeated throughout the existence of the Islamic state of Granada. The emirate never accepted subordination to Castile, and the status of vassalage was an on/off affair, often interrupted by the emir's support of Muslim rebels in Christian territories. The agreement stated that Granada's vassal status would initially last for just twenty years but it would be renewed by the Castilians and rejected by the Granadans many times in the long history of fighting between both sides.

Muhammad I showed loyalty to his overlord by giving Ferdinand III five hundred men to help his siege of Seville in 1248, instead of helping his fellow Muslims, and in 1246 the emir relinquished the city of Jaén in an act of feudal submission. But we also know that he made repeated acts of submission to Muslim rulers too, such as the caliph of Baghdad and the ruler of Tunis. No Arabic source mentions Muhammad I as a vassal of Christians, although Christian chronicles repeatedly describe Granada as a subject state. Politically speaking, Muhammad I must have needed to manoeuvre very fast in order to survive. As the scholar of Islamic Spain, L. P. Harvey, points out, it was a time of kaleidoscopic reversals of alliances, and there were no Muslim leaders in Spain who had not done deals with the Christians. Muslims fought for Christians and vice versa, and so to speak of treason or of apostasy on either side has little value in the context of the precarious balance between the two civilizations.

The second pivotal aspect of Muhammad I's agreement with the Christians relates to religion. The scholars of Muslim religious law, the *ulamā*, wielded a powerful influence on public opinion at all times and tended to favour fighting to the bitter end over diplomacy and compromise. Although religion appeared to play a minor role in the rise and fall of the Nasrid state, this hard-headed approach of Muslim theologians created great difficulty for its secular leaders. As a result, it was tricky for Muhammad I to make his peace treaty with a Christian monarch and not lose public support incited by the disapproval of the *ulamā*. This tension between politics and religion in Muslim Granada would become a significant factor in the final years of Nasrid rule. The Granadan emirs took religious matters very seriously, and were not liberal or tolerant, but all the Nasrids had to weigh the threat of defeat by the Christians against losing the support of Muslim opinion in a state whose fundamental existence depended on Islam.

On 21 January 1273, Muhammad I fell from his horse on his way to meet a group of army leaders near Granada, caught a chill and died in the Alhambra the same day. He was aged seventy-eight and was buried in the old cemetery on the Sabika hill. Muhammad I had reigned for almost forty-four years and his achievements were remarkable. Undeterred by the greatest defeat suffered by the Muslims of Spain at that time, the loss of Cordoba to the Christians in 1236, he came out of nowhere to forge a comparatively safe refuge for Islam in the peninsula, built on perhaps unheroic but effective compromises with the enemy, and hindered by discords caused by the alienation of his supporters. In the Alhambra, he left a building that would become the iconic symbol of Muslim Spain, yet his legacy would be a need for perpetual vigilance in dealing with the Christians, a willingness to compromise and switch alliances as political power shifted, all and anything required to maintain Granada's survival.

The first emir's third son, Muhammad II, stepped into his father's shoes in 1273 and reigned for almost thirty years until 1302. Despite his patronage of poetry as a tool for political propaganda, Muhammad I had been a soldier, not a scholar, and had told his sons that the Nasrids had not come to power by reading books but through rebellion. In contrast to his father's blinkered view of culture, Muhammad II was highly educated, interested in medicine, astrology and philosophy, and wrote poetry and music. His urban upbringing fostered his intellectual aspirations and he created a literary court at the Alhambra whose sages perceived and admired the immense learning of the Muslim, Jewish and Christian scholars at the court of the Castilian king Alfonso X ('the Wise').

Muhammad II also had a deep knowledge of politics but he was unschooled in a crucial element of the politics of the emirate that came into play at this time: namely the power of lineage. Granadan aristocrats up to the late fifteenth century traced their ancestry back to some of the thirty-six lineages established by tradition, which came directly or indirectly from the tribes of Arabia. The rest of the population was said to be descended from other famous lineages, which gives us an idea of the practical and psychological importance of the agnatic link, in which persons were connected through descent from the same, usually male, ancestor. The Muslim scholar, jurist and historian Ibn Khaldun wrote about this solidarity of descent in the fourteenth century, coining the new word *asabiyyah* to describe the group feeling, the cohesive force of the tribe or clan, that contributed in his view to social unity. Group honour, custom and feud provided the cultural connection for clans, the ancient tribal structures of Arab peoples which Islam was able to accommodate, while privileging religious identity over tribal loyalty. For the kin group to function as a support network, its members must have an intimate knowledge of their lineage, a consciousness of their ancestry, in order to forge deep alliances. Harmony in the clan was maintained by the constant threat of the blood feud, by ancient rivalries with the potential to escalate.

One clan or *Banū* closely associated with the early Nasrid sultans was the Banū Ashqilūla, whose leader had supported Muhammad I in his ambitions, but who after his death fell into a feud with his son, caused by the dead sultan's decision to exclude them from power in his new kingdom. The first sultan had enlisted the help of some Castilian noblemen against the clan rebellion but the king of Castile, the learned Alfonso X, craftily aimed to re-enlist the nobles on his own side instead of that of the Muslims. Muhammad II was at risk of losing some influential support from the Castilians, so he had the brainwave of talking to Alfonso X himself.

The *Chronicle of Alfonso X* [47] tells us how Alfonso cunningly misled Muhammad II:

> There came to Seville with them the king of Granada (Muhammad II) and Prince Philip and Don Nuño, and all the other nobles who had been in Granada, and the king received them well, and did them great honour, especially the king of Granada, and on this visit he knighted him. The king of Granada pledged him his friendship as firmly as could be, as had already been agreed in negotiations with Don Ferdinand and the queen, and promised to be Alfonso's vassal for all time, and to pay him from his revenues

300,000 maravedis in Castilian money. All through his stay in Seville, Alfonso did great honour to the king of Granada.

But once this agreement had been concluded, the queen and the nobleman Don Ferdinand pressed Muhammad to grant a truce to the Banū Ashqilula:

> The king of Granada was much grieved at this, for he could see what they wanted was to protect the Banū Ashqilula, whereas they had already taken his money, paid over to them on the understanding that they would abandon that cause.

Muhammad II learnt not only to beware of the power of the clan, but also how dangerous it was to trust the Castilians. He was undeterred, however, and skilfully took forward the project begun by his father to create a place that Andalusian Muslims could call their own. Then suddenly, in April 1302, the second sultan of Granada died in gruesome circumstances, amid rumours that he had been poisoned by a cake made for him by his son and heir, Muhammad III.

This third sultan is recorded as a superstitious, unpredictable man with a schizophrenic personality, prone to brutish cruelty. In the words of the historian Ibn al-Khatib:

> At the outset of his reign, he had a group of his father's household troops, about whom he had formed an adverse judgment, arrested in a sudden swoop. He had them imprisoned in the dungeons of the Alhambra and he kept the key, threatening with death anybody who threw them food; there they remained for days, raising their voices in the agony of their hunger, and those who died first were eaten by those left alive: finally from sheer weakness and exhaustion all fell silent. One of the guards set to watch at the mouth of the dungeon, moved by compassion, threw down to them a small leftover crust of bread. Somebody reported on the guard and orders were given for his throat to be cut on the brink of the pit, so his blood would flow onto the prisoners.

Muhammad III's short reign was ravaged by an instability and violence which would last for over a hundred years. His undue haste to make peace with the Christians, and the political error of trying to control the port of Ceuta, which alienated his north African allies, resulted in his deposition in a palace revolution on 14 March 1309 led by his brother Nasr, and in his departure to internal exile in Almuñécar. Over the next twenty-four years the kingdom of Granada was ruled by three different sultans. Nasr, the fourth emir, ruled for just five years, in which time he successfully defended the coastal towns of Almeria and Algeciras against Castile and Aragon, who had made a concerted effort to crush Granada. This defeat halted the Christian Reconquest for many decades but Nasr, last of the direct line of the Banū al-Ahmar going back to Muhammad I, was overthrown by his cousin Isma'il, who took the throne in 1314, and Nasr ended his life in exile in Guadix, leaving no heirs.

Isma'il, who had the same ancestor as Nasr but through a different line, was cheated of a long, successful reign by violent death. One of Isma'il's cousins took offence at some harsh words and plotted to kill him, leaving the emir's eldest son, a young boy, to become Muhammad IV in 1325. The paradigm of violence and bloodshed became more firmly entrenched when the sixth Nasrid sultan's eight-year reign ended with his murder in 1333 as he was returning to Granada from Gibraltar. Whether as a result of a plot from north Africa or from Castile, Muhammad IV, like Isma'il, died through treachery.

The winds of change were blowing when the reign of Yusuf I (1333–54) began a glorious age of Nasrid cultural achievement. The arts were cultivated and many of the foremost writers of the time graced the royal court. It was in Yusuf's reign that the Alhambra came into its full glory and there will be more to say about that great citadel in the next chapter. It was customary, when an emir or caliph became established, to shelter his royal personage in a palatine city,[48] which also lodged his court, key personnel and often his army. A citadel of this kind would have all that was needed to function as an autonomous unit. When Muhammad I founded his new capital, he created such a city in the Alhambra, whose urban structure was already clearly laid out by the time his son Muhammad II came to power. In Yusuf I's reign the monumental Gate of Justice was built on his order, as was the Comares palace, containing rooms for royal receptions, with its enormous rectangular patio, fountain and wooden roof representing the Islamic conception of heaven, one of the supreme examples of Nasrid carpentry. Under Yusuf I, Granadan architecture reached its zenith.

But Yusuf could not relax. Wedged between Castile and north Africa, the Nasrids had to be constantly wary but this circumspection did not prevent hostility. Like his predecessors, the sultan made a truce with Castile, and then entered into an agreement with both the Castilians and the north African Marinids, placing Granada as a pawn between two strong powers. During his reign the most significant reversal of the Muslim cause in Spain before 1492 took place, in the Battle of Salado in 1340. A decisive factor in the Christian victory was weaponry, as it would be in the last battles of the Nasrids to save their city. The Castilian Christians pounded the enemy with heavy cavalry charges, a form of fighting favoured by western European aristocratic society. In contrast, the Muslim cavalry was lightly armed and manoeuvrable, which did not cut the mustard on the day. To make matters worse, the Castilian king Alfonso XI's crusading zeal inspired him to have another go at capturing Algeciras in 1342–4. Once again, the machinery of war was crucial. The siege of Algeciras was the first major engagement in the Iberian Peninsula in which cannon were used, and one of the earliest anywhere. It was in fact the Muslims who introduced the new weapons, not the Christians, as the latter made out in their own chronicles. In the end the Muslims did not give in, and after the long siege of Algeciras, a ten-year truce was agreed in 1344.

Yusuf I's reign had a terrible end. As he was praying in the Great

Mosque in Granada in 1354, an assassin, described as a lunatic in Arabic accounts, stabbed him to death. It was as if the Nasrids had a curse of violent, bloody death upon them. Yet Yusuf's genius as a ruler allowed his kingdom to last one hundred and fifty years more, and established its reputation as one of the great sites of Islamic cultural achievement in the world.

His son and successor, Muhammad V, was the first Nasrid sultan to experience what has become known as the phenomenon of the interrupted reign, which was to be a critical feature of the final years of Nasrid rule. Only sixteen when he took the throne, just five years later, in August 1359, Muhammad V was replaced by another Nasrid prince in a palace coup which sharply prefigured future events. The Alhambra became a hotbed of sedition and treachery. A grandson of the emir Nasr, named Isma'il, and his mother Maryam, had their ambitions thwarted when Muhammad V was proclaimed the new ruler, though Isma'il was foolishly allowed to continue living in the Alhambra. His conspirators somehow scaled the mighty palace walls while Muhammad was outside and powerless to get back in, forcing him to flee to Guadix, with Isma'il II now on the throne thanks to his mother's money and cunning plot. His reign would not be a long one, however. In 1360 Isma'il was assassinated in a new intrigue in which his brother and court circle were also murdered. Muhammad VI, 'the Red', a nephew of Yusuf I, now took the throne. Meanwhile, Muhammad V, a staunch vassal of Castile in true Nasrid fashion, received the help of King Peter I of Castile against Muhammad the Red, whom Peter imprisoned and murdered, leading him out to a great field in Seville mounted on an ass and clad in a scarlet robe, where he ran him through with his lance. Muhammad V won back the kingdom of Granada in April 1362 and negotiated a series of truces that led to the longest period of peace Granada had experienced in its history, during which he reigned for nearly thirty years until his death at the age of fifty-three. Under his direction, the Alhambra took on the appearance it has today; the

Court of the Lions, and many of the beautiful royal buildings whose style has never been equalled were the work of his architects and craftsmen. The eighth Nasrid sultan died in Granada on 16 January 1391. It was a pivotal moment of transition from an era of unparalleled intellectual, literary and architectural abundance and beauty to a time of waning power, incessant conflict, violence and threat from within and beyond the frontier, sinister harbingers of the decline and fall of Nasrid Granada.

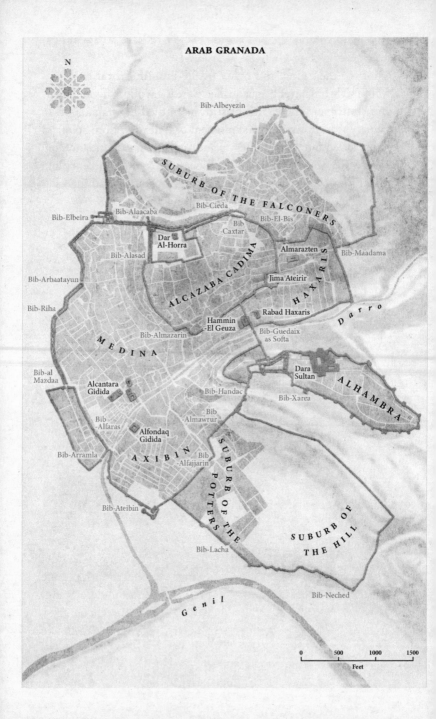

ARAB GRANADA

N

Bib-Albeyezin

SUBURB OF THE FALCONERS

Bib-Elbeira

Bib-Alaacaba

Bib-Cieda

Bib-El-Bis

Bib-Caxtar

Dar Al-Horra

Bib-Alasad

ALCAZABA CADIMA

Almarazten

Bib-Maadama

HAXARIS

Jima Ateirir

Bib-Arbaatayun

Bib-Riha

Rabad Haxaris

Darro

Hammin -El Geuza

Bib-Almazarin

Bib-Guedaix as Softa

MEDINA

Dara Sultan

ALHAMBRA

Bib-al Mazdaa

Alcantara Gidida

Bib-Handac

Bib-Xarea

Bib Almawrur

Bib -Alfaras

Alfondaq Gidida

Bib-Arramla

AXIBIN

Bib Alfajjarin

SUBURB OF THE POTTERS

Bib-Ateibin

SUBURB OF THE HILL

Bib-Lacha

Bib-Neched

Genil

0   500   1000   1500

Feet

4

PARADISE AND PERDITION

❖❖❖❖❖❖❖❖❖❖❖❖❖❖❖❖❖

'ETERNAL PARADISE OF PERMANENT HAPPINESS'

Built on the Sabika hill where eagles once nested, the red fort rises resplendent in its harmony of stone and landscape, natural beauty and human inspiration. A mountain refuge, an oasis of perfumed gardens and flowing waters evoking the image of paradise penned by the great court poet Ibn Zamrak, the Alhambra is a site of power. That power takes many forms – architectural, political, religious, historical and cultural – all permanent reminders of Granada's incarnation and heritage as a Muslim city, encapsulated in the iconic image of the Islamic fortress. Even so, that great walled citadel is not what it seems. Those concepts of *engaño*, meaning 'illusion' or 'deception', and *desengaño*, the awakening from that illusion to a realization of truth, were ubiquitous in the written and visual culture of medieval and early modern Spain. They inhere in the deceptive appearance of Granadan topography, architecture and decoration, and nowhere more so than in the Alhambra. It harbours secrets, illusions, mysteries; it is a place of the hidden and unexpected, of strange contrasts, contradictions and ambiguities. Perceptions can change radically depending on one's standpoint, and perspective is everything in an edifice abounding in windows and belvederes, from which the view is all-important and compelling.

Looking down from outer space, a satellite view of the Alhambra would show us the irregular shape of the palatine city on a hill which is one of the rocky projections of the Sierra Nevada. The Sabika is the loftiest of these craggy outcrops around Granada, and almost unassailable from the north and west, while to the south-east, we would see a narrow, very deep ravine separating the spur from its mountain. The aerial perspective reveals both the Alhambra's superb natural defensive position and also its potential weakness: since it lacks its own water supply, it is reliant on cisterns or aqueducts, which are vulnerable to attack.

Neither the earliest settlers nor those who followed, including the founder of the Nasrid dynasty, needed a satellite to explain the virtues of the Sabika hill, using instead their instinct, wisdom and experience to raise a fortress there. Viewed from the ground, and from a distance, the Alhambra inspires awe in its monolithic majesty, and its imposing military configuration speaks to us of conquest and victory. The great red fortress anchored on the hill-top is a symbol of the power of the Nasrid dynasty of Muslims who created this building, looking down on the city and interacting with it as a dominating Islamic presence. A celebrated fifteenth-century ballad, *Abenámar*, recounts how the Christian king John II of Castile brought his army within sight of Granada in 1431 and marvelled at the buildings rising on the distant hill before him. He asks the Moorish captain Abenámar: 'What castles are they, so tall and shining?' ('*¿Qué castillos son aquellos? ¡Altos son y reluzían!*'). When the Moor explains that they are the Alhambra, the mosque and the Alixares palace, the king exclaims: 'Granada, if you wished, I would marry you, and give you Cordoba and Seville as a dowry' ('*Granada, si tu quisiesses, contigo me casaría:/ darte yo en arras y dote a Córdoba y a Sevilla*').[49] His proposal is firmly rebuffed, King John is enraged and battle ensues. Never had the contrast been greater at this time between the drab brownness of Castile and Nasrid Granada, brightly coloured and luminous on its green pedestal above the *vega*. This ancient poem shows us how the Christians associated Granada and its buildings with femininity and how, despite being on enemy territory, a Christian king could admire a city and culture alien and inaccessible to most Spanish Catholics.

Moving closer, the massive walls of the Alhambra's stone and brick ramparts, towering hundreds of feet above the river below, the twenty-two towers and huge entrance gates, all reinforce the image of an unassailable fortress. The most important entrance, the Gate of Justice, was erected in 1348, during the reign of Yusuf I. The ceremonial purpose evident from its deep, wide porch is matched by a symbolic purpose, displayed in its unusual decoration in the form firstly of a hand, whose open palm, presented to the viewer in the centre of the arch of the porch, symbolizes protection, authority, power and strength. In popular lore, the hand is identified with the *hamsa* or 'hand of Fatima' – daughter of the Prophet Muhammad – an amulet still used by Muslims to represent the five pillars of Islam and to ward off the evil eye. A key with a cord attached is carved in the centre of the inner archway, signalling opening, victory, the symbol of entry into a consecrated place. There is a legend that when the hand touches the key, the Alhambra will have fallen and the end of time will come. Three conch shells crown the arch, evoking their watery origins and the pearls they form, symbols of fertility, creation and wealth. The message to the observer is clear – this is a place of Muslim authority, martial power and abundant riches, and its keynotes are defence, water and the Islamic faith.

Crossing the threshold to the inside lays bare the first illusion – the stern exterior hides the secrets of an astonishing interior, of a citadel transfigured into a palace. This is a place of mystery, camouflage and ambiguity. Perfect proportion and symmetry suggest order and harmony, which is constantly unsettled by the perplexing spatial complexity. There is the disturbing sensation of being in a maze. Courts and rooms are set at odd angles to each other, with access through inconspicuous doors or gloomy passages, and winding, offset approaches lead to inner chambers. No portals or vistas lead from one part to another. For the visitor, this dislocation of their spatial awareness is disorientating; there is no sense of the overall ground plan. Perhaps in Nasrid times it created in outsiders a feeling of vulnerability, of potential surprise at any moment. The sultan was inaccessible and therefore powerful. Only those in the know could navigate the entrances and exits to inner courtyards, creating a suspicion of intrigue heightened by interior passage-ways and shifting levels. This intentional confusion is mirrored below ground in the 16 kilometres of underground galleries, some leading to dungeons, others to secret passageways down which the sultan could flee in dire circumstances. The Alhambra has many strata whose multiple perspectives allow glimpses, impressions and contained observations of individual spaces – but never reveal the overall picture. Its architectural design speaks clearly of the obsession with defence of a dynasty of rulers who lived in perpetual fear of attack.

As if in defiance of this ever-present threat, the Nasrids created a palace of mythical style and opulence, a dream-like setting for the pleasure and refuge of those who lived there, but conceived on an intimate, human scale. All its spaces were fashioned to be seen from their centre, not from the outside or through a façade, and its open-air patios with rooms leading off them obeyed the cultural concept of the domestic space in Islam. Nasrid rulers lived much of their lives outdoors, hunting or inspecting their flocks and smallholdings, so while the palace was a quiet place by day, occupied only by women of the court, it came alive at night, lit at ground level by vast standing candelabra to welcome the return-ing sultan. In a similar way to medieval European cathedrals, no plans exist of its design, nor records of its architects and builders, anonymous masters who worked their magic with running and still water, reflections of light and shadow, scented and colourful plants, marble, stucco and wood. Unlike those cathedrals, few of the Alhambra's halls had stained glass and what did exist was destroyed in a gunpowder explosion in 1590. Instead, spectacular living views of the city and mountains are framed by open window spaces, or by *miradores,* viewing places often set low in the wall, their ground-level height dictated by the fact that in daily life the Nasrids sat on mats or cushions on the floor. The views in the fourteenth century would have been even more stunning than they are today. Then, the hill of the Albaicín was studded with many mosques, their minarets presiding over the large estates of court officials and nobles, each with its verdant gardens, enclosed courtyards and pools reflecting the light. Nowadays we might get some idea of the views they enjoyed by sitting on the ground ourselves but what is much more difficult to appreciate is the original visual splendour inside the palace.

The Alhambra today is a spectral echo of its former glory. Much of its magnificence resided in its lavish carpets, cushions and wall-hangings, colourful silk and wool textiles made in the royal workshops of the Alhambra city. They embellished the halls on festive occasions as draperies or floor coverings, all set amid interior spaces whose varied materials, stucco, wood, marble, glass and ceramics, were vibrantly coloured from wall to ceiling, as conservation work shows. The palace shimmered with vividly painted doors and walls and coloured ceramic tiles decorating the lower areas, their surfaces reflecting the light, the whole a vision of intense, all-embracing colour. Rich blue pigment made from lapis lazuli, deep red created from cinnabar (a toxic natural compound mined in Spain) and vermilion made from mercury sulphide ornamented the background of the plasterwork decoration, gilded with gold leaf on its foreground shapes. Black, turquoise and green pigment from malachite adorned small details. These were the colours and pigments of the early Gothic cathedrals and of medieval illuminated manuscripts, whose hues and tints took on an extra brilliance in the strong Granadan sunlight. The refinement of palace life is enshrined in the exquisite marquetry-work of its furniture and in the famous Alhambra vases, one of which graces the Alhambra museum. Like the floor-standing candelabra of Nasrid times, these huge vases were meant as ornaments to combine with low furniture, so were seen most often from floor level. Painted in metallic lustre and cobalt blue, they are covered in delicate foliage and calligraphic designs, whose shining gloss and aesthetic purpose attest to the enormous wealth of the sultan.

Qal'at al-hamra, meaning 'the red fort' in Arabic, shortened to Alhambra, speaks to the senses but also to the intellect. Beauty and the sacred meet there in the written word, which transforms the palace literally into a great stone book whose many texts ornament the walls and translate the fortress into a consciously learned monument. This is the largest known collection of classical Arabic mural poetry. It is also inseparable from the conception, construction and symbolism of Muslim palaces, and forms a visual record of medieval Islamic ideas about the ideology of the ruler. The many religious inscriptions taken from the Koran contradict the idea that the Alhambra was an entirely secular palace. In combination with the extensive epitaphs relating to royalty, they proclaim the elevated religious and political mission of the sovereign, his lineage and his noble attributes of morality and magnanimity. On the walls of his palace, the sultan is lauded as builder of the unsurpassable architecture around him; here the walls appear to talk to the viewer in verse, often written in the first-person female voice, often recording historical events, or the creation of new or renovated spaces, and evoking their surroundings in splendid images of paradise. Only about thirty poems remain, roughly half the original number, some wrought in plaster, but also on wood and marble, outlined in gold on a blue background, or white outlined in black on a red ground. Written in angular Cufic or more flamboyant cursive script, literature, sculpture, painting and architecture harmonize in this remarkable exaltation of the word.

Two other decorative motifs frame these writings. One conjures up plants in the stylized forms of the palmette, palm leaf, and pine cone, reminiscent of the palm trees of the East and the conifers round Granada, making a visual connection with the gardens of the Alhambra they frame or overlook, and an imaginative link with their place of origins. The other harnesses geometry in designs of staggering complexity that embrace the science behind ornamentation, based on repetition and symmetry, whose unending, overwhelming pattern seems to echo the interest of medieval Arab mathematicians in exploring infinity. The boundlessness of the heavens is the illusion created by the famous *muqarnas* or honeycomb-like forms suspended from the ceilings of the Alhambra halls, which were a feature of architecture in Muslim lands from the eleventh century. In the Hall of the Ambassadors, the sultan sat as if beneath the dome of the limitless Heavens, studded with a multitude of stars painted to resemble mother-of-pearl and silver. The three-dimensional volume of the *muqarnas* fosters the impression that things are not what they appear to be. In this building of perpetual surprises, the honeycomb form of the great ceilings and arches deliberately confuses the solid and the void, the positive and the negative. Once again, perspective and illusion urge us to question the evidence of our own eyes and ponder the meaning of its ambiguities.

The natural world that inspired the stone structures and decoration of the palace is transformed into a work of art in its own right in the patios and gardens of the Alhambra. Sitting today on the café terrace of the monument's National Parador, a state-run hotel created out of the old convent of San Francisco, we can take in the broad sweep of the landscaping as it blends into the hillside above and beyond, but much has changed and much is long gone. Abundant orchards once flourished on the neighbouring slopes, tended using the plant wisdom handed down by expert Muslim botanists like Ibn al-Baytar (1197–1248) from Malaga. But manuals of husbandry were all written in Arabic, and would later be lost, at a time after the fall of Granada to the Catholic Monarchs when the mere possession of a page of script in Arabic counted as heresy. This and centuries of deforestation and soil erosion created an arid landscape of exhausted soil barely sufficient to sustain stunted olive trees. Back in Nasrid times, the historian Ibn al-Khatib enthused over the farms and gardens around the city, luxuriant and verdant, with 'winds that exhaled perfumes bringing Paradise to mind'.[50] Inside the walled citadel of the Alhambra, it is hard to imagine the romantic gardens of the Generalife in their original incarnation as part of a fortress, which boasted extensive orchards belonging to the sultan, behind whose hedges 'white battlements gleamed like stars amid the verdure',[51] making it virtually invulnerable to assault by canon or siege engines.

In the fourteenth century, when the Alhambra was at its zenith in the reign of Muhammad V, its interior allusions to paradise were matched by those of its gardens, whose water, scent and colour blended to create a sensual Eden blessed with moisture and shade. For all its martial dimension, the Generalife was a place of contemplation, where the sounds of running water and the song of nightingales brought to mind the paradise of the Koran. Even in the inner patios themselves, this idea took literal form in still pools of water or moving fountains often divided into four in a symmetry harmonizing with palace architecture and representing the four rivers of Paradise of the prophetic tradition. Here sensual delight anticipated the spiritual pleasures of the afterlife. The patios also evoked the memory of ancient nomadic life, dependent on the life-giving water of the oasis. Water, light and shadow wove their spell, once more confounding the senses and confusing the eye – the poet Ibn Zamrak remarked of the Court of the Lions that in its fountain 'liquid and solid appear to be fused, so that we do not know which of the two is moving'.[52]

Mountains, water, gardens, stone; these natural features mark the twin poles of the Alhambra as a bastion of defence and a refuge of seclusion and delight, a fusion of human genius and nature that magnetizes the countless visitors from all over the world who continue to tread its paths. What does this enigmatic emblem truly signify and why is it so important not only to Spain's past but to its present and future? As the Arabist Robert Irwin points out, compared with the opulent palaces of the caliphs of Baghdad and Samarra, the Alhambra was 'a shadow of a shadow'.[53] Yet this sole Muslim palace to survive from the Middle Ages stands not in the lands of Islam but in western Europe, a testament to the distinctive history of Granada and of Spain. The walled palatine Muslim city of the Alhambra with its own mosque, madrasa, baths and housing was a microcosm and symbol of the more extensive Muslim city around and below it, ever vigilant to frontier attack.

The citadel is suffused with a nostalgia for the past – rather than striking out in a new direction, those who built its palaces harked back to the glories of eleventh-century Cordoba and thirteenth-century Seville before they fell to the infidel Christians, while the memory of the earlier architectural marvels of Damascus under the Umayyad dynasty, and of Baghdad under the Abbasids also lingered in their minds. Even the mural poetry was intentionally archaic, revelling in the forms and familiar hyperbolic, metaphor-laden style of classical Arabic verse. This longing to hold on to and recreate the past finds a potent echo in the nostalgia of many Syrian and Lebanese Arabs of today for the glory days of the Alhambra and Granada under Muslim rule.

In the proportion and symmetry of its architecture and the fusion of literature, art and science in its decoration, the Alhambra gives material substance to the most advanced Muslim learning of fourteenth-century Granada, and to the traditions of the past through which the Granadans strove to preserve a unique Hispano-Arab identity in Spain. Even so, Granada was not closed to other cultural influences. On the ceiling of the Alhambra's Hall of Justice are three oval paintings commissioned by Sultan Muhammad V, depicting elegant maidens with long, blonde hair standing in Gothic towers, admiring warriors both Christian and Muslim, one of whom is killing the hairy wild man of European folklore. There are no known Arabic precedents for the dramatic visual story-telling of these paintings and they were in fact created by Mudejars, Muslim artists living under Christian rule, lent to the sultan by King Pedro I of Castile. They may seem out of place to us now in a Muslim palace but their main purpose was to show that Muhammad V was up-to-date with fashionable European inno-vations. What they also reveal is the degree of cultural reciprocity between Muslim and Christian rulers in this era, accentuated by their singular presence in an archetypally Islamic setting.

If multiple perspectives play a crucial if disturbing role in the onlooker's visual and spatial experience of the Alhambra, they are equally vital in grasping its cultural significance. This is a site of immense power in so far as it looks, Janus-faced, towards East and West. Its essential Muslim and Arab identity sets it in the context of the Islamic civilization of the Orient, yet it exists on the very fringe of western Europe. As such it has profound meaning for both civilizations, as the epitome of Muslim culture, the symbol of Granada that underscores the enduring influence and value of that culture in Europe and the Arab world.

RED DEATH: THE DARK SIDE OF PARADISE

The malignant and destructive internal politics of the Nasrids cast a deep shadow over the brilliance of Granada's cultural achievements. The colour red that gives the Alhambra its name and defines its first sultan, Ibn al-Ahmar, the Red, takes on a ghastly hue in the phrase *Mawt al-Ahmar*, the Red Death, which signifies the violent demise of at least seven sultans and several viziers across the 262 years of the dynasty's existence.[54] The political power of the Muslim ulamā, warring clans, betrayals, murders, the tendency to multiple reigns, and the intense and prolonged discord at the heart of the royal family all played their part in destabilizing Granadan political life and weakening the city from within. The lives of two great and powerful men, both viziers, bear witness to this discord, and embody the uneasy, bitter-sweet alliance of scholarship and politics under Muslim rule in Granada.

To be a vizier brought great prestige but also great peril. In Granada it was not usual to have a chief vizier, or prime minister, as it was once in Cordoba, though a single vizier was usually in overall command. He was entirely at the mercy of the sultan, who appointed and dismissed his key minister at will, but his power was great since most viziers were personal friends of the monarch. Similar to the relationship between the old British monarchy and the prime minister, the sultan delegated administrative power to his minister, who conveyed and fulfilled his orders, organized administration, drew up decrees and official correspondence, and headed diplomacy as well as the Granadan section of the army. The minister carried out the sultan's dirty work on his behalf, often incurring the hatred of offended clans and lineages. But he had to defer to the emir's judgement, could not interfere in decisions of religious authorities, and had no right of succession. A vizier did not need to have noble lineage – the most fundamental qualification for the job was a high level of culture and education.

Sultan Muhammad V's first vizier, Lisan al-Din ibn al-Khatib, was born into an aristocratic Yemeni family on 16 November 1313 in Loja, an important town to the west of Granada, where his grandfather preached at the mosque. He became the disciple of Ibn al-Jayyab (1274–1349), secretary to the royal chancellery, who began the custom of inscribing his poetry on the walls of the Alhambra, and sang the praises of the Nasrid sultans for nearly half a century until he died peacefully in bed aged seventy-five. Ibn al-Khatib, whose felicitous first name Lisan al-Din means 'Tongue of the Faith', became a master wordsmith, succeeding al-Jayyab as court poet and secretary to Sultan Yusuf I and rising to a highly prestigious post in the Nasrid administration as head of the chancellery. This was the official press office of the sultan established originally by Muhammad II, where all state documents were written on the traditional red paper denoting the Nasrid line. As court poet at a time when poetry was political propaganda, his role was to write *qasidas*, poems of praise in honour of the sovereign, penned for official celebrations, the circumcision of emirs, military campaigns and funerals. He also composed many *muwashshahs*, poems about love's cruelty and hopelessness, consisting of five to seven verses and composed to be set to music and performed.

Ibn al-Khatib's literary talents were not solely those of a poet – his scholarship, range of knowledge and prolific output are remarkable, comprising some sixty or so works in total, encompassing travel writing, treatises on political theory and medicine, biographical dictionaries and the histories for which he became famous. His complex, highly ornate letters written as head of the chancellery contrast with the scientific stringency of his remarkable treatise on the plague. Written about 1362 and perhaps inspired by the eleventh-century polymath Avicenna, in it he explored the idea of transmission of the disease through contagion, five hundred years before the first vaccinations against infectious diseases became widespread. In north Africa, he became sufficiently fascinated by Sufism to set out his own mystical ideas in *Rawdat al-ta'rif bi al-hubb al-sharif* (*The Garden of Instruction in Noble Love*), expressing the belief that love literally makes the world go round. But his crowning glory was the great historical work *al-Ihata fi akhbar Gharnata* (*The Complete History of Granada*) of 1369, which tells his own life story, describes the city and kingdom of Granada and recounts its history. In it he gives us an invaluable portrait of its inhabitants; these were people, he says, who were not slaves to luxury, but were happy, orderly, bourgeois folk who spent summer in the country estates of the *vega*, were orthodox in their faith, paid their taxes on time and dressed elegantly. The women tended to be plump and short in stature, and were lavish with jewellery. Ibn al-Khatib likened the *vega* to the countryside around Damascus, boasting that it was the talk of travellers and a conversation point of evening gatherings. It was, he said, spread out:

> like a carpet on a plain furrowed by streams and rivers, where farmhouses and gardens cluster together, in the most delightful situation, and with the greatest abundance of sowing and planting – a space of forty miles bounded by hills and girded by mountains forming two thirds of a circle... Five hills and a vast plain mark the position of this great city, spreading out in the distance, cultivated everywhere, without any barren or desolate space, to the very limits where the bees have their nests.[55]

Known as 'the Man of Two Lives', Ibn al-Khatib's scholarly side was matched by an equally intense career as a politician and statesman, in which his relationship with his protégé and nemesis Ibn Zamrak was key. This Andalusian of precocious talent was born on 29 June 1333, the year that Sultan Yusuf I took the throne, and came from a poor family who had fled to Granada when Christians claimed their land, and lived in the Albaicín. An unconfirmed story tarnished his name, which claimed that his father, who was a blacksmith and also rented out donkeys, had been killed by a blow to the head from his own son. Ibn Zamrak was brilliant from the start, devoted to study, probably at the new madrasa of the Alhambra opened in 1349, and pupil of a glittering generation of north Africa and Granadan scholars, including Ibn al-Khatib himself. Like his most significant mentor, he harboured ambitious political aspirations alongside his literary prowess. He became secretary of the north African Marinid prince Abu Salim Ibrahim, until Ibn al-Khatib found him a niche in the Granadan royal administration. Both men were on excellent terms with each other, to the extent that Ibn al-Khatib dedicated his great history of Granada to his pupil, who in turn wrote eulogies about his mentor.

But, as we saw in Chapter 3, violence and intrigue took centre stage. The murder of Sultan Yusuf I in October 1354 was followed in 1359 by the deposition of his eldest son Muhammad V by his half-brother Ismail II, whereupon Muhammad fled to Morocco. Ibn al-Khatib and Ibn Zamrak followed him into exile and were well received at the Marinid royal court, from where the young scholar, now twenty-six, took advantage of the situation to travel round Morocco, and study in Fez. Here he witnessed the visit to court of some Sudanese diplomats who brought the sultan the gift of a camel. His natural talent for poetry stands out in his witty description of the beast:

> It has yellow patches like a border of daffodils,
> planted on high banks where the water vipers roam the streams.
> It moves its feet like palm trunks,
> And the lofty mountain of its neck rises
> Crowned by the light of its eye.[56]

Muhammad V crept back to Ronda to await his chance, taking Ibn Zamrak with him, and in 1362 regained his throne from the next usurper, Muhammad VI, with the help of Pedro the Cruel of Castile. As private secretary to the sultan, and now court poet, the next ten years passed tranquilly for Ibn Zamrak, still considered the greatest poet of the Alhambra, whose verses appear in the Patio of the Myrtles, the Hall of the Two Sisters and on the bowl of the fountain in the Court of the Lions. Expert in the secrets of cadence and symmetry, his grammatical perfection and impeccable musicality betoken a master of his art. Ibn Zamrak was unique as a poet in witnessing the completion of the palace buildings. His lyrical descriptions of the place, though conventional, are often sublime, evoking the natural world, gardens, flowers and life's pleasures, which were standard topics of Arabic poetry. He often expressed his preference for artifice over nature, which combined in perfect measure in his eulogy of the city:

[Granada] is a bride whose garland is the Sabika,
And whose jewels and garments are the flowers…
Her throne is the Generalife;
Her mirror, the surface of the pools,
Her ear-rings, the pearls of dew.[57]

Meanwhile, Ibn al-Khatib had not fallen under the shadow of his beloved student, and carried on writing his great history of the city, and advising the sultan as his chief minister in the complexities of Granada's politics. In a letter to Ibn al-Khatib which begins: 'Father and source of my knowledge, author and renewer of my benefits, polisher of my perfections, fountain of my hopes…'[58], Ibn Zamrak showed his deep gratitude to and affection for the man who educated and employed him. Or so it appeared.

The year 1371 brought dramatic news. The chief vizier, Ibn al-Khatib, who had been sent to study the frontier fortresses, had sailed from Gibraltar to Ceuta under the protection of the Marinid sultan Abd al-Aziz in Tlemcen in modern-day Algeria. Rumours had been circulating that Ibn al-Khatib was plotting the Nasrid sultan's overthrow and Muhammad V immediately replaced him with Ibn Zamrak, who now attained the defining goal of his political career. In Marinid Morocco, Abd al-Aziz died in 1372 and his successor arrested Ibn al-Khatib on trumped-up charges of heresy. He was interrogated by a special commission from Granada, who tortured him then sentenced him to death. Late that same night, henchmen from Granada broke into his prison and strangled him; the following day his body was dug up from its burial place and burnt by his enemies. It was the ignominious murder without fair trial of a great man for political reasons. Even more dastardly was the fact that the head of the special commission and its henchmen was his chosen and favourite disciple, Ibn Zamrak.

We may never know for sure whether Ibn al-Khatib did plan to betray his sovereign, nor ever establish the true reasons for Ibn Zamrak's treachery. Was he torn between loyalty to his old master and loyalty to sultan and country? Was he himself under threat if he failed to take action, or was he eaten up by political power and ambition? In the years that followed, Ibn Zamrak pursued his political intrigues, recording all the events of the Nasrid court in his verse, but over time his influence waned along with his reputation, and he came to be viewed as the Judas of Muslim Spain, while the dead Ibn al-Khatib grew in stature. He was naturally hated by the murdered vizier's son, who spread the story that Ibn Zamrak had killed his father and had, he said, a despicable nature and base appearance. When Muhammad V died in 1391, the famous court poet got nowhere with his son, Yusuf II. Imprisoned in the fortress at Almeria, Ibn Zamrak was released in July 1392 and when Yusuf died a few days later, the new ruler Muhammad VII immediately dismissed him from his post as chief vizier, appointing him as *kātib* or secretary instead. Then one night, probably in 1393, the sultan's thugs attacked Ibn Zamrak while he was at home reading the Koran with his two sons. They were all murdered, in front of his wives, daughters and servants.

So, one terrible assassination was avenged by another, and politics destroyed the lives of two exceptional scholars. Incited by intrigue, treachery and ambition, Ibn Zamrak's bloody Dance of Death finally extinguished Arab Andalusian poetry, one of the brightest lights in western Muslim culture.

THE PATH TO PERDITION: THE END OF MUSLIM RULE

By the start of the fifteenth century, Granada had become more oriental than ever. This Arabic-speaking Islamic state on the edge of Europe mirrored the customs and even institutions of the Marinid dynasty of north Africa with which it had strong ties. Before, Granadans had rubbed shoulders with the Christians to the extent that their ways of dressing and the arms they used looked similar, and Muslims rarely wore turbans in al-Andalus. But now Granadan troops wore Moorish armour and golden helmets, and used Arab saddles, leather shields and light Moorish lances.

What kind of place was Granada at this time? What did it look like, who lived and worked there, and what did daily life consist of? The cityscape of Granada was typical of other Andalusian and north African Islamic cities, with a walled central nucleus or *medina* where the main religious, commercial and military buildings were situated, next to the main royal palace and fortress of the Alhambra. The city we know today was then two cities, the royal one on the Sabika, Madinat al-Hamra, and the city of the people, Madinat al-Gharnata, beneath it. It expanded around the core of its great fortress, and its original residential area, the old Casbah on the right bank of the Darro, spread out in concentric rings of new suburbs created to house the influx of Muslim refugees from the rest of Spain. New districts flourished around the *medina*, some big, some small, each with its own gates, normally open all day for the purpose of collecting taxes on the merchandise coming in or going out, but closed at night to isolate and protect the city dwellers. The names of some of these suburbs came from the place of origin of their first inhabitants, such as the district of Gomeres at the present-day entrance to the Alhambra, named after the black Berber tribesmen who lived there, and who had come from Morocco to fight for the Granadans. Some reflect their profession – the Albaicín, or al-Bayyazin, means the district of the falconers.

The street layout so characteristic of Muslim cities was one of winding streets with many smaller streets branching off the main routes, twisting and undulating and often leading to dead ends. Some of the streets were, and still are, so narrow that a single soldier wearing armour and holding a lance couldn't walk down them. Passages linked the upper floors of houses above the street, many of which had attics that protruded outwards, creating sharp contrasts of light and shadow that accentuated their irregularity. The separation and isolation of the districts, the narrow tortuousness of the streets, the many labyrinthine passageways, mighty walls and entry gates all point to a primordial need for defence against attack. They suggest a society closed off from the outside world, living with the ever-present threat of assault and persecution. Such a mindset is entirely understandable, given the long history of Christian Reconquest, a threat which had pushed the boundaries of the Islamic kingdoms further and further south until only Granada remained.

This closed-in quality also had an effect on the houses of its inhabitants, of which there were about fifty thousand at the end of the fifteenth century. The majority of Granadans lived in very restricted, enclosed spaces. The records left by the Christian con-querors show that their families often needed between two and six dwellings of the size used by the same number of Muslims. The sheltered nature of Muslim houses reflected their concept of urban domestic life as a refuge from the hubbub of the street. The houses in the Albaicín were remarkable for their beauty, each a small oasis to counteract the heat of the city, with courtyards and orchards, pools and fountains with running water. Nowadays few true Moorish houses survive, the best preserved being 16, Calle del Horno de Oro (Gold Oven Street), near the River Darro. With their inner central patios, fountains and potted plants surrounded by living areas and bedrooms, these dwellings were places of intimacy away from prying eyes and the fierce summer weather, with few windows facing outside, often just balconies with wooden shutters. Most houses had a water supply system using irrigation channels from rivers and streams, and water closets running into an external drain. Their furniture was poor and sparse, mainly consisting of low tables or dressers, chests, mattresses and cushions, carpets and rugs. There were copper or clay pots, rarely glass, and better-off families had oil lamps, bedclothes and table coverings. The crowning glory of the Albaicín was the *maristan*, a hospital for therapeutic treatment of the insane, built in the reign of Muhammad V in 1367 round a central pool and courtyard.

It is the first record of such a hospital in Europe and is a source of pride to Muslims.

Outside, in the town, the main buildings bespoke the importance of trade. Its outer walls marked the frontier between the urban and the rural, a place of transition where goods from the *vega* and further afield were transformed in city workshops and sold in the bazaars. The main thoroughfare, Zana qat Ilbira, now the Calle de Elvira, ran north to south the length of the city and still survives, as does Calle Zacatín, the clothes market where street-traders sold second-hand clothes and just about everything else from rush matting to hosiery. The *alcaicería*, situated near the main mosque, was devoted to commerce, particularly buying and selling the beautiful silk that was one of Granada's most important products. It was a large area full of stalls and small shops, almost two hundred in all, with ten access doors, and was owned by the sultan, who collected tribute from the stallholders. The historian Bermúdez de Pedraza, writing in the sixteenth century, captures the essence of the commercial heart of Granada, in the *alcaicería*, the original silk market:

> ... it is like a square city surrounded with a wall and ten gates with chains so that no one can enter on horseback, with so many streets and lanes that it resembles the Cretan labyrinth, and it is even necessary to tie a thread to the door to find the way back. Its shops are innumerable, wherein is sold every kind of silk, woven and in skein, plus gold, wool, linen and merchandise made from them.[59]

Today, the old silk market sells tourist trinkets but its labyrinthine quality remains.

The *alhóndiga* or *fundaq* was a kind of corn exchange where grain was stored and sold, as well as other merchandise. The building known as the Corral del Carbón in modern Granada is the only old corn exchange preserved in Spain. There was also a specialist *alhóndiga* called the Zaida, which sold oil, honey, cheese and dried fruit. The third area devoted to trade was the *zocos*, the permanent or regular markets, of which there were many in the streets and squares of the *medina* and in the city suburbs, and they were inevitably the noisiest, busiest places in Granada. The city also had many mosques. The German traveller Hieronymus Münzer estimated that there were over two hundred when he visited Granada in 1494, though most of them were small, private places of worship. All the large mosques were converted to churches when the city came under Christian rule and none have survived apart from two minarets, converted to the bell-towers of the churches of San José and San Juan de los Reyes. The madrasa, the Muslim higher education school, is still in Calle Oficios (Trades Street) near the cathedral today, and continues to fulfil its original function as an educational institution, now part of the University of Granada.

A wide variety of people lived inside the city walls. Rich Muslims who were landowners, merchants or members of a distinguished family lived in big houses in the suburbs, while the majority of the population consisted of artisans, many of whom lived in specific streets or *barrios* according to their areas of expertise. Most of the professional army lived in the city, along with artists, men of letters, lawyers and religious leaders. A large part of the Granadan lower class was made up of agricultural workers from the *vega*, who lived outside the city walls in small communities and villages. A number of native Castilians, either captive or free depending on their religious status, had an influence on politics. Many religious renegades, or *elches,* who had converted to Islam and escaped from Castile, found asylum and important positions in the Nasrid army and at court. There were no Christians native to Granada because the *mozárabes,* or Christians living under Islamic rule, had disappeared from the area before the emirate was formed. A Jewish community numbering no more than three thousand people lived in the city and on the coast, working as craftsmen and traders, as well as doctors and interpreters. Granada was a thriving cultural, religious, commercial, artisanal and agricultural centre, in a privileged position of access to the ports of Malaga and Almeria, with north Africa within easy reach. Genoese merchants called regularly at these ports and eagerly bought local silk, sugar and fruit; the economy would have flourished if the Granadan treasury had not had to pay enormous sums of tribute money to Castile.

The typical Muslim city was a living organism, as the scholar James Dickie describes it, with the mosque at its heart as the centre of spiritual nourishment, and the *suqs* or markets, the digestive system of the urban structure.[60] The deep connection between commerce and religion is reflected in Muslim city life as an entire circulatory system, where sacred and profane co-exist in everyday dealings and in the environment of civic and religious buildings. Granada was a living, breathing model of the Islamic city, whose everyday bustle and comfortable abundance spoke of wealth, confidence and power.

The curtain falls on this commanding spectacle and rises again for the final act of the drama of Muslim Spain. The sky is stormy, the terrain rocky and barren, the colours drab, tawny, grey, black and white. A turbaned man shrouded in a white cloak stands with his back to us, gazing out across the plains towards a far-off city among mountains swirling in mist. Behind him, a train of horses and mules struggle up the steep slope, led by a band of Muslims who gaze at the turbaned figure with worried faces. A servant holds his white horse, which also stands gazing into the distance, its haunches and richly decorated saddle dominating the scene. Two men kneel to stare afar, one of them carrying an oud evoking merrier times, but the mood is of shock, sadness and desolation. This scene painted by the Spanish artist Francisco Pradilla in 1892 depicts 'The Moor's Last Sigh' (*El suspiro del moro*), the legendary moment when Boabdil, the last Muslim sultan of Granada, is said to have turned and looked back on his lost city and wept. The conquered sultan's horse faces back in the direction it came, suggesting its master's longing to turn back to Granada. All of the personages have turned away from the viewer, their gaze intent upon the hazy, distant image of the paradise they have left behind. The dun tones of the image, the turbulent sky, the suggestion of wind and the rocky outcrop which dominates the foreground, reflect the impoverishment of the defeated Muslims and the barren future ahead. How was it that this final act came to unfold in such a dramatic way?

It took three hundred years for Granada to reach its zenith as a Muslim city. Its nadir came in just one century, hastened by the Nasrids' bloody feuding and instability inside the city, and by the threat of Christian attack on its frontiers. After the great Muhammad V died in 1391, sultans came and went at a bewildering rate, and their history reads rather like something from tales of the Arabian Nights. Over the next twenty-six years, into the fifteenth century, three sultans reigned briefly. Yusuf II, Muhammad V's son and Boabdil's great-grandfather, reigned very briefly indeed, for just two years, dominated by his father's faithful minister Khalid, who went from tyrant to victim in a ghastly execution after Yusuf II suspected him of a plot to poison him. Ironically, Yusuf himself died a terrible death soon after, when according to Christian accounts, he put on a poisoned gold tunic sent to him by the King of Fez.

Muhammad VII succeeded the poisoned sultan in 1391 and reigned for sixteen years until his own death in May 1408. As the Nasrids continued to indulge their fatal predilection for palace intrigue and bloody violence, the strength of the Christian kingdom of Castile was growing. Castile had recovered from the Black Death, which had ravaged the peninsula from mid-century, and was developing the formidable power which would eventually lead it to dominate both Europe and the New World. The skilful diplomacy that had previously enabled the kingdom of Granada to stand up to Castile grew less effective as the Christians began to wield their muscle and refused to accept the kind of easy truces made in the past.

While Muhammad VII was sultan, his elder brother had

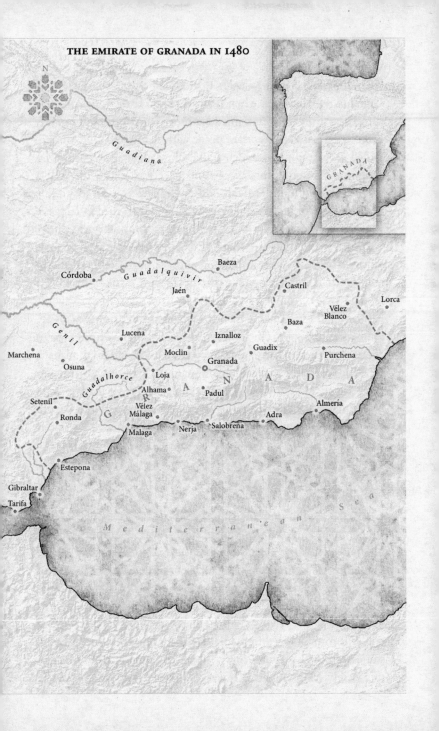

THE EMIRATE OF GRANADA IN 1480

Guadiana

GRANADA

Córdoba

Guadalquivir

Baeza

Jaén

Castril

Lorca

Vélez
Blanco

Genil

Lucena

Baza

Iznalloz

Marchena

Osuna

Guadalhorce

Moclin

Guadix

Purchena

Granada

Loja

G   R   A   N   A   D   A

Alhama

Padul

Setenil

Vélez
Málaga

Adra

Almería

Ronda

G

Ronda

Malaga

Nerja

Salobreña

Estepona

Gibraltar

Tarifa

Mediterranean Sea

N

been imprisoned in the castle of Salobreña on the coast south of Granada. Finally freed when Muhammad VII died, he took the throne as Yusuf III and reigned for nine years from 1408 to 1417. Yusuf tried hard to negotiate peace with Ferdinand I of Aragon, but in 1410 Ferdinand struck a vital blow against the Nasrids by capturing the border fortress of Antequera, which gave the victors encouragement and demoralized the Granadans, who lost a fine town and a fertile growing region. When Yusuf III died in 1417, the issue of clan warfare resurfaced startlingly to disrupt the next thirty-five years, which provided what L. P. Harvey describes as an extreme example of the Granadan phenomenon of multiple interlocking reigns.[61] It is mind-boggling that up to 1453, Muhammad VIII reigned twice, from 1417 to 1419 and from 1427 to 1429, while Muhammad IX, 'the Left-Handed', reigned three times, 1419–27, 1429–45 and 1447–53. In addition, Yusuf IV reigned from 1430 to 1432, Yusuf V in 1445, 1450 and from 1462 to 1463, and his son Isma'il III from 1446 until 1447. What are we to make of this? Apart from revealing the dizzying political instability of the Granadan state, both internally and externally – due to the continued interference of Castile and Aragon – it suggests something was cracking under pressure. That pressure came from a new destructive factor, the fierce fighting between clan factions in Granada itself, principally between the Banū Sarraj, known as the Abencerrajes, and the Banū Bannigas, known as the Venegas.

In 1419 a coup d'état led by the Abencerrajes brought down Muhammad VIII and put Muhammad IX on the throne. He was not in direct line of succession, and this lack of legitimacy to rule sparked a profound conflict which continued until the end of the emirate. By destroying the direct legitimacy of succession, the Abencerrajes hoped to bring in a political system based on respect for the power and privilege of their lineage group, and their feuding family is romanticized in medieval ballads and sixteenth-century stories, reminding us of the importance and influence of lineage in this society. Muhammad VIII was reinstated in 1427 and promptly changed his ministers – the Abencerraje government was replaced at its head by Ridwan Venegas, whose clan supported legitimate succession. Ridwan had been the great enemy of Muhammad IX in the Granada ruling elite and proposed a third candidate for the throne, Yusuf IV, supported by John II of Castile, whose story is told in the Castilian ballad *Abenámar*. But by the time Muhammad IX died in 1453, the Abencerrajes had found a new pretender to the throne, Abū Nasr Sa'd, the grandson of Yusuf II. It turned out to be a disastrous move on their part.

Sa'd would be fifty-five when he became sultan in 1453, supported by the Abencerrajes and also by the new Castilian king Henry IV, who came to the throne in 1454. But before Sa'd's accession, there was a confused period of two years or so when there were two rulers in Granada – the son of Muhammad VIII, Muhammad X (known to the Castilians as el Chiquito, the Younger) occupied the Alhambra, all Granada, Malaga and Almeria, but proved so unpopular that he had to flee, falling into an ambush set by Sa'd's son, after which he was suffocated to death inside the Alhambra, along with all his heirs. At this point in 1455, Sa'd entered the Alhambra himself and promptly rejected all Castilian demands for truce, vassalage and tribute, in spite of having their support.

A first-hand account, written from the point of view of the Christian enemy, confirms Sa'd's bellicosity and daring, although it also speaks volumes about the horrific cruelty of the Christians. In 1457, a Swabian knight, Jorge de Ehingen, travelled to Spain in the service of Duke Albert of Austria. While he broke his journey at the French court, news came that King Henry IV of Castile was preparing an expedition against the Muslims of Granada, and Ehingen left to take part. He recounts that 'a solemn embassy from the king of Spain arrived asking the king of France to participate in the great crusade he intended to lead against the Moorish king of Granada (Sa'd), because the latter, with the help of the king of Tunis and other Moorish sovereigns from north Africa, had made many ruinous raids throughout Spain, and if they were not restrained, worse would happen'. He describes the beautiful suits of full armour each man was given, as well as one hundred crowns and a letter of recommendation for the king of Spain. He continues: 'We went in the direction of Granada (in Spring 1457) winning all the castles and small populations of this kingdom, because the Moors feared taking on so many troops. We had to assault most of the fortresses and towns and put all the Moors to death, and their assistants and servants were ordered to knife to death the women and children, which they did. We continued to the city of Granada, ready to fight, as we suspected that the Moors, with so many soldiers, would come out to meet us. They didn't let us get close to the city but sought us out, to no advantage since we had better munitions than they did.' After this Jorge and the troops crossed the kingdom of Granada, 'bringing blood and fire to everything we found'.[62] He escaped with his life, although his leg was badly injured during an assault on the town of Jimena, near Jaén.

The year 1461 is remembered with horror in the history of Granada as the time when Sultan Sa'd, who then lived and reigned in the Alhambra, ordered the assassination of the Abencerrajes, who had always been his supporters and promoters. Sa'd's motivation is unclear: either he wanted to deflect attention from the fact that he had failed to keep the Castilians at bay, or perhaps he was enraged that the Abencerrajes had in reality kept some tribute money for themselves which should have been paid to the Castilians. Whatever lay behind his decision, the demise of the Abencerrajes was swift and brutal: Sa'd invited them all to a banquet at the Alhambra and had nearly the entire clan slaughtered there, including his own minister Mufarrij. Those few individuals fortunate enough to escape fled to Malaga.

Then, in a bizarre turn of fate, Sa'd was overthrown by his own son Abu l'Hasan in a midnight coup in late August 1464. Banished to Salobreña castle under house arrest, he died there on 20 April 1465. Abū l-Ḥasan had his father's cruel and warlike nature, and a weakness for sensual indulgence. To keep the ūlama happy, he showed defiance to the Christian enemy, always favouring fighting over diplomacy, and refusing at one point to pay the tribute which denoted subservience to the Castilian crown because, he claimed, the places in Granada where coins were minted were forging lance-heads to make war.

Abū l-Ḥasan's kingdom nonetheless enjoyed a long period of peace and prosperity from 1465 to 1481, while the sultan maintained constant raiding attacks on the Christians, forcing the enemy to sign a series of truces. So far so good. Abū l-Ḥasan's militant politics allowed his kingdom to flourish. But events conspired against the continued peace of the Nasrid state in the form of two new and very powerful monarchs, Isabella of Castile and Ferdinand of Aragon, who had married in 1469. Isabella had assumed the throne of Castile in 1474 when her brother Henry IV died in his palace in Madrid, thereby ousting her rival, the king's allegedly legitimate daughter Juana la Beltraneja. When the king of Aragon, John II, also died in 1479, his son Ferdinand took his place, and the two kingdoms were united. In the same year, civil war in Castile ended and peace was made between Castile and Portugal. These circumstances proved fatal to both the Nasrid kingdom and to Andalusian Islam, as Ferdinand and Isabella could now concentrate on war against Granada. Their aim was to extinguish the Muslim state forever.

The Arab historian Al-Maqqarī tells us of ominous warnings given to the Granadan Muslims of their imminent divine punishment and ruin. He recalls that ancient weathercock in the old Casbah of the city, which bore the notorious rhyme foretelling some dreadful calamity that would ruin both the Alhambra and its owner. The historian and Jewish convert to Christianity Hernando de Baeza also describes the appearance of a comet, broad and long like a sword, which appeared from two hours before dawn until daylight, for a period of thirty days. The king's astrologers told him this was a portent of war and destruction. The year

1478 brought another omen. Eager to increase his military might, Abū l-Ḥasan had amassed more cavalry, artillery and other weapons than any of his predecessors, and his soldiers were confident and not intimidated by Castilian military prowess. In April 1478 he decided to organize a great parade and inspection of all his troops, a marvellous public spectacle to demonstrate his military might, and surreptitiously to prime his people to accept a tax increase. But the sultan's triumphal parade, which lasted for days on end, culminated in disaster. Al-Maqqarí gives us a vivid description of what happened:

> On this occasion the soldiers were clad in suits of polished steel armour, dressed in gorgeous silken robes, mounted on fleet steeds, and having their swords, spears and shields richly embossed with gold and silver. One day when the sultan was as usual seated under the pavilion and the troops were passing before him, the summit and the sides of the neighbouring hill of As-sabíkah being crowded with spectators who had left their dwellings for the purpose of witnessing the pageant, God permitted that all of a sudden the rain should fall down in torrents, and that the river Darro should overflow its banks. Such was the fury of the devastating element, which came pouring down from the neighbouring mountains, carrying along large stones and whole trees, that it destroyed everything on its way, and that houses, shops, mills, inns, markets, bridges and garden walls were the prey of the devastating flood. The water reached as far as the square where the great mosque stands. So frightful an inundation had never before been experienced in the country, and the people naturally looked upon it as the harbinger of the dreadful calamities which awaited Muslims in just chastisement for their perversity and their sins.[63]

The catastrophe had a terrible effect on Abū l-Ḥasan, who seems to have suffered some sort of breakdown. The anonymous Arabic author of the fifteenth-century chronicle known as the *Nubhdat*, the only contemporary historical source existing in Arabic, declares that from this time on the sultan grew confused and began to decline. He reviles him for devoting himself to pleasure and lust, and amusing himself with singing and dancing girls. No doubt the sudden shock of the flood did adversely affect Abū l-Ḥasan but his abandonment to sexual pleasure was nothing new, and his naturally lustful nature had intense and far-reaching consequences for his family, and for his kingdom.

Just a few years before Abū l-Ḥasan had overthrown his father, his first son, Abu Abdallah Muhammad b. Ali, known to the Christians and to posterity as Boabdil, was born in the Alhambra, in either 1459 or 1460. From the start a dark shadow of destiny lay over him, as court astrologers predicted that he would suffer great misfortune, to the extent that he also became known to the Christians by the nickname *El Zogoibi,* 'the unlucky one'. The opposing poles of Boadil's early years were the beauty and protection of the great palace and fortress, and in disturbing contrast, the climate of danger and fear that pervaded the citadel and therefore his youth. At the madrasa of the Alhambra he learned Arabic grammar, poetry, logic, algebra, science, history, law and theology. Boabdil's schooling was designed to make him an educated and widely read man, an image hinted at in Christian chronicles. A future sultan also needed practical expertise and we know he became a highly skilled horseman adept at hunting, a pursuit that was a measure of his nobility as well as excellent training for fighting, which made him deft in battle. The twin focuses of his life were his Islamic education and his immersion in the arts of horsemanship, hunting and war.

His mother, Abū l-Ḥasan's legitimate wife Aixa, was an important and powerful Nasrid princess, daughter of Sultan Muhammad IX and allegedly descended in a direct line from the Prophet Muhammad. Her first husband, Sultan Muhammad X, had been executed by Abū l-Ḥasan on behalf of his father Sa'd. Despite this melodramatic background, their marriage was harmonious for twenty years, during which time their three children Abd Allah, Yusuf and Aixa were born. But harmony turned into hatred when another woman came into Abū l-Ḥasan's life. A young Christian girl captured during a raiding party was taken to Granada and sold into the king's household. She was given the task of chamber-maid, sweeping the royal chambers. Abū l-Ḥasan somehow became involved with the girl, using one of his pages as a go-between, but Aixa's ladies found out that she had visited the king's royal chamber and gave her a beating which left her half dead. Outraged, Abū l-Ḥasan ordered beautiful clothes to be made for her, and gave her magnificent jewellery fit for a queen. On the next festival day, he ordered his people to pay homage to 'la Romía', the name used to describe a Christian woman who had become Moorish.

The young Christian captive was Isabel de Solís, daughter of the knight commander of the town of La Higuera de Martos, Sancho Jiménez de Solís. She converted to Islam and took the name Zoraya from the name of a star in the Pleiades cluster. Legend has created an image of her dazzling beauty that bewitched the sultan, although Hernando de Baeza, who lived at the royal court, wrote that he knew her many years later and didn't think much of her appearance or character. Whatever the case, something about her must have captivated Abū l-Ḥasan, for he gave her land, houses and a privileged position at court, apparently bribing certain judges into legalizing a new marriage, which created furious resentment in Aixa and her sons. Baeza continues that from then on, the sultan made his life with her, recognized her as queen and never spoke to nor saw his wife Aixa again.

To a proud noblewoman like Boabdil's mother, such an insult must have been hard to bear, and we learn from the chronicles of Aixa's bitter jealousy. To be scorned as queen by her husband and substituted by a young girl with no social status, a renegade Christian to boot, created enmity between Abū l-Ḥasan and his legitimate wife, his family and members of his court. Because of the emir's impetuous, cruel and angry nature, Aixa feared for her children, so she let things pass for a time, while he indulged in his passions. What forced her to act was the threat posed to her first son Boabdil by Zoraya's two young sons, Sa'd and Nasr, considered as royal princes from birth, and treated as such at the Granadan court. The position for Aixa was intolerable – she lived in the rooms surrounding the Court of the Lions with her children, loyal servants and advisers, while Zoraya lived with Abū l-Ḥasan in the Comares tower of the Alhambra close by. Like the rest of the royal family and court, her two sons Boabdil and Yusuf sided with their mother, and being clearly ambitious for her eldest child, she saw the danger to Boabdil's succession to the Nasrid throne, fearing his father would favour one of Zoraya's sons over his legitimate heir. But Aixa had a very important card up her sleeve. As a Nasrid princess, she could transmit rights to the throne, rights which she exercised as mother of the next true Nasrid sultan. As a young man of twenty-two, amid this family crisis between his father and mother, Boabdil married Moraima, daughter of the governor of Loja, in 1482 and lived with his own young family in the Alhambra. But events had reached a tipping point and a new drama was set to be played out on the political stage of Granada.

Abu l'Hasan's seizure of the Christian town of Zahara in December 1481 and the retaliatory Christian capture of Alhama in February 1482 began a ten-year struggle between the two sides, and discord in the Granadan royal family would become a key factor in the final outcome. Boabdil was incited to revolt against his father by the once again powerful Abencerraje family, with his mother's support, and was proclaimed Sultan Muhammad XI in 1482. The man who had ousted his own father was overthrown by his son in turn, and he fled to Malaga. Yet despite their enmity, father and son continued to fight the Christians vigorously. Boabdil was unlucky to be defeated and captured at the battle of Lucena in April 1483, enabling his father to recapture Granada in his absence. The young emir was obliged to pay the price of his freedom by pledging homage and fealty to the Catholic Kings, who had taken his tiny son Ahmed as hostage, and promising to collaborate with them against his father.

Ferdinand used that deadly antagonism between father and

son to win a diplomatic victory but Isabella wanted to go further, insisting that the time was right to conquer the kingdom entirely. The Castilians began a policy of relentless aggression against Granada in 1484. Boabdil, who had returned to the city, was forced to flee again to Cordoba, which was in Christian hands, when his uncle, Muhammad Ibn Sad, el Zagal, seized control and deposed his brother, Boabdil's father, who died in 1485. El Zagal ruled from 1485 to 1487 as Muhammad XII; but Boabdil and this second rival for the throne, his uncle, decided to present a united front against the intensifying Christian campaign. Boabdil was captured once more, this time at Loja, and forced to renew his vassalage to Ferdinand and Isabella. By 1487, the Christians had gained such a major advantage in El Zagal's territory in the south-west of the kingdom that he lost support and withdrew to Almeria, leaving Granada in his nephew's hands. Obliged to agree to surrender Granada in 1487 in exchange for a lordship, Boabdil reneged on the agreement and continued to resist.

But by 1490 Ferdinand and Isabella had built a military head-quarters in their newly constructed town, Santa Fe, just west of Granada, allowing them to sever the city's communications with the outside, and facing it with the spectre of starvation. Rather than suffer that fate, Boabdil opened secret negotiations and reluctantly decided to surrender, finally agreeing to the terms of the capitulation on 25 November 1491. His royal chancellery prepared a long document on behalf of the sultan setting out his proposals for the surrender of Granada, which would only take place once Ferdinand and Isabella agreed to them. First and foremost, on the day that they received the Alhambra, they must release Boabdil's son, still prisoner in Moclín, and hand him over to his father, along with all the other hostages and their servants, without delay.

There followed a long series of practical conditions and religious stipulations. In essence, all Granadan Muslims should be allowed to keep their religion, mosques and leaders, and the muezzin's call to prayer should continue, for all time. Boabdil also stipulated that

1. Colourful pomegranate plate from the local Fajalauza ceramics workshops.

2. Sewer cover in Granada embossed with a pomegranate.

3. A statue of the Infant Jesus holding a pomegranate (detail).

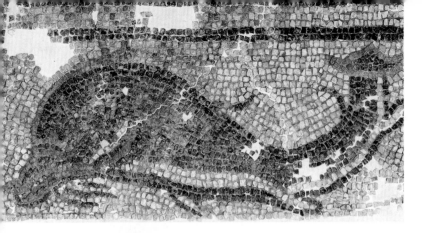

4. Dolphin mosaic dating from AD I, found in Calle Primavera in the district of El Zaidín in Granada, on the site of the Roman villa of Los Vergeles.

5. Bronze sculpture of a man wearing a toga dating from AD I, found near Piñar in Granada province.

6. The fortress and palace of the Alhambra set against the backdrop of the Sierra Nevada mountains.

7. The Nasrid shield carved on the wall of the Alhambra, inscribed with their dynastic motto 'Only God is conqueror'.

8. Elaborate
Nasrid tilework
on the walls of
the Alhambra.

9. Inside the
fortified residential
tower or Qalahurra
of Sultan Yusuf I.

10. Patio or Court of the Lions in the Alhambra, the main courtyard of the palace, famous for its twelve white marble lions. It is said to be an architectural image of paradise.

11. Coin minted in the reign of Sultan Muhammad V.

12. One of the famous Alhambra vases painted in cobalt blue and lustre. Their imposing presence and lavish decoration represent princely grandeur and divine perfection.

13. Gilded inscriptions on the walls of the Alhambra, displaying the beauty of Islamic art.

14. *opposite* Anonymous fifteenth-century portrait of Boabdil. His posture, kind expression and melancholy eyes convey dignity, royal composure and respectfulness.

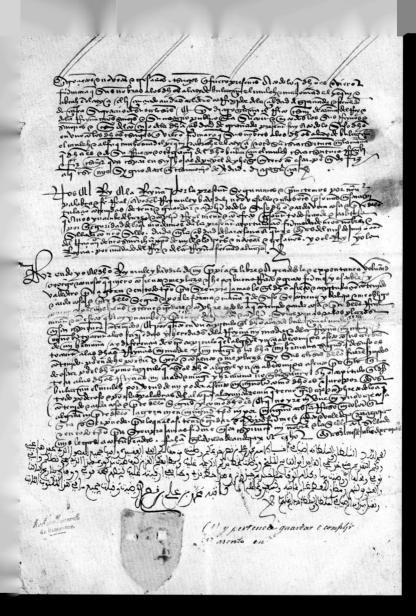

15. The page from the Capitulations or terms of surrender
of Granada showing the signatures of Sultan Boabdil, King
Ferdinand and Queen Isabella, dated 25 November 1491

Jews living in Granada should have the same rights as Muslims under the terms of the surrender. His desire to preserve the religious life and customs of his people, both present and future, and to negotiate a situation which would allow them the greatest possible freedom and tolerance is plain to see. He was sensitive to their feelings and took pains to try and avoid any sense of the inferiority of Muslims under Christian domination, stipulating that no Christian would have the right to speak cruelly of the past. The practice of Islam and its material manifestations of the mosque, minarets and muezzins, were paramount, as was the *aljama* or Moorish quarter of the city, from where Muslim lawyers, judges and community leaders operated. Boabdil's inclusion of the minority group of the Granadan Jews in the terms of surrender, where he states that they 'should benefit like us from these terms', is particularly poignant when just months later in the spring and summer of 1492, all Jews, not just those from Granada, would be expelled from their native Spain by Ferdinand and Isabella.

On 2 January 1492, Boabdil surrendered the city of Granada to the Christian monarchs King Ferdinand and Queen Isabella. It was a moment that has captured the imagination of writers and artists up to the present day, initially as a day of supreme conquest and later because of the extreme pathos of that moment of transition and loss. As Boabdil handed the keys of his city to Ferdinand, he said in Arabic: 'God loves you greatly. Sir, these are the keys of this paradise. I and those inside it are yours.' The story of the Moor's last sigh portrayed in Pradilla's painting was perhaps a Morisco tradition, and may be truth or invention. Legend has it that when the retreating Moors reached the town of Padul, which is farthest place from which Granada can be seen, Boabdil began to sigh heavily, invoking the Muslim god of war, and began to weep. His harsh and unkind mother is said to have upbraided him with the words: 'You do well, my son, to cry like a woman for what you couldn't defend like a man.'

Boabdil's wife Moraima died in internal exile soon after at the estate in the Alpujarras granted them by the Catholic Monarchs, and in October 1493 the last sultan set sail for exile in north Africa. Mystery surrounds the date and place of Boabdil's death – some say he died soon after in Fez, others that he lived on and expired in Tlemcen in modern-day Algeria. Overtaken by political and cultural events beyond his control, the man destined to relinquish the last Islamic state in Europe played the foil to King Ferdinand as hero, and where his life was retold in fictional stories of conquest, he was cast as the betrayer. Boabdil was both the Muslim invader and also the native Hispanic self, and he encapsulates the enduring quandary over Spain's cultural distinctiveness. In defeating Boabdil, the Spaniards defeated a part of themselves and denied their Muslim heritage and a part of their own identity.

Boabdil, the last Muslim ruler of the medieval Islamic state of Granada, changed the course of Spain's future.[64] He was a key figure at a crucial crossroads in world history, and many of the current tensions between Islam and the West have their roots in the history of Granada, the kingdom he lost, a calamity which has been seen as the prelude to the economic depression and decline of the Muslim world. Deprecated in the past as a cowardly traitor or tragic victim, he has become a potent symbol of resistance to repression, always preferring negotiation and diplomacy over violence and war. His reign marked a crucial moment in the centuries-old clash between two great religions and cultures, and symbolized the epoch-changing transition of the kingdom of Granada from Islamic state to Christian territory, a moment which set Spain on a course to become the greatest power in early modern Europe.

GRANADA
THE PEOPLE I

5

GARNATA AL-YAHUD

City of the Jews

• • • • • • • • • • • • • • • • • •

THE RISE AND FALL OF THE STAR OF DAVID

The rooms are dark inside the House of the Forgotten. Ethereal strains of plaintive Jewish music hover in the air, merging with the gloom to intimate that this is the abode of the unseen, the hidden. But what brings tears to your eyes is the tangible, oppressive atmosphere of sadness and fear. This stately museum house at the top of a small alley off the Carrera del Darro is a place of absence, a shrine to the Jews of Granada, who have vanished almost without trace. Its façade bears an anonymous shield, the details obliterated long ago, allegedly to hide the Jewish identity of its sixteenth-century owner. The exhibits are disturbing in their disparity. Jewish cooking utensils, domestic paraphernalia, small home-made toys, all tell the story of home life in a culture in which women played a central role in educating their children. Alongside, there are lavishly embellished Torahs, one dating from the fifteenth century, an oil lamp from the second century AD, sacred scrolls emblazoned with the Star of David, and the gold seven-branched candelabrum of the Menorah, all evoking a people whose twin poles were family life and a learned religion. Yet turn the corner and the shock is instant as you come face-to-face with gruesome weapons of torture. Here are the *garrucha* or pulley to stretch and dislocate the limbs, the *toca*, a strip of linen used in water torture, and the *potro*, a rack on which bodies were bound ever tighter by a series of cords. These were the instruments of choice of the Spanish Inquisition, employed to extract confession from those former Jews converted to Catholicism and known as *conversos*, whom the inquisitors deemed to be heretics. The encounter between the holy, the homely and the ghastly implements of violent suffering in these sharply divergent exhibitions epitomizes the history of the Jewish people of Granada, who settled in the region two thousand years ago, flourished there, suffered persecution and were finally expelled never to return.

The story of the Spanish Jews is punctuated by silences and composed of fragments, partial accounts, glimpses and myths. Like the earliest history of Spain and of Granada itself, realities are overlaid with legend. No one knows exactly when the Jews arrived, although the Jewish scholars of medieval Spain claimed their forefathers had come on Phoenician ships from Tarsus in the time of King Solomon, ten centuries before Christ. Much later, they may well have fled to Hispania from Rome soon after the Jewish rebellion against the Roman Empire in AD 66, followed just four years later in AD 70 by the destruction of much of Jerusalem, including the Second Temple, by the Emperor Titus. Jewish people also came ashore in Baetica from the south, since there was a flourishing Jewish population in north Africa from ancient times. There is a legend that a Jewish soldier, Pirus, came to Spain with many other Jews as early as the sixth century BC, after the destruction of the first Temple, and that with their help he founded Granada and Toledo. These inherited stories may have some truth in them but they also served to justify the right of all Jews to remain in Spain when they were threatened by exile. A man called Justinus, who lived in Mérida in south-west Spain and came from the Palestinian town of Flavia Neapolis, is named in an inscription from the second century AD that gives us the first concrete proof that Jews lived in the peninsula.

The short Old Testament Book of Obadiah is a prophecy in the form of Obadiah's vision of the people of Israel returning from exile to claim the land they had lost. He mentions a land of unknown whereabouts called Sepharad, where the people of Jerusalem had been banished. Perhaps as early as the second century AD, the Jews adopted this word, Sepharad, to denote Spain and Portugal, a land that they viewed as their second home, another place of refuge from exile, whose name future generations would adapt to identify themselves as the Sephardim. Strangely, very little solid or tangible remains of a people so deeply attached to their new abode. In Granada, Jewish traces are inexistent in its urban structures – there are no synagogues, no street names, not from the early years after Christ, nor from the thousand or so intervening years until the Jewish expulsion of 1492. Nevertheless, we can detect their presence in and around Granada in the early fourth century through the material evidence of the written word. Turning back to the decrees or canons of the Christian Council of Elvira, convened in Iliberis at the very beginning of the fourth century to solve specific religious issues of the time, we find that at least four of these decrees refer explicitly to Jews. Canon 16 expressly prohibits mixed marriages between Christian women and Jewish men; if parents married their daughters to Jews, they were refused Holy Communion for five years. Such a ruling suggests that relations between the followers of both faiths was very close, and that this kind of mixed marriage happened fairly frequently. No mention is made of Christian men married to Jewish women, although Canon 78 excommunicates any Christian man who committed adultery with a Jewish woman. The Church feared the religious influence of Jewish women, considered as dangerous as any pagan.

Other relationships between members of the two faiths were

also penalized. Canon 48 forbids any crops grown by Christians to be blessed by Jews, upon pain of perpetual excommunication. The Christians seemed to believe that Jewish blessings had a special, mysterious virtue which enabled crops to flourish, and may have feared them as magicians or sorcerers. In Canon 50 a similar punishment befell any Christian who shared his table with a Jew. Since Saturday is a day of rest and enjoyment of good food in Judaism, Canon 26 orders Christians to fast on this day of the week, presumably to underline their religious difference. The early Church leaders clearly feared such intimate and binding relationships with a people close to, but different from, orthodox Christianity, and the cautionary decrees of the Council of Elvira on Christian–Jewish relations were echoed by Bishop Gregory of Iliberis in his five *Treatises* (*Tractatus*), where he examines these ties and condemns in particular the practice of circumcision and the celebration of the Sabbath.

These insights into the life of the people of Iliberis in the very early fourth century bring certain important aspects to light. The strictures of the evolving Catholic Church presuppose the existence of an already substantial Jewish population in the city and its outlying rural districts, a population which had regular, friendly contact with the Christian community, and which was large enough to pose a religious threat to Catholicism through its propaganda. Even at this early stage in the life of the city, future discrimination against and oppression of the local Jewry were plainly prefigured.

After the time of Gregory, the Jews of Iliberis are silent for four hundred years. We can dimly glimpse their unquestionable presence up to the eighth century, a span of almost half a millennium during which the Visigoths renounced Arianism for the Catholic faith, with distressing results for the Jewish population. Under Arianism, the Jews could marry Christian women, employ them as servants and buy them as slaves, but when King Reccared converted to Catholicism in 589, laws were modified and persecution began, with varying degrees of intolerance. Christianity played a key role in the newly unified Visigothic state and, as before, the Jews were perceived as a threat to that unity. Ervigius (680–7), the king most hostile to Jewry, prohibited any Jewish books and teaching, and punished non-pork-eaters with head shaving and a hundred lashes. Many Jews were forced to convert or emigrate. Discontented and desperate, they were about to take a vengeance with long-lasting repercussions.

All sources agree that the Jews rebelled, assisting and welcoming Tarik and his Muslim army when they arrived on the south coast in 711. Arab sources agree that Iliberis was captured violently sometime between 711 and 713, and was crucially involved in this rebellion against Visigothic rule, as Tarik left a Jewish garrison in the town to guard it while he advanced further north.[65] Their support for the Muslims turned out to be a good move, as things improved considerably for the Jews under Islamic rule. They were *dhimmis*, people of the Book, whose faith was one of the three Abrahamic religions, and as such they were allowed to practise their religion freely in synagogues and choose their own leaders, subject to a payment of tax. By the tenth century, the Jews may have had the biggest population of any community in al-Andalus, borne out by the words of Sultan Abd Allah, who wrote that in the first years of the Zirid kingdom, the majority of the inhabitants of Granada and its tax inspectors were all Jews.[66] There is a story that the Jews founded and renamed the city of Granada, which has become its most popular foundation legend. It comes from a casual remark made by the Arab historian and geographer Ahmed al-Razi, known as the Moro Rasis, who visited the place in the tenth century and claimed that the township was called 'Garnāta al-Yahūd' 'Granada, city of the Jews', because they lived there in large numbers.

The stones of Granada hide some of the secrets of this Jewish settlement. The ancient parts of the bell-tower of the church of Saint Joseph in the Albaicín, still partly preserved, were built in the eighth century. Later overlaid by the minaret of a mosque, which then became a Christian bell-tower, it was known as the tower of the Jews and marks the site of an early Jewish quarter in the heart of this district on the right bank of the River Darro, close to the protective citadel. The unknown numbers of Jewish people living in this community were most likely small farm-owners, artisans and traders, who earned their livelihood from local resources. By the eleventh century, three hundred years of violence, wars, revolts and banditry had left the settlement of Granada in ruins and diminished, until the Berber chieftain of the Zirids, Zawi ben Ziri, conquered it easily in 1013, founding his new city-state, a refuge also for Jews fleeing from the sacking of the *alhama* of Cordoba. In the eleventh and twelfth centuries, Granada's population has been estimated at 15,000 inhabitants, a quarter of whom were Jewish, making them the most numerous group in the peninsula. From this time on, Granadan Jewry began to flourish.

Skilled in agriculture, tanning, dyeing, silk-making and metal-working, they traded what they grew in the rich lands of the *vega*, especially sugar cane. They practised as doctors and were influential as intellectuals and poets, but their most striking talent was their skill in finance. They monopolized tax-collecting and exerted enormous political influence, as we will see later in this chapter in the case of the Granadan magnates, the Nagrela family. This fascinating and important era of Jewish history was interwoven with the history of the Spanish Zirids. The ascendancy of the powerful Jewish viziers Samuel Ibn Nagrela and his son Joseph Ibn Nagrela in the eleventh century, and the peaceful prosperity of the Jewish Granadans at this time, went hand-in-hand with the rise of the Zirids to become the most powerful princes of al-Andalus. Jewish power and prosperity in the city had reached its zenith.

Then disaster struck. In 1056–7 the young Jew Yusuf Ibn Nagrela inherited an immense fortune from his father Samuel, who had served as vizier to the Zirid emir. Yusuf also inherited his father's political ambition and became vizier in turn, but he lacked Samuel's experience and shrewdness. In the next section we will see exactly how he became embroiled in dangerous court intrigues and soon found himself out of his depth. When the emir's much-loved heir Buluqqin died in 1064 at the age of just twenty-five, Yusuf was suspected of having poisoned him. His scheming aroused a climate of increasing hostility towards his people which led to his assassination on New Year's Eve 1066 in the first pogrom in the history of Spain, when three or four thousand Jews were murdered in the city. From then on, details of the life of the Granadan Jews become ever more elusive. The surmise is that the Jewish quarter of the city recovered quickly after the storm had passed, but another was brewing. This was the century of the First Crusade, and Christians in the north of the Iberian Peninsula, inspired with zeal to fight the holy war, were gradually gaining strength. The Almoravids – the fierce, veiled Islamic warriors from north Africa – answered the call of Spanish Muslims to help fight King Alfonso VI of Castile after he wrested Toledo from the Muslims in 1085. Their leader Tashufin subdued Granada, by then famed in the Muslim world for its beauty and known as the 'camel's hump' (whose meat was considered the tastiest part of the camel), and the Jews of the city rushed to help their new rulers in the losing battle against another north African sect, the Almohads, who invaded al-Andalus in the middle of the twelfth century and proposed to destroy all remaining churches and synagogues in the region.

Against the odds, some Jews survived these persecutions and worshipped at the mosque of the Converted in Granada, the present-day church of San Juan de los Reyes (Saint John of the Kings). Yet they were distinguished from true Muslims by the yellow turbans the Almohads forced them to wear; in 1199, they were also obliged to wear blue by the Almohad leader al-Mansur. As Almohad power waned and the new Nasrid dynasty of Spanish Muslims sprang up in the thirteenth century, a small community of long-standing Jewish residents hung on in their old quarter in the Albaicín. In the two hundred and fifty years of Nasrid rule of city and province ending in 1492, there is no sign that they ever persecuted the Jews. Many Jewish newcomers from north Africa settled in the new community at the foot of the Mauror hill, under the Vermilion Towers (Torres Bermejas) and the Old Fortress or Alcazaba Cadima, while others continued to live in the Albaicín. Both Jewish *aljamas,* which were self-governing communities, lived on in an increasingly heavily populated city with its resplendent Islamic civilization.

The city of the Jews had become the city of the Muslims. No Jewish voices speak to us from that time, no direct Jewish testimony remains; once again, their covert presence can only be detected by piecing together the scarcest of evidence. In the late twelfth century, the great Jewish philosopher Maimonides from Cordoba, who himself feigned conversion to Islam for a time, had reacted angrily to the forced conversion of the Jews by the Almohads, declaring that a persecuted Jew could publicly adopt Islam, while secretly following his original faith. In doing so, he legitimized crypto-Judaism. Over the next two hundred years the Jews of the Iberian Peninsula fared little better under Christian rule. England had expelled all its Jews in 1290, and France followed suit in 1306. Tolerance held out for longer in Spain but the religious fanaticism stirred up in the south in the late 1300s by the uncompromising archdeacon of Écija, Ferrant Martínez, exploded in anti-Semitic hatred as hundreds of Jews were murdered in Seville in 1391, and their *aljama* was destroyed. From that moment, Granada once again became a land of refuge for the Jews, a place where many fled to save their lives and regain their identity. Yet their numbers were tiny – of about 300,000 inhabitants of the province of Granada, only 3,000–5,000 were Jewish, and by the end of the fifteenth century they made up about 1 per cent of the population of the capital city, just 550 individuals.[67]

Once in Granada, they struggled to keep that identity as they initially appeared no different in dress from their Muslim neighbours, whose rulers, ironically, eventually obliged them to wear yellow hats and a humiliating badge on their outer clothes in order to distinguish them. Instead of denoting pride in their Jewishness, these measures shamed them in public. So, recalling the advice of Maimonides, they merged into the community as inconspicuously as possible. Many wealthy Jews appeared to convert inscrutably to Islam, yet followed their faith behind closed doors. They left no traces, no synagogues, no street of the Jews. Yet when Sultan Boabdil agreed the terms of his final surrender of Granada to the Catholic Monarchs in November 1491, he stated that all Jews of his kingdom 'should benefit like us from these terms'. It was a gesture of inclusiveness and tolerance on the part of the last Muslim ruler of Granada that clashed starkly with the attitudes of his Christian conquerors, who had established the Spanish Inquisition in 1480 to root out heresy among *conversos* or Jews converted to Christianity. Those who had not converted soon realized that they too were in the line of fire.

The Jewish people who had found a sanctuary in the city and kingdom of Granada in the fifteenth century had not been touched by the Inquisition. Granada had been the last Islamic state in Spain, Arabic-speaking, independent and not subject to Christian jurisdiction in any way. These Jewish refugees, from a race of people who were never conquerors but always victims fleeing from persecution, had thought they were safe in a second promised land, citizens of a city that in their later historical memory would become one of the great capitals of their geographical map of nostalgia and uprootedness. In January 1492 they watched the surrender of their beloved city with heavy hearts, not knowing that in a matter of months, their world was to fall apart.

STATESMEN AND SAGES:
THE GOLDEN AGE OF THE JEWS

On the eve of catastrophe, if the Granadan Jews could have looked back at their long history in that place, lasting almost fifteen hundred years, they would have felt great pride and gained some consolation from knowing that their people had made a permanent and illustrious contribution to the life of Granada and of Spain. That brilliant heritage was enshrined in the lives of four prominent individuals who lived in the Golden Age of Hispanic Jewish culture in the eleventh and twelfth centuries. The first rose from a humble shopkeeper to become one of the most powerful and influential men in medieval Spain. As we have seen, Samuel ben Yosef ibn Nagrela ha-Naguid (993–1055), known as Samuel ibn Nagrela, started life in Cordoba, although his family came from Mérida. In the city of his birth he gained a full education in Hebrew and Arabic culture before he was obliged to leave in haste for Malaga to escape the Berber assault on the city. There he opened a shop selling spices but his fame as a calligrapher in Arabic soon spread. The Jewish historian Abraham ibn Daud tells us in the *Book of Tradition*[68] (*c.*1160) that his shop was near the palace of Abu l'Qasim, vizier of the Zirid sultan Habus ibn Maksan, who heard of Samuel's skill at letter-writing from one of his servants. He was so impressed with his multilingual talents and the artistic composition of his letters that he took him back to court in Granada, first as a tax collector, then as a secretary and finally as assistant vizier to Habus himself, and likely administrator of the royal finances. Samuel was not only very learned in his literary and scientific knowledge but was also a fine Talmudic scholar. In 1027, he was appointed as Nagid, or leader, of the Jewish community in the kingdom of Granada and its representative before the sultan. As the highest-ranking Jewish courtier in the whole of Spain, he became extremely influential. The Nagid saw himself as

God's messenger, sent to make Granada a fortress and stronghold for his oppressed people. He was convinced that God had sent him to fight, and that the angels and patriarchs would intercede for him. Samuel's militancy led to his becoming general and commander of the Muslim army, of which he remained in charge for seventeen years. It was an astonishing feat for a Jew to be made head of a Muslim army. To hold high public office at the same time was very rare, since Jews were not normally allowed to hold such positions in Islamic nations.

When Sultan Habus died during Ramadan 1038, we can recall that Samuel was influential in achieving the succession to the throne of Habus's first-born son Badis, whom he supported against a younger son, Buluqqin, who fled to Seville. The Jew was not only Badis's chief vizier but was also responsible for foreign policy in the kingdom of Granada until his death. He has the image of a powerful statesman and diplomat, hated and respected by the Muslims, loved by the Jews and feared by neighbouring kingdoms, a man of exceptional character and quality, as the Arab historian al-Qurtubi (d. 1076) declared in a remarkable portrait of the Jewish vizier:

> That accursed Jew was a superior kind of man, although God misinformed him about the true religion. He was very knowledgeable and tolerated insolent conduct patiently. He combined a solid, wise character with a sharp mind and a polite, friendly manner. Blessed with exquisite manners, he was capable of taking advantage of any circumstance to praise his enemies and calm his hatred with affable conduct. He knew the literature of both peoples. He had a deep knowledge of the Arabic language and knew the work of the subtlest grammarians. He spoke and wrote classical Arabic with the greatest ease, using this language in the letters he prepared in the name of his sultan. He used the usual Islamic formulas, the praise of God and of Muhammed, our Prophet, and recommended the addressees of the letters to live according to Islam. He was distinguished in his knowledge of the science of the ancients, in mathematics and astronomy, and also

in the field of logic. He beat all adversaries in debates. Despite the vitality of his spirit, he spoke little and thought a lot. He owned a wonderful library.

Ibn Nagrela made a clear distinction between his private life as a Jew and his official post as the vizier of a Muslim ruler, and at all times he used diplomacy and gained respect among nobles and common people alike. An anecdote from his life makes this clear:

It is said that a spice merchant who lived near sultan Habus's palace always showered Samuel with insults when he went past his house in the sultan's company. The sultan was outraged at this behaviour and ordered Samuel to punish the man by cutting out his tongue. Instead of carrying out such a cruel order, Samuel made some enquiries about the man and found out that he was short of money. He sent him a large sum to get him out of his difficulties. Soon after, the king and his vizier went past the spice merchant's door, and instead of the old insults, the merchant showered blessings on them. Astonished and irritated at the same time, Habus asked Ibn Nagrela why he had not punished him. 'My lord,' the Jew replied, 'I followed your orders religiously, because the truth is that I have indeed taken away this man's evil tongue, and replaced it with another much better one.'[69]

Master of language and nuance, Nagrela the statesman was also an exceptionally fine poet, one of the most famous bards writing in Hebrew in the Middle Ages. His great innovation, born of his deep knowledge of both Hebrew and Arabic literature, was to use the techniques and tropes of Arabic poetry while writing in biblical Hebrew. But his subject matter ranged from religious verse to homoerotic poetry, and even the poetry of war. When he celebrated his victory over the allied armies of Seville, Malaga and the Berbers on 8 September 1047 in verses of thanksgiving addressed to his son, few war poems could have been so beautiful nor so eloquent:

Send a homing pigeon, although it cannot speak,
with a small letter tied to its wings,
reddened with saffron water and perfumed with incense.
And when it flies up and away, send a second after it,
in case a falcon takes the first, or it falls into a trap,
or returns at its leisure, so that the second gets there faster,
and as it nears Yosef's house, it will coo from the rooftop;
And when it flies down to him, he must treat it like a bird
And free its wings so he can read this letter:

    'My son, you must know that the cursed enemy
    Has scattered in the mountains like chaff blown by the
        storm,
    Or on the highways like sheep without a shepherd,
    Without finding in their enemies what they were
        expecting.
    As we went to destroy them, they fled in the night,
    Some died, and some killed each other in the ford.
    Their hopes of winning the walled city were dumbfounded,
    They were ashamed like a robber caught in the act.
    Shame covered their faces like a blanket,
    Ignominy stuck to them like the liver to its lobe,
    They drank opprobrium in glasses, they sipped from the
        inebriating cup,
    My heart trembled like that of a woman who gives birth
        the first time,
    But God laid his balsam on it, like rain in the drought.
    Then my eyes shone whilst those of my enemies clouded over.
    I sing with joyful spirit, while they are bitter with weeping.
    To you, my Rock, my Fortress, to You my soul sings;
    To you their cries of anguish were directed.
    My son, pay attention to the magnificent hand of my God.
    Arise and speak my praise to the assembled townsfolk.
    Wear it like a phylactery, tied to your hand,
    And write it on your heart with a pen of iron and lead.'[70]

The real voice of Samuel ibn Nagrela speaks in this poem, in which
the at times biblical tone and reference to Jewish tradition shows

his piety, modulated by metaphors which are Arabic in style. Here the soldier meets the father, the man of arms meets man of letters. Samuel left a rich written legacy in the form of correspondence, a biblical dictionary in Hebrew and Aramaic, an Arabic work on the contradictions of the verses of the Koran, which aroused a heated argument with the famous poet and philosopher Ibn Hazm (994–1064) of Cordoba, and a fine body of poetry. His war poems, including the one above, were considered to be the first war epics in Hebrew literature.

Samuel headed a Hebrew Renaissance in Granada, and many great Hebrew thinkers and poets gathered round him. The philosopher Ibn Gabirol (1020–70) moved to Granada from Zaragoza, where he wrote his famous *Fountain of Life*, a theory of Neoplatonism based on the concept of divine love and the union of the human with the divine. Nagrela was also a generous protector of his fellow Jews, a patron of traditional Jewish culture who helped impoverished scholars by buying their books for them so they could study the Torah, the Mishnah and the Talmud, the main religious texts of Jewish tradition. This great medieval Jewish polymath, warrior and poet died of natural causes around 1055 at the age of sixty-two, a very wealthy, influential man whose name will always be remembered in Jewish culture.

Samuel's son Yusuf ibn Nagrela ha-Naguid (1035–66) had a hard act to follow. He was only twenty years old and inexperienced when his father died, so Sultan Badis chose Ali ben al-Qarawi as successor to Samuel in the role of chief vizier. But Samuel had left a poisoned chalice. He had carefully groomed his son to succeed him and instructed Yusuf upon his father's death to engineer the downfall of two rival viziers, revealing the deep rift between the Arab Sinhaya clan and the Granadan Jews. After Yusuf bribed al-Qarawi to influence the sultan in his favour, Badis made Yusuf a secretary, from which he rose to direct the royal treasury.

The son was very different from his father. Well-educated and proficient in Arabic and Hebrew, he had led a sheltered life and was prone to nerves and melancholy. His only known poem, written on a military campaign with his father in 1045, expresses his longing for home and family in Granada. Ibn Gabirol wrote a fascinating description of that home, possibly built by his father Samuel on the hill where the Alhambra now stands. He was awed by the strong Arabic sense of beauty it exuded, with its plasterwork of plant ornamentation, marble paving, glass and the play of light which gave the sensation of movement in its domes. There was also a pool, like the Sea of Solomon, he said, with lion and gazelle fountains surrounding it. This vision of the eleventh-century Jewish palace gives us our first real insight into the appearance of the urban landscape of the city. For the first time a major building, striking in its Jewish origin, graced its highest hill, and its architectural themes would later be echoed in the Muslim palace of the Alhambra.

Yusuf employed many Jews as tax collectors in his financial administration, and like his father, he was soon made Nagid, or leader of the Jews of Granada. He used his wealth to acquire an outstanding collection of Hebrew and Arabic books in all known branches of learning, and took on two assistants whose sole job was the copying of books for his library. Also like his father, he was devoted to Jewish learning and provided generous funds to support Jewish scholars. But he did not have Samuel's diplomatic and negotiating skills. Yusuf ingratiated himself with Badis, alleging that his vizier al-Qarawi was plotting to overthrow him. The sultan sacked al-Qarawi and appointed Yusuf instead. Yet the young vizier's big mistake was to cultivate the friendship of Buluqqin, one of Badis's sons, rather than relying on the sultan in times of trouble.

There are differing views of Yusuf. Some scholars think he was a good governor and an intelligent administrator skilled in foreign policy. Others accuse him of provoking uncontrolled violence, of which he was the first victim. All agree that he lacked his father's prudence and judgement, as well as the respect of the people.

Contemporary sources are unanimous in stating that Yusuf was guilty of the murder of Buluqqin sometime between the end of 1063 and 1064. The vizier invited the young heir to a drinking party and poisoned his wine but Badis took vengeance on his son's servants instead of on Yusuf. Nagrela found himself in a dangerous situation. The Islamic jurist al-Ilbiri had been expelled from Granada and wrote a famous poem attacking Yusuf and the Granadan Jews, reproaching his confidence in 'men of impure race, devils with horns, bastards and villains'[71] and inciting Badis to kill all the Jewish infidels. Al-Ilbiri's poetic intervention was regarded as the main factor in Yusuf's downfall, hastened when things came to a head on 31 December 1066.

Yusuf had lost some influence at court because of his intrigues and had only narrowly escaped when his long-time ally Sultan Badis ordered his murder in a fit of drunken rage. The Jewish community advised him to transfer his wealth to a safe hiding place and leave the city, but Yusuf asked the ruler of Almería, Ibn Sumadih, for help by encouraging him to attack Granada. When he saw the mighty ramparts of the city, Ibn Sumadih changed his mind but at a drinking party on New Year's Eve 1066, Yusuf let slip the falsehood that the Almerian forces were approaching the city. Thinking Badis was dead, one of the drunken guests rushed out of the palace shouting that the Jew had betrayed the sultan. The reaction was swift and brutal. Granadans of all kinds – nobles and common folk, Arabs and Berbers – fell on the Jewish quarter, as Yusuf tried desperately to stop the attack by exhibiting a very much alive Badis. The vizier took fright and fled in disguise but his charcoal-blackened face was recognized and he was murdered, his house plundered and his library destroyed. Three thousand Jews were massacred in Granada in Spain's first pogrom. The Nagrelas' rule had ended and the decline of the Granadan Jews had begun.

Was the arrogant, pretentious Yusuf to blame? Perhaps only in part, as the influence and wealth of the Jewish community aroused an ancient envy and hatred that had reached boiling point. Sadly, Samuel Nagrela's dream of a cultural, artistic and even political Solomonic kingdom uniting all Jews in Granada – embodied in Yusuf's fortified palace, grander and more impressive than the Alcazaba Qadima of Sultan Badis – undermined the authority, status and culture of the Zirids. It shone too brilliantly in the conflicted, multiracial society of the eleventh-century city.

The poet and philosopher Moses ibn Ezra (*c.*1055–1135) followed in the footsteps of the great Samuel ibn Nagrela as one of medieval Spain's greatest bards, ahead of his time in his theories on the nature of poetry. Born and raised in Granada into a wealthy and cultivated family, he had three brothers: Isaac, who was married to one of Yusuf ibn Nagrela's daughters, Joseph and Zerahiah, all distinguished scholars themselves. In his youth he went to Lucena some one hundred kilometres west of Granada, then a centre of Hispano-Judaic culture and a city of poetry, to study at the rabbinic academy of Isaac ibn Gayyat (*c.*1030–89) and gain a solid knowledge of Arabic and Hebrew. Moses returned to Granada, at that time the illustrious centre of literary innovation in the peninsula, where he met his lifelong friend, the poet Judah Halevi, and won important administrative positions in Sultan Abd Allah's government.

As a young man, influenced by the Arab lyric verse he read in Lucena, his favourite themes were love, friendship, wine and gardens, but when he grew older his poetry became more melancholy and focused on life's brevity. Moses was a revolutionary poetic theorist who believed poetic metaphor should be used to interpret the divine being. This concept became a crucial aspect of medieval Jewish ideology and conflicted with the views of the great Maimonides, who used metaphor for philosophical explication. A master of both sacred and secular verse, Moses also wrote songs, dialogues and recollections, and his treatise *Hebraic*

Poetics, written in Arabic, was translated into Hebrew in the early twentieth century.

His happiness in Granada did not last. When the Almoravid ruler Ibn Tashufin conquered the city in 1090, the Jewish community there was almost destroyed and Moses ibn Ezra's family lost their jobs and had to flee to Toledo. His own words describe his feelings at being left abandoned in Granada:

> I didn't complain when they stole my fortune; it didn't bother me that it disappeared and evaporated. I didn't lament the fact that my opulence had ended, nor did I feel ill when my servants deserted me... How could I not mock destiny? How could I not laugh at its dirty tricks? I had known success all my life and my fortunes took flight like a soaring eagle; the work of my hands took wing to show that the hand of God is powerful. Yet tears flow from my eyes and pain overcomes me at being left alone in my native land, without a friend at my side. I feel like a foreigner and outsider; no one from my family is near, no one from my father's house. I stay on in Granada like a stranger, I'm here in this city whose bustle and splendour have declined, like a sparrow who's lost his nest; in this misguided and corrupt generation, I'm like an exiled bird. There is no refuge for me, and no one here remains who remembers me or takes an interest in my wellbeing.'[72]

In 1095, Moses ibn Ezra left for the Christian kingdom of Castile, some say because of a threat to his life, others that he had a love affair with his niece that was opposed by his brothers and nephew, though the lament above seems to contradict that idea. He spent the rest of his life travelling around Castile and remained bitter about his exile, remembering his native city with sadness and nostalgia as 'the most delicious of lands' and 'Granada the glorious'. He likened the mountains of the Sierra Nevada to the snow-capped Mount Hermon in Israel. He died far from home in 1135 but lives on in his verse, much of which is recited in the High Holidays service in Sephardic congregations.[73]

The Jews were resilient people. A few must have remained in the city after 1090, which we can deduce from the life of the fourth great Granadan Jew of the Golden Age, Yehuda ibn Tibbon, born in the city around 1120. Yehuda was expert in Arab and Hebrew culture and owned a large library, so Jewish life there must have held some promise and vitality under Almoravid rule. Ibn Tibbon was also a physician and translator into Hebrew from Arabic, and in his lifetime he translated works by Ibn Gabirol and Judah Halevi, among others. He was sensitive to the difficulties of translation and his views on the task would not be amiss in a twenty-first-century translator's guide. He recommended writing a strictly literal version of the original in the first instance, then reworking it to read as if it were written by the translator himself.

Ibn Tibbon did not escape the fate that befell so many Jewish people, which was to flee from persecution. The Almohads – synonymous in Jewish tradition with destruction, persecution and forced conversion – conquered the city in 1156, and Yehuda fled to the south of France, to Lunel, where he was reported by traveller Benjamin of Tudela to be working as a doctor. He had a son and two daughters, whose marriages caused him great anxiety, and he died around 1190 in Marseille. Luckily, against the odds, his will survives, written in a plain, conversational style that speaks eloquently of the wise, pious nature of the man. In it, he addresses his son Samuel, also a scholar and translator, whom he chides for hiding so much of his life from him, for never sharing his literary or business affairs with him or asking his advice. He urges Samuel to practise writing in Arabic regularly, citing Samuel ibn Nagrela as a man who achieved greatness as a result of his superb skills in Arabic. Yehuda urges his son not to neglect the study of the Torah, alongside science and medicine, and to read grammatical works on Sabbaths and festival days; he encourages him to eat a healthy diet, so as not to fall ill and set a bad example to his patients. His father writes of his library as being his greatest treasure and companion, as the most beautiful garden of pleasure. Here is his advice to Samuel about that library:

> I have collected a large library for your sake, so that you never need to borrow a book from anyone. As you know yourself, most students run back and forth searching for books without finding them... Look over your Hebrew books every month, the Arabic ones every couple of months, and the bound books every three months. Keep the library in order so that you won't need to search for a particular book. Draw up a list of books on each shelf, and place each book on the correct shelf. Take care of the loose, separate pages, because they contain exceedingly important things, which I have collected and written down. Lose no writing or letter that I leave you... Cover your bookshelves with beautiful curtains, protect them from water from the roof, from mice, and from all harm, as they are your greatest treasure.[74]

Ibn Tibbon's line of intellectuals lived on, and honoured him. In 1988, the Mexican philologist and historian Gutierre Tibón (d. 1999), a direct descendant of the Granadan Jew, donated a statue of his illustrious ancestor to the city of Granada. The tall, upright sculpture presides at the place where two streets, Calles Pavaneras and Colcha, meet at the entrance to the old Jewish quarter of Realejo. It was created by the Granadan sculptor Miguel Moreno (b. 1935), when the socialist mayor of the city was Antonio Jara, current president of Caja Granada, a foundation that oversees the heritage and culture of the city. Heedless of the occasional cigarette that mischievous pranksters set between his teeth, Ibn Tibbon has his right hand on his heart and holds aloft a book, a symbol of his learning and profession, as he welcomes passers-by to the ancient district of the Jews. He would perhaps be amazed to know that he is the patron of the Granadan Tibónidas group, who fight for the visibility and rights of translators today.

No tangible traces remain of the Jews of Granada in the eleventh and twelfth centuries save for Ibn Tibbon's poignant memorial, the only obvious visual reference to the city's Jewish past. Samuel and Yusuf ibn Nagrela, Moses ibn Ezra and Ibn Tibbon testify to the powerful and influential cultural, religious and political heritage of the Jewish population in the city and province of Granada, and to the at times violent but mostly fruitful relationship between Jews and Arabs of this era. But their paradise became a place of torment; Jewish learning, diplomacy and wealth could not hold back the tide of religious persecution, and the worst was yet to come.

EXILE, ENMITY AND REMEMBRANCE: THE SEPHARDIC JEWS

On a warm spring day at the end of March 1492, a few months after Sultan Boabdil had stipulated in the terms of surrender of the city to Ferdinand and Isabella that all the Jews of his kingdom should benefit like the Muslims from the deal agreed, his conquerors sat in state in his former throne room in the Alhambra to give their final approval to the Edict of Granada. Sometimes known as the Alhambra Decree, this new law stated that all Jews must either become Christians or leave the kingdoms of Spain by 31 July 1492. The Catholic Monarchs reconvened a month later on 30 April 1492 at the palace in Santa Fe, the new town they had built near Granada as a launchpad for their final siege upon the city. Amid a trumpet fanfare, the edict was proclaimed, giving the Jewish population three months exactly to convert to Catholicism or pack up and leave. As Christopher Columbus prepared to set sail on his first voyage of discovery to the Americas in August, the Jews of Spain were boarding ships taking them into exile.

In just four months, from January to April, two events had happened that altered the course of Spanish, Portuguese and European history. This decree of expulsion, following so quickly on the heels of the fall of Muslim Granada, represented the ultimate failure of the inter-faith existence that had contributed so much to Iberian life. It ended a Jewish presence in Granada, and in Spain overall, going back to the Roman era, the last of a long series of expulsions that deprived Latin Europe of most of its Jewish communities. In December 1491, Ferdinand and Isabella appointed Jewish tax officials to act for 1492–4, and as late as April 1492, Jews are still recorded buying and selling property from and to Christians around Toledo, so there was no inkling of the impending disaster. The monarchs even employed Jewish physicians. What could have provoked a sudden decision of such magnitude? In a letter to a Galician aristocrat, the Count of Ribadeo, the king and queen suggest their motive was fear of religious and moral corruption. They told the count they had been informed by Inquisitors and others that measures to remedy what was perceived as the Jewish problem, such as relegation of Jews to ghettos and regional expulsions, had failed, and that only complete expulsion would prevent Christians from being 'perverted' by Jews. Other letters hint that the idea of the expulsion was the brainchild of the terrifying Inquisitor General, Tomás de Torquemada.

The text of the Edict is ruthless:

> We have decided to order all Jews, men and women of any age, alive, well and finding themselves in our kingdoms and dominions, to abandon these same kingdoms and dominions before the end of the coming month of July of the current year, in the company of their sons and daughters, manservants and maids, and Jewish members of their household, young and old of whatever age; they shall not have the audacity to return nor shelter here, upon pain of death and confiscation of their goods… Moreover, we give licence and authority to the said Jews, men and women, to take from all our kingdoms and dominions their goods and possessions by land or by sea, on condition that they do not take gold, silver, coins nor other things prohibited by the laws of our kingdoms, with the exception of merchandise or authorized letters of exchange.

The decree gave the Jews three months to choose between baptism and abjuration of their faith, and being exiled in poverty, and they saw it as a catastrophe on the scale of the biblical flight from Egypt or the destruction of the Temple of Jerusalem. The best estimate is that about 100,000 Jews were expelled from the peninsula,[75] many of whom came from Granada. Spanish historian Miguel-Ángel Ladero Quesada has delved into detailed embarkation records to give us a vivid snapshot of the traumatic expulsion of the Granadan Jews.[76] There were some 3,000 individuals living in the old emirate in 1492, and in June of that year, 1,485 Jews from 268 households in the province of Granada were sent into exile in north Africa. A committee had been formed to register all the households embarked and to value their property, so that Customs could charge them a tithe of 10 per cent of its overall value, with extra duty on any silk item. Three Portuguese merchant ships, a three-masted *nao* and two *carracas*, had been provided by a veteran of the last stages of the Granadan war, Garci López de Arriarán, to carry the Jews into exile.

' Over half the households came from the city of Granada itself, sixteen from Guadix, thirteen from Almuñécar, six from Motril and seventeen from Malaga. Taken by surprise by the order of exile, nearly all of them embarked without any household goods or furniture. The wealthier households, over eighty of them, took light, easily transportable silk with them to sell profitably in north Africa, though some fell prey to the prohibition on taking money, gold or precious stones – one record shows an unlucky man deprived by customs officials of the eleven ounces of gold he had hidden in the covers of a book. Among the poorest Jews to embark were women, some of them widows, and men like Salamon Aben Ami, who boarded a ship with two other people whose total property only amounted to a measly twenty *reales*, barely enough to buy a dozen eggs. These people from the old city of the Jews left behind their houses, small synagogues such as the one that probably existed where the Iglesia de San Pedro (Church of Saint Peter) now stands, and small plots of land, all of which were put up for sale after the expulsion. They left behind clothes and jewellery in the form of rings, beads and small objects of silver and gold, though some people managed to carry flour, corn and oil on board ship.

Despite his fierce anti-Semitism, the chronicler Andrés Bernáldez, priest and chaplain to the Archbishop of Seville, could not help being moved by the dreadful plight of the emigrating Jews:

> And so they abandoned the land where they were born. Big and little, young and old, on foot, on donkeys or in carts, each one making his way to the port designated for embarkation. They stopped by the roadside in the middle of their journey, some dropped with exhaustion, others were ill and even dying. Everywhere they passed, the people urged them to be baptized, but their rabbis encouraged them to reject this, and to support them they made the women and children sing with a tambourine as accompaniment. When those who were to embark at Cadiz and Puerto de Santa María saw the sea, all of them, men and women, began to wail heartrendingly, lamenting and imploring the Almighty for mercy and hoping he would send a miracle. They remained there prostrate with grief and wishing they had never been born.[77]

Tragically, the fate of the Jews of Granada who stayed behind and converted to become Catholics was just as deplorable. Ferdinand would not let them rest. In May 1511 he issued a royal warrant forbidding *conversos* from living in the Alpujarra region because, he said, it was 'very inconvenient for the peace and tranquility of other residents'. No newly converted Jew could enter or live in any Alpujarran village, and those who did live there had one hundred days to leave.[78] Once again, Jewish life became hidden, secret and forbidden, as many new Catholics covertly worshipped as Jews. Soon after, the Inquisition finally came to Granada. It had been created as a tribunal separate from that of Cordoba in 1499 and began to operate in 1526 in response to the increasing problems with assimilating the converted Muslim population. Its favourite prey was the Moriscos but converted Jews also became victims.

The first public *auto de fe* or act of faith took place in 1529, when there were eighty-seven convicts consisting of three Moriscos and eighty-four *conversos* accused of practising Judaism clandestinely.

Public *autos* were initially held in Plaza Nueva, New Square, outside the Chancellery building, while private *autos* were held in the church of Santiago, in the Santo Oficio parish. The records show that over a period of sixty-five years, the Holy Office saw 1,716 convicted prisoners, of whom 221 were judaizers; among their number were people from all walks of life, including doctors, merchants, moneylenders, spice dealers and silversmiths.[79] What the Granadan Tribunal regarded as their great benevolence meant that only 11 per cent of these were burnt at the stake. In the 1571 *auto*, Beatriz Pérez, wife of a Granadan silk dealer, was accused of fasting with her mother and only eating when the stars came out. They ate fish stew, not meat, prayed at a window by starlight and pretended to eat bacon but actually threw it under the table. Beatriz denied this, claiming that her mother was ill and often could not eat. In the end, she hanged herself from the door of her prison cell with a girdle from her underskirt after trying unsuccessfully to slit her throat and wrists. The public prosecutor pursued the case, and Beatriz was 'relaxed in effigy', the euphemism the Inquisition used when a convict died before they could be burnt alive at the stake. The tribunal ordered the body to be dug up and the remains burnt at the next public *auto*.

Today, the Bib-Rambla square in the old city is a popular haunt of tourists and locals, a hotspot for restaurants, bars and gift shops. Over four hundred years ago, it had an altogether more sinister purpose. There exists an anonymous eye-witness account of the build-up to an *auto* held in the square on Ascension Day, 27 May 1593, a stark, lucid description that captures the solemn piety, foreboding and morbid spectacle of the occasion:

> A very high scaffold was built in Bib-rambla square... near Gomeres street. It was as high as the roof timbers, alongside the

city council buildings, right across the front of the houses, fifty feet long. Three wooden steps were built on top of the scaffold, attached to the balconies of those houses. Then two pulpits were made for the secretaries… three feet apart. Another scaffold was made twenty feet wide, with two seats facing, ten feet apart, where the convicts sat, with their family members and other persons involved sitting at the sides.

There was a narrow passage two feet wide between the two scaffolds, and a private place for bodily needs also between the scaffolds. The religious orders sat on the wooden steps, with lay people friendly with officials. The Inquisitors and Court sat inside the city council building, with the President below. At the top was a city model of Granada. On Ascension Day, there were scaffolds in Elvira and Zacatín streets, in all the doors of houses, and entrances to streets so that people could see and allow the procession to go past. A palisade was erected from the entrance to the Zacatin as far as the main scaffold for the same reason, to allow the procession past. There were many ladies at the windows, and people on the scaffolds, all unarmed as the Holy Office decreed.

At seven in the morning the procession of convicts came out, preceded by many of their family members, and it is said over 20,000 people were watching in the crowd. Then three crosses were carried out, their arms draped in black taffeta. The convicts filed past, each between two family members, and most of them were women, wearing the insignia of their penitence. Half an hour later, the Inquisitors, Court and city representatives followed, headed by the chief magistrate and head of the city council, then the Chancellery, constables, court mayors, clerks and judges… and finally the President. At the scaffold, the Augustinian Father Castroverde from Cáceres preached, addressing the convicts, condemning their sects and insulting their apostles. Then the *auto* began.

The persecution of *conversos* through *autos de fe* persisted into the eighteenth century and there are records of public burnings at the stake in 1606, 1615, 1641, 1672, 1721 and 1723, after which the victims' *sanbenitos* or penitential garments were hung in the cathedral for all to see. The archive of the Granadan Inquisition was allegedly burnt in 1823, for fear that it might give rise to further enmity.

The Sephardim of the province of Granada who survived their journey into exile probably fared better than those who chose to stay and convert. In the Ottoman lands, they were treated as *dhimmis*, as they had been under Islamic rule in Spain, protected by Sultan Bayezid II and his successors. A family of doctors from Granada travelled as far as Istanbul, where they settled and became famous. José Hamon, whose father Isaac had been the personal physician of the Nasrid Sultan Abu l'Hasan, became the doctor of Bayezid II and also of his successor Selim I, who took him with him on his victorious campaigns in the Middle East. The Hamon dynasty flourished – José's son Moisés, a scholar and author of a treatise on dentistry, was a powerful doctor at the court of Suleiman the Magnificent in the first half of the sixteenth century, and his own son, also José, found favour with Selim II, who allowed him to treat the sizeable Jewish community of Salonika in 1586, where the doctor was able to exercise his patronage of Jewish poets.

Many Jews from Granada went less far afield, settling in Badis, a port city on the Moroccan Rif that had traded with Muslim Malaga for over a century, while some went to Tangiers, and others ended up in Tétouan, as those epigraphs still legible on their elaborately decorated tombstones reveal. In these places, like the Muslims before them, they tried to recreate the lifestyle and cultural life of their homeland, even keeping their language, Ladino, which is medieval Judeo-Spanish. The Sephardic Jews of Tétouan preserved a large number of poems and songs that their ancestors had sung in Spain, and the last Sephardic poet, the Granadan scholar Saadiah ibn Danan, took refuge in Morocco only to die in Oran a few months after the expulsion, in December 1492.

The ballads of the Sephardic Jews are kept alive today and performed regularly.[80] They are full of longing for their homeland, for their Spanish past. In these sung poems, Granada is a symbol, a fantasy place of the geographical imagination, exotic and distant, a city strewn with pearls, a place of splendour, riches and marvels, the most valued prize of kings. Granada is the setting in some ballads for magical, mysterious events, and for fleeting romances. Above all, it is a paradise, the *locus amoenus* of Classical verse, a place of fecundity and enchantment, evoked in the Moroccan Sephardic ballad 'The slander of the queen', where the beautiful Briana magically becomes pregnant:

> The count has a wife, Briana was her name,
> Who went for a walk one day in the orchards of Granada,
> Among roses and flowers, carnations and sweet basil,
> Where in that orchard lies a fountain of clearest water.
> Seven jets cascade from it, each one of silver,
> Three of soft water, and four of salt water;
> The woman who drinks this water soon finds herself pregnant.[81]

522 years later, that nostalgia and longing for a lost paradise was in part allayed by the new Spanish law which came into force on 1 October 2015 conferring Spanish nationality on the descendants of the Jews exiled in 1492. This gesture of reconciliation on the part of the Spanish government was greeted with joy by all Sephardic Jews, without hatred or rancour, as recognition of their belonging, and of their enduring love for what they consider to be their native land. Prior to this, in 2011 the mayor of Granada, José Torres Hurtado, had met the Great Sephardic Rabbi of Israel, Shlomó Moshé Amar, the chief religious authority on those expelled by the Alhambra Decree in 1492. It was the first time a figure of civic authority from Granada had met a figure of Jewish religious authority for 519 years.

Eight years later, the covert Jewish heritage of Granada started to become visible again. Jewish Heritage Tours is run by a local firm, Cicerone Granada, and has its specialist tour guide, Fernando Abril. For him, Granada has great resonance because it was the final place of refuge for the Spanish Jews, but also the place where the Edict of Expulsion was signed, so it is deeply charged with melancholy. There are two Sephardic museums, the House of the Forgotten, where this chapter began, and the Sephardic House Museum in the Realejo district, run by the family of Beatriz Chevalier, daughter of a Jewish woman exiled in France. It was at the doors of this museum, tucked away in a tiny, narrow alley, that the haunting summons of the *shofer*, the ceremonial horn sounded by the Jewish people as a call to prayer at the start of the Sabbath, was heard recently for the first time for half a millennium. Not far away, the Jewish tourist route takes in the proud statue of Ibn Tibbon and passes by the Rodrigo del Campo cistern, the last original water store of the Granadan Jewry, which supplied residents of the Realejo district. The only other vestiges of Jewish life in the city are the ancient, worn tombstones used to build the walls of the Convent of the Carmelites in the Cuesta de Rodrigo del Campo. A few illegible names on a wall, a lone cistern, the sound of an age-old horn, a single monument to Hebrew learning, these are the tangible fragments of remembrance of the once peerless Jewish people of Garnata al-Yahud, who endure in the written word, in their scholarly writings, in historical records, and in their poetry and song, adding a rich but subliminal layer to the multicultural strata of Granada.

GRANADA

THE PLACE II

1492–1700

6

SITES OF POWER

City of the Christians

● ● ● ● ● ● ● ● ● ● ● ● ● ● ●

TRANSFORMATION: THE NEW
URBAN LANDSCAPE AND
MINDSCAPE OF GRANADA

Stepping inside from the dazzling light and heat of the city, the interior seems dark and chilly. You can hear the silence. Then all at once the gleaming gilded surfaces, the black ironwork, the life-like bleeding statues and cold marble take on shape and colour. The unexpected simplicity and modesty of the architectural structure are perfect foils for the profusion of artistic forms that honour the Royal Chapel, built to house the sepulchres of Ferdinand II of Aragon and Isabella I of Castile. As Europe's greatest medieval queen lay on her deathbed in October 1504, she dictated her will, whose very first clause stated 'I want and order my body to be buried in the monastery of Saint Francis in the Alhambra, of the city of Granada.' Isabella expired on 26 November of that year and her wishes were obeyed; twelve years later in 1516, Ferdinand died and his body was laid beside the queen's. The monastery, dedicated to her beloved Saint Francis, had been built at her orders on the site of one of the Nasrid palaces, which had boasted its own prayer room. In this former Muslim space they remained until 10 November 1521, when their bones were transferred to their final resting place in the Royal Chapel, the cortège passing down the Cuesta de Gomeres and past Plaza Nueva in the greatest ceremonial spectacle the city had ever seen.

Soon after Isabella's death, Ferdinand had ordered the construction of the Royal Chapel, under the direction of the master architect Enrique Egas. By 1517 it was nearly finished, decorated with the Queen's collection of paintings of the Virgin, Christ and the Crucifixion, alongside the heraldic devices, coat of arms and initials of the monarchs that boasted their Christian devotion and military power. The Chapel made a bold statement as the first Gothic building in Moorish Granada, rising in the very heart of the Muslim city. Its visual message of stark Christian piety vies with Baroque exuberance as, high above, our gaze alights upon the extraordinary altarpiece by Felipe de Vigarny with its sumptuous sculptures lavishly polychromed to give the illusion of living actors playing their parts on a stage whose framework, entirely covered in gilded figures, foliage and flowers, echoes the profusion of Islamic decorative art. Like the lacework of leafy designs on the great Renaissance ironwork grille closing the nave at the transept, their style is plateresque, a term deriving from *platero*, the Spanish word for 'silversmith'. Their intricate craftsmanship evokes the age-old Muslim mastery of metalworking in Granada.

On ground level, the huge sepulchre of the Catholic Monarchs looms in the centre of the transept, next to that of their daughter Juana and her husband Felipe. Its sober grey Carrara marble fashioned by the Italian sculptor Domenico Fancelli immortalizes the mortal in the effigies of the two stately monarchs that lie side by side on a bier adorned with Classical figures and motifs. Their Latin epitaph is unequivocal: 'Here lie Ferdinand of Aragon and Isabella of Castile, husband and wife, called Catholic, who overthrew the Mahometan sect and annihilated heretical depravity.' Although their bones do not in fact lie under the marble sepulchre, but in the almost shockingly stark crypt, Fancelli's monument in this Granadan pantheon is a material testament to that epitaph, a symbol of a crucial moment in Spain's history, and of a victory through which they gained a longed-for prize, marking their power and Christian devotion. It represents the tangible, visual super-imposition of one religion on another, an assertion of religious difference and dominance. Yet there is also an unconscious irony, as in breaking with royal family tradition in choosing Granada as her burial place, Isabella ensured that she and Ferdinand would be identified with the conquered – but still resoundingly Muslim – city for evermore.

On that day of conquest on 2 January 1492, Catholic Mass had been heard for the first time in one of the magnificent royal chambers of the Alhambra, a moment of ritual transformation of the Islamic into the Christian. As Boabdil departed from Granada to lead his family into internal exile, Isabella and her retinue, that included Christopher Columbus, had looked up and seen a cross paraded from the Tower of Comares in the Alhambra, alongside the flag of Saint James, the Moor-slayer, signalling the transition of the Alhambra from Muslim to Catholic ownership. Ironically, it looked as if the Christian royalty and knighthood had in fact turned Muslim, since all were wearing Moorish dress, decked out in brocade and silk tunics and the waist sash or *marlota*. This purported to be a mark of respect, a visual statement to placate, reassure and suggest commonality, which pretended to say 'Yes, we are like you, you are not being taken over by an alien people, we are the same, and nothing is going to change.' To a Granadan watching in fear from the city vanquished after a long period of siege, it did not seem that way but felt more like an act of insolent appropriation, of absorption of what was Moorish by the Catholic enemy. It was an entirely ambiguous symbolic act, hinting on the one hand at the centuries-old covert Christian admiration for Moorish culture, for what was forbidden to them and which militated against the entire ethos of the Reconquest, and on the other betraying a longing to usurp and eliminate that culture and religion.

Ferdinand and Isabella soon made arrangements to make sure the Alhambra, the ultimate trophy of victory, was maintained, and its towers and ramparts repaired, and they lived there for short periods between 1492 and 1501. It was an exemplary monument and at the same time the epitome of a vanquished but still living heresy. But Granada only nominally became a Christian city in January 1492 – it was rather a Muslim city under Christian political control. The creation of Christian Granada was a gradual historical process, and an incomplete one at that. Granada has never severed its ties with its Islamic past, and today remains the most clearly Islamic of Spanish cities. For the next eight years, Islam remained the religion of most of the inhabitants, the muezzin still called the faithful to prayer from the two hundred or more mosques that rose in the urban landscape, and the great Mosque with its imposing minaret dominated the skyline until it was demolished in 1588. The mood changed at the turn of the sixteenth century, when a Muslim rebellion in the Alpujarras region was quashed by a royal order that all Granada's Muslims must convert to Catholicism or leave the city. Mass baptisms obliged all Granadan residents to become technically Christian but often the conversion was superficial. A climate of dissimulation and secrecy began to prevail.

To remould Granada in a Christian image was to hark back eight hundred years to the Visigothic city whose inhabitants had converted from Arian to Catholic Christianity in the sixth century. The blend of tradition, transition and renovation which characterized that society also marked the urban and cultural evolution of sixteenth-century Granada, although some things did not change. First and foremost, it was still a political and military frontier. For decades, those in power feared either a greater rebellion by those Muslims forced to convert, known as Moriscos, or an Ottoman invasion from over the sea. City and province also remained a cultural and religious frontier, where Spanish Islamic and Christian practices met, blended and often collided. Not least, post-conquest Granadan society was fluid and dynamic, quite different from that of most of Spain's other major cities. The immigrants crossing the border into the former Islamic state were not now Muslims fleeing Christian persecution, as they had been under Nasrid rule, but Christians, tens of thousands, merchants, soldiers, artisans and bureaucrats, all moving south to seek their fortune in what they perceived as a kind of Eldorado of limitless opportunity.

Some were lucky. Juan de la Torre grew up in Toledo with his parents, wealthy *converso* merchants. His family had a dark history of rebellion, and two of its members had been hanged for forcing entry into Toledo cathedral and fighting with Old Christians,[82] while another met the same fate for an alleged plot to murder the local inquisitors. But Juan was a clever businessman and in 1493–4 he set up as a moneylender in Granada, loaning money to such distinguished clients as Archbishop Talavera, and to Ferdinand and Isabella's royal secretary and right-hand man Hernando de Zafra. Later Juan became a tax collector to the local silk trade and amassed a huge fortune, enough to maintain a house in his native Toledo and to become lord of a village south of Granada in 1553. Domingo Pérez de Herrasti had a far less privileged background, coming from an impoverished Basque noble family. He ended up as a soldier, fighting in the final battle for Granada under the Catholic Monarchs, and was duly rewarded with two public offices, one as scribe for Granada, another as a non-voting official at municipal council meetings. Despite being accused of shady dealing, Domingo cleverly curried the favour of some powerful families, and was granted possession of lands near the city. Some immigrants had no luck at all, like husband and wife Pedro Sánchez and Juana González from Plasencia, who tried their hand at trading but ran up enormous debts. In her will of 1577, it states that poor Juana ended up begging in the streets of Granada.[83]

The transformation in the city's populace was reflected in the transformation of the urban landscape, but that process took far longer. Foreign Christian travellers to Granada up to the 1530s spoke of a city both sublime and yet flawed. The Italian chronicler Peter Martyr of Anghiera wrote to the Archbishop of Toledo in March 1492 claiming that '... among all the cities I have seen under the sun, Granada must be the most preferred'.[84] He praises its climate, location, abundance and running water, and declares that the *vega* called to mind the Elysian fields. The Flemish traveller Antoine de Lalaing in 1502 and the Venetian Andrea Navagero in 1526 echoed Peter Martyr's words, affirming that Granada was the best city in Spain. Alongside these superlatives a certain unease comes through – Granada belongs to a world that is not theirs, which disturbs them. Its location, climate, flora and fauna are incomparable, yet the urban structure appears strange to them in equal measure. Its tangle of small streets, often dead ends, the lack of order, the anarchic accumulation of interlinked houses, was unsettling to men from the North. Even Hieronymus Münzer, the German physician fulsome in his praise for the city, wrote in 1494 of the narrow, labyrinthine streets and intricate network of alleys.[85] The Western Christian visitors who came to Granada felt the full shock of the revelation of a different civilization, and so did the Catholic authorities in charge of the conquered city, who believed they had a mission to reconstitute the urban landscape. Granada seemed intolerable to them in its Muslim incarnation, and in their eyes, it needed to be made safer, more beautiful, nobler. The aim of Christian councillors and urban designers was to impose order and cleanliness on the Nasrid capital, as if they were physicians healing the morally sick body of the city through regeneration.

While the Royal Chapel was the first permanent statement in stone of Catholic dominion, two important buildings, the cathedral and the palace of Charles V, established sites of Christian power by appropriating Muslim spaces. This strategy, born of the same desire to obliterate the memory of Islam as a feature of local and national identity, reared its head in historical writing of this time. The construction of the cathedral struck at the architectural heart of Granadan Islam. The original plan was for it to sit inside the Alhambra but Isabella wished it to be built on the site of the city's main mosque. The great Renaissance building created during the sixteenth century by Diego de Siloé and Alonso Cano, a symbol of the birth of modernity in architectural style in Andalusia, was two hundred years in the making and remains an enduring monument to the power of Catholicism in Spain, and to the political might of the Catholic Monarchs. This all-encompassing omnipotence is reflected in the symbolic location of the cathedral, a ritual architectural object visible from viewpoints of 360 degrees, which speaks to all quarters of the city, including the Alhambra, the Sacromonte and the Albaicín, from where the painter Velázquez drew it. It gives the illusion of ancient, enduring solidity, as if it had always stood there. Yet the urban area of the cathedral complex was of fundamental functional and symbolic importance in Muslim Granada. The Nasrids had converted it into a religious, administrative and commercial zone, the *Madinat Garnata*. The mosque with its eleven naves and stone minaret occupied the space that is now the Iglesia del Sagrario or parish church, next to the madrasa built by Yusuf II in the fourteenth century. When the pale pillars of the cathedral and the new nave were built, the ancient mosque was demolished and the administrative buildings and baths destroyed. Diego de Siloé was its architect and worked on the temple until his death in 1563, when Alonso Cano, Ambrosio de Vico and Juan de Maeda took over. Prey to doubts, interruptions and changes in design, the new landmark was not finished until 1704.

Charles I of Spain (1500–58), also known as Holy Roman Emperor Charles V, 'the Caesar', was the grandson of Ferdinand and Isabella and son of their daughter Juana I of Castile. In 1526 he married Isabel of Portugal in Seville, and the newly-weds spent several months in the Alhambra. Deeply impressed by the palace of the African kings, he hit on the idea of making it his main residence but strictly on his own terms. A brand-new palace was to be built in the Alhambra precinct, at the end of the Patio of the Myrtles, where a pavilion was demolished near the Tower of Comares to make way for a building that was designed as a tangible representation of triumphant universal Christendom, at the centre of the acropolis of the Nasrids. For Charles and many Spanish rulers, architecture was a vehicle of ideology. He thought the Italian Classicism of his time recreated the ideas of ancient Imperial Roman art, the supreme expression of absolute temporal power. The ground plan of the new building was a geometrical abstraction, a circle, the sign of creation, within a square symbolizing the earthly world, a form illustrated by Leonardo da Vinci's Vitruvian Man. It was the design of Pedro Machuca, who had trained in Italy as a painter but found his architectural talents as creator of the royal palace, which he began in 1533 but never lived to see completed. Charles V's palace was not fully finished until four hundred years later in 1930, and it now houses the Museum of the Alhambra. It remains a controversial building. Viewed from the air, it dominates the main site of the Alhambra, incongruous in its monolithic style set against the graceful elegance of Nasrid architecture, despite its exceptional location.

The superimposition of Christian upon Islamic architecture in these great buildings was echoed throughout the city, where mosques gradually became churches, and Muslim cemeteries, of which there were many outside the city walls, became the sites of new parish churches or convents. At the same time, the city space changed. Islamic cities have few open spaces, as their houses look inwards for privacy and protection, aided by a narrow maze of tiny alleyways created for defence. Now new squares appeared, like Plaza Nueva, where the Chancellery was erected. Plaza Bib-Rambla was enlarged, narrow streets were widened and the porches and protruding balconies of Moorish houses were dismantled to make more open space. The new urban structure reflected the firm desire to make Granada a Christian capital, fit to accommodate the royal court, which was established in September 1500, thereby converting Granada into the political capital of Castile. In the sixteenth century, it was a city under construction, although the Albaicín, which had 30,000 inhabitants in 1560, held on to its closed-off, inextricable, disturbingly Islamic cityscape.

Like a living organism, Granada flourished, withered and revived. The terrible Morisco uprisings of 1568–70, which will be described in Chapter 7, left shops and dwellings abandoned, their wooden structures used as firewood by the royal army. Many houses tumbled down in violent storms and there was a general air of dilapidation. By 1620, the Albaicín had shrunk to a mere 5,000 residents. It was at this time that the city took on the appearance we know today. More Moorish dwellings or *cármenes* (meaning 'God's paradise' in ancient Hebrew) sprang up, as the original rural suburbs were absorbed into the inner nucleus; these were uniquely Granadan city houses with their own enclosed leafy gardens hidden behind high white walls. The famous Paseo de los Tristes running alongside the River Darro was constructed in 1600 and is described by the historian Enríquez de Horquera as '... the viewing place of the city, where on summer evenings, with minstrel music, gentlemen riding ferocious brutes stroll for their amusement... where Granadan ladies take the cool air in well-equipped coaches'.[86]

The *carmen* was a transitional space between city and country-side, whose limits were not clear-cut, where the rural seemed to encroach on the urban. The thriving figure of the market gardener symbolized the osmosis between the two worlds and reflected the intense, coherent relationship between Granada and its *vega*. There has never been a liminal industrial area round the city, perhaps due to its vibrant silk industry, the sugar industry in the coastal towns of Motril and Almuñécar, and the artisan and horticultural trade of the *vega* itself. The city in the sixteenth and seventeenth centuries was an enormous market, whose corn exchange, the Alhóndiga, was vital to maintaining a supply of corn for the twenty-five to thirty tons of bread consumed daily in the city around 1550. Meat was plentiful, fish came along the 'fish road' from Motril to Granada, and wine, olive oil, fruit and vegetables rolled in from the *vega*.

Water, more precious even than bread, flowed from its two rivers that channelled the melting snow of the mountains to water the crops and gardens, and supply houses and the trades of dyeing, tanning and milling. The old Islamic baths were gradually destroyed, although they would remain a feature of the cityscape until the late sixteenth century. Water had always been a defining element in the life of the city, criss-crossed with irrigation channels and abounding in wells, cisterns and fountains. Today there are still at least twenty underground cisterns in the Albaicín in working use. All houses had a constant water supply conveyed through a system of pipes, and the largest dwellings had at least three fountains. These complex water systems had been in place since the time of the Zirids in the eleventh century, and had been gradually improved by later generations of Muslims. The Christians added little.

Visions of the new cityscape were captured by foreign artists from a number of perspectives – panoramic vistas, views from *miradors*, views from above, landscapes suffused with emotions and ideas. The panoramic picture presented Granada from a distance and emphasized its walls, churches and houses as dominant features. A Flemish artist, Joris Hoefnagel (1542–1600), drew three colourful panoramas of the city between 1563 and 1565, exaggerating the size of the cathedral to increase its impressiveness and dominance. In the foreground are scenes from everyday rural life, snapshots of local customs and dress of Christians and Moriscos. Another Flemish painter, Anton van den Wyngaerde (1525–71), was also in Spain in the 1560s and his sepia-toned panoramic view of Granada dated 1567 shows the urban spread obliquely, from an imaginary, elevated, almost mystical viewpoint that guides our gaze to admire from afar the city rising on its hilltops like Rome.

Around the turn of the century, Ambrosio de Vico, the master mason and architect who worked on Granada cathedral, created the first ever street map of the city, known as the *Plataforma de Granada,* engraved by the Flemish printer Francisco Heylan. It was complete, detailed and accurate, and as such it is an invaluable record of the urban layout around the year 1600. This important street plan had a hidden agenda. Vico had been commissioned to draw it by the Archbishop of Granada, Don Pedro de Castro, to illustrate a new book, the *Ecclesiastical History of Granada* (*Historia eclesiástica de Granada*) by an Augustinian friar, Justín Antolínez de Burgos. His history was written as a lengthy justification of the legitimacy of the Catholic religion in Granada, going back to its apparently ancient Christian roots and entirely eliminating its Islamic history. The tacit purpose of the map was to represent the streets of the city as a great religious stage where Christian ceremony was performed. In the imagination of its recent conquerors, Granada was a new Jerusalem, properly Christian again.

Yet strive as they might, the Catholic authorities in Granada could not change the fact that by the end of the seventeenth century, the city was still essentially Islamic, especially in the centre. The permanent, and perhaps lucky, co-existence of two opposing urban models created a place of unique and abiding charm, worth preserving at all costs. The local historian Francisco Bermúdez de Pedraza (1585–1655), writing in the seventeenth century, evoked the now familiar image of Granada as a utopia, a paradise of water, soft breezes, scented flowers and abundance. This image penned by Pedraza, a Catholic propagandist, is ironically reminiscent of the city created by its Islamic inhabitants and rulers. The marriage of urban and country remained a perfect association between mountain, plain and city.

DUPLICITY, DOCTRINE AND DEVOTION: HISTORY, EDUCATION AND FAITH

As the historic home to native Iberians, Phoenicians, Romans, Visigoths, Jews, Muslims and Christians, Granada is the epitome of a cultural hybridity which sat uneasily alongside the quest for Spanish national identity that took root in the aftermath of its conquest in 1492. The Muslims in particular were the 'other within': Spanish and yet not Spanish, feared, hated even, yet desired; and the opposition between Christianity and Islam took on a momentous role in the construction of Spain's history and essential nature. History writers in the sixteenth century resorted to invention to construct an identity for Granada that evaded the memory of Islam, and they hijacked the city's topography to do it. General knowledge of the ancient peoples of the province was shaky enough to be manipulated to serve the aims of a kind of sacred archaeology[87] that set out to show how Islamic monuments originated in primitive Christianity. Francisco Bermúdez de Pedraza, who was a priest and canon of Granada cathedral, and a native of the city, published an ecclesiastical history of Granada in 1638, in which he claimed that the Alhambra stood on the site of the city's earliest Phoenician temple.[88] He also compared Granada to Rome and to Jerusalem in its antiquity, and declared it to be superior to other Spanish cities not only in its beauty but because it witnessed the first Christian martyrs, whose relics were found on the hillside outside the city. One of those martyrs was Saint Cecilius, the earliest Bishop of Granada in the first century AD.

Hidden water was key to this strategic reformulation of the image of the city. The complex hydraulic system of the Arab *medina* with its network of cisterns and underground pipes inherited by the Christians became part of their symbolic transformation of the territory into a space of exceptional sacredness and antiquity. In this way not only the native inhabitants, but also the geography and history of the place underwent a forced conversion to Catholicism. Again, Bermúdez de Pedraza played a central part. He described a legendary bottomless well next to the old mosque, the deepest known in Spain. It had a circumference of twenty-six feet and a depth of 136 feet down to the water below, which had supplied the mosque itself.[89] The well was first mentioned in a letter dated 12 September 1509 from the governor of the Alhambra to King Ferdinand, stating that the new Royal Chapel had been orientated towards the north-east instead of the east, to avoid the destruction of a well in that place. It was allegedly so deep that it had no bottom and Pedraza recounts that a straw cast into it emerged in a fountain some two leagues from Granada. The well was part of a network of underground streams linking various miraculous sites, which sprang from a bottomless lake in the Sierra Nevada. It was also connected to the caves in which the remains of the martyrs had been found, and legends revealed that Saint Cecilius had fashioned it with his own hands. In the war of the Alpujarras (1568–71), the five thousand-strong army of Don John of Austria was parched and drank from it, and it was said that its level never wavered. Pure and uncorrupted conveyors of sacredness, Arab water channels had become holy and Christian.

Back in the city, Vico's street map shows twenty-six churches, twenty-nine monasteries or convents, three shrines, eleven hospitals and four colleges, with the Royal Chapel and cathedral at the heart of the ritual, sacred topography that overlaid Nasrid Granada. Monumental crosses sprang up everywhere to reinforce the holiness of specific places but the biggest innovation was the ornamenting of the façades and interiors of buildings with pictures to reinforce the doctrinal message. Later, in the eighteenth century, Granada would become a painted city, with a growing tradition of mural art, usually depicting cycles of the lives of patron saints, or instructional scenes from the life of Christ and the Virgin. There are still murals on the external walls in Calle Elvira, the Carrera del Darro and in Realejo, with major paintings on the inner dome of the Holy of Holies in the monastery of La Cartuja, and in the church and hospital of San Juan de Dios. The city was akin to a stained-glass window or an illuminated manuscript in which you could read the Christian message in pictorial form.

Education became a priority in the refashioning of Granada in the sixteenth and seventeenth centuries, inspired by the first seminary to train priests founded in 1492 by the Archbishop of Granada, Hernando de Talavera, which is still in existence. In all, nine religious colleges were set up, where students learned theology, canon law, grammar, liberal arts and song. But things got slack, and trainee priests spent their time playing cards and visiting prostitutes. Reform was needed. Talavera had been seen as an exemplary priest in Spain and abroad because of his enlightened views on teaching Muslim converts the Castilian language, and his insistence on priests learning Arabic so their message could be understood. He was the earliest of a group of influential religious reformers in Granada which probably had no equal in any other city of Catholic Europe. Located in a frontier zone on the very edge of the European continent, the city was remarkable in summoning up contributors to devotional reform movements that would transform sixteenth-century Catholicism worldwide at this time, harking back to the reforms of Gregory of Granada in the early fourth century.

Two figures stand out in the holy panorama of Renaissance Granada – San Juan de Dios (Saint John of God) and Luis de Granada. On 20 January 1537, Saint Sebastian's day, João Duarte Cidade was in Granada, where he heard a sermon by Juan de Ávila, the 'Apostle of Andalusia', an inspirational preacher later to become a saint. He was so deeply moved that he began to beat himself in the street, begging for mercy and repenting for the sins of his past life. He was taken to the new Royal Hospital where he was locked up and subjected to the latest treatment for insanity, which consisted of being chained up, flogged and starved. João had gone to Granada because he had seen a vision of Jesus, who had advised him to settle there, although he had been born in 1495 in the district of Évora in Portugal. His deeply pious family had grown poor, and to add insult to injury, one day when João was only eight, he disappeared, either kidnapped or inveigled into leaving by an unscrupulous visiting priest. His parents never found out what really happened, and soon after, his mother died of grief.

Somehow, the boy ended up in Oropesa, near Toledo, where he settled down as a shepherd, under the kind, watchful eye of a local farmer. Years later, when he was twenty-two, he joined the army to escape marriage to the farmer's daughter, and fought for Charles V's company against the French. During the campaign, he was set to guard a large hoard of booty, most of which had vanished on his watch. Suspected of theft, he was condemned to death but luck was on his side in the form of a benign officer who got him off the hook. He returned briefly to Oropesa but was lured back to fighting, serving as a soldier all over Europe for the next eighteen years. On finally returning to Spain and landing at La Coruña in Galicia, he journeyed south to stop off in his hometown, where he found his only remaining family tie was an uncle. He decided to head for Seville to work once more as a shepherd and think about his future, but could not settle down. This time, Africa called and he made for Ceuta to help free enslaved Christians there. But troubled and lost, he returned again to Spain, ending up in Granada where he distributed books produced by the newly available modern printing press. At this time, he began to be known as Juan de Dios, John of God, a name he claimed to have been bestowed upon him by Jesus in his vision.

During his incarceration in hospital, Juan de Ávila visited him and advised him to focus on others instead of himself. Soon after, he was discharged and began to work among the poor, but found himself isolated and alone, working day and night, a victim of the stigma of mental illness, until more charitable priests and physicians began to help with the needs of patients and with medical supplies. Stories abound of his many visions of the Virgin, and even of St Raphael who came to lighten his burden. Gradually, disciples were drawn to help him in serving the poor and needy, and he organized them into the Order of Hospitallers, approved by the Holy See in 1572. Juan died on his fifty-fifth birthday on 8 March 1550, which would become his feast day after his canonization by Pope Alexander VIII in 1690. In 1757 a magnificent Baroque church, called the Church of San Juan de Dios, was built to house his tomb. Now a basilica, it can be found in the street in Granada which also bears his name. Juan is the patron saint of the sick, nurses, firefighters, alcoholics and also of booksellers, and his legacy lives on through the Brothers Hospitallers of Saint John of God, who are present in fifty-three countries where they provide medical services, and are officially entrusted with the Pope's medical care. After an early life torn between caring and killing, Granada exerted a direct, tangible influence on this extraordinary man whose radical work with the sick left a legacy with worldwide impact.

Like Juan, Luis de Granada, born Luis de Sarria in the city in 1504, came from a poor Galician family who counted among the first immigrants to the newly Christian kingdom. His father died when he was five, leaving them penniless, but a stroke of good luck placed Luis under the protection of the powerful Count of Tendilla, Íñigo Hurtado de Mendoza, Captain General of Granada and governor of the Alhambra, who appointed the boy to be a page to his children. Luis was educated at the convent of Santa Cruz run by the Dominican friars, known for their very severe theological training and Aristotelian leanings, where he felt a religious vocation. He was accepted into their community at the age of nineteen, changing his name to Luis de Granada. The Dominicans' main role was teaching and preaching, and Luis devoted himself to these pursuits and corresponded with the main religious thinkers of the time.

Trusting, imaginative, sensible yet emotional, Luis's heart ruled his head. Although the Dominicans favoured the use of Latin, Luis wrote in vernacular Castilian and Portuguese as well because he wanted his words to reach the people they were aimed at. This created antagonism among his fellow priests, as did the popular nature of his work, which challenged the observation by the Dominican theologian Melchor Cano that it was dangerous to teach people things that were inappropriate for them. This difference of opinion reflected the contemporary debate in the Catholic Church about its mission, and about the role of the religious orders. Luis wrote more than forty-five works on the Scriptures, Church dogma, ethics, biography and Church history. His piece about the pomegranate quoted in the first chapter of this book gives us the informal, kindly flavour of his writing style. His first work, *Book of Prayer and Meditation* (*Libro de la Oración y Meditación*), was so unexpectedly successful that he decided to devote his life to writing for the people. *The Sinner's Guide* (*Guía de Pecadores*), published in 1555 and praised for its easy, inspirational style, was likened to Thomas à Kempis's *Imitation of Christ* and was a bestseller of its time, translated into Italian, Latin, French, German, Polish and Greek. It also invoked the displeasure of the Inquisition, and of the Inquisitor General Fernando de Valdés, egged on by Melchor Cano, who felt that Luis's conviction that everyone could aspire to saintliness smacked too much of Erasmianism. When *The Sinner's Guide* appeared in Spain, it contained more than a few modifications. Undeterred, Luis made a great deal of money from his writing, all of which he gave to the poor, and he lived his life in a cell with few possessions. He moved away from Granada in 1551, finally ending up in Portugal where he was offered the post of Bishop of Viseu, followed by the archbishopric of Braga, both of which he turned down. Some say he took refuge from persecution for his perceived Protestant leanings by moving to Lisbon, where he died in 1588, aged eighty-four, weakened by fasting, mortification and overwork.

In different ways, both Juan de Dios and Luis de Granada were deeply influenced by Erasmian humanism and the general spiritual developments of sixteenth-century Europe. Their devotional and doctrinal originality sprang from a city whose local religious culture grew out of a process of innovation and invention. Even so, religious learning was not the only kind of education fostered in Granada at this time. The main educational institution was the university, founded in 1531 by Charles V on the site of the former madrasa of Sultan Yusuf II destroyed by Cardinal Cisneros, and its foundation was confirmed by a papal bull in that year, with the Archbishop of Granada as 'protector'. Teaching began in 1532 and from the start there were five Faculties: Arts, Theology, Law, Canon Law and Medicine. One of its main aims was an ambitious educational programme to encourage the cultural and religious integration of the Moriscos, many of whom were students of medicine there. But it couldn't maintain its momentum, and a climate of growth and euphoria up to 1560 gave way to a long decline. Funding became tricky owing to the financial difficulties of its sponsor institutions, there were conflicts between the archbishop and the rector, and absenteeism of both professors and students was rife.

Amid this uncertain and depressing state of educational affairs, an exceptional individual came into the limelight, Juan Latino, a man born a slave, who rose to become a university professor. Even more remarkably, that man was a black Afro-European, the very first to write literary works in erudite Latin. Juan described himself as an 'Ethiopian Christian, brought from Ethiopia as a child. I was the slave of the excellent and unconquered Gonzalo Fernández de Córdoba, Duke of Sessa, grandson of Gonzalo, Great Commander of Spain.'[90] Juan was born around 1518, though probably not in Africa but in Baena in the province of Granada, the invented story of an Ethiopian origin distancing him from Islam and from any suspicion of heresy, since Ethiopia was then believed to be the land of the Christians converted by the legendary Prester John.

Juan may have been the illegitimate son of a nobleman and grew up in the household of the illustrious Córdoba family, where he was educated alongside his friend, the young Gonzalo. His mother was Magdalena, a black slave to the Duchess of Sessa, who was freed and continued in the employment of the Duchess. Many slaves from sub-Saharan Africa lived with noble families at this time, so Juan's presence was not unusual but his talent was. In contrast with his social condition as a slave, he was said to have a free, liberal mindset. He shone intellectually and is mentioned in the first Acts of the university, dated 2 February 1546, when he was awarded his school graduation certificate. He had already learnt

Latin by carrying Gonzalo's books to the university where they both studied, and so Juan chose Arts, which covered Grammar, Latin, Greek and Rhetoric, as his university degree. He must have been an outstanding student. In 1563, two new professorships in Arts were established to quell students' complaints about the teaching on offer, and Juan was appointed to one of these, in what today would be the Faculty of Philosophy and Letters in Spain, or the Arts Faculty in a British university, on a salary of 30,000 maravedis. He taught Latin at Granada cathedral, effectively part of the university at that time, and close to its central offices in Plaza Bib-Rambla.

The new university colleges, such as Santa Cruz, housed about twelve students, plus a steward, cook and porter, and the university had a student library. These colleges embodied the mission statement of the university that appears in Latin on the windows of the old Arts building in Plaza de Alonso Cano: 'This university was founded to banish the shadows of the infidels, by order of the most Christian Carlos, ever august, King of the Spains...' Its plainly anti-Islamic ideology, promoted by Crown and Church, has a certain irony, as many of its sixteenth-century students were Moriscos. Juan tells us in one of his books that his promotion to the Chair of Grammar and Latin Language was a big step up. It was a position he enjoyed for at least twenty years and he was to play a full part in university life, eventually voting for examiners for undergraduate degrees, and for the new rector in the secret elections held each year. The last time his name appeared in Acts of the university was 12 March 1587, when he was about seventy.

Juan's personal life was equally surprising. Soon after his first graduation, he began teaching private classes and fell in love with one of his pupils, Ana de Carteral. She was an enlightened white woman of rank, keen to learn, interested in the Arts, and she admired Juan's learning and his many virtues. Juan was most probably a free man by then and the couple married sometime in the late 1540s. Their first daughter, Juana, was born in June 1549, and they bought a house in the Santa Ana district of the city in October of that year. Their marriage was one of the first of the few mixed marriages legally constituted in Renaissance Europe. There were other mixed marriages in Granada at this time but they were all between a white man and a black woman. Twelve years later, the family were still living in the same house and had two servants, Pedro and María García. Four more children were born to them, Bernardino, Ana and Juan, who died in infancy, then in 1559, when Juan Latino was forty-one, they had another son, also named Juan.

Their property, which was to become a source of great anxiety to them, was in a street next to the Church of Santa Ana, a converted mosque with its minaret preserved. It was a mainly middle-class Christian district, the abode of working folk such as spice traders, hosiers, midwives, carpenters, clergymen, black-smiths and cobblers. In 1564, Juan became involved in a long, drawn-out legal case over a mortgage on another house they had bought in 1551 as part of the same block of houses where they lived, which condemned him to pay an annual rent of 1,424 maravedis in perpetuity. Believing he had redeemed this amount when he paid the initial sum of 30,000 maravedis, Juan took on his own defence, facing up boldly to the public prosecutor and his accountants, and insisting that he was in the right. Sadly, in 1572 he lost the case after eight years of litigation and was obliged to pay the annual rent. Around this time, probably in 1573, Ana died.

Juan's learning gave him courage and confidence. In one poem, he wrote to the king in Latin that if his black face did not please his ministers, those of white men were not found pleasing in Ethiopia, where kings are black. He composed an epic poem entitled 'Austriadis Carmen' ('Song of the Austrias'), a tribute to the victory over the Ottoman Turks of Don Juan de Austria in the battle of Lepanto of 1571, written in the difficult Humanist Latin of his time, full of evocations of Virgil, and in grand rhetorical style. Juan translated the poets of Antiquity, and had a fondness for the playwright Terence, also a slave favoured by his master. In his lifetime the name Juan Latino became a popular phrase used to mean 'the learned man', 'the Latin expert'. He was so famous that the great dramatist Lope de Vega mentioned him in his play *A Lady of Little Sense* (*La dama boba*) as a man who married for love, and in the poetry at the start of *Don Quijote* Cervantes uses his name as a synonym for talent and wit. King Philip II had a portrait gallery of eminent celebrities of the time in his royal palace, where a painting of Juan Latino is described in the General Archive, probably from 1596–8. The painting is now lost but its inclusion in the royal collection shows how highly the king valued him.

When Juan died is uncertain, although Bermúdez de Pedraza claims he lived till he was ninety, and even when blind in old age, he walked the streets of Granada with his students who read out the Classics to him. Juan Latino is one of Granada's great heroes, a man who rose above the obstacles of racial and class prejudice through his innate talent and fine character. According to one anecdote, Juan was at home one day with his servants on his patio and was not fully dressed. Some visitors arrived who had not met him before, and when they saw him, asked if his master was at home. Juan said 'yes', went into his bedroom, put on a jacket, sat in a fine chair and asked the men to come in. They were full of embarrassment when they realized who he was but he merely told them that it did not matter at all.

THE BAROQUE CITY:
GRANADA'S RENAISSANCE

Visualize a square wooden frame 70 cm high and 85 cm wide, like a window opening. Where the view should be, there is pitch blackness. Suspended by strings hanging from an invisible hook at the top left of the frame are a quince and an upside-down cabbage; in the middle of the sill sits a melon cut open roughly to show its seeds and pale off-white flesh. Almost touching, but not quite, and at an angle to it, a slice from the melon is poised half on, half off the wooden frame. A small ridge cucumber lies on the right of the ledge, its end protruding into space. The arrangement of the objects describes a partial parabola, a curve set against the rigid lines of the wood. The fruit and vegetables are vividly lit from the side, so that these simple items acquire an almost mystical aura. They have a startling, vital presence, each isolated yet associated, their incongruous setting drawing out the mysterious uniqueness of their forms, intense and hyper-real. This is a masterpiece of still life, created in 1602 by the Baroque painter Juan Sánchez Cotán (1560–1627) a year before he left his life in Toledo to enter the Carthusian monastery in Granada as a lay brother.

Sánchez Cotán, who grew up in Orgaz, a town near Toledo, had a brother Alonso who was a sculptor, and two nephews, one a gilder and the other a specialist in 'estofado', the art of creating elaborate, expensive textiles in painted sculptural form. Juan enjoyed great success in Toledo, working for nearly twenty years for patrons among the city aristocracy, painting altarpieces and religious works, then portraits and his celebrated still lifes. In August 1603, when Juan was forty-three, he closed his workshop in Toledo to renounce the world and become a Carthusian monk. Once in Granada, he turned to religious subjects for his art, reaching his peak in 1617 with a cycle of eight great narrative paintings for the cloister of La Cartuja monastery in the city, which portray the foundation of the order of Saint Bruno and the persecution of monks in England by the Protestants. We know from his will of 1603 that he owned a few books, French tapestries and coats of arms, as well as a harp, vihuela and a book of music. Juan must have made a good living from his painting, as he often lent money to others, including the artist El Greco, whom he must have known from his Toledo days. He died on the feast day of the Virgin, 8 September 1627, in Granada. Juan was a prolific artist but only eleven of his works were still lifes, which, he explained, were offerings to the Virgin, portraying a monastic denial of worldly pleasure and richness. Yet they also seem to endow commonplace, humble, everyday items of food with an almost sacred reverence and beauty. They are now regarded among the greatest still lifes ever painted.

Granada is a city deciphered through the visual and when Sánchez Cotán arrived it was already an important artistic centre. Artists from all over Europe, from Italy, the Low Countries, France, had come there to ennoble the city, as contemporary accounts say, and in the first half of the sixteenth century art flourished in a way unequalled in the rest of Spain at the time. Around 1518–20, Alonso de Berruguete (the most famous sculptor and painter of the Spanish Renaissance), Bartolomé Ordóñez (also a sculptor), the Toledan architect Enrique Egas, Felipe de Vigarny (a sculptor and architect from Burgundy) and the Tuscan sculptor Domenico Fancelli were all in Granada, a constellation of major artists who shaped the triumph of Renaissance art in the city. They all left a testimony to their genius but did not remain there. Meanwhile, two other important artists, the Toledan Pedro Machuca, and Diego de Siloé from Burgos, arrived and put down roots. Machuca had studied with Michelangelo before arriving in 1520 and he made a crucial impact with his architectural work despite being a painter. For twenty-four years, from 1527 until 1550, he directed the construction of Charles V's palace and was succeeded by his son Luis. Diego de Siloé had been employed in Naples before he came to Granada in 1528, where he lived with his wife for thirty-five years, in a house near the cathedral. He worked on most of the important new buildings in the city, in particular the cathedral, and created much of the new urban skyline single-handed.

What had attracted so many highly gifted artists to the city? The answer lies in the deeply religious atmosphere which pervaded Granada after 1492, born of the determination to Christianize the city. This atmosphere informed all art and sculpture and gave these artists newly trained in the most up-to-date techniques of the Italian Renaissance a unique opportunity to display their talent through the religious themes of their work, mainly commissioned by the Church. Its profound religious spirit chimed with what we now call European Baroque, a style of art with a social aim, to delight, instruct and move the viewer or reader spiritually for a moral purpose. The Catholic Church was the driving force behind Spanish Baroque, which offered a striking counterpoint to the simple austerity of Protestant architecture and art. Exuberant, profuse, brilliantly coloured, majestic, it inspired awe and wonder through its ability to create lavish illusions. Baroque art in seventeenth-century Granada evolved in an original way. You only have to look at the altarpiece in the Basilica of San Juan de Dios to appreciate how the excess of gilded surfaces, intricate ornamentation and overwhelming detail covering every surface in some way constitute a Christian incarnation of similar features in Islamic art. Yet there was also an element of pared-down naturalism in Granada's religious paintings, with their sculptural figures and extreme contrasts of light and dark of the kind which strike the dominant note in Sánchez Cotán's still lifes, and echo the imagery of light and darkness in the famous mystical poetry of Saint John of the Cross, who was Prior of the Convent of the Martyrs in Granada from 1582 to 1588.

Envisage entering a dark room, barely lit, and coming face to face with the figure of a monk, his head covered in a cowl that frames his face like a halo. He is standing stock still, hands clasped together inside his sleeves, staring upwards as if in ecstasy, lips apart, skin deathly pale, his figure illuminated dramatically in the blackness. A shiver goes down your spine, as if you are in the presence of sanctity, for this person is uncanny, cadaverous, an intensely real apparition. Dare to move closer and you see that there are real ivory teeth in the mask-like face, the eyelashes are real hair, a real cord is knotted round his waist. Detailed inspection shows that this is not a living person but the eerie illusion of one. It is a shocking but profound representation of Saint Francis of Assisi (c.1181–1226) standing in ecstasy, created in 1633 by the Granada-born sculptor Pedro de Mena (1628–88). From October 2009 to January 2010, the National Gallery in London staged an exhibition of seventeenth-century Spanish painting and sculpture in which the image of Saint Francis was brought from its niche in the sacristy of Toledo cathedral to stand in its probably original glass case among an entire cast of holy and heavenly sculpted figures.[91]

In 1449 Pope Nicholas V ordered Francis's tomb in Assisi to be opened, and legend has it that the saint's corpse was discovered as if he were alive, standing up, feet apart, his soles firmly on the ground. Saint Francis was a popular subject for seventeenth-century sculpture and such works were specially blessed – if you recited an *Ave Maria* in front of them you would receive four days of remission from punishment for sins committed. When Pedro de Mena sculpted his great masterpiece[92] to illustrate the legendary incorruptibility of the saint's body, he was working in an ancient tradition of painted sculpture that goes back to Neolithic times, which took on a uniquely Spanish flavour as part of the technique of painting wooden sculptures that began in the Middle Ages in Europe. Baroque emotional intensity, three-dimensional colour and naturalism met in one of the crowning glories of Granadan art at this time, its polychromed sculptures, full-size figures carved from wood, coated in gesso and painted meticulously, then finished with a variety of materials – flesh, blood, cloth, wood, thorns, whose textures the viewer could feel. Favoured by the Church because they seemed almost living and breathing and could bring the viewer closer to the divine, these were three-dimensional simulacra of unsettling realism. Some sculpted figures were draped in clothing, often exquisitely carved and coloured, and had moveable limbs, glass eyes and real hair. Here the sacred was made real in a truly popular form that belonged to the world of everyday life.

Pedro de Mena rose to great heights: promoted to master sculptor of Toledo cathedral in 1663, he left his native city behind. Another great Granadan master, José de Mora, was born in the town of Baza in 1642, after which his family moved to the city, where his father and brother worked as sculptors until 1666. José left for Madrid in 1669 and was made court sculptor to King Charles II, finally returning to his father's workshop in Granada around 1680. He and his wife lived in the Albaicín in the beautiful Carmen de los Mascarones, the house formerly owned by the poet Soto de Rojas (1584–1658), which he had called his 'walled paradise'. Mora was never short of work and commissions flowed in from the cathedral and chapterhouse in Cordoba, and the convents of San Antonio in Granada and Guadix. His magnificent, imaginative sculpture of Saint Cecilius, the legendary but fabricated founder of Granada, graced its cathedral. José de Mora's life ended in tragedy: following his wife's death in 1704, he descended into a madness that would last for twenty years, until his own death in 1724. Many of his works were destroyed in the Spanish Civil War but his statues of Saint Bruno in the Charterhouse in Granada and the full-length Virgin of Sorrows in the church of Santa Ana are still greatly admired. There is a story that when in 1671 the Virgin was led by torchlit procession through the streets to be installed in the church at midnight, she miraculously healed a gravely ill woman as she passed by her house.

The life of the Virgin is the subject of seven monumental paintings displayed twenty-five metres above the floor on the second level of the rotunda that forms the Royal Chapel of Granada. Luminous and vividly coloured, they are the creations of Alonso Cano Almansa (1601–67), the 'Michelangelo of Spain', so called because like the Italian virtuoso he excelled in sculpture and architecture as well as painting. Born in the parish of San Ildefonso in Granada in March 1601 to a father who installed retables, the decorated frames and shelves above and behind a church altar, and a mother who had artistic leanings, Alonso's life reflected the drama, lights and shadows of his greatest works. Precociously talented, he went to Seville to join the workshop of Francisco Pacheco (1564–1644), tutor to Velázquez, with whom Alonso remained close friends. He qualified as a master painter in 1626 but just as fame began to call, tragedy struck when his wife María de Figueroa died in childbirth the following year. He found love once more with Magdalena de Uceda, daughter of the painter Juan de Uceda, and married her in 1631. Seven years later, he was in Madrid, where the powerful Duke of Olivares, King Phillip IV's favourite, appointed him court painter. Influenced by the recent works of his colleague Velázquez and by Venetian painting of the time, he became a colourist and elegant figural painter. But tragedy was lying in wait once more. In 1644 Magdalena was murdered and Alonso was accused of the crime, imprisoned and tortured, but there was no evidence to prove his guilt. He finally returned to Granada in 1651 to become a priest and was appointed canon of the cathedral.

It seems clear that Alonso, like the great Caravaggio, had a tempestuous, quarrelsome nature, and took part in duels. Despite earning large amounts of money, he was nearly always in debt, having to be bailed out by his friends. Alonso's magnificent artistic heritage has regrettably suffered more than most from irreparable losses due to fires, war, robbery and pillaging. Religion was the focus of most of his work, and the cycle of paintings in the Royal Chapel depicting the life of the Virgin are among the high points of European Baroque art, yet his most enduring legacy lies in his sculptures. His polychrome sculpture of the head of Saint John of God, made between 1660 and 1665, is a work of genius, carved out of a single, hollowed-out block of wood, with two glass 'cups' painted white and brown and inserted from inside into the eye sockets. He applied subtle tones of white, pink, red and brown on top of the white gesso base, painting over the sculpted hair and then adding individual strands with a fine brush to make the hairline seem natural, the whole comprising an exquisite and masterly fusion of painting and sculpture. Just months before his death in 1667, he was appointed Master of Works of the cathedral and designed its façade, but he did not live to see it finished. Alonso Cano lies buried in the crypt of the cathedral whose Baroque transformation he instigated.

In the two centuries that followed the Christian takeover of Granada, the keynote was transformation. Urban structural changes mirrored changes in politics, religion and in the mindset of the inhabitants. It was a transformation of outer appearances, which involved the creation of façades, surface superimpositions that attempted to reconstitute a Muslim city as a Christian one through appropriation. The urban landscape was partly reformulated through visual perspectives, through the creation of views and panoramas real and imagined, and through the imposition of dominant Christian sites of power epitomized by the cathedral and Royal Chapel. The history of the city was refabricated to match, in a faked Christian past in which holy relics would disclose the secret story of Granada's ancestry. The mindscape of the city in the sixteenth and seventeenth centuries can be charted through an obsession with piety and religious reform in which the role of art was crucial. Baroque altarpieces, polychromed sculptures, architectural overlays, all fostered the spirit of profound religiosity through a series of illusions, through a semblance of the divine which appeared lifelike, familiar and genuine.

Illusion enlivened the streets of the city in the form of public spectacles where the sacred and the worldly, even the pagan, rubbed shoulders. One of the earliest took place when Luis Hurtado de Mendoza took over the governorship of the Alhambra in 1561. He mounted the hill to the fortress astride a grey horse and wore sumptuous furs and damask silk woven with gold threads. Four hundred Moriscos came down from the Alhambra before dawn to take part in mock battles re-enacting the fall of the city, which were followed by a splendid feast in the Arab palace. Bullfights were held regularly in the Bib-Rambla square, reigniting the ancestral memory of the pagan bulls of early Iberian times, bringing thrills and mortal danger. During the bull-running at the *corrida* held in August 1609, thirty-six people were gored to death and over sixty wounded. In the same square, the nobles played *juegos de cañas,* a horseback combat game using canes for lances, a bizarre spectacle with its origins in the Arab military world. The main festival in the sixteenth century was the feast of Corpus Christi, held in June to commemorate the institution of the Eucharist. Still important today, Corpus Christi was both an act of faith and a theatrical performance, mixing holy and profane in its processions of polychromed sculptures of religious figures, carnival giants, dragons and devils. Royal visits too were occasions of high emotion and splendour. King Philip IV's entry into the city through the Rastro gate, on 8 April 1624, cost the town council a small fortune. He headed for the Alhambra amid great jubilation, fireworks, church bells and canon fire from the fortresses.

Since 1492, the flourishing Christian society of Granada had been forging a new identity, inventing a history, imagining a future in which the infidels played no part, a history in which the Jews and Muslims of al-Andalus, who in their time were as much a part of European civilization as the native Iberians, stopped being perceived as such. It meant identifying the West with Christian Europe, Christian Spain, and denying the place of those peoples in their history. Yet that new Granadan identity was a simulacrum, undermined by paradox and ambivalence. The flux of renovation and renewal that sought to obliterate the Jewish and Muslim past did the opposite. A society persisted that was covert, secret, underground, in which crypto-Jews and crypto-Muslims struggled perilously to hang on to their cultural and religious identity. Granada had become a brilliant city of the European Renaissance but it represented the ultimate *engaño*, a visual, political and historical illusion of triumphant Catholicism, beneath which latent, illicit rebellions simmered and intensified.

7

HOAXERS, HERETICS AND HEROES

The Moriscos of Granada

•••••••••••••••••••

'A WAR OF FIRE AND BLOOD': THE REBELLION OF THE MORISCOS

Hajj Hamadi Ben Ezzedine sits in his small workshop in the bustling *medina* of Tunis, peering intently as he puts the finishing touches to a crimson cap he is making. He works as a craftsman and earns a living making *chechia*, traditional Tunisian red woollen skullcaps with a black tassel. Hajj proudly explains that his forefathers had brought their *chechia* trade with them four hundred years ago when they were exiled from their Andalusian homeland. Abdelghafar el Akel lives a day's travel away from Tunis, near the Moroccan coast in the blue-tinted town of Chefchaouen. Over the fireplace in his house hangs an unusual artwork, a collage consisting of a large key, a lock and some fragments of wood. These objects have survived war, emigration and poverty, gathered together in an old sack as revered possessions of Abdelghafar's ancestors. They are all that remains of the door of the house his family owned in Granada, relinquished when his forebear Ibrahim Ben Ali fled in desperation to north Africa to escape religious persecution just before the city fell in 1492. To understand the histories of Hajj and Abdelghafar, who have the blood of the Spanish Muslims in their veins, and who still speak of Granada as their lost paradise, we must return to the city soon after 1492 and view things from a different perspective. If the Christian immigrants who came to Granada saw it as a place of opportunity and prosperity, for the native Muslims who remained it quickly became the abode of fear and despair.

The power of names can be significant. The Muslim population of Granada, folk whose families had lived for many generations on Spanish soil, and who considered it their native land, became *mudéjares* on 2 January 1492. This term redefined them as Muslims living protected under Christian rule, who could continue to follow Islam – yet the word, taken from the Arabic word *Mudajjan* meaning 'tamed', and originally used as a taunt, implied their subjection to Christian domination. On the surface though, at first Muslim life appeared unchanged, in line with the terms of the surrender agreed by Sultan Boabdil and the Catholic Monarchs, which safeguarded their religious and cultural freedom. In the spring of 1492, the Nasrid pomegranate symbol of Granada was incorporated into the royal shield of Castile and Leon, bright red fruit, green stalk and leaves on silver, a unique heraldic expression that linked Granada's Christian and Muslim peoples, created at the request of the leaders of the Islamic community, who had asked their conquerors to give a seal and noble status to the city.

When Hieronymus Münzer visited 'the great and glorious city of Granada' in October 1494, two years and eight months after Boabdil surrendered, he left a detailed and revealing travelogue that recorded important aspects of Muslim life under Christian jurisdiction. His doctor's eye perceived the advanced Muslim sewerage system with running water, as well as urns used as urinals, and plentiful wells of clean drinking water. He knew the captain-general, the Count of Tendilla, who took him to the Alhambra, where he saw its ceilings and cupolas made of gold, lapis lazuli, ivory and cypress wood. Tendilla told him that Boabdil had a helmet in the shape of a pomegranate, bearing the motto *Only God is conqueror*, a motif Münzer saw painted on many walls of the Alhambra in sky blue. He also described the splendid main Mosque, 66 yards wide and 113 yards long, with rush mats on the floor and a patio with a central fountain for ablutions, as well as nine rows of columns, thirteen on each side, plus 130 arches, and an enormous candelabrum bearing over 100 candles, used for festivals. 'We saw many beautiful lamps lit and priests wearing a white tunic and white headcloth chanting their hours in their own way, which was a very sad clamour rather than singing. The temple was made with extraordinary richness.' Münzer records over 200 smaller mosques in the city, such that at night the clamour from the minarets was so loud it was hard to imagine. He singles out the small mosque in the Albaicín, which he thought lovely, with its eighty-six free-standing columns, smaller but more beautiful than the main Mosque, with a pretty garden planted with lemon trees. He witnessed Muslim beliefs and rituals, the Friday prayer meetings, ritual washing before entering the mosque, and admired the diligence of the Muslims at prayer, as the muezzin called two hours before dawn, at midday and in the evening, as well as sometimes at two in the morning, he grumbled, which was the case in the mosque right next to his inn. His travel diary shows that over two and a half years since Granada fell, Islam was still thriving in the city. But beneath the surface, trouble was brewing.

Hovering in the margins of Christian perception was the fear of a new Muslim conspiracy or uprising, accompanied by the suspicion that the constant interaction of Christians with Muslims would somehow contaminate Catholicism. On 2 March 1498, it was decreed by the Catholic authorities that Granadan Christians were forbidden to sell wine to Muslims, or rent out houses to them, or use Muslim baths, or Muslim midwives, and each community must have separate storehouses for oil, honey, cheese, raisins and fruit. Soon, the Muslims found themselves ghettoized in the Albaicín, or moved out to the *vega*. By December 1499, the growing uncertainty in their besieged community over whether all Muslims, men or women, were safe from forced conversion to Catholicism was the straw that broke the camel's back. It was a state of affairs that confirmed the betrayal of the 1492 Capitulations and provoked a revolt by the exasperated Muslims living in the Albaicín between December 1499 and January 1500. Street fighting broke out, a Christian law officer was killed and the Inquisitor General Archbishop Cisneros, who had been staying in the city, fled from his house in the Alcazaba after being attacked. In the end, the Count of Tendilla restored law and order but it was a watershed moment. From the Christian point of view, it was this Muslim revolt that rendered the terms of the Capitulations null and void, and a new alternative was presented: the stark choice between conversion to Christianity or exile. From the Muslim perspective, they felt they had been hoodwinked over the guaranteed right to pursue their own religion, and violence was their last resort. This crucial moment marked the end of Islam as a public religion in Spain, the start of the Morisco era and the birth of crypto-Islam.

The Muslims had been redefined yet again, no longer as Mudejars but as Moriscos, a word that in twelfth-century Castilian Spanish derived from the word 'moro', both an adjective and noun meaning 'Moorish' and 'Moor' respectively, and which referred to them as either north African or Muslim. 'Morisco' is also both noun and adjective, and its diminutive ending has a pejorative sense. The later meaning of 'Morisco', which came into being in the sixteenth century precisely because of these events in Granada, is much more specific. It describes the Muslims who remained living in Spain as baptized Christians but who were, crucially, forced and unwilling converts. At least 8,000 individuals were converted in Granada around the turn of the century and one of the most shocking events associated with this was carried out on the orders of Cardinal Cisneros. He had become the foremost religious figure of authority in Spain and had decided on a programme of evangelization of Granada using strong-arm tactics, his obsessive zeal for conversion making nonsense of the Capitulations already treacherously abandoned by the Catholic Monarchs. In 1501, the Plaza Bib-Rambla became the scene of one of the most dramatic and devastating spectacles for the Moriscos, remembered vividly even today. Cisneros gave the order to burn all the books and manuscripts written in Arabic that his men had gathered throughout the city, as part of a series of measures to eliminate all external features of an Islamic nature. Juan de Vallejo, Cisnero's servant, described the scene in his *Memorial of the life of Brother Francisco Jiménez de Cisneros* (*Memorial de la vida de Fray Francisco Jiménez de Cisneros*):

> In order to uproot them from their perverse and evil sect completely, he [Cisneros] ordered the Muslim expounders of the Law to take their Korans and other private books, as many as they owned, and build large fires and burn them all; and among them were an infinite number with silver bindings and other Morisco patterns on them, worth eight or ten ducados, and others worth less than that. Although some of the Moriscos besmirched themselves in taking them and availing themselves of the parchments, paper and bindings, his Very Reverend Lordship expressly ordered none to be taken. So they were all burnt, without leaving a trace, as they say, except for the books of medicine, of which there were many, which he ordered to be kept; of which his Lordship ordered thirty or forty volumes to be brought, which today are in the library of his distinguished college and university of Alcala.[93]

So it was that in just five years, the peerless Granada where Islam still flourished, described so clearly by Münzer, had become a place of continued trauma for its Muslim inhabitants, as contemporary evidence showed. The New Capitulations, or solemn agreement, dated 26 February 1501, aimed to ensure that Islam was eliminated as soon as possible. The choices it announced were brutal: remain and accept baptism, refuse baptism and become a slave, or emigrate and become a refugee in an Islamic country. This was followed by a Royal Decree of 12 February 1502, just ten years after the fall of Granada, which obliged all inhabitants of Castilian territories to become Christians as they were forbidden to remain Muslims. What could the Muslims do? The rest of western Europe had celebrated the Christian victory, which was seen as revenge for the loss of Constantinople to the Ottoman Turks some forty years earlier, so there would certainly be no help for the Moriscos from that quarter. The only option was to rely on Muslims abroad for help but appeals to the Egyptian Mamluks and the Ottomans proved fruitless, as neither was in a position to make a successful strike against Spanish territory. The crisis deepened, its great irony being that Spain, a world imperial power at that time, felt threatened from within its borders by a minority group who, without substantial overseas aid, could never have posed a military problem for them.[94]

In the first half of the sixteenth century, a young man of unknown name from the town of Arévalo in the province of Ávila in Castile lived as a crypto-Muslim, continuing to practise Islam clandestinely after the forced conversion decrees of 1501 and 1502. He wrote in *Aljamiado,* a secret language invented by crypto-Muslims, which used the Arabic alphabet to express Castilian words. The Young Man of Arévalo (*el Mancebo de Arévalo*) was learned and expert in Arabic, Hebrew, Greek and Latin, and his body of work includes the fundamentals of the faith and rites of Islam. What is particularly interesting is the record of his interviews with several of the survivors of the fall of Granada, which gives us a deeply personal interpretation of the tragedy of the Muslim community in Spain at this time.[95] His encounters with some of the most prestigious figures of Morisco society reveal their pain, hopes and fears as they struggled to cope with the reality that faced them. With a modern-day journalist's eye for detail and for the circumstantial, the young Muslim describes in full the conversations he had in the aftermath of the surrender of the city.

One extraordinary figure he interviewed was a very elderly woman known as the *Mora de Úbeda*, a Moorish woman originally from the town of Úbeda on the border between Granada and Castile. When he met her, she was ninety-three years old and lived in the Albaicín, close to the Puerta de Elvira. She had a powerful physical presence, with a body and limbs so large they scared the young scholar, who had never seen anyone like her before, a woman whose little finger was bigger than his middle finger. She wore rough twill clothes and esparto grass sandals and lived alone in great simplicity, although she had been very influential in the time of Boabdil and his fifteenth-century predecessors and was a prestigious commentator on the Koran. She couldn't read but could argue with great judgement and wisdom. The young Morisco tells us that despite her rough, coarse speech, no one could equal her in teasing out the most transcendental meanings of the Koran. The *Mora* no longer fasted during Ramadan, prayed sitting down and did not leave her house because of her great age; since things had changed for the worse for Muslims, he recalls how she had withdrawn from public life into the shadows of her unhappiness to weep over the fall of the Islamic state. Before this she had maintained a privileged role at the Nasrid court, signing and sealing the books of the sultans of Granada, and she was given certain books by Boabdil when he went into exile. This ancient sage was greatly afflicted by the fall of the city, during which she lost all her relatives except for a niece, Aixa. She had witnessed the terrible destruction of Arabic books in the Bib-Rambla square, and was greatly moved by it, sensing that she was in effect present at the destruction by edict of the culture of her elders. The young man reports her very words: 'I saw the Holy Book in the hands of a merchant who was tearing it up to use as paper for children, and I gathered up all the pieces, which broke my heart.'

The young man met another distinguished figure in the local community, an Islamic teacher, Yūse Banegas, whose classes on the Koran he attended, held in the strictest secrecy and at risk to their lives. Yūse had an expert knowledge of Arabic and Hebrew, and his possession of books in those languages shows that their prohibition by the Christians was scorned by the Morisco minority. He was a person of some material as well as cultural wealth, and was possibly a member of the prestigious Venegas family of Granada, which was involved in the surrender capitulations. That family enjoyed certain civil liberties, including in all likelihood religious freedom. Yūse clearly perceived the tragedy that had struck down the Moriscos. He describes his personal losses and the enormous pain and indignation he felt in witnessing the shaming and selling of Muslim women at public auction. In a sermon delivered out in the *vega* beside a stream, Yūse laments:

> In my opinion nobody ever wept over such a misfortune as that of the sons of Granada. Do not doubt what I say, because I am one myself, and an eye-witness, for with my own eyes I saw all the noble ladies, widowed and married, subjected to mockery, and I saw more than three hundred young women sold at public auction. It is more than I can bear to tell you any more. I lost three sons, all of them died defending our religion, and I lost two daughters and my wife, so just one daughter was left to be my consolation, though she was only seven months old at the time.

These eye-witness accounts are privileged insights into the sadness and despair of the conquered Granadans in the immediate aftermath of Boabdil's departure, and count as priceless personal testimonies, given the virtual absence of other contemporary historical accounts written from a Muslim perspective. In the next decades, sadly, their plight worsened as it became bedeviled by contradiction. The apparent desire to assimilate Moriscos wholeheartedly into the Catholic fold clashed with an equal desire to contain, control and isolate what was perceived as the alien element in the new Granada. Soon, the converted Muslims fell prey, like the *conversos*, to the involvement of the Inquisition, hell-bent on obliterating the whole inherited culture of the Moriscos, as the Christians contemplated violent solutions to the perceived problem.

Meanwhile, the mufti of Oran, an expounder of religious law, had pronounced a Fatwa, or considered legal opinion, in 1504, setting out for the benefit of persecuted Muslims in Spain a list of modifications they could legitimately introduce into the religious obligations they must observe under circumstances of oppression. It is an exceptional document, still known today throughout the Muslim world, which essentially permitted Muslims to stay in Spain by allowing them to pretend to be Christians while maintaining their inner determination and intention to be Muslims. It gave detailed instructions on how this double life could be led.

In the secrecy enforced upon them by external pressures, the Moriscos invented a new written language, the one used by the Young Man of Arévalo, known as *Aljamiado* or *Aljamía*, in essence Spanish written in Arabic characters – similar to the phenomenon of Ladino, the Spanish written in Hebrew characters adopted by the Jews prior to their expulsion in 1492, which had continued to flourish after this date in the diaspora. Unlike that language, the use of *Aljamía* ceased after the Morisco expulsion that began in 1609. The creation of a new Morisco language was an exceptional achievement, in which their choice of Arabic instead of Latin was not only an assertion of loyalty to their religion and culture but also a vital way of maintaining their threatened Islamic identity. The invention of *Aljamía* was also an act of great courage as its use flouted the sixteenth-century ban on writing in Arabic script; so anyone possessing such a manuscript was immediately placing themselves in a dangerous position. In effect, the message lay in the medium, which asserted the precedence of Arabic culture over Latin. But that message was ambivalent – the use of Arabic marked cultural difference, yet the Spanish vocabulary showed that Moriscos were also Europeans too. The new language expressed their embracing of two cultures, their Spanish identity as well as their Arabic and Islamic origins.

The ever more threatening attitude of the Christians and the clandestine lives of the crypto-Muslims built towards a conflict that would end in violence, as falsity and ambiguity, friendship and betrayal, reigned in everyday life. Just before 1560, a petition was drawn up by Christian lawyers insisting on the revision of all property titles in the kingdom of Granada. This move was disastrous for Moriscos, who were obliged to show ancient title deeds from the time of the Nasrid dynasty dating from the thirteenth century. If they could not, they were stripped of their land and property, which was put up for sale. In 1567 the Granadan authorities made the decision to ban not only the use of Arabic but also Arab names and the use of Moorish baths, while wearing Moorish clothing was officially prohibited in January 1568. Granada had become a place of panic and terror for the Moriscos. At this time, prophecies or *jofores* containing obscure predictions circulated freely and Moriscos met secretly to debate the situation. They decided to resist and in an upsurge of enthusiasm for all the external symbols of Islam and Arab culture that had been repressed in recent generations, the Moriscos began their first rebellion at Christmas 1568.

Suddenly Granada was no longer a safe, pacified place, but a city engaged in devastating strife and conflict once more. The Morisco Uprising (also known as the Rebellion of the Alpujarras) lasted for nearly two years, until November 1570, and involved great cruelty and appalling atrocities committed by both sides. On Christmas Eve 1568, despite the planned main attack being cancelled by atrocious snowfalls, a daring rebel, Farax ben Farax, led one hundred and fifty men through the city gates to incite an uprising. His efforts failed but were taken as tantamount to a declaration of war by the Moriscos, whose wild enthusiasm for their cause expressed itself in anarchic violence and released the terrible rage of a persecuted people. They robbed and burned churches, pulled down altars, dragged priests through the streets naked, then shot them with poisoned arrows. They invented terrible new torments, setting the priest of Mairena alight after forcing him to swallow gunpowder, and burying another priest half alive and then using him as an archery target.

In their many campaigns outside the capital in the Alpujarras, longtime refuge of bandits and outlaws, the Moriscos fought under local Granadan commanders headed by the last indigenous Muslim pretender to rule in al-Andalus, Fernando de Válor, alias Aben Humeya, assisted by foreign military experts sent by the Turks from Algiers. Aben Humeya's claim to be a descendant of the Umayyads who first ruled in Spain sent the strong message that his rule had a legitimacy predating any claimed by the Christian House of Austria. He and his men were up against the Christian might of royal troops and urban militia led by more than six generals, including Don John of Austria, the half-brother of King Philip II, who went on to command the Spanish troops as Admiral of the Fleet in the Battle of Lepanto in 1571. While the Moriscos sorely lacked manpower and firearms, they knew the rocky mountain passes, mule trails and deep valleys of the Alpujarras like the back of their hands, and were often able to outwit and outmanoeuvre the royal troops, who lacked experience of the terrain or mountain weather conditions. But in the middle year of the conflict, disagreements in the Morisco camp, which had a tendency to divide into factions like the Nasrid rulers before them, became murderous, heightened by sexual jealousy and drug-taking. The Christians did not need their own initiatives to succeed as long as the Moriscos shot themselves in the foot. The rebels finally turned against their own leader, and Aben Humeya was strangled in October 1569. At this moment, Phillip II removed all restrictions on rape and plunder on the part of the Christian army, giving his troops free rein in what he declared to be 'a war of fire and blood'.

In January 1570, Don John of Austria took a sledgehammer to crack a nut. Amid the smouldering ruins of small towns in the *vega*, he led 12,000 Spanish troops and heavy artillery to lay siege to the large, ancient village of Galera, 150 kilometres from Granada, famous now as the place where the Phoenician sculpture of the Dama de Galera was found but of no strategic importance then. The locals numbered about 3,000 men, armed only with rocks, rubble and the few weapons they had, plus an indomitable spirit.

As heavy cannons blasted gaps in the walls, the Christian knight Juan Pacheco rushed through the gap into the village, where he was promptly hacked limb from limb. Enraged at the terrible casualties among his professional troops inflicted by mere civilians, Don John ordered the slaughter of over 400 women and children, an atrocity that speaks as much about John of Austria as it does about the extraordinary courage and determination of the Morisco villagers, whose resistance was inevitably overcome. Despair prevailed. On 15 March 1571, the last Muslim ruler of any part of al-Andalus, Aben Abóo, was murdered with the butt of a gun by one of his own men, who slung him over a pack animal and took him to Granada. En route, he began to stink, so they removed his entrails and packed him with salt, and on arrival in the city his body was handed over to the Christian authorities in exchange for a reward. Aben Abóo's degrading demise sounded the death knell of Muslim resistance in Granada.

What the Morisco rebels did not know was that around March 1570, it had been decided to deport the entire Muslim population of the Kingdom of Granada to destinations in the Kingdom of Castile, where they were unlikely to cause a threat. Don John of Austria had returned personally from the Alpujarras campaigns to the city in June in order to direct the critical first stages of the deportation. On 23 June in the afternoon, squadrons of royal soldiers rounded up all Morisco men and boys aged between ten and sixty and barricaded them into parish churches, where they spent the night under armed guard and in great terror. That night proved a long ordeal, ending in violent scuffles as the quaking captives were marched next day into the confines of the Royal Hospital outside the city walls. After questioning and the compiling of an inventory, some were set free and permitted to stay – artisans and craftsmen whose expertise was thought essential to the city's economy, together with merchants who were permitted to settle their accounts before departure. The rest were left in detention, awaiting their fate. The Granadan soldier and chronicler Luis del Mármol Carvajal was moved by the plight of his neighbours in the Albaicín: 'It was a miserable spectacle to see so many men of all ages, heads held low, hands crossed, their faces bathed in tears and their expressions sad and suffering as they left their comfortable homes, their families, their homeland, their native identity, their possessions, without knowing for certain if they would keep their heads on.'[96]

The deportation began in June and carried on into the harsh Castilian winter, during which these internal exiles suffered cruelly from the effects of heavy snowfalls, cold and typhus, and many died on the way to their new homes. Those who survived found it hard to make a living in the north, where they often received a frosty welcome. Every single Muslim inhabitant of Granada was relocated, with the exception of artisans and a very small, privileged elite judged to be useful to the Crown.[97] Yet against all expectations, there emerged from this minority band a group of men who brought hope to the crypto-Muslim community of Spain, not this time using arms, but words.

'As precious as the Ark of the Covenant': the Lead Books of Granada

Nearly twenty years after the first banishment of the Moriscos, the archaeological artefacts known as the Lead Books were unearthed on a hill outside Granada,[98] mysterious objects that harboured a secret as compelling as the occult lore that cloaks the Turin Shroud and the lost Jewish Menorah. Their story rests upon theology and history and weaves together the lives of some exceptional people of opposing race and religion, among whom one individual stands out, his shadowy life inescapably bound up in the enigma.

In late March 1588, Armada year, a dark-haired Morisco sat at a low table in his house in the Sacromonte neighbourhood of the city, poring over a large parchment by candlelight. He was wrapped in a thick cloak against the spring chill, and all was quiet as he worked late into the night, deep in concentration and showing no sign of fatigue. From time to time he stopped to listen to the smallest sound from outside, his eyes alert and anxious, as if he feared an intrusion. His name was Miguel de Luna, translator from the Arabic to King Philip II, and he had a major task on his hands. Only a week before, on 19 March, as workmen were demolishing the minaret of the former great mosque, known as the Torre Turpiana, to make way for a third nave in Granada's cathedral, they unearthed a lead casket amid the broken masonry whose contents surprised them. Inside was a small panel bearing an image of the Virgin Mary, a fragment of linen, a small piece of bone, a folded parchment and some blackish-blue sand. At first glance, these seemed to be Christian relics of some kind, and their discovery aroused great excitement in the city. What caused the greatest commotion was the parchment, on which a text was written in Latin, Arabic and Castilian, which described the contents of the casket as the bone of the first Christian martyr, St Stephen, the cloth the Virgin dried her eyes upon at the Crucifixion, and a prophecy by St John the Divine relating to the end of the world. The writing on the parchment proved so difficult to decode that eventually expert translators were called in to decipher the full script. Among them was Miguel de Luna, who was summoned because of his expertise in Arabic. He took the parchment home to work on for a week, then his colleague Alonso del Castillo, another Morisco, studied it separately.

Luna and Castillo deciphered a great revelation – it transpired that the prophecy of St John, which told of the advent of Muhammad In the seventh century, the division of Christianity into sects and the coming of the Antichrist, had been translated into Castilian by one Saint Cecilius, who described himself as the first Bishop of Granada during the first century AD. Despite the conundrum posed by such an early saint being able to write not only in Arabic but also in Castilian Spanish, a language that did not exist in the first century, the inhabitants of Granada were delighted to learn that he was their first bishop.

The genuineness of the relics and parchment seemed to be borne out when in 1595, treasure-seekers digging on the Valparaíso hill outside Granada, later known as the Sacromonte, came across a strip of lead engraved in archaic Latin, which claimed that the cremated remains of an early Christian martyr were buried there. Immediately the site began to be excavated and revealed two more lead plaques, one of which announced that Saint Thesiphon, one of the seven bishops of Rome, who was apparently an Arab convert to Christianity, had written a book on lead tablets called the *Fundamental Doctrines of the Church* or *Fundamentum Ecclesiae*. Amid great excitement, ashes, presumed to belong to the saint, were discovered on 13 April 1595, and then on 22 April, something even more unprecedented happened.

The first of the strange Lead Books of the Sacromonte was discovered beneath a large stone, still visible today. It was wrapped in a lead cover and was made up of five round plates 10 centimetres across, hinged together by a twist of lead. The plates were inscribed in Arabic on both sides, with the Latin title on the inside, which translated into English as *The book of the fundamental doctrines of the church written in the characters of Solomon*. This was a book written by Saint Thesiphon and referred to in the Torre Turpiana parchment. The new revelation was celebrated with parties, fireworks, artillery salutes from the Alhambra and general bell-ringing. No one had yet read the book but this did not seem to matter. Soon after, the lead plaque relating to Saint Cecilius himself was found, and the Sacromonte was destined to become a famous place of pilgrimage. Even the celebrated poet Luis de Góngora wrote a sonnet in honour of the forest of wooden votive crosses erected on the site.

Over a period of many months, a total of twenty-two lead books were found on the hill. Owing to the complexities of the texts, written in ancient Arabic, professional translators were called in, once more including Miguel de Luna, who declared that the books contained doctrinal material of the greatest importance, including the instructions and sayings of the Virgin Mary, St Peter and St James, as well as references to the doctrine of the Immaculate Conception of the Virgin. Experts of all kinds, including scribes, parchment-makers, anatomists and charcoal-burners, were called in to scrutinize the relics. For the Granadans, the decisive proof that the finds were genuine were the strong supernatural predictions of their discovery. As long as fifty years before the excavations took place, mysterious lights had repeatedly been observed over the site and this was considered conclusive evidence of the impending divine revelations.

King Philip II was fascinated by this affair that had required the services of his royal translators, but rumours began to circulate that the relics were not authentic and a number of scholars and churchmen appeared to corroborate this. Yet a group of local theologians, including the new Archbishop of Granada, Don Pedro de Castro, had already decided that the relics and texts were genuine. The scholar and poet Arias Montano wrote to Archbishop Castro in 1597 that the finding of the relics and lead disks was 'a very serious matter… the most important in the world today and perhaps there has been none more important for many centuries'.[99] It was inevitable but unfortunate that the Vatican got involved and firmly applied pressure to have the finds investigated further. After several decades of resistance, the Lead Books were taken to Madrid for examination in 1631, forcibly removed to Rome amid great protest in 1642, and finally condemned as heretical Islamic writings in 1682. The Lead Books had caused a religious sensation in Granada as well as in Catholic Europe. Many of those involved ignored the Vatican's damning judgement, including Diego de Yepes, the king's confessor, who deemed them to be as precious to Granada as the Ark of the Covenant was to the Israelites. Even so, the tangled web of intrigue and enigma that surrounded them begs some crucial questions – what precisely were these texts and relics?

How could they appear authentic to Catholics, yet be denounced as Islamic texts? And who had made them, and why?

To look at, the Lead Books seem more magical than sacred. Their archaic script is the kind used on amulets and seals in magical writings that circulated among Spain's Muslims, and the Seal of Solomon, the Morisco star which adorns most of the lead discs, was familiar in Arabic, Islamic, Christian and Jewish cultures as a sign having powerful associations with alchemy and black magic, though in the Lead Books it also emphasizes their divine truth.[100] Their cryptic, ambiguous, often indecipherable language heightened the mystery of these objects, which possessed all the features of the talismans made by Moriscos in sixteenth-century Spain. These were artefacts cleverly designed to resonate with the spirit of the time. Primed by perceptions of 1588 as a year of strange, prophetic events, the Torre Turpiana finds foretold the major discoveries on the Sacromonte, forming a combined body of relics and texts that exalted the divine authority of the Virgin Mary, a central figure in both Christianity and Islam, while paving the way for a very non-Christian message.

Their sensational impact was heightened by cultural elements that converged to truly astonishing effect, elements that came together in three motifs of vital importance, the sacred mountain, the cave and the idea of treasure as a book. For the everyday folk of Granada, mountains were revered places linked to revelation and instruction, and their accompanying caves were ambivalent, often sacred, ritual spaces offering protection and shelter, as we saw in the case of the skeletons found in the prehistoric Cave of Bats near Albuñol. In popular Spanish culture and writing of the time, caves were sites where buried treasure lay, which often took the form of a written text, a talismanic book.[101]

These perceptions converged with the obsession with prophecy that prevailed in Granada and also throughout Spain and Europe, conspiring with an almost wilful blindness to fakery, and an ambience of secrecy, to mould the mindscape of the Catholics and crypto-Muslims of Granada. At the same time, Catholic Granada was under the spell of another obsession, the cult of relics, which had thrived in Europe since the Middle Ages. Fake relics of saints were essential religious and political propaganda, and the ashes of Christian martyrs burned to death were greatly prized. All manner of bones, body parts and other relics of dubious origins were credited with miraculous powers, and had a counterpart in the profusion of false histories and chronicles circulating in Spain, which aimed to establish holy and ancient origins for Spanish cities, like the chronicles of the ecclesiastical sage Román Jerónimo de la Higuera, whose invented history of the Church identified Toledo as a place of unbroken Christian heritage. In this climate of prediction, forgery and concealment fostered by religious piety and folklore, illusion clashed with truth, lending inordinate power to the Sacromonte discoveries, in which complex cultural forces met in the arena of political and religious conflict.

Archbishop Pedro de Castro passionately espoused the cause of the Lead Books, or *plomos* as they were known, and assured Pope Paul V in 1611 that they were one of the greatest things to happen since Adam and Eve. Castro was profoundly involved in the whole Sacromonte affair, commissioning the translators to work on the Lead Books and arranging the testing of the relics, with the encouragement of royal and religious authorities. The fact that their message involved rewriting Church history to provide Granada with a Christian heritage that long predated its Islamic incarnation was a marvellous boost to the project of transforming the city from Islamic state to Christian enclave. In April 1600, Pedro de Castro had called a meeting of forty-nine Church elders in the cathedral to authenticate the relics. They unanimously agreed that the relics were genuine and Granada literally went crazy, putting on a spectacle that lasted several days in the Plaza Bib-Rambla involving imitation ships, knights, serpents and fireworks. The Archbishop began to foster the cult of the Sacromonte, insisting on keeping the relics there on the hillside in a small chapel, later to become the Abbey of the Sacromonte, which he founded in 1610 on the site of the discoveries and conceived as a sanctuary to house the bones of the first Christian martyrs and ultimately the Lead Books. The Abbey remains a highly significant institution, housing one of the most valuable libraries in the city, and probably in Spain.

The Vatican has never challenged the authenticity of the relics of the Sacromonte martyrs to this day. In stark contrast, for the eighty-seven years between the discovery of the Lead Books and their condemnation in 1682 by the Vatican, a genuine intellectual and religious conflict sprang up between those denouncers of the finds, known as *antilaminarios*, and those who were apologists for them, the *laminarios*. Eminent scholars declared the lead texts to be fakes on the basis of their inaccurate version of history, the clumsy Arabic used to masquerade as an antique tongue, and their esoteric magical dimension. Among the apologists was the Catholic Marquis of Estepa, who even learned Arabic in order to translate the texts himself and supported them ardently. But from the start, the out-and-out apologists for the *plomos* were their first translators, the Moriscos Alonso del Castillo and Miguel de Luna, who step into the limelight as the main protagonists in the affair.

Miguel de Luna is the most fascinating, mysterious and complex of all the personages who play a part in the drama of the Lead Books. When he sat in his Sacromonte house translating the Torre Turpiana parchment he was about thirty-eight years old, born in Granada around 1550 into a noble Morisco family originally from nearby Baeza. As a young man he learned Arabic and studied medicine at the newly founded university in the city. He worked as a physician in Granada but it was authorship that became fundamental to his life as the vehicle through which he conveyed his radical, subversive views. Luna's treatise on bathing, written in 1592 and reflecting the latest medical thinking, was a thinly veiled political and religious statement about the importance of restoring the prohibited Morisco practice of taking baths, which purported to discuss their therapeutic value from a solely scientific, pragmatic perspective. His ulterior motive was unsuccessful as the treatise was never published, but the very opposite was the case with a work written in the guise of his other profession of translator. The *True History of King Roderick* (*Verdadera Historia del rey don Rodrigo*) was published in 1592 as a crucial reinterpretation of the events surrounding the Muslim invasion of Spain in 711, which sought to render the Arab Muslims comprehensible and acceptable to Christian culture. Luna alleged that his history was the translation of an unknown Arabic source he found in the library of El Escorial. The account was very popular, with seven reprintings and translations into other European languages, but it transpired that this 'true history' was in fact a colossal fabrication, which fooled many learned people including the two Inquisitors who assessed whether it should be censored or not. Boldly dedicated to King Philip II, Luna's alternative history aimed to give political and religious legitimacy to the Moriscos' claim that they had the right to live in Spanish territory, and was written at a time when the Church was acting fast to close out any traces of religious otherness. It ventured towards a utopia of mutual tolerance between Arabs and Christians by capitalizing on Spain's Achilles heel, the inability to distinguish between illusion and truth.

For Miguel de Luna, words were power at a time when Moriscos in Granada, as well as those in internal exile, were a powerless minority. The most crucial aspect of his life was his ambiguous involvement with the Lead Books, initially as their translator in his capacity as a converted Muslim member of the elite Christian royal establishment. He began work on translations of the first two lead texts in May 1595 and issued a very persuasive report for the king in October, adamantly supporting their antiquity because, he asserted, the great age of the lead they were made from proved they were too ancient to contain any reference to the Koran, which might have cast them as Islamic texts instead of the Christian documents they purported to be. According to Luna, their script predated Koranic language. It was, he claimed, 'Solomonic script' of the kind he claimed he had seen in ancient magical books like the *Key of Solomon*. He also declared that no one alive in Spain could have faked them, as no Moor was sufficiently learned or adept at such a script. But, in fact, Miguel de Luna himself was just such a person.

Luna was native to Granada and loved the place, which he described in his *True History of King Roderick* as '...a small city built in a high place, from which a very pleasant and delightful fertile plain could be seen, with a very beautiful, fast-flowing river running through it, the surrounding mountains full of groves of trees and fresh breezes, so that it seemed to be a paradise on earth'.[102] His vision of the city seems surely to reflect the author's personal feelings about Granada as an earthly garden of delights, yet less than ten years later, in February 1611, in a letter from Luna to the Archbishop of Granada, his paradise had turned into purgatory. Fearful of the expulsion that had overtaken his fellow Moriscos, he describes himself as being on the verge of the same fate: 'the authorities entered my house to remove arms and exert other extortions, which has made me so furious that I can't sleep at night for thinking about these offences'. In the same letter he lamented 'the injustice of wanting to take away my property, lineage, honour and the value of services I have rendered'.[103] Miguel de Luna lived his life in a liminal space between joy and suffering, torn between his desire to belong to the Christian establishment and the urge to remain true to his Morisco roots. In the end he succeeded in acquiring the status of a nobleman, thereby avoiding deportation, and Archbishop Castro wrote that his faithful translator lived as a Catholic and died a good Christian death with all the sacraments in his beloved Granada in the summer of 1618.

But startling documents from the Inquisitorial trial of a Morisco shopkeeper, Jerónimo de Rojas from Toledo, in 1601 tell a very different tale. His statement includes the revelation that Miguel de Luna never ceased to be a Muslim, living a double life, outwardly as a Christian doctor and translator and covertly as a learned crypto-Muslim. At secret meetings with other crypto-Muslims, Luna expounded on the Lead Books, which he used as evidence that Jesus was not divine but a prophet. He presented the purpose of the *plomos* not as upholding the longevity and power of Christianity in Granada, which he had so vehemently defended when in the city, but as polemical Islamic texts presenting an improved version of Christianity and implying that the perfect religion was Islam. This document reveals that Miguel de Luna lived on a knife-edge, risking his life on a daily basis. He was certainly a heretic, who lived publicly as a Christian but secretly as a Muslim, definitely a hoaxer, and almost unquestionably the author of the Lead Books and Torre Turpiana parchment, in concert with others, including Alonso del Castillo.

After a nine-hundred-year ancestral presence in Spain, the right of Luna's fellow Moriscos to consider themselves native Spaniards was undermined by the new Catholic regime, their cultural and religious customs were condemned, and they were finally forced to leave their homeland. The fabrication of the Lead Books is a story of resistance and creative ingenuity in the face of overwhelmingly powerful religious and political forces, a resistance embodied in a hidden network of courageous, idealistic men who fought to defend their culture and language. Miguel de Luna was never denounced in his lifetime and never suffered exile. Daring, radical, recorded in official documents and testimonies as a good Christian, we know for sure that he was a dyed-in-the-wool Muslim who had underground contacts in various locations outside Granada and worked tirelessly in secret for his people. Working at the heart of the Establishment as the king's translator from Arabic, Miguel de Luna was a prolific wordsmith who delighted in the art of ambivalence, in constructing an outer appearance contrary to the inner reality, in using language as a compelling yet subversive weapon in the desperate fight to reinstate Morisco cultural and religious values in Spanish society. A heretic and a hoaxer, but also a hero, he walked a tightrope between subversion and conformity that allowed little scope for failure. But in the end, neither arms nor words were enough to prevent the cataclysm of expulsion that Christian Spain inflicted on its Morisco population, an act of cultural and religious hatred that entailed physical and emotional cruelty, exile and death.

ABANDONING PARADISE: THE TWILIGHT OF MORISCO GRANADA

On the last evening
we contemplate mountains surrounding the clouds,
invasion and counter-invasion,
the ancient era handing our door keys over
to a new age.
Enter, O invaders, come, enter our houses,
drink the sweet wine of our Andalusian songs!
We are night at midnight,
no horsemen galloping toward us
from the safety of the last call to prayer
to deliver the dawn
Our tea is hot and green – so drink!
Our pistachios are ripe and fresh – so eat!
The beds are green with cedarwood
give in to your drowsiness!
After such a long siege, sleep on the
soft down of our dreams!
Fresh sheets, scents at the door, and many mirrors.
Enter our mirrors so we can vacate the premises
completely!
Later we'll look up what was recorded in our history
about yours in faraway lands.
Then we'll ask ourselves,
'Was Andalusia
here or there? On earth,
or only in poems?'[104]

This excerpt from the poem 'The Last Evening in this Land' is part of the book of verse *Eleven Planets in the Last Andalusian Sky* by the Palestinian poet Mahmoud Darwish who died in 2008. Darwish was the national poet of Palestine, whose family fled from their home in Galilee to Lebanon to escape the Israeli armed forces during the 1947–9 Palestine War. No one knew better than he the pains of exile. Palestine and Andalusia became metaphors for a lost Eden in his poetry, which expresses the anguish of dispossession and banishment, and Darwish felt a deep affinity with the dispossessed Muslims of Granada, whose profound sorrow is movingly evoked in this poem. Its final lines capture the illusory nature of the Moriscos' own lost Eden, an idea that took root in the hearts of the Spanish Muslims of Granada who lived in great anxiety in the years leading up to 1609, and whose nostalgia and longing for their ancestral land still lingers in the hearts of modern Muslims like Hajj Hamadi Ben Ezzedine and Abdelghafar el Akel, with whom this chapter began.

Amid the intrigues and drama of the Lead Books affair, the Spanish monarchy and the Catholic Church worked doggedly at a solution to what they perceived as the Morisco problem. Their chosen policy of methodically expelling all Muslims from Spain was foreshadowed not only by the expulsion of the Jews in 1492 and the expulsion of Jews and Muslims from Portugal in 1497 but also by the internal exile of the Granadan Muslims. The desire to banish the Moriscos, who were objectively native Spaniards who had converted to Catholicism, was fuelled by a racial and religious antipathy that went back a very long way, to the Muslim invasion of 711. Expulsion was to be the final stage of reversing that ancient historical turning point, and such a measure reveals how deeply unsatisfactory the apparent completion of the Reconquest in January 1492 had been. Islam had not disappeared, and both secular and sacred authorities were nonplussed. The Christian perspective was that despite all efforts at conversion, the Moriscos could not be assimilated into the Catholic scheme of things. Everyone knew they were still Moors – 'as Moorish as the Algerians' became the refrain. The proposal for a solution sent to King Philip II in 1587 by the Bishop of Segorbe, Martín de Salvatierra, shrank from a prior recommendation to send the Moriscos to sea and drown them, suggesting instead that they could all be deported to America, the males castrated and the women sterilized, so they would die out quickly. The fact that this horrifying scenario was prompted, the bishop stated, by the fear of a Morisco alliance with north Africa that might see them launch an attack on Spain underlines how potent the ancient horror of invasion continued to be in the Christian psyche.

Yet not all Christians in Spain were unanimously in favour of a policy of expulsion, and some hoped that true conversion might still be achieved. Miguel de Luna could have taken some comfort from the fact that the Sacromonte discoveries had a noticeable impact on the royal court. If the Lead Books were genuine, then relics of immense importance to Spain and the Christian world had come to light, in Phillip II's kingdom, and Morisco expertise might be needed to interpret them as they were in Arabic. Maybe that fact might also encourage them to change their minds about Catholicism, so it did not seem the right moment to banish them entirely. Soon after 1605, the Moriscos made their own last-ditch attempt to halt the tide by appealing to the Moroccan sultan Muley Zaydan for help – a forlorn hope as he was too beleaguered by conflict in his own lands to be able to intervene on their behalf. But the appeal put the fear of God into the Christians, who saw it yet again in terms of the 711 invasion and of a potential second coming of the Muslims. The die was cast. On 4 April 1609, King Philip III, who had come to the throne in 1598, decided in conjunction with his Royal Council that expulsion was the only way to avoid war with the Islamic world.

Over the next five years, like the Jews before them, the marginalized, persecuted Moriscos were banished region by region and herded onto galleys at ports round Valencia to be taken to north Africa, initially to Oran in present-day Algeria. It should be said that there were a few who greeted their exile joyfully and looked forward to returning to the land of their distant ancestors. Most of the Granadan Moriscos had already been sent into internal exile in the 1570s but they had not settled in, and many had managed to find their way back to Andalusia where there was work. Some had even illegally slipped back into Granada itself. The Edict of January 1610 ordering the expulsion of all Andalusian Moriscos was designed to stamp out any possibility of rebellion by blackening the name of those Moriscos who had returned to the city by accusing them of traitorous connivance with the Turks. These Moriscos were to be expelled without exception within thirty days, taking no money with them, only permitted goods. It was a move that had made Miguel de Luna's application for noble status even more urgent. By March 1611, there was really no escape – Moriscos from the city who had not left when summoned, including former slaves and even those who possessed a formal statement that they lived as good Christians, were forced to leave. The process of ethnic cleansing was complete, and Islam, which had first come to Spain in 711, was finally driven out in 1614, after nine hundred years.

Best guesses estimate that 300,000 Moriscos were exiled from the Spanish realm, plus some ten or twelve thousand who died en route. Of those who survived, many were scattered across sub-Saharan Africa, some even reached the Americas, but the vast majority ended up in what are now Morocco, Tunisia and Algeria, where their agricultural know-how, artistic and cultural heritage and Hispanic family names live on today. The transition was a hard one, since they were Spanish and their language, customs, way of life and even religion did not blend in easily with north African ways. Their expulsion, and that of the Jews before them, is little known and rarely talked about or denounced as something that should never happen again. It was an act of intolerance, fanaticism, religious prejudice and cultural racism that lies buried below the surface of the collective historical memory of modern Spain, revealing a society still not reconciled with a dark chapter of its history.

By 1614 Granada had been transformed into a Spanish-speaking Castilian kingdom with almost no native Muslims. Or at least that was the theory. The practice was quite different. In the first half of the eighteenth century, the Inquisition in Granada rooted out several hundred crypto-Muslims, all married and living within their own community completely incognito, many of whom were silk dealers, artisans, livestock-breeders, sugar-traders and leasing agents. Alongside these middle-class Moriscos, a new elite group of families lived on – including the heirs of Miguel de Luna – who had become more or less integrated into seventeenth-century Granadan society. Often they were wealthy, competing with and even surpassing the Old Christian elite, and working in public offices as scribes, law enforcers, doctors, castle governors and even as priests, some of whom attained a high rank in the Church. Such people had been able to acquire nobility by establishing a legal case, like Miguel de Luna, who belonged to one of at least ten Morisco families who used fake documents and genealogies to concoct a plausible ancestry. They were all protected by a network of powerful local Christian aristocrats who enabled them to hide in plain view. Between 1728 and 1731, the Holy Inquisition[105] persecuted about 250 of these Moriscos, some of whom fled to Istanbul and Tunis, while others lost their possessions, were imprisoned for years or exiled, but none was burnt on the pyre. Yet it is astonishing that the majority of those on trial stayed on living in Granada, either in the city or in the kingdom, and to all appearances became completely integrated into the community by the late eighteenth century.

Try as they might, the Spanish Church and monarchy never entirely eradicated the Spanish Muslims from Granada, nor could they obliterate their cultural traces. Donning the disguise of a great Renaissance Christian city, Granada unmasked still bore the indelible imprint of its Muslim heritage in its lineages, in its architecture, in its very cityscape. Nowhere is this split personality more apparent than in the Abbey of the Sacromonte, perched high on the hillside and built as a shrine for the worship and protection of the relics and Lead Books discovered there. The Abbey, the Alhambra and the cathedral form a topographical triangle where both Christian and Islamic pasts meet in the present. If the Alhambra stands as testament to the military and cultural power of the Moors and the cathedral embodies Catholic conquest and domination, the Abbey of the Sacromonte overlooks both the Alhambra and the cathedral, and endures as an enigmatic symbol of the encounter between Muslims and Christians in Granada. The Lead Books revealed an agenda of rebellion that nevertheless brought the Abbey into being as a paradoxical testament to the vexed relations between the two religions and ways of life, and to the dread and fear in which converted Christians lived in what should have been their paradise. Its recent abbot, Juan Sánchez Ocaña, described it as a hallowed site, a religious and cultural institution unique in Andalusia and a place of great spiritual and cultural significance for Granada. It is a significant and defining landmark in the artistic and religious history of the city,[106] combining pious intentions with hidden desires to alienate. In spite of its ambivalence, it came to be seen as the most important independent institution on the cultural horizon of Baroque Granada. Did the Abbey stand for a certain mutually beneficial relationship between Catholic and Muslim in late sixteenth-century Granada? For the Moriscos, the Lead Books were an attempt to stave off their inevitable expulsion through the creation of texts that to a degree blurred Islam and Christianity and justified the Morisco presence on Spanish soil. Yet they also had great importance for the Christians, who suddenly saw their city established in the history books with a Christian lineage.

A walk through the Sacromonte district, up the winding road past the Alhambra, leads to the Abbey buildings high above, well off the beaten tourist track. From the outside, the monument is imposing and severe but step inside through the ancient wooden door into the inner courtyard of the Abbey and you find a beguiling refuge complete with Moorish-style arches, plants and a cooling central fountain. This Catholic enclave echoes the domestic architecture of the Moriscos, an architecture of the interior, turned away from the world outside and centred upon private spaces. It shows in a direct way a merging of secular urban Morisco style with that of the Christian religious cloister.

Further inside, the Abbey holds more surprises. It is decorated on nearly every surface with the sign of the seal of Solomon, its six-pointed star inlaid in floors, walls, ceilings and furniture, as well as adorning the outer railings of the Abbey. Archbishop Pedro de Castro even used it on his personal shield and it was adopted by the Abbey as its own emblem. This symbol, ever present in the Lead Books, betrays an enigma with unexpected implications, since it has meaning for Jews, Christians and Muslims. In medieval legends of all three faiths, the seal was a magic ring possessed by King Solomon that gave him immense power over demons and bore the hexagram often known in Jewish culture as the Star of David. Its upward-pointing triangle is an ancient sign for the power of a king, while the downward-pointing triangle represents the power of the priest, established in heaven and reaching down to Earth, and combining spiritual and secular power. The contemporary German mystic and alchemist Jacob Böhme saw it as a symbol of Christ and believed it was the most meaningful symbol in the universe. Zótico Royo Campos, abbot of the Sacromonte in the 1960s, also believed the seal represented Christ, stating that the shape of the triangles was a symbol of divinity, interlinked to represent Christ's human and divine aspects, an explanation he uses to justify its predominant presence in the Abbey.

Yet it was also an ancient symbol in the Arab world. Many Arab works translated in medieval Toledo were treatises on magic, the best-known being *The Key of Solomon the King*, containing spells and magical formulae, the seal of Solomon and pentacles aimed at controlling the spirit world. A prohibited text referred to in the trials of the Inquisition, copies of it were often burned. One of the Lead Books deals specifically with the history of the Seal of

Solomon, recounting how the Devil stole it, how it was regained and how it represented justice, power and wisdom. The seal also appears in Arabic manuscripts on magic preserved by Moriscos hoping to recover the mythical power of Solomon and use it for their benefit. A sign that gave hope to the Morisco minority crushed by Christian power,[107] it was also dangerously heretical and prohibited.

If the star of Solomon in the Abbey shows a merging of Christian and Morisco identities, it is not a symbol of mutual benefit for Islam and Christianity. Miguel de Luna's utopian vision of a future in which Islam would be reinstated in his native country of Spain confirms that the star of Solomon was a symbol of the power and justice of the Moriscos and of Islam, quite the opposite to the Christian meaning it purports to enshrine in the Abbey of the Sacromonte. The very existence of the Abbey makes a statement about the power of Catholicism in Granada but cannot avoid alluding to the plight of the Moriscos that inspired the Lead Books and brought the building into being. In adopting the seal of Solomon as the dominant motif of the Abbey, unwittingly or not, Archbishop Castro drew attention to the conflicts and rebellion of the crypto-Muslims. It is a symbol that poignantly expresses the vexed, complex relationship between Catholicism and Islam in Granada at that time.

GRANADA

THE PEOPLE II

8

MYSTERY AND MAGIC

Gypsies and flamenco

• • • • • • • • • • • • • • • • •

LIVING HISTORY: THE LANDSCAPE
OF THE SACROMONTE GYPSIES

The Sacromonte, the Holy Mountain of Granada, is a place where the picturesque meets the sacred and transforms it into a unique cultural site. Known before the late sixteenth century as Monte Valparaíso, the Mountain of Paradise Valley, this name with biblical yet pagan resonance associated the area with Eden and the pastoral life. It lies on the borders of the city along a route that takes you past the grand architecture and busy bars of Plaza Nueva, along the narrow, cobbled street running beside the River Darro, with its lofty houses, part Moorish, part Renaissance, to a point where the scale of buildings and streets changes as the path turns right towards the Sacromonte neighbourhood, up the steep, winding lane of the Cuesta de Chapiz. Here low cave dwellings are cut into the hillside, their intensely white walls contrasting dramatically with the dark holes of their doorways and windows. These ancient houses perch at a precarious angle on the sheer slopes, their whiteness relieved by the greenery of succulent plants and occasional pink and red geraniums. As the dusty road snakes its way up the mountainside, the scale changes once more. The land towers high above, and the vegetation becomes sparse and spiky, the tall banks lined with *chumberas*, the huge prickly pear cacti whose pip-ridden fruit are sold on the market stalls in the city below.

Up here it is peaceful, far from the noise of traffic, a privileged location from which to contemplate the splendid landscape – the Alhambra, the valley of the Darro, the city and cathedral, the *vega* and the Sierra Nevada – a panorama that takes in the vital elements of Granada's history and topography. Higher still, stone wayside crosses announce the approach to the Abbey of the Sacromonte, a site of power of great significance to Moriscos and Christians alike, which looks down over the city beneath. Its extensive Renaissance buildings mark the third point of a topographical triangle completed by the Alhambra and the cathedral. Up there, the harsh grandeur of the mountain is mellowed by the shelter and protection offered by its caves, at once practical, geographical features and mythical spaces that have moulded its identity as a sacred place.

Among the prickly pears and fig trees, the gypsies of Granada made their homes in the age-old caves of the hillside, working in times gone by as smiths, lit up at night-time by the flames of their forges like so many Vulcans transfiguring base metals with their fire. There the gypsy cave-dwellers of the Sacromonte, both demonized and romanticized, created a famous community of flamenco artists and a tradition that flourishes today. The Sacromonte district is a surprising, fascinating place, which manifests the tangible, material history of the gypsies who arrived in the city long ago, a history that comes alive in the caves, statues, museums and flamenco clubs that typify the urban landscape. High above the road to the Abbey, the Barranco de los Negros (Ravine of the Negros) is home to the Museo Cuevas del Sacromonte (Museum of the Sacromonte Caves), which evokes the life and history of the gypsies through a series of caves recreated to look as they did when they were lived in. The spaces are small, even claustrophobic, with one tiny bedroom, a room for sitting and for eating, and a tiny kitchen at the entrance; the furnishings are sparse but the decorations speak volumes. Copper pots and pans hang from the walls along with devotional pictures and family portraits, testaments to the skill in metalworking, the religious piety and the vital importance of kith and kin so fundamental to the gypsy way of life.

These simple material possessions are crucial to the history of a people who have left no written records, few works of art or literature, no distinctive religious liturgy, no representative institutions. The story of the Romany people, like that of the Jews of Granada, is partial, plagued by gaps and absences. Like them, in legend they were a people cursed to wander. From the nature of their language, we know that the gypsies originally came from north-east India around the year 1000, where they may have been soldiers working as mercenaries. As they travelled across Europe, they began to evolve their traditional lifestyle and mixed with the non-gypsy population, so their identity became truly European. There are many legends about their origins, one story claiming the gypsies forged four nails to crucify Christ but stole one to lessen his suffering. Their punishment for assisting in his crucifixion and also for stealing was to wander for seven years. Another apocryphal story about their anti-Christian attitude gave their origins in Egypt, where they refused to shelter the Christian holy family who had fled there. The Spanish word *gitano* for 'gypsy' is a derivation of the word *egipcio/egipciano* meaning 'from Egypt', now deemed to refer to their likely route to Spain, either via Cyprus, Syria or parts of Greece or Turkey, which were known as Lesser Egypt. On their pilgrimage of redemption, the gypsies needed safe-conducts or permission to enter new countries, and the first documentary evidence of their presence in Spain dates from 1425, when King Alfonso V of Aragon gave permission to a gypsy called Juan of Egypt to travel in his dominions, accompanied by a group of about 80 to 150 people. In total, probably one to two thousand gypsies at least entered the country in the fifteenth century.

As their survival strategy was to present themselves as Christian pilgrims or penitents, the gypsies met no antagonism in Spain, where they were viewed as exotic and were treated with kindness and understanding for some seventy-five years. But in 1499, hot on the heels of the expulsion or conversion of the Sephardic Jews in 1492, Ferdinand and Isabella issued a Decree proclaimed in the town of Ocaña ordering the expulsion of all gypsies from their kingdoms. Its stipulations were all too familiar and displayed the same fanatical drive to eliminate difference that had led to the fall of Granada seven years earlier. The main problem was perceived to be the itinerant lifestyle of the gypsies, which made it harder to bring them to account or include them in the workforce, and which, effectively, enabled them to live outside the law. The terms of the 1499 Decree were cruel to the gypsies, replacing the relative freedom granted them by the safe-conducts with repression and systematic persecution. They had to take up residence in one of a limited number of locations and join the workforce or leave the country. They were given sixty days to do this, after which time non-action would be punished with a hundred lashes. A second infringement was punished by cutting off their ears, sixty days in chains and exile; a third meant a lifetime of slavery if they were caught.

Unfortunately, this was the situation facing the gypsies who had served Ferdinand and Isabella as metalworkers to their troops during the last stages of the conquest of Granada. By happy chance, Granada was on the official list of cities designated as places where gypsies could live, and a good number of Romany people chose to make their home in the Sacromonte caves, an area outside the city limits and therefore beyond the jurisdiction of the civic authorities, with whom they had a longstanding relationship of conflict and distrust. Little evidence exists of the details of their life in the city during the sixteenth century, though records reveal their involvement in the dancing and singing that was their lifeblood and their greatest artistic expression. In Granada in 1531, 1607 and 1618, official documents show that they danced and tumbled during the Corpus Christi processions, one act consisting of nine gypsy women and a tambour.[108] The municipal department of the city drew up contracts stipulating the exact number of male and female dancers, tumblers, singers and musical instruments involved, usually tambourines but occasionally guitars. The contracts also stipulated that women should be dressed suitably in gypsy style, with the addition of a farthingale, the fashionable fifteenth-century Spanish invention of hooped underskirts. Payment was not just in money but might also include a sheep, sixteen litres of wine and a bushel or so of wheat. These official arrangements between gypsies and the Establishment show the great popularity of their performances among ordinary people in a city where visual spectacle was, and remains, powerful.

Not surprisingly, in a country where difference was no longer tolerated, the gypsies were defined by the distinctness of their language, dress and occupations, for which they were persecuted. Their appearance was exotic – the oldest testimonies from the fifteenth century describe gypsy men and women as having one or both ears pierced and wearing gold hoop earrings, and women also wore necklaces, bracelets and anklets, as well as colourful clothes, including printed tunics over long yellow or white blouses with sleeves exposing part of their breast or legs, for which pious Catholics condemned them as prostitutes. The vivid colours of gypsy women's dress were also offensive to moralistic Spanish society, and a notice posted in Madrid on 13 June 1592 forbade them to wear coloured clothing or head-dresses. Men had beards and long hair, and dressed more soberly, often in striped tunics belted with a wide fabric sash, with coloured leggings and boots or shoes embroidered in gypsy style. They wore jaunty hats adorned with a feather, and military-style jackets harking back to their ancient occupation of soldiery.

The Roma were first-class linguists and records show they knew Castilian Spanish perfectly by the sixteenth century, but their own Romany language set them apart. A tongue that originated in

Sanskrit, it gave the gypsies a collective identity and was known as *caló*, a fusion of Spanish regional dialect with Romany words that has almost faded out today. Similar to the *Ladino* of the Jews and *Aljamiado* of the Moriscos, some Romany words and phrases were expressed using Castilian grammar but their idiom was dismissed in Spanish accounts as *jerigonza*, jargon or gibberish, or even worse, the language of thieves. The discordant appearance and impenetrable language of the *gitanos* aroused fear and hostility, aggravated by their choice of jobs suited to their wandering lifestyle, which lent itself to agricultural work, horse-dealing, trading and travelling performance. Accountable to no one, the gypsies worked outside the established system and avoided taxation, and soon they began to be demonized as unscrupulous villains. The Toledan professor Sancho de Moncada, writing in the early seventeenth century, considered them 'a sect of rogues, atheists and whores, less useful than the Moriscos, as they do not know how to plough or sell, only rob and flee'.[109] In a law of 1586 King Philip II prohibited gypsies from selling anything without signed testimony of a public scribe, otherwise their wares would be considered as stolen goods.

In the 1600s things went from bad to worse. Death came with an outbreak of plague across Spain, and bad harvests brought famine to Andalusia, which combined with the expulsion of the Moriscos to cause a dramatic drop in the population and a failing economy. Suddenly, the gypsies were needed to contribute to the workforce. Two years before he died, King Philip III passed a law in 1619 obliging gypsies to settle in towns of over 1,000 inhabitants or leave the country within six months. Failure to comply incurred the death penalty. His successor Philip IV took more severe steps to integrate the *gitanos* into the community, with a Decree dated 1633 punishing any gypsy who wore their traditional dress, spoke *caló*, attended fairs or worked in any occupation forbidden to them with 200 lashes and six years as galley-slaves, while women were to be exiled. In this way, the law obliged gypsies to abandon Spain or exchange their roaming ways for sedentary lives in urban areas. By

16. Alhambra decree.

17. Partial view of Granada drawn in pen and brown ink by the Flemish artist Anton van der Wyngaerde in 1567.

18. Ambrosio de Vico's *Plataforma de Granada*, a late sixteenth-century map of the city engraved by Francisco Heylan, and the first to show the city layout in detail.

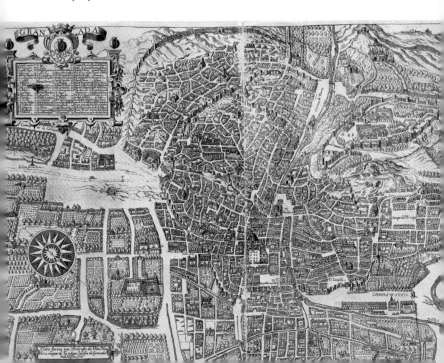

19. Portrait of
Fray Luis de
Granada drawn
by Francisco
Pacheco around
1599.

20. Morisco
costume from the
costume book
of 1530 created
by the German
artist Christopher
Weiditz.

21. Chest containing the funerary relics of the martyrs on the altar of the collegiate church of the Sacromonte.

22. Aerial view of the Abbey of the Sacromonte.

23. Seals of Solomon, commonly known as Morisco stars, found in the Lead Books.

24. Lithograph from 1850 showing the Alhambra from the Cuesta de los Molinos, a cactus-lined lane in the Sacromonte.

25. Gypsy cave on the Sacromonte, now the dwelling of a former picador, with his bullfighting posters on the walls.

26. A gypsy zambra, showing gypsies dancing and playing music on the Sacromonte, painted by Spanish artist Mariano Bertuchi.

27. *Cartloads to the Cemetery* by Francisco de Goya evokes a tragic scene all too common during the outbreaks of cholera in Granada in the nineteenth century.

28. *A Street Scene in Granada on the Day of the Bullfight* by John Frederick Lewis, dated 1834.

the middle of the eighteenth century, any gypsy found outside their designated dwelling places for longer than a fortnight was declared a public bandit and could be legally killed even if unarmed.

In this way, the Spanish gypsies became an underclass of outlaws and marginalized poor, persecuted for their perceived heretical practices, the colour of their skin and their tendency to rove, a repression that they countered with pride, rebellion and disobedience. In the old kingdom of Granada, *gitanos* and Moriscos, both rootless and oppressed, struck up an alliance early on, united against a common enemy, the Old Christians of Castile. As far back as 1533, the Archbishop of Granada had written to the king accusing the gypsies of teaching Moriscos sorcery and superstition, and in addition, he complained, they robbed the clothes from their backs and the beasts from their fields, much to their outrage. Yet gypsies and Moriscos intermarried, some Moriscos joining the gypsy ranks unnoticed, perhaps to avoid being banished. The majority of gypsies, uneducated and constrained, prohibited from owning land or acting as financiers, were obliged to work as labourers or metal craftsmen, though some made a living from dancing, trading at local markets, begging and palmistry. Others had little choice but to rob, steal livestock or trade in defective wares, which debased their image and forged a lasting negative stereotype.

For the Roma, the nadir came on 30 July 1749, in what was known as the Great Raid. In a single night, 9,000 gypsy men and women were arrested with the aim of ridding society of them and putting an end to the 'gypsy problem' that the government deemed a threat to the social order. They were kept imprisoned in various centres to await further action, while their few belongings were sold for their upkeep in prison. This black and forgotten episode in Spain's history ended fourteen years later when King Charles III ordered their release in 1763.

After almost three hundred years of subjection to laws and policies designed to eliminate them from Spain as an identifiable group, the *gitanos* were assimilated into society. The censuses of 1783 and 1785 show that in Granada, and other places, gypsies worked at a wide range of familiar jobs, often as carpenters, smiths, builders and bricklayers, cobblers, mule-drivers, water-carriers, sailors, musicians and bullfighters. There are frequent records of gypsies working as sheep-shearers and horse-dealers, roles that they had mastered as travelling people. Their talent for sale and negotiation was curbed by their prohibition from attending markets or fairs, a law that if flouted resulted in their being branded on the shoulder for a first offence, a slight improvement on previous punishments of cutting off the ears and death. The Granadan gypsies still buy and sell today, although now they trade mainly in cars and textiles.

Despite their ancient guise of Christian penitents who took part in the sacraments of baptism, marriage, confirmation and extreme unction, gypsies were not churchgoers and were suspected of being impious pagans by upright Catholic society until the end of the eighteenth century. Surprisingly, very few were pursued by the Inquisition – only a matter of 170 or so in the seventeenth and eighteenth centuries, maybe because they owned nothing of value to confiscate to offset the expenses of their arrest. There are records of forty-eight gypsies tried by the Tribunal of Granada, one of whom was Gabriel Chaves, who attempted to cross to north Africa from Marbella in 1608 and was arrested under suspicion of renouncing Catholicism in favour of Islam. Although Chaves was tortured twice, he denied the accusation but the Inquisitors believed he was lying and sentenced him to a hundred lashes and six years as a galley-slave on the Spanish treasure galleons. In 1625, a gypsy woman, María Hernández, was accused of sorcery in Granada in cahoots with a group of Jewish sympathizers. When Juan Escudero from near Seville was tried by the tribunal for fornication, he claimed his intention to have sex with a female prisoner and her daughter was not sinful. He was prone to blasphemous outbursts in which he threatened to burn all the crucifixes he could find when he was released. But the tribunal also knew that he had already served ten years in the galleys for hurling a rock at a boy and killing him, so he was sentenced to a further six years at the oars. María de Montoya was also accused of gypsy sorcery in Granada in 1697 but escaped with just a warning.

All the efforts to force the *gitanos* to conform or leave bore little fruit, as is confirmed by the numbers of gypsies who escaped the traps set for them and remained in Spain. From the eighteenth century onwards, the Sacromonte *gitanos* were the regular inhabitants of the caves, which they made internationally famous. These rebels who came from the East, indifferent to the law and possessed by the pagan spirits of dance and song, were the polar opposites of all the Catholic Church of Granada stood for. They embodied absolute non-conformity, yet were powerless in a land where, like the Moors and Jews before them, they were seen as outsiders despite having lived there for centuries. Even so, a remarkable metamorphosis was about to take place in the very heart of the Sacromonte of Granada, which was set to convert the gypsies from demonized pariahs into an idealized icon of Western culture. It would also refashion the singular identity of the city.

MANUFACTURING THE GYPSY MYTH: TOURISM, TRAVELOGUES AND TRAUMA

In the seventeenth century, flour was weighed at the Peso de la Harina (Flour Scales) at the bottom of the Cuesta de Chapiz, where the Sacromonte district begins. In 1995 the site was remodelled into a small square, a place to relax before embarking on the walk uphill, with benches, hedges and a small fountain near the old cistern dating from Arab times. In the centre of the square stands the statue of a man known as Chorrojumo, Prince of the Gypsies, sculpted by Antonio Salazar in forged iron, in the style of Granada. His name means 'jet of smoke' in Granadan colloquial speech, which suggests the swarthy colour of his skin, further darkened by the smoke of the Sacromonte forge where he worked as a blacksmith, alluded to by the material of which his statue is made. Chorrojumo lived in the nineteenth century and became a cult figure of his time. His real name was Mariano Fernández Santiago and he was born in Granada in 1824 into a gypsy family. In 1843, when Queen Isabella II was on the throne, he was called up aged nineteen to serve in the royal army, and was very proud to be one of the few gypsies to have done so. On his return, he married Dolores Román, also a Sacromonte gypsy, and they had six children who begged from the foreign tourists visiting the Alhambra in order to earn enough for their daily food, while he worked as a blacksmith.

Unexpectedly, destiny was poised to save him from his hard, impoverished life. In 1868 when the blacksmith was forty-six, the internationally renowned Catalan painter Mariano Fortuny (1838–74) went to Granada on his honeymoon and returned to live there for more than two years in 1870. As he was strolling in the Sacromonte one day, he saw three men working at a forge, beating the red-hot iron with hammers. He noticed one in particular, his skin the colour of old leather, with enormous sideburns and piercing eyes the colour of steel, who turned out to be his namesake, Mariano Fernández. Fortuny had a penchant for the exotic and he put it to the gypsy that he might make a living other than working at the forge by virtue of the striking and unusual figure he cut. The artist asked him to pose for him and supplied him with a bizarre outfit that consisted of a sugar-loaf hat with pompoms, frilled shirt, a short blue jacket with silver buttons, a scarlet sash, close-fitting black trousers and a metal-tipped walking stick. Mariano the blacksmith liked his new outfit, agreed to be the artist's model and the myth of Chorrojumo was born.[110]

Armed with postcards of his portrait with the title 'Prince of the Gypsies', Fortuny's model abandoned the forge and took to walking each day in the grounds of the Alhambra, where he was photographed by tourists in exchange for a few coins, sold his postcards and served as a guide. He became a professional gypsy, so popular that tourists queued up to have their picture taken with him. Basking in his success, Chorrojumo upgraded his title to King of the Gypsies, rather than Prince, and even acquired a kingly sceptre fashioned of almond wood. Visitors to the Alhambra loved his stories, told in his rich, attractive voice, many of which had been written by the American Washington Irving, though he made them sound as if they were his own. Thanks to his new role as a tourist attraction, he made enough money to move from the Sacromonte to a humble house in the Callejón Niños del Royo (Niños del Royo Alley). At the start of the 1900s, in his late seventies, he wrote to the governor of the Alhambra complaining that he had been imprisoned several times for cheating the tourists, which he denied. By this time Chorrojumo had competitors too, who dressed like him, fooled the visitors and poached his livelihood. Now partially blind, the old gypsy's business began to fall apart. On 10 December 1906, aged eighty-two, the Lord of the Alhambra Woods suffered a fatal stroke as he climbed the road to the Nasrid palace, where he dropped dead as if struck by lightning.

Chorrojumo is one of Granada's most famous gypsies, whose extraordinary presence and personality in some ways defined and drew the attention of the world to his people and to his birthplace. His glamorous life and image chimed to a remarkable degree with the mood of the time – with the Romanticism of the nineteenth century, and with the increasingly popular vogue for European travel and tourism, when visits to the Sacromonte caves became an established component of the Grand Tour, to the degree that the Andalusian gypsies themselves enthusiastically embraced the creation of the Romantic gypsy myth by writers and artists enchanted by the exotic and the Oriental. The interest in Spanish gypsies came into the spotlight through the work of a man who lived at almost exactly the same time as Chorrojumo, the Englishman George Borrow (1803–81). Borrow was born in the quiet town of Dereham in Norfolk and lived most of his life in East Anglia, but unexpectedly became a crucial figure in the story of the

Spanish gypsies when he was employed by the Protestant British and Foreign Bible Society to spread the word and sell copies of the New Testament in Spain and Portugal. Borrow's *The Zincali – An Account of the Gypsies of Spain* was written mostly at the inns he stayed in on his travels between 1835 and 1840 while he was trying to sell Bibles, a task at which he was apparently hopeless. In contrast, when his own book came out in 1841 it was an immediate success, with six further editions printed, and had a lasting impact on later accounts of gypsy life.

Borrow was fearless in his encounters with gypsies in remote, dangerous locations and he paints a very different picture of the *gitanos* of Granada from the one portrayed by Chorrojumo. He speaks of the large numbers of gypsies in the city, whose condition was miserable and wretched: '... Granada itself is the poorest city in Spain; the greatest part of the population, which exceeds 60,000, living in beggary and nakedness, and the Gitanos share the general distress.'[111] Borrow visited the Sacromonte caves, describing the gypsy families who lived and worked in them in vivid language:

> To one standing at the mouth of a cave, especially at night, they afford a picturesque spectacle. Gathered round the forge, their bronzed and naked bodies, illuminated by the flame, appear like the figures of demons; while the cave, with its flinty sides and uneven roof, blackened by the charcoal vapours which hover about it in festoons, seems to offer no inadequate representation of fabled purgatory.[112]

Borrow also recounts the story of a tragedy that took place in Granada around the 1820s caused by the deadly rivalry between two gypsies, Pindamonas and Pepe Conde. Pepe was a notorious smuggler who had fled to north Africa to escape punishment for some heinous deed and became a Muslim. After some years, when his crime was almost forgotten, he returned to Granada where he resumed his old professions of horse-dealing and smuggling. Pindamonas was a wealthy, highly respected gypsy in the city, who wielded great influence, which partly accounts for the great jealousy that existed between the two men, as proud, untamable Pepe did not take kindly to a perceived superior among his own people.

One day, Pindamonas and Pepe Conde were in a coffee house with their friends when a terrible row broke out over who should pay the bill. This was a matter of honour, privilege and superiority, and to Pepe's outrage, Pindamonas offered to pay first. He countered this with his own offer but Pindamonas insisted and flung the money onto the table. In a fury, Pepe Conde produced a flick knife and with one ghastly swipe opened up Pindamonas's abdomen and killed him. The murderer fled and was not seen for some time, although the cave where he lived was kept under watch, until early one morning he was seen to enter it. Soldiers were called and the gypsy fled to the rocks and ravines of the mountains with the soldiers in hot pursuit. When he refused to surrender, they shot him dead. Borrow himself received a personal letter from Pindamonas's nephew, in prison for stealing a pair of mules, begging for money and advice, and invoking the vicious murder of his uncle to elicit sympathy.

A few years after Borrow's travels in Spain, the French writer Alexandre Dumas *père* arrived in Granada in 1846 with an entourage of artists and writers, including Eugène Giraud and Auguste Maquet, to see the reality of gypsy life in the Sacromonte. Victor Hugo had published his great novel *Notre-Dame de Paris* in 1831 and France had fallen under the spell of his heroine, the gypsy girl Esmeralda, who reflected the Romantic idea that gypsies symbolized freedom and spontaneity. But Dumas' accounts of his experiences suggest both a fascination with and dislike of the Granadan *gitanos*. He wrote of the mutual hatred between the other inhabitants and the gypsies, who numbered, he said, around twelve thousand on the Sacromonte. Dumas described gypsy girls with water pitchers on their shoulders in the fashion of antique statues, their parents standing motionless outside their caves like caryatids, in 'an extraordinary atmosphere of strangeness and poverty'.[113] He saw two beautiful but dishevelled young gypsy dancers with sepia skins, velvety eyes and unkempt, matted hair, dirty clothes and ill-matched shoes, and was at once bewitched and repelled by a dance spectacle organized by a local guide, which, he complained, was sensual and incestuous. The gypsies of the Sacromonte provided Dumas and his artist friends with plentiful inspiration as they brought them vividly to life in words and paint, which often portrayed the glamorous ideal rather than the painful reality.

Three years later, another French traveller, Alexis de Valon, saw that reality only too clearly in the gypsy women he came across in Granada: 'A dozen atrocious females, as hideous as they were filthy, with the profiles of goats and the hands of field mice... tell us please that Esmeralda and Carmen were not Granadan bohemians!'[114] In the mid-nineteenth century, the French artists Alfred Dehodencq, Gustave Doré and Edouard Manet visited Spain and filled their sketchbooks with images of the gypsies, whose perceived liberated lifestyle appealed as an escape from the growing oppression of industrialist and capitalist society – surely just as sordid in its own way as the actual living conditions of the Granadan *calés,* the name given to the gypsies of Granada, whose extreme poverty drove them to crime. Perhaps the best travel writer of the nineteenth century, the poet and artist Théophile Gautier, visited Granada in the 1840s and published his *Voyage en Espagne* (*Travels in Spain*) in 1843. These are his impressions of the Sacromonte and its inhabitants:

> Gigantic Indian fig-trees and enormous nopals raise their prickly heads, the colour of Verdigris, along its impoverished and white-coloured slopes; under the roots of these unctuous plants... are dug in the living rock the dwellings of the gypsies. The entrance to these caverns is white-washed; a light cord on which hangs a piece of frayed tapestry, serves as a door. It is there that the wild race swarms and multiplies; there, children, whose skins are darker than Havana cigars, play in a state of nudity before the door, without any distinction as to sex, and roll themselves in the dust uttering sharp, guttural cries. The gitanos are generally blacksmiths,

mule-shearers, veterinary doctors and above all, horse-dealers. They have a thousand potions for putting mettle and strength into the most broken-winded and limping animals in the world... Their true trade, however, is that of stealing.

The gitanos sell amulets, tell fortunes, and follow those suspicious callings inherent to the women of their race. I saw very few pretty ones, though their faces were remarkable both by their type and character. Their swarthy complexion contrasts strongly with the limpidness of their oriental eyes, the fire of which is tempered by an indescribable and mysterious melancholy... Nearly all of them possess so much natural majesty and freedom in their deportment, and are so well and firmly set, that in spite of their rags, their dirt and their misery, they seem to be conscious of the antiquity and purity of their race...[115]

Gautier wrote as a man of his time, with a certain disdain mixed with admiration, and captures the vital spirit and the desperate plight of the Sacromonte *calés,* a name taken from the local word for their language. That plight had been worsened by social change, which had started promisingly for the gypsies in 1812 with the new Spanish Constitution of Cadiz, the founding document of liberalism in the country that recognized them for the first time as Spanish citizens. The legislation of subjection was abandoned, although prejudice and discrimination were not. On the basis of the new constitution, gypsies began to find work as blacksmiths and horse-traders in Andalusia, and started to give up their nomadic life and settle on the outskirts of towns, as they did in the Sacromonte. But Spain was not immune to the industrial revolution, and the gradual mechanization of agriculture made many of the gypsies' favourite rural professions redundant, leaving many families in abject poverty. Rates of child mortality were high, life expectancy was low and illiteracy rife. One day at the end of 1888, Father Andrés Manjón, a priest who had great sympathy for the marginalized, was walking through the Sacromonte when he heard some illiterate children reciting the *Ave Maria,* an experience that inspired him to found the *Escuelas del Ave María* (*Hail Mary Schools*) to educate gypsy children from poor families. It was such a success that today his schools are a way of life in eastern Andalusia, with at least three in Granada itself. Generations of gypsies learned to read and write and achieve a good standard of living thanks to Father Manjón, and were able to take their first steps towards social integration.

When Andrés Manjón walked past the singing gypsy children in 1888, he was a canon at the Seminary of the Abbey of the Sacromonte, where he died in his austere cell in 1923. Twin poles of the sacred hill, the Catholic Abbey and the gypsies have long had an unlikely connection. Inside the Baroque church of the Abbey, visitors today can see the famous sculpture of Christ crucified called the Most Holy Christ of Solace, better known by its popular name of the Christ of the Gypsies, in a chapel of the same name, close beside the eighteenth-century statue of the Virgin Mary of the Sacromonte. The magnificent Christ figure was sculpted in 1695 by the Baroque sculptor José Risueño, born in 1665 in the Sagrario district of the city, and is one of the images most beloved by the people of Granada, especially those who live in the Sacromonte and Albaicín. During Holy Week, probably Granada's most important religious celebration, a simulacrum of the original Christ of the Gypsies, made by the Granadan sculptor Miguel Zúñiga Navarro in 1987–9, makes his appearance on Ash Wednesday in an atmosphere heavy with incense. The gypsy brotherhood known as the Guild of the Christ of the Gypsies, with its headquarters at the Abbey, is the first to pay homage to the effigy, which is mounted on a platform and leaves the Church of the Heart of Jesus in the late afternoon and arrives home at the Abbey of the Sacromonte in the early hours. The heavy float is carried by bearers, often penitents, who inch along under its terrific weight, following the winding uphill path to the chapel, where they arrive about three o'clock in the morning. Bonfires are lit, candles twinkle in the darkness to light the way and the mournful religious songs of great power known as *saetas*, originally meaning 'arrows' or 'darts', are sung to accompany the procession by members of the brotherhoods. These songs are performances of great emotional intensity, like arrows which pierce the onlookers with their sorrowful lamentation, hence their name. The procession of the Christ of the Gypsies is one of the most unforgettable and moving experiences of Holy Week in the city.

The age-old story of Christ and the Romanies that is perpetually re-enacted during Easter week was remembered in the celebrated collection of verse *Fields of Castile* (*Campos de Castilla*, 1912) by the Spanish poet Antonio Machado (1875–1939). His poem 'La saeta', inspired by a popular refrain, recalls the close association of the gypsy people with Christ:

> Who will lend me a ladder
> to climb up on the Cross
> and unnail Jesus of Nazareth?'
> Oh, the saeta, the gypsies'
> song to Christ,
> always with blood on their hands,
> always bent on unnailing him.
> Song of the Andalusian people,
> who each Spring beg a ladder
> to climb up on the Cross.[116]

The ancient tradition of the four nails made by the gypsy black-smiths to crucify Christ, resulting in their unabsolved guilt, is dramatized each year on the first Lenten day of repentance, Ash Wednesday, in the procession of the Christ of the Gypsies along the cross-lined road to the Abbey, in which penitents perform the agonized laments of the gypsies before the crucified Jesus in a kind of repeated expiation of their legendary sin.

By the end of the nineteenth century the myth of the Andalusian gypsy had been forged in Granada by the travelogues of the new tourists and it had become a source of international fascination, sought out by foreign visitors who wanted to experience an alluring,

authentic spectacle and were willing to pay for it. As a result, the
Sacromonte caves were regarded as a tourist trap by the 1880s, a
place where the unsuspecting visitor fell prey to the hawkers who
lay in wait. For better or worse, out of the persecution, hatred
and oppression of the past, the Granadan gypsies had somehow
risen to prominence partly by virtue of their own talents and
independence. What had come to the fore was their unmatched
talent for performance of all kinds, penitential and pagan, a
talent that emerged as long ago as the sixteenth century in their
entertainments at the Corpus festivals in Granada. The procession
of the Christ of the Gypsies and the larger-than-life character of
Chorrojumo are two sides of the same coin. The gypsies were
illusionists in a city of illusions, masters of dramatic art, who
were about to take the world of song and dance by storm.

'A SPELL, DIABOLICAL AND DREADFUL': FLAMENCO, DEEP SONG AND GYPSY WOMEN

Nightfall brings changes both subtle and dramatic in the atmosphere
of the Sacromonte. The tranquil feel of the district is transformed by
throngs of passers-by, tourists and locals, who pack out the streets
and small bars. Lights begin to glimmer over the hillside as the caves
come alive in the darkness and there is an energy, an excitement
in the air. Somewhere in the blackness an anguished voice begins
to sing, hands clap, guitar chords strike an urgent, thrilling tone.
The Sacromonte itself becomes the stage for a performance. The
crowds head for the *peñas* or flamenco clubs, in particular the
thriving Peña La Platería (Silversmith's flamenco club) in the Placeta
de Toqueros, near where the Albaicín merges into the Sacromonte.
The Platería is one of the most important *peñas* in Spain and was
the first flamenco club to open in 1949 at the height of Franco's
regime. Its logo is the pomegranate, which adorns the bar, the gate

and the plaques commemorating local flamenco artists, giving it a specific Granadan identity that symbolizes the importance of the city as one of the birthplaces of flamenco.

Like other caves where flamenco is performed, when you enter the Peña La Platería you see a bar and eating area, and an area for performances, usually a stage at the back of the cave, or an area with the audience on either side. The atmosphere inside is intense, almost hallowed. Every inch of wall is covered in posters, photos of artists and celebrities, which create a sense of heritage and collective memory. In the early days, it was a meeting place for fans of traditional flamenco, a place where the minutiae of style and mood were debated. Now, it is open to the public, mostly international tourists, for packed performances every Thursday starting at ten o'clock at night and boasts a full programme of local and international flamenco interpreters, as well as advanced courses on flamenco guitar and song.

Worldwide, flamenco music and dance evoke a familiar image of Spain, conjuring up the romantic notion of gypsies, exotic women dancers, fire and passion, and symbolizing the cultural identity of Andalusia. Flamenco is the great dramatic art of the gypsies of Granada and Seville, a people who have left no literature, no painting, no sculpture, nothing tangible save their creative skill in metalwork. Flamenco came into being at the end of the eighteenth century, although it was only performed in secret in family circles until the mid-nineteenth century. The army colonel José Cadalso (1741–82), a leading writer in the Spanish Enlightenment, provided the first written reference to gypsy music as flamenco in 1774 when he described a song performed at a private gypsy party.[117] Yet its origins are ancient and shadowy. Few provinces of Europe have had such a rich and chequered history as Andalusia, and few cities have been moulded by so many different peoples and cultures as Granada. Its musical heritage is inseparable from a view of life that is both tragic and anarchic, that marked the history of the gypsies and of flamenco, the latter formed of a mix of musical elements. Old Indian systems of musical notation brought to Andalusia by the Persian singer-poet Ziryab in the ninth century, Moorish song and dance, Jewish synagogue songs from the ninth to fifteenth centuries, and the folk songs called *zambras* and *jarchas* of the Moriscos all brought an influence to bear on flamenco. It has two distinct strains – gypsy song, *cante gitano*, developed by the gypsies after their arrival in Andalusia in the fifteenth century, and Andalusian folk song, *cante andaluz*, a musical fusion of the influences of its many peoples, adopted quite late by the gypsies. The fandango is typical of Andalusian folk music, while the tango and melodies such as *soleá* and *bulería* come from the gypsies.

No one is certain how the name 'flamenco' came into being. The word is an adjective meaning 'Flemish' in Spanish but Andalusian gypsy music did not come from Flemish lands. At the end of the seventeenth century, a good number of Andalusian gypsies aged between fifteen and forty were enrolled in the forces of the Spanish army in Flanders. Those who returned alive were given a document proving their services to the king, which in theory meant they had the freedom of the Spanish kingdoms. The gypsy soldiers who went back to Andalusia came to be known as 'Flemish gypsies' and later 'flamencos', and it seems most likely that their song and dance were given the same name, so that *música flamenca* came to mean 'gypsy music'.[118] Nowadays, 'flamenco' can also refer to something flashy, vulgar and gaudy, perhaps harking back to the sixteenth-century dislike and prohibition of the gypsies' vividly coloured clothes.

In its oldest form, flamenco relied on a single singer, usually male, and very basic accompaniment, which was traditionally beating time with the knuckles or with a small stick, or with rhythmic clapping, performed in intimate settings such as rural inns and taverns. The guitar was not used as a solo flamenco instrument until much later. The close ties between the Moriscos and the gypsies of Granada created a dance unique to the Sacromonte, the *zambra*, from the Arabic word meaning a boisterous performance of music and song. It is thought that the *zambra* took place before Morisco weddings and was expressly prohibited by the Inquisition during the sixteenth century. After the Morisco expulsion, the gypsies of the Sacromonte kept the tradition alive and made it their own as part of the gypsy marriage ritual in which the *zambra* consists of three dances, each symbolizing a specific moment in the gypsy wedding rite. In the 1860s and 1870s, a gypsy from the town of Itrabo in the province of Granada, Antonio Torcuato Martín, 'El Cujón', made the modern *zambra* famous. A blacksmith with a forge in the Plaza del Humilladero near the River Genil, Antonio was an astute businessman. Realizing that one of the rooms of his forge was large enough for dances, he started up regular performances of *zambras* there and gave contracts to the best gypsy talent in the city as well as playing the guitar and singing himself. But his success was cut short when a robber stole all his savings, leaving him in poverty. Later, the Amaya family would carry on the same tradition in the heart of the Sacromonte. Today, the picturesque Zambra María la Canastera at 89, Camino del Sacromonte, a cave where gleaming beaten copper pots, pans and ceramic ware typical of the neighbourhood adorn every wall and ceiling, offers performances of the famous gypsy dances in memory of its namesake María, the daughter of a basket-maker born in Granada in 1913, who became a celebrated dancer of the *zambra*.

Antonio Torcuato was a pioneer of what would become known as *cafés cantantes*, live-music cafés, which became the rage all over Spain in the 1860s, providing food and flamenco performances and offering a real source of income to gypsy artists, who had regular, fixed salaries and an interested, critical audience who appreciated their talents. The Café de Cuéllar and the Café Comercio were popular live-music cafés in the city, where flamenco took on a new lease of creative life. At the same time, non-gypsies also began to perform gypsy music, starting a commercial trend that diminished the authentic and traditional art. From the late nineteenth century onwards, flamenco flourished as it became more and more orientated towards foreign tourists, yet in doing so, its essential nature was at risk. It was this perceived degeneration of genuine flamenco that led to one of the most important cultural events in Granada's modern history.

In September 1920 the Spanish composer Manuel de Falla went to live in Granada. He moved with his sister into a beautiful *carmen* in Calle Antequeruela near the Alhambra, with spectacular views of the *vega* and the Sierra Nevada,[119] where he lived for nearly twenty years, until the end of the Spanish Civil War in 1939. The presence in the city of Spain's finest composer made Granada an important place on the musical map of Europe, and Falla had a profound effect on its artistic life. He struck up a friendship with the Granadan poet and dramatist Federico García Lorca and his circle, who often visited him in his *carmen*. A frequent subject of conversation was the decline in authentic flamenco. A close friend of Lorca's, Miguel Cerón Rubio, suggested holding a great competition in Granada in which exponents of genuine flamenco from all over Andalusia could take part. It would mean the renaissance, conservation and purification of the old *cante jondo* or deep song of the gypsies, as flamenco was known among experts, in which the protagonist would not be a person, but flamenco itself. Falla and Lorca greeted the suggestion enthusiastically, and the first ever Cante Jondo festival, sponsored by the Granada Arts Club, was arranged for 13–14 June 1922, in Granada's spiritual epicentre, the Alhambra. The attention of the artistic world in Spain and abroad was focused anew on Granada and the rare musical heritage of southern Spain.

A few months before, in February 1922, Lorca gave a lecture to the Arts Club on the deep song of the Andalusian gypsies.[120] What he said was memorable in its beauty and in its intuitive illumination of the nature of *cante jondo*. The song, he said, was purely Andalusian, not purely gypsy, as it did not exist in gypsy communities outside Spain and bore traces of the ancient Byzantine liturgy and the music of the Granadan Moors. It has a lack of harmony, a repeated, even obsessive use of a single note, similar to certain formulae for magical spells; the song is a kind of sung prose with no feeling of metrical rhythm, and expresses the most infinite gradations of pain and sorrow in the purest, most exact form. Lorca described its strong influence on the Spanish composers Albéniz, Granados and Falla, and also on Debussy, who considered Granada to be a true paradise. The poet emphasized its deep roots: 'It comes from distant races, across the graveyard of the years and the fronds of withered winds. It comes from the first weeping and the first kiss.'[121] The themes of deep song are sorrow, the wind and weeping, and the tone is melancholy; it is always sung at night, 'an all-encompassing night with a multitude of stars'.[122] Lorca believed that the guitar had fashioned and deepened the dark oriental muse of the ancient Jews and Arabs: 'The guitar has westernized flamenco song and created peerless beauty, the positive beauty of the Andalusian drama, of East and West in conflict, which make it an island of culture.'[123]

Four months later, in June 1922, a huge, gaily dressed audience filled the Plaza de los Aljibes in the Alhambra to capacity, many of them dressed in silks and satins in the style of the 1830s and 1840s, the Spain of Gautier and George Borrow. There were two unforgettable evenings of *cante jondo*, the second of which was interrupted by a heavy downpour. The great surprise of the competition was the performance of Diego Bermúdez Cañete, known as 'El Tenazas', 'The Pincers', an old, almost forgotten *cantaor* or flamenco singer who was said to have walked all the way from Puente Genil in the province of Cordoba, a hike of at least 80 miles. On the first night he sang with memorable *duende*, the spirit that possesses true performers of authentic flamenco, and was in the lead but his lack of inspiration on the second night was put down to a day's drinking, probably sponsored by his rivals. He was awarded a thousand pesetas for the first night's efforts. Another prize-winner was eleven-year-old Manuel Ortega, 'El Caracol', 'the Snail', destined to become one of the greatest *cantaores* of the century. The festival proved a great success and managed to revive the artistic heritage of the gypsies. It continues to be held each year.

After the Spanish Civil War of 1936, the new dictatorship under General Franco encouraged commercial flamenco because it projected an image of the cheerful poor in Andalusia that fitted its ideology, but no social criticism was permitted in any flamenco song lyrics. The cult of national flamencoism of the 1940s seemed to transform the gypsy from a despised pariah into a prized national icon. Their stereotypical folk image was used to promote tourism but the reality of their life under Franco's regime was quite different. Gypsies did not on the whole take sides during the Civil War, though they were badly affected by situations and conditions they could not avoid, and the worst afflicted were gypsy women.

High up along the Camino del Sacromonte, a simple cave houses the Ethnological Museum of the Gypsy Woman (Museo Etnológico de la Mujer Gitana). It was founded in 2006 by the Association of ROMI Gypsy Women, who organize cultural and social events there. Inside the cave is a permanent exhibition that demonstrates the contribution of women to gypsy life and culture, displaying artefacts relating to gypsy spirituality, culture, medicine and daily life. One room is devoted to basketry, one of the main occupations of gypsy women, and another displays a magnificent traditional white lace wedding dress. The museum is a moving and significant tribute to the Romany women of Andalusia, many of whom suffered severe persecution after the Civil War. At the end of Franco's military occupation of the south, repression began by means of War Councils, which threatened anyone who did not demonstrate their allegiance to the ruling right-wing Falange party. Political allegiance is rare in the gypsy world, especially among women, who had no access to education or culture because of their nomadic lifestyle. They lived as family carers, basket-makers, washerwomen, cooks and cleaners, or sold fabric from door to door, reaped and picked olives and on occasions begged. Yet even that degree of agency and independence challenged the Francoist view of women's duties, and they were seen as disobedient, non-submissive and disrespectful. Large numbers of gypsy women were punished as common criminals, not as the political prisoners they really were. In 1935, the Ministry of Justice built a women's prison in Granada, which had an astonishing 23,232 inmates by 1939, where poor food and overcrowding caused disease and death.

Two incidents that took place in Granada tell a sad and tragic tale of persecution and violence. The gypsy Josefa Carmona Ortega was married to Pedro Quero Robles, one of the most wanted guerrilla fighters in the province of Granada during the Civil War. On 15 June 1939, Josefa was arrested for marrying a man who would become a rebel. Fortunately, her employer, a woman of right-wing loyalties, issued a statement saying that Josefa was of sound character and had never belonged to a leftist political party, and the gypsy was set free in 1940. But Josefa was arrested again in 1945 along with two other gypsy women because of their association with the Quero family. It happened that the Civil Guard, who kept the gypsies under close surveillance at all times, found out that Mariano Delgado Borlán, who lived in a remote part of the Barranco de los Negros in the Sacromonte, had sheltered some members of the Quero family there. Mariano was arrested, and informed the guards that the Queros were hiding in the cave of a woman called La Josefica.

At dawn on 10 July 1945, armed forces stationed themselves outside the cave in question, and at 7.30 a.m. ordered those inside to come out into the street. Josefica came out and told the troops there were no strangers hiding inside but at that moment Modesto Hidalgo, of the Quero band, dashed past her and headed for the nearby prickly pears. He was shot dead before he even reached the cacti. Josefica was arrested for harbouring a rebel, as were other Quero supporters, including Josefa Carmona Ortega, who was lucky to be released once more in October 1945 by the Captain General of Granada. This affinity between the gypsies and the guerrillas in Granada was less ideological and more a case of two marginalized groups uniting against a common oppressor, in which women were often unsuspecting victims, put on trial because of their relationships with anti-Francoist fighters.

Less than twenty years later, the Sacromonte gypsies suffered yet another great trauma in the form of terrible floods that hit the mountainside in 1963. The ancient caves collapsed in the torrent and became uninhabitable, forcing many poor gypsy families to move out to other districts of the city, into impoverished areas like Almanjáyar, Cerrillo de Maracena or La Chana. Over time, those gypsies with longstanding family ties in the Sacromonte made their way back little by little, reclaiming their caves, many of which were converted into performance areas for flamenco, out of which their owners made a living. The plight of so many gypsies, the Granadan *calés* included, sparked the emergence of gypsy associations in the 1970s to address basic issues such as dwellings, work, health and education. In 1971 the landmark first world conference of the International Romany Union was held, where the green, blue and red gypsy flag and the gypsy hymn were inaugurated, and the Annual Day of the Gypsy People was designated as 8 April. It is celebrated each year in Granada in a special ceremony in which red petals are thrown into the River Genil and candles are lit to honour the gypsy race.

In 1976, a year after Franco died, a new piece of flamenco theatre caused an uproar. Its author was a young gypsy poet, José Heredia Maya, born in Las Albuñuelas in the province of Granada in 1947, who started his career in the Sacromonte and became the first gypsy ever to become a professor in Spain, at the University of Granada, in the same year that his dramatic spectacle *We want to speak* (*Camelamos naquerar*) was performed for the first time. It was choreographed and interpreted by the *bailaor* or flamenco dancer Mario Maya, whose statue stands in the Paseo de los Tristes beside the River Darro. Heredia's drama was put on from Granada to Paris between February 1976 and April 1977. The performance was a manifesto intended to empower the Spanish gypsy but at first it suffered boycotts, racist threats and prohibition even in

Granada itself. The film director Miguel Alcobendas made a short documentary in 1976 based on *Camelamos naquerar*, a brilliant, powerful interweaving of images of the daily life of gypsy families in Granada, clips of performances of the original show and the solemn reading of the laws of oppression and persecution of the gypsies, starting with Ferdinand and Isabella's decree of 1499. It reinforced the importance of José Mario Mayo's work as a milestone in the dignification of the Spanish gypsy and of their flamenco art.

In twenty-first-century Granada, life has improved for the gypsies but not all their problems have been solved. The so-called 'dark zone', the poverty-stricken district of Almanjáyar,[124] is just three kilometres from the city centre and despite efforts to dispel the stigma, to many local people it represents drugs, marginalization and armed violence. It is home to a good number of gypsy families, the descendants of those who abandoned their hillside homes in the floods of the 1960s, and many have been driven to the drug-peddling that has had such a devastating effect on Romany society. Almanjáyar is the other side of the coin from the Sacromonte, the negative and positive poles of gypsy life in the city today, which still expose the gap between the cruel reality of poverty, poor housing and social stigma, and the glamour and international appeal of gypsy song and dance in a unique setting.

Just 12 kilometres away in the Sierra Elvira mountains, the ancient village of Albolote is the site of Paleolithic and Roman settlements, and became a village in Nasrid times. Today it is the location of a large prison that regularly detains enough gypsies to take part in the national 'flamenco in prisons' competition inaugurated almost twenty years ago to recognize the talent of gypsy prisoners who sang flamenco to ease the long hours inside, and to express deep sorrow and a cry of consolation. That deep gypsy song of grief and sorrow shapes the emotional tone of Federico García Lorca's *Gypsy Ballads* (*Romancero Gitano*), a collection of poems written between 1924 and 1927. In 'Ballad of Black Sorrow' ('Romance de la pena negra'), the poet gives their anguish a unique quality:

Pure sorrow, and always alone,
Oh sorrow of hidden waterways
and remote early mornings![125]

The age-old clash between gypsies and the law is played out in Lorca's 'Ballad of the Spanish Civil Guard' ('Romance de la guardia civil española'). The guards are black, bloodstained and waxen, with skulls of lead and souls of patent leather. They have no feelings. Silently they bring destruction, fire and violence to the ephemeral gypsy city they raze to the ground in the midst of its festival:

Oh city of the gypsies,
Who could see you and not remember?
City of pain and musk,
With towers of cinnamon.[126]

Lorca's strong sympathy for the gypsies lay in his deep feeling for marginalized, persecuted people of all kinds. Although the *Gypsy Ballads* relates clearly to the gypsies, Lorca wrote that its main subject, its true protagonist, was Granada itself. It is a statement that suggests the profound connection between the gypsies and the identity of the city in the poet's mind.

The story of the gypsies of Granada is told in stone, statues and sound, in the caves, museums, monuments and music of the Sacromonte. It has left a powerful visual imprint on a city that imparts so many of its secrets through the visible. Like much of the history of Granada, the history of the gypsies is one of truth and illusion, of outer appearance and inner reality. Their persecution and repression were overlooked and forgotten until more recent times but the city has been at the forefront of action to right those wrongs. It is the home of the Andalusian Gypsy Social and Cultural Centre (Centro Sociocultural Gitano Andaluz), whose agenda is not only to promote the culture and history of the gypsy people but to foster understanding and cooperation between them and the wider community. At the same time, the international fame of the flamboyant performance art of the gypsies of the Sacromonte led to flamenco being recognized as the Intangible Cultural Heritage of Humanity by UNESCO in 2010. For some, Granada is the birthplace of flamenco, and its Granadan style is unique in the world. It carries with it a historical and cultural legacy, a nostalgia and an almost utopian image of the Sacromonte that has formed a distinctive part of the character of the city. The gypsies, mavericks and natural outsiders, both nomadic and sedentary, are a vital layer in the deep strata of Granada's diverse cultural bedrock.

GRANADA
THE PLACE III

1700–1950

A PARADISE OF THE MIND

*Travellers' tales from
a changing city*

◆◆◆◆◆◆◆◆◆◆◆◆◆◆◆

THE RIVER AND THE RUINS

Long before human habitation, before the creation of the urban settlement of Granada, river water tumbled down between rocky crags and chasms from its source in the mountain springs of the Sierra de Huétor in the north-east, creating a tributary of the greater River Genil, which merged with the watercourse of the Guadalquivir before it reached the sea. In Roman times men searched for legendary gold in the stream from the sierra and called it Aurus, meaning 'gold', translated by the Arabs as Hadarro, which the Christians converted into its final name, Darro. The fast-flowing river 16 kilometres long runs like a silver spine through the centre of Granada. It is not a mighty waterway, like the Thames or the Tiber, and its rock-strewn, downhill riverbed makes it unnavigable, so it was never a river of commerce but it was life-giving. In Muslim times, its waters supplied the Alhambra and Generalife via a system of aqueducts and its presence was later crucial to the tanners and dyers whose workshops lay on its banks, and who easily disposed of their waste residues in the torrent.

The revitalizing waters of the Darro were part of the picturesque image of the urban space, a central feature of the Romantic cityscape of nineteenth-century Granada that defined its character. Flanked by the Alhambra on one side and the historic Albaicín on the other, the river now runs from Plaza Nueva along the narrow, cobbled seventeenth-century street that takes its name, the Carrera del Darro, its course spanned by small pedestrian bridges. Opposite the river are palaces, convents, churches and archaeological remains from the Nasrid era, all leading to the Paseo de los Tristes, where its valley opens out to offer a celebrated image of the Alhambra, before the river rises on the leafy banks of the Sacromonte hill. Here stones, buildings, bridges and water speak of eight hundred years of history, reflected in the coloured façades of some fifty historic structures. It is a street considered one of the most exceptional in universal architectural heritage, whose scenic perspective has been praised by all manner of artists and writers, including the gruff Somerset Maugham, who wrote in his work *Andalusia: The Land of the Blessed Virgin* of 1930 that it was 'the most beautiful half-kilometre in the world'. Its layered, interwoven history comes to the surface in the church of Santa Ana, built on the foundations of the old Aljama mosque, opposite the narrow pavement where small Arab houses rub shoulders with Renaissance buildings, alongside the convent buildings of Zafra and San Bernardo, and where what is believed to be the oldest Arab bath in Spain, el Bañuelo, is still in use. The vista of a street unique in Spain captures a Romantic portrait of Granada, its coloured lime plaster façades offering the artist deep ochres and siennas, shades of white and blue, the greens of chrome or cobalt oxide, the warm reds of iron oxide, those colours of the sky and landscape with which they blend.

Granada is a living entity that moves and changes with time, with its singular laws of life and growth, watched over by its feminine principle and *genius loci*, the River Darro, that swells the River Genil on the eastern border. In the nineteenth century, this fragile combination of water, landscape and history became the focus of an almighty clash between ancient and modern that saw the erosion of old ways of urban life, and the transformation of the very structure of the city through the reorganization of its physical configuration. To grasp the nature of the reforming zeal that gripped the city and altered it forever, we must look back to the early eighteenth century, the start of Spain's modern era, to understand the political upheaval that left Granada looking ahead, albeit with both feet anchored firmly in the past.

On 1 November 1700, King Charles II, known as 'the Bewitched' owing to his innumerable illnesses and physical misfortunes, died aged just thirty-eight, ending the Habsburg dynasty of the Hispanic monarchy and sparking a War of Succession provoked by the rival claims to the throne of Philip of Anjou, son of the Bourbon king Louis XIV of France, and Archduke Charles of Austria. Granada toed the Bourbon line and supported Philip, who finally became King Philip V of Spain in 1724, and its citizens prepared for a new chapter in their history with great hope. Some things stayed as they had been in the seventeenth century – the unique connection between the city and the *vega* that was vital to the main economic pillar of agriculture meant that there was no agricultural revolution, as there was in other parts of Europe. Granada's fertile soil continued producing beans, linen, corn, tomatoes and potatoes, and in the 1750s linen and sugar cane production took off, while sheep- and goat-rearing flourished. What did change was the ownership of the agricultural land. What had belonged to the Moriscos in the *vega* before their rebellion in 1568 had been snapped up by the Church, which owned over half the growing land by the eighteenth century, while the rest was fragmented between wealthy landowners who lived in the city itself and local peasant farmers. Silk-making, a craft fundamental to the economy of Granada since Muslim times, virtually disappeared.

The social structure of Granada had barely altered in the last two hundred years. Nobility and clergy still dominated the upper classes, though by the 1750s about 12 per cent of the population were either intellectuals, lawyers, doctors, teachers or administrators, who along with merchants and traders, formed middle-class society. The lower classes continued to work as labourers and day-workers, many sorely persecuted gypsies among them. In 1788, 580 *gitanos* laboured in Granada as livestock workers, sheep-shearers and slaughterhouse workers, all the jobs most repellent to the rest of the inhabitants. It was a community where wealth, aristocracy and the Catholic Church still ruled supreme, in which life was governed by a typically bureaucratic city, bogged down by administration and legality. Yet despite the apparent rule of order, under the surface, the vestiges of past conflicts survived and were finally unmasked. In 1727, a son denounced his father Nicolás Díaz, spiritual leader of a clandestine Morisco community, to the Inquisition. In October of that year, 226 people accused of professing the Islamic faith were arrested and later condemned in different *autos de fe* held in the city between 1728 and 1731. The victims belonged to about fifty families linked to the textile industry or to other middle-class professions, in particular the Aranda, Chaves and Figueroa families. The existence of these crypto-Muslims hidden in plain sight as late as the eighteenth century begs the question of whether other such families persisted far beyond that time.

While the organization of society remained stuck in the past, everyday living and leisure took on a new aspect. Although many city streets were dirty and unpaved, and drinking water was in short supply in some districts, new buildings and outlying areas began to appear. By 1796 there were 10,000 habitable houses and 300 caves in the city; the houses in the Albaicín were in a poor state of repair owing to their wooden framework, in light of which the town council prudently created a fire-fighting unit as a precautionary measure. The Baroque architecture of many buildings, including the Church of San Juan de Dios, the last great commemorative work of its kind, was overtaken by Neoclassical style, imposed by a royal decree of King Charles III (r. 1759–88) that found form in the fine palace of the Conde de Luque in Calle Puentezuelas, today the School of Interpreting and Translating of the university.

The evening *paseo* or stroll became the popular pursuit along the newly created broad promenades on the banks of the River Genil, the Paseos del Salón and la Bomba, and later the Paseo del Violón, and similar walkways were made in the Alhambra to honour the visit of King Philip V to Granada in 1730. In a bold move, Granada's first dedicated bullring was authorized by the Royal Armoury and built in 1768 near the Hospital Real in the Campo del Triunfo, despite the monarchy's attempt to prohibit bullfighting. The *corrida* was much loved especially by the working classes, harking back to the ancient tradition of bull-running practised in Muslim times in the Bib-Rambla square. It was a tradition that evoked the primitive taurine culture expressed in the stone bull of Arjona six centuries before Christ and that reached its zenith in the nineteenth century, when Granada's most famous matador, Salvador Sánchez Povedano, known as the legendary Frascuelo, was born in 1844 in Churriana de la Vega, eight kilometres from the city. His father was a soldier-turned-gambler whose debts inflicted poverty on his family, until Salvador and his brother began to take part in bullfights in towns around Madrid, where they had moved when their father died. He performed in the Madrid bullring aged just twenty-three and quickly made his name, taking part in sixty bullfights a year. In late spring 1868 he returned to Granada to take on the equally famous El Lagartijo, with whom he had a longstanding rivalry. All the great bullfighters of their era fought in the Granada bullring until it was ravaged by fire one night in 1876, just when Frascuelo was at the height of his fame. It took three years to build a magnificent new arena in the Triunfo esplanade, which was opened in April 1880, boasting three storeys and a capacity of 15,000 spectators, making it one of the best in the land. The bullring poster for

3 April 1880 showed El Lagartijo, Frascuelo and another famous matador, Cara Ancha, with bulls provided by Antonio Miura. The most glorious moments in Frascuelo's career took place in that bullring, while his rivalry with El Lagartijo became a national obsession. On one occasion he fought on his own and gave his earnings, some 80,000 reales, to the needy folk in Granada and in his home village. Frascuelo ended his career at the age of forty-six in Madrid. Indomitable, handsome, clever and powerful in the fight, he dared to do what no one had before, or since, but he died too young, just eight years later in 1898, of pneumonia[127].

Theatre proved to be even more popular than bullfighting for the middle classes in Granada, where a special royal dispensation to put on plays had been granted, contrary to the regular virulent clamp-downs on their performance by the Church and monarchy. A memorandum from a clergyman writing in the late eighteenth century denouncing the sinfulness of theatre gives the flavour of the accusations levelled at play-going, through which, he said, a young lady learns 'that to allow courting and flirting is not indecorous… that it is gallantry to disobey her parents' wishes and do as she likes… that it is discreet to deceive one's parents by allowing a pretender to enter their house. The devil is in these plays, the ruin of custom, the inconstancy of young women and the discrediting of what is honourable.'[128] Theatregoers ignored these kinds of diatribes and flocked to the playhouse in great numbers. Outside the theatre, in the streets and squares, entertainers such as jugglers, tightrope-walkers and musicians fed the Granadans' love of spectacle, and punctuated the tranquil monotony of daily life in the city during the century of Enlightenment.

At the time of the conquest of the city by Ferdinand and Isabella in 1492, Granada was one of the richest, most densely populated cities not only in Spain, but in the known world. By the start of the eighteenth century, it had proportionally fewer inhabitants than it had three centuries earlier, largely because of the expulsion of the Moriscos and the effects of various kinds of poor government. A century later, its commercial power had waned as the silk industry had been run down, and nineteenth-century growth and wealth were counterbalanced by an insidious decadence.

The geography of the province, balanced between tropical and alpine, influenced every aspect of its evolution, and the extraordinarily intense relationship between city and country shaped its material and spiritual personality, as agriculture remained the most important industry. The *vega* was watered by four rivers, the Darro, Genil, Monachil and Dilar, that supplied an Arab irrigation system at once simple and complex, regulated from the city by the ringing of the bell of the Watchtower, the Torre de la Vela. The river water that vitalized the crops was the lifeblood of Granada's economy and in Muslim times water had brought an unprecedented degree of sophistication to city life. The Muslim supply network had reached such perfection that most houses had running water, with cisterns and two separate pipes, one for drinking water and one for toilets. By the nineteenth century the old network was still in place but was in need of repair, so as the population grew, the water became more and more unhealthy. Often the houses had no running water or baths, and for this reason, the age-old trade of the water-sellers became crucial. They collected water from the wells in the Patio de los Aljibes in the Alhambra and carried it in demijohns on their backs or strapped to a donkey, trekking down to the city every day to offer it fresh and cold to their customers. Another familiar figure of the time was the 'snowman' who supplied the city with ice. In the late evenings these intrepid entrepreneurs could be seen climbing up the Sierra in a line, bearing panniers which they would fill with snow, returning before dawn with their icy treasure to sell for ice-creams and sorbets.

The Muslim structure of the city endured. The River Darro ran as it always had but its waters grew polluted with waste from local industries, while women washed their dirty clothes on its banks. The complex maze of narrow, winding streets failed to maintain the most minimal standards of sanitation, and mass burials often took place in churches inside the urban area. Soon, subsistence became a major problem as poverty crippled the population, which fell in 1804 to 54,962 inhabitants, and lowered its resistance to devastating epidemics of cholera. The first came in 1833, spread by two Polish refugees in Portugal, bringing fear and confusion to Granada, where the symptoms of joint pain, diarrhoea and in some cases instant death were quite unknown to its inhabitants. The cholera outbreak lasted for a year, until the autumn of 1834, with dramatic effects on population numbers. Further outbreaks followed in 1853 and 1885, when 5,000 people died. Those who escaped with their lives found refuge in everyday normality. Houses in the narrow, sunless streets where no vehicle could pass sported brightly coloured curtains and flowers on the balconies, and women sat at their front doors watching children play. Inside, houses were dark and cool, often cluttered with furniture and knick-knacks, and most had living rooms, intimate spaces where women sewed, wrote letters and received close friends. In the winter they were heated by braziers. Life was tough if you were a maid in service, as one account reveals, in which an employer instructs her maid, newly arrived from a nearby village, in her duties each day:

> Get up at 5 a.m., light the fire, go down into town for bread and milk; then bring me my chocolate, then the master's chocolate. While I get up, sweep the drawing room, sitting room, dining room and reception room, clean the windows, dress my daughter, give her breakfast, take her to school, and when you get back, go to the square for shopping at 11 o'clock promptly... make the beds... we eat at five when you bring the children home from school.[129]

A series of pen sketches of life on Sundays in Granada by Nicolás de Roda,[130] written in 1841, paint a vivid picture of how a day of leisure was spent. The upper classes went to Mass, then took a leisurely stroll, read the newspaper and chatted, then went home for lunch about 2 p.m. The almost sacred duty of the after-lunch siesta was followed by coffee and a change of outfit, as it was not done to be seen wearing the same thing twice. The preferred place for a pre-theatre stroll in the evening was the Paseo del Salón or la Bomba; others enjoyed an ice-cream at the trendy Café Suizo or a cold drink at the Café Juan Hurtado. Some went to *tertulias,* evening gatherings where folk talked, played the guitar or piano and drank chocolate. Working-class people wore their best, clean clothes, went to Mass, then straight to the inn, or for a stroll with their girlfriend, stopping for lunch in some small tavern. A card game was nearly as sacred to the working classes as the siesta to the upper classes, and usually involved drunkenness and altercations. At night, they went dancing, but often there were rows, and the law was called.

The veneer of jollity disguised the stark realities of early nineteenth-century life, when hunger, empty purses and epidemics had taken their toll. There were underlying political tensions too, including the persecution of the Granadan liberals, all those who spoke directly, or indirectly against the Crown. The forced abdication early in 1808 of King Charles IV was followed by the short-lived reign of his son Ferdinand VII and the occupation of parts of Spain by French troops. The popular uprisings that broke out after Napoleon installed his brother Joseph as king of Spain marked the start of the Peninsula War. For the first time for many hundreds of years Granada was invaded again. When the French General Sebastiani and his troops entered Granada on 28 January 1810 it was a calvary for the city, whose submission to the French was total and complete. Sebastiani demanded a contribution of several millions to fortify the Alhambra, which his army had seized, thereby emptying the city's coffers and intensifying its dire financial straits. By the time the French departed from Granada on 16 September 1812, its inhabitants had lived through a nightmare.

In their four-year occupation, churches had been demolished to provide building materials and many were converted into stores, stables or soldiers' lodgings. The invaders ransacked works of art, paintings, statues both religious and profane, and took them with them. Worst of all was their terrible devastation of parts of the Alhambra, including the destruction of ten towers on the upper parts of the site in their mania for rebuilding. It was an irreparable loss of part of the city's history and of its ability to reconstruct the past.

As the century advanced and the material culture of the city began to crumble, the distance between social classes grew greater. While the middle classes started to gain confidence and live calm, fairly comfortable lives, the working classes faced the spectre of unemployment, one of the endemic problems of the city that would mark its future development. Religion acted as a panacea, and the celebrations of the important Corpus Christi festival – held in May or June depending on when Easter fell – which honoured the presence of Christ's body in the Holy Wafer, converted Granada into a fairy-tale setting. The holy procession set off from the Bib-Rambla square, led by little Devils, exquisitely dressed up, and the entire city was illuminated by huge candles, chandeliers, cornucopias and street lights. The crowds enjoyed sorbets sprinkled with cinnamon and garnished with strawberries at the popular bar Botillería del Callejón, and at the Café de León in Calle Mesones you could get exotic drinks to wash down the sponge cakes and ice-cream cornets made in nearby patisseries. Brilliant lights, magnificent processions and lavish refreshments briefly disguised the darker side of mid-nineteenth-century Granada, unhygienic and in ruins, where many of its residents lived in squalor. The stagnation of the eighteenth century had finally turned into dilapidation and decay, and the River Darro, whose pure waters had been vital to life, became polluted and deadly. The utopia of the Muslims and early travellers to the city had declined into a dystopia, and Granada had reached a crossroads.

THE OUTSIDER'S GAZE:
EARLY TOURISM AND TRAVELOGUES

Oddly enough, it was precisely the ruinous state of parts of Granada that appealed to the gaze of foreigners. A view arose of a romantic city elevated in the imagination of outsiders to the paragon of a place whose past was plainly visible in its ruined monuments, a past that had more value and interest than its present or future. This point of view came about as a result of the convergence of specific ways of thinking with the evolving phenomenon of early tourism. From the late eighteenth century to the 1850s, the mindset of Romanticism suffused cultural endeavours throughout Europe, embracing a rejection of industrialization in favour of the ideal of rural life and the beauty of nature, and finding its inspiration in Nature's powerful, unpredictable sublimity and capacity to transcend baser reality. Over a similar period of time, young men, and sometimes women, from the European upper classes, along with artists and writers, undertook a traditional rite of passage, the Grand Tour, an educational trip to the great cultural sites of continental Europe to seek the legacy of Classical civilization and the Renaissance. They recounted their experiences in travelogues and sensational tales that inspired the Western interest in all things foreign. The Grand Tour, now seen as the start of modern tourism, had started as early as the seventeenth century and usually took in France, Germany, Switzerland and Italy. Spain was not initially part of the established route but in the nineteenth century that all changed – suddenly it was the trendy place to visit, and Granada became the high point of the experience.

The fascination with the objects and culture of the East attracted people of the Romantic cast of mind and found expression in the imitation or presentation of the Oriental world in art, literature and architecture that focused on the perceived differences between Eastern and Western civilizations. It led the first early tourists to

Andalusia. Among them was Wilhelm von Humboldt, founder of the University of Berlin, who travelled to Spain with his wife Caroline, and arrived in Granada in the middle of February 1800, perhaps not the best month to visit the city for the weather is cold and the days are still short. Humboldt was keenly aware of the otherness of the place and his precise, factual account at times expressed a dislike of what he saw. The Court of the Lions in the Alhambra was not to his taste, typically Arabic, but 'decidedly not beautiful'. Humboldt's words would find an echo in the observation of Walter Gropius, founder of the Bauhaus school of architecture, who likened the structure of the Alhambra patios to a campaign tent whose hanging carpets were the intermediate arches and the pillars the tent poles. It was the style, he declared, of a nomad people in a country of burning heat. The British baronet Sir Arthur de Capell Brooke expressed a rather different view in his *Sketches in Spain and Morocco* of 1831, which affirmed the city's international fame at that time: 'Who has not heard of Granada, and does not long to climb its mountain barriers and visit this romantic city, once the last refuge of an enlightened and high-minded people, who... reached that height of civilization so remarkable when contrasted with the barbarism of the rest of Europe...'[131] Despite this, Sir Arthur still criticizes the steep, uneven streets of the Moorish part of the city and remarks on the cracks and frailty of the walls of the Alhambra, which he said was tolerably preserved, while other nearby buildings were neglected and ruined. What interested him most, though, was the nature of the Granadan Muslims, whom he considered to be culturally superior to other Europeans, and the difference between the Catholic Spain of his time and its Muslim past, a contrast about which he was scathing: 'It is true that Christianity has taken the place of the religion of Mahomet; but how much lower on the animal scale does the bigoted Spaniard of the present day appear when compared with the enlightened and liberal Mussulman of former ages!'[132] He was not the only traveller to Granada at this time who criticized contemporary

Spanish Catholicism, to the extent that, rightly or wrongly, the Alhambra came to personify racial and religious tolerance, and to express medieval culture's highest degree of civilization.

The Alhambra also became the focus of an extraordinary polemic on the Islamic roots of Gothic architecture. In his work *Parentalia*, published in 1750, the architect Sir Christopher Wren set out his theory of the Saracen origins of Gothic style, the crucial feature being the pointed arch, which he believed the Crusaders had brought to Europe from Jerusalem. Around 1800, as more European travellers explored Spain, a debate arose surrounding the idea that the origin of Gothic actually lay in the Spanish Muslim kingdoms, and not the Near East. British visitors went to Spain with that preconception and searched for evidence of the theory in the Muslim architecture of Andalusia, and of Granada specifically. When the Scottish painter David Roberts, newly elected as president of the Society of British Artists, embarked on his first trip to Spain in 1831, he returned to London with a portfolio filled with sketches among which were several views of a 'Gothicized' Alhambra. These were used as engravings for Thomas Roscoe's book *The Tourist in Spain* (1835), images that Roscoe claimed 'transformed the Alhambra into a set for a Gothic novel',[133] lengthening the perspective and the height and size of its pointed arches to create a sense of the sublime. The perception of the Alhambra as a source of Gothic inspiration was far-reaching, as its influence on the Great Exhibition of 1851 reveals in a design for stained-glass windows, in which the inner area was decorated with Christian symbols as well as acanthus motifs that echoed not only Roman but also Nasrid style, with borders embellished with ornamental patterns inspired by the Alhambra. It was a triumphant cultural exchange between East and West in glass and stone.

In 1831, around the same time that Arthur de Capell Brooke and David Roberts were in Granada, another British traveller, Richard Ford (1796–1858), arrived in the city. Ford was born in Chelsea, London into a wealthy family, and after a first-class education at Winchester School and Oxford University, he trained as a barrister, though he never practised, and remained a staunch Tory and anti-Liberal. He married Harriet Capel in 1824 and they had six children in the space of eight years, three of whom had died in infancy by 1832. Not surprisingly, Harriet's health was causing concern so they decided to spend time in Spain's warmer climate, staying in Granada during the summers of 1831 and 1833. Ford's account of his time in the city is a masterpiece of travel writing, in which his sharp eye for detail, intuitive understanding of his subject and his dynamic, poetic style make compelling reading. He wrote from a privileged position as a resident of the Alhambra, where the governor lent him a suite of rooms in the palace above the Patio de la Mezquita (now the Mexuar), and this first-hand knowledge lends great authority to his opinions. His personal reflections on the dire consequences of the occupation of the city by General Sebastiani sheds light on the precarious state of the Alhambra after the Peninsular War.

Richard Ford rekindled the image of the province of Granada as a paradise, divided by its wealth-bringing river water, like a Rubicon, from the desert beyond the *vega*, green and fruitful while all beyond is barren and tawny. His descriptions of its geography abound in strong contrasts in a place where, he says, eternal snow and the blood-heat of Africa mingle, and with fulsome enumerations of its natural abundance, from the hardiest lichen to cotton plants and sugar cane, from precious minerals to priceless marble mined in the Alpujarra mountains – the Switzerland of Spain, according to Ford, and a source of inspiration and fascination to artists, geologists and botanists alike.

Ford voiced strong opinions about the history and society of Granada. This is his view of the city at the time he was writing: 'Under the Moors, Granada was rich, brilliant, learned, industrious and gallant and now it is poor, dull, ignorant, indolent and dastardly. The Spaniards have indeed laboured hard to neutralize the gifts of a lavish nature, and to dwarf this once proud capital down to a paralysed provincial town.'[134] Although his overall perspective was a Christian one, he condemned Philip III's expulsion of the Moriscos as a great crime, rather than a great glory. Ford and his wife had been based in Seville for most of their stay in Andalusia, and he remarked on the longstanding mutual hatred between that city and Granada, whose society he criticised as dull and less well-dressed, lively or intelligent than the Sevillians. Granada was stagnating in bookless ignorance, he complained, and had neither letters, arts nor arms, while education was at a low ebb and the lack of proper roads hindered commerce.

But on entering the Alhambra site, the traveller, Ford included, came under 'the magical jurisdiction of this fairy palace',[135] despite its neglected and ruinous condition, a prolonged degradation dating in his view from 2 January 1492 when the Catholic Monarchs ordained the whitewashing of walls to remove Moorish symbols. Less than twenty-five years before Ford's visit, in 1808, Don Ignacio Montilla had been appointed governor and his wife kept her donkey in its beautiful chapel of Santa María and converted the Mexuar into a sheep pen. Ford laments the destruction caused by the French troops under Sebastiani, who converted the palace into an arms store, tore up the paving of the Court of the Lions to make a shrub garden whose roots damaged the underground pipework and – as a parting shot – blew up eight towers. They had intended to blow them all up but thanks to the quick thinking of an invalid soldier, José García, who disabled the rest of the unlit fuses, the remainder were left standing. The Court of the Lions was impassable in its ruined state and some of the stone lions lay broken on the ground. Ford recalled how the second founder of the Alhambra, as he described her, Francisca de Molina, stepped in. Francisca, known as Frasquita, was a peasant whom governor Montilla had appointed as porteress, and she lived in the Alhambra with her niece Dolores and one Mateo Ximénez. The Englishman shared the Alhambra with them for two summers and found Frasquita short-tempered and crabby, Dolores ill-favoured and mercenary, and Mateo a chattering blockhead. Frasquita made a bit of money showing visitors round and providing picnic dinners, but she also set to work to repair the ravages wreaked by the French, placing the lions back on their feet and clearing away the rubbish. While Ford was there, he witnessed the galley-slaves in chains who resided in the palace grounds tearing down Moorish tapestries, paintings and tiles and casting them over the battlements. The dereliction of the Alhambra and the nature of its inhabitants were a symbol, in Ford's mind, of the parlous state of Spain, as his vignette of the Plaza de los Aljibes reveals: 'In front the massy towers of the Moors frown over ruins and neglect. The uneven, weed-encumbered court is disfigured by invalids, beggars and convicts, emblems of Spanish weakness and poverty.'[136] He remarked ironically that the Granadans themselves did not admire the Alhambra – their hatred of the old rival, the Moor, was not extinct, and they resented the preference shown by foreigners for its Moorish heritage over the palace of Charles V, which they saw as representing their own culture. Ford had a timely visit from the British ambassador in Madrid, Henry Addington, who fortunately persuaded the Granadan authorities to remove a live powder magazine on the site, averting the catastrophe of the complete destruction of the monument.

The French poet and journalist Théophile Gautier (1811–72), who wrote so eloquently on the gypsies of the city, had a different temperament from Richard Ford, and certainly a more optimistic perspective on Granada. Gautier grew up in Paris in the era of Romanticism, developed a wide circle of literary friends including Victor Hugo and Gérard de Nerval, and made a name for himself as a writer and advocate of the doctrine of Art for Art's Sake, although he originally aspired to be a painter. Among his many travels, he visited Spain in 1843 and spent time in Granada, staying in a boarding house run by a Frenchwoman in Calle Párraga near the Carrera del Darro. His account of his stay in the city is filled with everyday detail and close observation. The river made a strong impression on him and inspired a description which gives a valuable insight into the appearance of the Darro in the 1840s:

> ... the Albaycín is situated on a third hillock, which is separated from the others by a deep ravine choked with vegetation and full of cactuses, coloquintidas,[137] pistachio trees, rose-bays, and tufts of flowers, and at the bottom of which flows the Darro with the rapidity of an alpine torrent. The Darro, which has gold in its stream, traverses the city first beneath the open sky, then under bridges so long that they rather merit the name of vaults, and joins itself in the Vega, at a little distance from the parade, to the Genil which is contented with containing silver.[138]

He added that the river was wearing away its banks, causing landslides. His poet's ear was attuned to the music of the city's water, a constant murmur that accompanied the hum of crickets, water which sprang out from tree trunks, cracks in old walls, the hotter the weather the more abundant the springs of melted snow. Like Ford, Gautier saw a paradise in Granada: 'This mixture of water, snow and fire renders the Granadan climate unparalleled throughout the world, and makes Granada a real terrestrial paradise.'[139] He recalled the Arabian saying 'He is thinking of Granada', which expresses sadness or longing.

Gautier was amazed by the rich colour and ornamentation of the houses in the city, which he felt lent it the quality of a theatrical set. Those of the well-off were painted in:

> the most fantastic manner with imitations of architectural embellishments, sham cameos on grey grounds, and false bas-reliefs... with a medley of mouldings, modillions, piers, urn-like vessels, volutes, medallions ornamented with rose-coloured tufts... bits of embroidery, pot-bellied cupids supporting all sorts of allegorical figures, on apple-green, bright flesh-colour or fawn-tinted backgrounds.[140]

It was, he thought, the height of bad taste. In contrast, the women showed good taste in sporting their black lace mantillas and flouting the latest fashions in order to wear traditional dress, which Gautier applauded as a stand against the uniformity that masqueraded as progress, and for the picturesque. In contrast to Ford's scorn for the people of Granada, Gautier admired the happy calmness and tranquil dignity of the faces he saw around him, and the leisurely pace of a life, as he saw it, filled with conversation, siestas, promenades, music and dancing.

The Generalife perhaps delighted him most of all, with its over-whelming perfume of aromatic plants, their abundance creating a luxuriant disorder that rubbed shoulders with the clipped formality of yews, all irrigated by the ever-present running water. The Arab skill in hydraulics was a sign to Gautier of the most advanced state of civilization, and he claimed that the sophisticated irrigation system in the city had created its reputation as the Paradise of Spain. His poetic evocation of the Sierra Nevada at sunset recalls the exquisite eulogies of the medieval Arab bards:

> The Sierra Nevada… assumes the most unimaginable hues. Its whole steep and rugged flank and all its peaks, struck by the light, become of a rose-colour, dazzling to behold; ideal, fabulous, shot with silver and streaked with iris and opal-like reflections… the hues of mother-of-pearl, the transparency of the ruby and the veins of agate and aventurine that would defy all the fairy jewellery of the Thousand and One Nights… the mountain seems to have put on an immense robe of shot silk spangled and bordered with silver; little by little, the bright colours disappear and turn to violet mezzotints, darkness invades the lower ridges… while the silver diadem of the Sierra still shines out in the serenity of the sky, beneath the parting kiss sent it by the sun.[141]

Gautier was not alone in his admiration for the Generalife, which are the oldest Western gardens in existence. There are few places in the world where a traveller can contemplate gardens created in the fourteenth century, even if the planting has changed since then. The earliest travellers to the Alhambra, like the sixteenth-century Venetian ambassador Andrea Navagero and the Arab visitors who had admired Granada as much as Damascus, marvelled at the abundance of water and vegetation, and the beauty wrought out of technical, topographical and botanical skills. Yet over time, the palace and gardens evolved into the idealized space of the imagination, outside time and normal human experience. In 1777, the French traveller Jean-François Peyron saw the gardens as a great amphitheatre, a privileged place in nature, although by his time, sad and deserted, defeated by another government and set of customs that, he said, had destroyed its glory.[142] By the nineteenth century, a gap had developed between the real place and the representation of it, between the crumbling, neglected citadel and the idyllic, imagined palace and its grounds. The Generalife became a cultural icon, a mythical place conjured up by Romantic writers such as Gautier, René Châteaubriand and Prosper Merimée, whose magic spread across Europe and manifested itself in recreations of the Alhambra gardens in the properties of the rich. Nineteenth-century travellers, including Alexandre Dumas *père* in his eulogy of the paradise-like Generalife, were struck by its modest scale in real life, by its natural simplicity of line and form, by the sheer number of orange trees, roses and jasmines flourishing in a relatively small area. Above the city, yet never losing it from view, part of its appeal lies in its uniting of opposites, of heat and water, snow and fire, or, as Gautier put it, 'an eternal Spring under African temperatures'.

The Alhambra became picturesque, poetic in its dereliction. It became a place of veneration and pilgrimage. If you walk up the steep slopes of the Alhambra woods today, about half way to the top you come across a very welcome stone bench where you can rest your legs under the watchful eye of the elegant statue of a man with a book and briefcase, bearing the inscription 'Son of the Alhambra'. This is a monument to the New Yorker Washington Irving (1783–1859), sculpted by Julio López Hernández and inaugurated in 2009 to commemorate the 150th anniversary of his death. Irving is considered the first American Hispanist, famous for intensifying the romantic image of Granada and the Alhambra adopted by nineteenth-century travellers, and much loved in the city, where the bookshops all stock his *Tales of the Alhambra*. Irving was given permission to stay in the Alhambra for a short time in 1829, and returned to Spain in 1842 as US ambassador for four years, writing several more important works on Spanish subjects such as Christopher Columbus and the conquest of Granada in 1492. His captivating descriptions and stories inspired by the Moorish fortress tell a sorry tale of the desolation and ruin of the buildings, where no fountains played. Irving was spellbound by the 'old dreamy palace' as he called it, whose 'peculiar charm' is its power to conjure up '… reveries and picturings of the past, thus clothing naked realities with the illusions of the memory and the imagination'.[143] To him as to other travellers, it was a sacred place: 'To the traveller imbued with a feeling for the historical and poetical, the Alhambra of Granada is an object of veneration as is the Kaaba or sacred house of Mecca to all true Moslem pilgrims.'[144] Granada and its famous palace had become a place of poetry, dreams and fantasy, a paradise of the mind and a unique destination for those who hoped to find or rediscover a lost Eden there.

THE CLASH BETWEEN PROGRESS AND THE PAST

Ancient and modern came into conflict in the middle of the nineteenth century. The history, tradition and beauty beloved of the Romantics clashed with renovation and reform in Granada, where for once the city was refashioned not by the demands of creed and clan but by those of commerce and cleanliness. The silver backbone of the city, the River Darro, became the focal point of that refashioning and its transformation was irrevocable. Ironically, tourists' fascination with Granada was partly responsible for the drive to modernize, so the 'romantic city' espoused by a significant element of city society conflicted with the 'healthy, geometric city' that middle-class liberals tried to impose by structural reforms. Another reason was the way trade really began to flourish, especially the newly important sugar-beet industry in the *vega*, which supplied sugar factories linked by that symbol of nineteenth-century urban modernity, an electric tram network, that ran between Granada and the smaller outlying towns. Manuel Rodríguez Acosta, born in 1840, became leader of the Granada Conservatives and a councillor until his death in 1912. Much loved and admired by the citizens, he provided a great deal of capital for the sugar-beet trade, as did his contemporary, Julio Quesada Cañaveral, born in 1857, a politician and entrepreneur whose most lasting achievement was building the Alhambra Palace Hotel.

In 1846 José Giménez Serrano, a professor and journalist from Jaén, published his *Manual for the artist and traveller in Granada* (*Manual del artista y del viajero en Granada*), an early tourist guide to the city. It contains a lengthy description of the trades and wares that prospered around the mid-century:

> In spite of everything, there are still two iron and copper-beating workshops, two factories making continuous paper which will soon have their goods for sale, namely various papers, coarse brown and white; cotton weaving factories, rope makers, producers of sailcloth, serge, cashmere for trousers, mixed with silk for jackets; wool sashes, coarse wool cloth, covers and blankets, ordinary cloth, some made out of silk... two places that weave embroidery canvasses, glove makers, fabric makers producing thick flannel, cleaning cloths, linen for mattresses, table-linen, drill, ticking and woven damask; more than twelve vermicelli-makers, manufacturers of hard and soft soap, earthenware jars, metal mouldings, bricks, flagstones, Granadan glazed tiles, brandy, licquors and chocolate; two making wallpaper, others making combs, lead pipes and sheets, wax and tallow candles, gut strings, matches, fans, umbrellas, glue, fabric for engraving, foundry and cupellation work, linseed oil, elastic items, buttons, cutlery, mirrors, buckskin, pianos, hats, mats, sandals and trappings for

horses; canvas-makers, a considerable number of tanners, starch mills, more than three lithographic presses, relief, copper and steel engravers and at least eight other presses.[145]

This is the word portrait for foreigners of a vibrant city – bang up-to-date, affluent and prolific in its trades and services; but it came at a price. Factories that produced toxic products – tanning residues, starch, tallow, ink, waste from slaughterhouses – tipped their black residual water into stinking drains and sewers, and often into the River Darro, which tended to overflow and flood the streets with its reeking effluent. The narrow, airless streets festered, their broken drainage systems overflowing with rainwater mixed with sewage. The habit of many Granadans of using open spaces such as the Bib-Rambla square, Pasiegas and the fish market as a public toilet exacerbated the problem, and soon the inhabitants fell prey to what was known as 'the Granadan trots' or *diarreas granadinas*. The local press complained loudly about 'streets converted into animal graveyards, where filthy rubbish lay strewn in disgusting drains'. One journalist composed a 'hymn to the swine' as a protest at the intolerable stench that pervaded the place. Disease spread and the situation in hospitals and prisons grew lamentable, with overcrowding and illness converting them into death-traps, while corpses mounted up in the cemeteries where the remains were often dug up by scavenging dogs. To make matters even worse, many buildings were in a state of ruin and large areas of the city had to be demolished. Places that had been preserved for centuries suddenly disappeared forever. Many Arab and Mudéjar houses of the Albaicín once owned by nobility came under the axe, obliterating the traces of beautiful Moorish patios where Arab, Gothic and Renaissance elements combined in harmony. Some of the best houses in the Albaicín were sold for demolition, their materials going for a paltry 35 *duros*[146]. The same happened in the lower parts of the city, where typical Andalusian houses also vanished. The change was dramatic enough for one German tourist, G. Honrsttuns, to remark: 'I've heard that day by day Granada is losing its characteristic appearance, and that neither the town council, nor corporations nor individuals give a toss about whether Granada, which those of us who know it will never forget, perishes, and with it, unique and considerable beauty.'[147]

At this crucial time in Granada's history, the keynote was ambivalence. The picturesque corners of an enigmatic city shrouded in legend that had beguiled Romantic engravers were understandably seen by local authorities as unsanitary places that endangered the health of their residents. The question was how to deal with them. The first reform plans of the modern middle-class city were motivated by concerns for hygiene, public health and urban enhancement; they were based on the Geometric Plan of the architect José Contreras, whose pioneering ideas on Neo-Arab architecture were absent from his restructuring design for the city, which used a system of geometric grids harking back to the earliest urban grid layouts of Hippodamus the Greek. The Geometric Plan was fundamentally a project of road-straightening as far as was feasible, which encompassed improvements to water supplies, and urban lighting in the form of gas and oil lamps that transformed the way of life in Granada and gave it a whole new perspective. Public markets were built where certain convents had been demolished, notably in the Plaza de las Capuchinas and Plaza de San Agustín. The new infrastructure created a modern city equipped for the needs of its citizens, and guaranteed food supplies.

From the 1840s onwards, the Generalife was not the only public garden in Granada. Part of the nineteenth-century concept of a modern urban space involved what was known as 'public green', *verde público*, squares with gardens or large parks for public use, and it became very important in the middle-class transformation of Granada. The poplar plantations in and around the city close to riversides were converted into garden spaces that contrasted with the geometric alignment of roads in their natural sinuousness, complimented by the wide variety of trees, shrubs and rare species and by exotic, varied scenery. The walkways along the banks of the Darro and Genil, and the Triunfo esplanade were transformed into extensive groves of luxuriant vegetation. Gardens were created in the main squares: the Plazas de Lobos, Trinidad and Mariana Pineda. The Bib-Rambla square, where in past times bulls had run and markets had traded, became a shopping area with bars and cafes, with an English-style central garden. Giménez Serrano remarked favourably on new gardens on the banks of the Genil: 'The various reforms carried out by the Town Council in the fifteen years after 1830 have greatly increased the beauty of these avenues which an illustrious traveller has compared to those of Versailles.'[148]

The most momentous restructuring of all in Granada began in 1854 and it struck at the heart of the urban landscape. The Romantic vision of the city had focused on the River Darro as a picturesque motif, part of the aesthetic of the ruin, like the Alhambra. The entrepreneurial middle-class residents failed to see the charm, however, and saw the river as a physical obstacle that hindered the trading connection between the main areas of the city such as Bib-Rambla square, the Town Hall and the Plaza del Campillo, where a new theatre was being built. To make matters worse, the noxious state of the river waters and banks was the cause, it was felt, of the sharp drop in the value of property in the urban centre. So it was that the municipal authorities contrived their solution to the problems arising from modern urbanism by endorsing a monumental project to cover over the River Darro, known as the *embovedado* or vaulting of the river. It was to be a spectacular transformation of the historic quarter, with no equivalent in any other Spanish city, and took thirty years to complete. It involved concealing the course of the river beneath the streets, starting at the Plaza de Santa Ana at the end of the Carrera del Darro, past Plaza Nueva, down to the Plaza Isabel la Católica, along the street that is now Reyes Católicos down to Puerta Real and along the Acera del Darro, where the river re-emerges shortly after to flow into the Genil. Today, the Darro runs underground along one of the main shopping streets of the city, past the fashion shop Zara then down past the main post office. Its disappearance from sight was intended to allow a more favourable arrangement of urban space, allowing higher rents to be charged for buildings in a modern commercial street. The new alignment also connected the Town Hall with the Bib-Rambla square. The journalist Francisco Seco de Lucena hit the mark when he wrote in his *Guide to Granada* (*Guía de Granada*) of 1909 that what the road had gained in healthiness, convenience and hygiene, it had lost in characteristic, archaic originality.

The stretch of the river below the asphalt became a latent presence, a residual, undefined space forgotten beneath the newly paved streets. The guardian spirit of the Darro now lay mostly in shadow, absent from the heart of Granada and excluded from the living space of many generations. Its invisible, concealed course created a parallel cityscape, a newly formed stratum whose topography embraced both the revealed and the hidden, where the vitality of the historic Darro coursed underground beneath the city crowds. Nowadays, most people are unaware that they can be seen from below when they cross the traffic lights at Puerta Real. There, a drainage grid creates a point of connection between two worlds, the city centre and its parallel subterranean universe, a place completely unknown to the majority of citizens. Beneath their feet lies a whole network of water channels, weirs and water-falls like the one beneath the corner of Calle Sancti Spíritu, whose cascade is nearly three metres high, amid the remains of the historic city of the Alhambra. The underground trajectory is walked several times a year by firemen who check the state of the current and look for signs of damage. Down there, eight metres underground, it is dark and the river stretches the width of the main channel, its banks formed of the residual soil the water drags along with it. It smells fusty but not foul, and the water is almost clear, swollen by the rivulets running downhill from the Alhambra woods. No rats live there. Below ground, when you are underneath Calle Reyes

Católicos, you can hear the buses but you can actually see people crossing the road at Puerta Real, where the only light and air that enters this forgotten world filters through the large drainage grid.

While the River Thames in London and the River Nile in Cairo formed vertebral axes essential to metropolitan revitalization through trade, Granada's urban renewal tamed the lively waters of the Darro with concrete and bitumen and reconfigured the urban topology forever. The obliteration of this unique aspect of Romantic Granada was denounced by artists and intellectuals alike but the tide of liberal urban reform that promoted throughout Europe an ideal of the healthy, geometric city as superior to any previous urban form was relentless. Granada's second major reconstruction began in 1895 with the creation of the Gran Vía de Colón (Great Columbus Avenue). One of the most important internal road reforms in Spanish cities before 1905, both in terms of cost and scope and in its singular nature, this new major city artery was funded by the new Chamber of Commerce and the Town Council. The Gran Vía de Colón was intended to clean up the central area, which had the highest mortality rate in Spain at the end of the century. The ancient urban structure of the *medina* of Muslim Granada had the highest cultural and historical value but was described by promoters of the new road project as 'a filthy network of small streets, the most imperfect, nauseous, unhealthy and ugly part of the city'.[149] Work began in 1895 to create a long highway extending from the Plaza Isabel la Católica almost as far as the Jardín del Triunfo, a broad main boulevard straight as a Roman road. Overall, 244 irreplaceable medieval houses were demolished along the route, including the house of the Renaissance architect Diego de Siloé and the Cetti Meriem palace. The disappearance of a large part of the old Muslim city was welcomed by the project promoters, many of whom had financed the enormous undertaking from the wealth of the sugar-beet trade and sugar factories, the most important industrial enterprise in the *vega*. These men were the epitome of late modernity, enshrined in an economic and industrial growth that heightened class divisions between rich and poor, and they were funding a process of urban reconfiguration that would drag Granada kicking and screaming into the twentieth century. The building of the Gran Vía also coincided with the initiative to create what years later would become the city's first ring-road, the Camino de Ronda.

Like the vaulting of the Darro, the Gran Vía project provoked a storm of criticism from Granada's intelligentsia, who rejected the urban modernity it embodied. Their outrage was inspired by an anti-modern manifesto written by one of the most important literary figures of Granada, Ángel Ganivet (1865–98). It rejected the modern urban progress in Granada, which Ganivet envisaged as an ideal city, 'what it could and should be, though I don't know if it ever will be',[150] preserved in a golden age in which any contemporary transformation was an act of aggression. Ganivet's yearning for the deep essence of his native city took root when he began work as a consul outside Spain. His father died when he was ten, which put paid to any special education but he read constantly and was a natural linguist, studying Philosophy, Letters and Law, followed by a Ph.D. in Madrid. While he was posted in the Belgian cities of Antwerp, Ghent and Bruges, in 1897 he wrote *An Interpretation of Spain* (*Idearium español*), which wrestled with the subject of Spain's national decline and proposed solutions to it in a theory that became known as regenerationism. His theory was based on his most well-known book, *Granada the Beautiful* (*Granada la bella*) written the year before, where his vision of the ideal city became a paradigm for those who denounced the disappearance of its historic infrastructure and buildings, including intellectuals such as Manuel Gómez-Moreno and Antonio Almagro y Cárdenas, who fought strongly against the loss to Granada's architectural and historical heritage, with no success. For all his idealism, Ganivet met a dreadful fate when he drowned himself aged thirty-three in the Daugava river in the Latvian city of Riga while he was consul there, because of a doomed love affair.

Not all the vestiges and traditions of Old Granada disappeared. Artisans, qualified workmen, minor business-owners or labourers took to living in small *cármenes*, less luxurious than their eighteenth-century incarnation but similar and less pretentious. They spread out at the foot of the Torres Bermejas and the Martyrs' Cross, through the uphill districts of Mauror, the old Jewish quarter, and the district of Antequeruela, which those Jews exiled from Antequera in 1410 had made their home: 'Quiet houses, closed to the street, where the only note of colour is the railing on the whitewashed façade, they open fully to intimate family life, to the garden where beside the small orchard the most lovely flowers grow.'[151] Amid tortuously narrow, twisting streets, little-changed today, around a corner a magical view of the *vega* suddenly appeared; up there, silence reigned, fragments of city walls emerged butted up against misshapen houses, garlands of overhanging roses perfumed the air. The Sacromonte also kept its character. Its location and street layout, like that of the Albaicín, confounded any idea of straightening and modernizing. Each cave continued to shelter a family, the children in rags, their home shared with domestic animals, but each day its inhabitants were treated to one of the most beautiful panoramas in Granada, the green hillside dotted with white *cármenes*, the *vega* with its myriad colours in every shade of green and red, and above it all, the immutable silhouette of the Alhambra. Lower down in the city, by the end of the nineteenth century, traditional Arab Granada, with its small squares and picturesque corners, ancient houses and sonorous fountains had all but vanished, to give way to a reconfigured city that looked like so many others.

Over the seven hundred years between the thirteenth and the late nineteenth centuries, Granada had undergone radical religious and cultural metamorphoses that manifested themselves in its city-scape, transformations that took it from Muslim state to Christian kingdom to modern European metropolis. The conversion of a settlement created by Arab Muslim minds into a Catholic community demanded profound reorganization and repurposing of city spaces, an appropriation of the markers of Islam that remade them as Christian objects. In this latest incarnation, Granada remained a staunchly Catholic society but history and tradition had clashed with practical progress, the picturesque had run up against the necessity for hygiene and sanitation, with irreversible consequences. The desire to imitate other modern European cities overrode any interest in preserving and restoring certain unique city sites. Modernization brought undeniable and essential benefits to the health and wealth of the inhabitants but the price paid was the irreparable loss of part of the city's history, and of its unique urban scenery. Always ambivalent, always divergent, Granada's outer appearance spoke of its readiness to meet the challenges of the imminent twentieth century but a part of its identity was concealed underground and its former townscape existed only in the engravings and paintings of foreign artists. Strangely, that ideal Granada, that paradise of the imagination, lived on in the perceptions of travellers, strangers who had come from faraway places to imbibe the legendary magic of the city. It was not the Christian cathedral, nor the broad avenues of the Paseo del Salón, nor the fine streets and pavements over the Darro that lingered in their minds, but the memory of an Arab past that had forged the myth of a Muslim utopia, watched over unflinchingly by its ever-present tutelary spirit, the Alhambra.

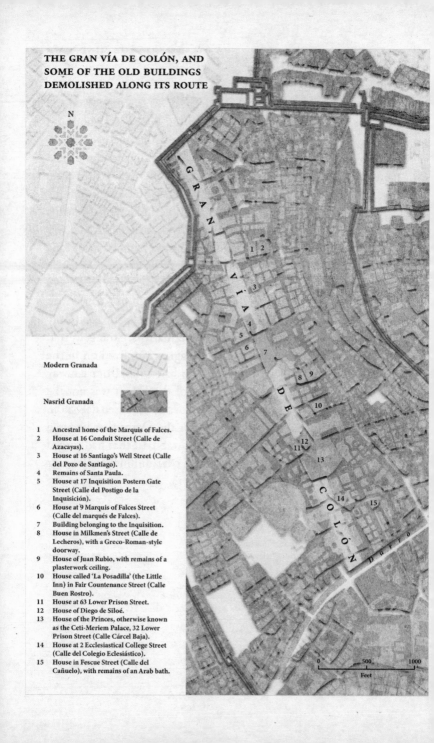

THE GRAN VÍA DE COLÓN, AND
SOME OF THE OLD BUILDINGS
DEMOLISHED ALONG ITS ROUTE

N

Modern Granada

Nasrid Granada

1   Ancestral home of the Marquis of Falces.
2   House at 16 Conduit Street (Calle de
    Azacayas).
3   House at 16 Santiago's Well Street (Calle
    del Pozo de Santiago).
4   Remains of Santa Paula.
5   House at 17 Inquisition Postern Gate
    Street (Calle del Postigo de la
    Inquisición).
6   House at 9 Marquis of Falces Street
    (Calle del marqués de Falces).
7   Building belonging to the Inquisition.
8   House in Milkmen's Street (Calle de
    Lecheros), with a Greco-Roman-style
    doorway.
9   House of Juan Rubio, with remains of a
    plasterwork ceiling.
10 House called 'La Posadilla' (the Little
    Inn) in Fair Countenance Street (Calle
    Buen Rostro).
11 House at 63 Lower Prison Street.
12 House of Diego de Siloé.
13 House of the Princes, otherwise known
    as the Ceti-Meriem Palace, 32 Lower
    Prison Street (Calle Cárcel Baja).
14 House at 2 Ecclesiastical College Street
    (Calle del Colegio Eclesiástico).
15 House in Fescue Street (Calle del
    Cañuelo), with remains of an Arab bath.

0   500   1000

Feet

10

THE DESCENT INTO HELL

*Modern Granada and
the Civil War*

◆ ◆ ◆ ◆ ◆ ◆ ◆ ◆ ◆ ◆ ◆ ◆ ◆ ◆ ◆

ALL MOD CONS: NEW PERSPECTIVES IN A NEW CENTURY

In the darkness of a late December afternoon two small boys pressed cold noses against a shop window, fascinated by the spectacle of a beautifully backlit nativity scene that glowed in the gloom, its tiny crib with the baby Jesus, the miniature clay figures of Joseph, Mary and the bejewelled Wise Men on camels displayed against a background of small white houses and Moorish arches. There were other figures too – gypsies dancing, smugglers and saints, toy donkeys, sheep and even a small cat, all standing round the holy infant, who was lying on a little bed of straw in a manger made of matchsticks, nestled on a bed of moss. The houses and arches were constructed from cardboard, the Three Kings were adorned with glass beads and their costumes glittered with tinfoil. It was Christmas 1899, the eve of the new century, and Granada was holding firm to its traditional custom, the Christmas crib scene, lovingly created and proudly exhibited at home, on market stalls and in shops. All around Calle Mesones in the city centre as far as the wide Carrera de la Virgen, a motley range of booths sold fruit and sweets, hot chestnuts, castanets, drums, ancient instruments like shawms, rebecs and tambourines with a distinctly Moorish feel, typical local pottery known as Fajalauza, live turkeys and chickens, the kiosks interspersed with children's swings and fairground-style stalls.

The bars and taverns in Calle Mesones were jammed with strangers and labourers with their baskets of produce for sale, and a legion of persistent touters for trade inhabited the alleys and squares. All of Granada seemed to be out in the streets, fathers with small children pleading for toys, teenagers, grand local officials, ancient nobility come down in the world, landowners, day workers, pickpockets and the destitute, and Spanish soldiers in their now ragged blue and white striped uniforms. The crisp, cold air was filled with shouts, children crying, laughter and the chorus of merchants plying their wares, above which floated the strains of Christmas carols. Up the hill on the Sacromonte, the best *cantaores* in the city welcomed the season in the flamenco bars while 'John the Gypsy' and the old 'Habichuela' and her daughter sang in the inns El 32, Los Manueles and the fabled Los Altramuces. The Albaicín and the caves of the Sacromonte resonated with the music of guitars and flamenco carols such as this one: 'The bell of the Watchtower / struck twelve, / so that God could be born / beside the Alhambra.'[152]

Shops and businesses struggled to cope with the tide of Christmas shoppers, especially those that sold typical seasonal treats like almond cakes, almond and hazelnut shortbread, chocolate or cheese puffs, pies from Baza, iced doughnuts, the almond delicacy known as *turrón*, pine nuts and special rice from Játiva. But the poor still ate potatoes for Christmas dinner while the wealthy feasted on turkey. The tradition of inviting a poor person off the street to share the Christmas meal had fallen by the wayside, though the convention of giving a Christmas box or *aguinaldo* still flourished. It was originally a present given by the powerful to the humble, which recalled Queen Isabella's gift to Pope Alexander VI of an *aguinaldo* in 1492, after the fall of Granada. The gift took the form of a silver model of the Alhambra. Isabella's gesture was ambiguous, however, in that it appeared to stress the victory of Christianity over Islam, while at the same time it revealed an admiration for the precious prize of the conquered. In turn-of-the-century Granada, the less grandiose Christmas box was in some measure a gesture of goodwill to the less fortunate, albeit one which came with many complaints that nowadays the postman, the baker, the night watchman, and even the street sweepers all demanded their share.

Midnight Mass was at the heart of the celebrations. The dark, ice-cold cathedral was illuminated by countless sparkling candles, as the packed congregation joined in sung Matins, after which Holy Mass began. Officiating priests, altar boys and churchgoers were decked out in their finery, and the solemn organ music soared above the racket from drums and tambourines in the streets outside. At the same hour, in the intimate confines of Granada's multitude of whitewashed convents, the intense hours of silence were broken by perfectly intoned carols and Christmas songs.

Alongside the centuries-old traditions of Christmas, the new century brought new perspectives. In a city enamoured of the visual, the advent of cinema in Granada at the start of the 1900s aroused great excitement, but also some trepidation. The movie theatre of the Lumière brothers had been part of the festival of San Isidro in Madrid in mid-May 1896 and later the same year there were projections using Edison's early motion picture device, the kinetoscope, on the terrace of the Teatro Principal in Granada. Movies proper arrived at Christmas 1900, after a request was made of the Town Hall to install a cinema on the covered part of the Darro. Naturally local residents on the Acera del Darro complained at the ugliness of the cinema booths, which they considered 'inappropriate for the ornamentation of the city, because of the trouble they would cause, the scandal that would arise and because they would block the view from the ancient houses'.[153] The Granadan writer and journalist Melchor Fernández Almagro, who went to the cinema as a child, gave his less than favourable opinion on the experience:

> ... a strange, huge organ, at the entrance to the booth, made a thunderous trumpeting noise, with a figure made of wood or some such, representing the conductor of an orchestra with a tiny beard, among Solomonic columns decorated with glittery paint, that gyrated incessantly, so that the whole picturesque and excessive musical altarpiece was stupefying in effect... Please go in, gentlemen, please go in! ... Inside, another figure explained in a loud voice what was happening on the screen, which was often off square and cut the projection in two halves... Close your eyes from time to time, as the cinema is not good for one's sight...[154]

In 1904, one of the first permanent cinemas was built in the newly created main thoroughfare of the Gran Vía, but at first films were shown only at Christmas and during Corpus Christi.

The front page of the local daily paper *Defensor de Granada* (*Champion of Granada*) of 1 January 1900 offers a verbal snapshot of everyday preoccupations and interests in Granada at the dawn of the new era. It presents an incongruous mix of consumerism, culture and Catholicism. The main advert at the top of the page promotes the script of a play, *The Triumph of the Ave Maria* (*El Triunfo del Ave María*), attributed to the Baroque playwright (and governor of Granada jail) Cubillo de Aragón, which dramatizes the surrender of the city to Ferdinand and Isabella in 1492. The play was traditionally performed on 2 January, the festival of the *Toma* or capture of the city, and now it was available to read in a handsome volume of 200 pages costing just one peseta. The fact that there was a presumed market for such a book reveals just how significant the Christian conquest of their city still was to its inhabitants over four hundred years later. Reading a play was second best to watching an actual performance, and the *Defensor* announces two plays showing at New Year, *Los amantes de Teruel* (*The Lovers of Teruel*) by the Golden Age playwright Tirso de Molina, at the Teatro Principal, and a *zarzuela* or light opera in three acts, *The Tempest* (*La Tempestad*), by the nineteenth-century composer Ruperto Chapí, at the Teatro Isabel la Católica. If theatre was not to your taste, you could go daily to the trendy Café de León in Calle Mesones to watch dancers performing *sevillanas* while enjoying beer, tea or fizzy drinks for 30 cents, or 35 cents if you had sugar in your tea. More pious Granadans could celebrate the Circumcision of the Lord with a sung Mass in the cathedral at 9.30 a.m., or attend services at any of the other ten churches listed by the broadsheet.

The adverts on the two-page *Defensor* highlight the latest innovations in everyday life at this time. Electric light had come to Granada around 1892 with the foundation of the General Electricity Company, which had its offices in the Zacatín. On 1 January 1900 the company was offering electric light installation work for five, ten or sixteen bulbs at varying prices. The new modern chemists at Calle Príncipe 10 gave free medical consultations between 1 and 2 p.m. daily; dentists advertised the latest dentures at 100 pesetas in advance. Don Vicente Ruiz from Madrid presented the wonderful invention of the hearing aid, Dr Herrera's digestive potion cured all manner of stomach ailments and nervous disorders, and an ointment was available for impotence. Consumers could purchase up-to-the-minute men's suits in pure wool, ties, fans, the very best cognac, sherry from Jerez, the purest drinking chocolate, sweets, and local eau-de-cologne from Orive near Cordoba, better and four times cheaper than many foreign brands, at 3 *reales* a flask. As befits a provincial newspaper, there is little foreign news and much space devoted to the New Year's lottery numbers.

The new perspectives on life created by the cinema, by medical and technical innovation, and by up-to-date consumer products were mapped onto the most fundamental change in structural perspective that Granada had undergone since its rebuilding as a Christian city, and even exceeded it. A decade after the completion of the vaulting of the Darro, Jose Contreras's geometric plan for the city found its fullest expression in the radical transformation of the urban centre to create the Gran Vía de Colón (Great Avenue of Columbus), named after the explorer who discovered the New World, his voyages given the royal seal of approval by the Catholic Monarchs in 1491 in Santa Fe just outside the city, weeks before its final surrender. It was a name perhaps meant to echo the pioneering spirit of the great adventurer.

The project was provisionally finished in 1903, when the first shop opened on the Gran Vía, but as we have seen, it had plenty of detractors, including Ángel Ganivet, who had been outspoken in his abhorrence of the vaulting of the Darro and equally outraged at the destruction caused by the new central avenue. He had proposed that the ancient winding, irregular streets of the Muslim city obeyed the need to create shade for protection against the burning sun and brilliant light, and to act as windbreaks, whereas broad streets were typical of cold countries like Scandinavia, where shade was to be avoided. Ganivet's views were ahead of their time, but they were not in vogue in the early twentieth century and it would be a long time before his ideas made an impact. Decades later, in a new journal called *Renovation*, Antonio Gallego Burín put forward his own theory of urban planning, based on Ganivet's ideas and motivated by the desire to make the city more beautiful in order to attract more tourists, whose potential contribution to the city's economy was just beginning to be glimpsed. Gallego Burín was to become the first mayor of Granada to support Franco's regime, which tainted his attempts to revive sacred festivals under the aegis of the state religion of national Catholicism.

Either inspired or incited by the dramatic changes to the urban landscape, culture in Granada flourished for the next thirty years, reflecting similar cultural developments in the rest of the country, to the degree that the first three decades of the twentieth century were dubbed the Silver Age, a modern version of the great Golden Age of Spanish culture of the sixteenth and seventeenth centuries. The buzz of new ideas was in the air in Granada – the university saw a big improvement in its buildings and its intellectual renovation was reinforced by the reopening of the Artistic Centre, which had been closed due to lack of interest in 1898, and now aimed to maintain and preserve the purest traditional essence of the city. These were the golden years of Federico García Lorca and the other young intellectuals, including José Mora Guarnido, a close friend of Lorca's, and Manuel de Góngora who belonged to the Centre. At the same time, the famous literary *tertulias* held at the Rinconcillo bar in Plaza del Campillo became a hub for artists, writers, journalists and thinkers, where educated chat, anecdotes and ideas were exchanged. The Granada press was vibrant, boasting four dailies at the start of the century, the *Defensor de Granada* already mentioned, the *Heraldo Granadino* (*Granada Herald*), *La Publicidad* (*Publicity*) and *El Triunfo* (*Triumph*), as well as the renowned review *La Alhambra* (*The Alhambra*) that printed articles on the city's past as well as on literature.

In 1909 the celebrated guitarist Andrés Segovia's very first concert at the age of sixteen was organized by the Artistic Centre and held in the city, in which he played works by Spanish composers Francisco Tárrega and Isaac Albéniz. Up-and-coming painters like Joaquín Sorolla and Santiago Rusiñol began to frequent Granada and gave new life to its visual art. Granadans themselves began to value the beauty of their city, in which they saw a note of intimacy, melancholy, a yearning for the past or perhaps a disenchantment with the present. By the 1920s, Granada was no longer a provincial, withdrawn city but one transformed into a hive of activity, a creative hub that was often in the vanguard of Spanish culture, reclaiming its birthright as a bridge between ancient and modern, between Christian, Muslim and Jewish heritage.

Monochrome landscape photographs of Granada replaced the old black-and-white engravings of the city, the old focus on the cathedral and on churches built after the Christian conquest of the city superseded by images dominated by the crisp, straight lines of its newly remodelled urban centre. Even so, the eye of the camera at times wandered to the older quarters, still atmospheric, still romantic, still seemingly impervious to the efficient, bureaucratic system born of the contemporary state. The old Muslim city was always present, and the new currents of regionalism flowing through Spain in the 1920s reinforced interest in Granada's past. Political regionalism was strong in the Basque country and in Catalonia, while in Granada it manifested itself in terms of Andalusian culture, in a sense of its difference from the rest of Spain, rather than in a belief in Andalusian autonomy, which came later. The interest in historical works of art and architecture as part of national heritage was revived, and polarized in Granada into a clash between those who wanted to restore ancient monuments and those who wanted to conserve them exactly as they were. The Basque architect Modesto Cendoya, who had come to Granada in the 1890s to help rebuild the town of Alhama de Granada when it was damaged by the severe Andalusian earthquake of 1884, became director of conservation of the Alhambra between 1907 and 1923, and was firmly in the 'restore' camp. But professor and architect Leopoldo Torres Balbás, who was on the 'conserve' side, was sent from Madrid to replace him and swept away earlier capricious and destructive renovation work to create an Alhambra much like the one we know today.

The 1922 Cante Jondo festival had defined the deep feeling for the culture of Granada at that time by uniting the popular and the educated under the umbrella of flamenco music, in a common effort to place city and province in pole position in national culture. Granada's contentious Muslim heritage came to the fore in 1924 when another ambitious plan was mooted, this time to hold a Hispano-African exhibition rivalling the international exhibitions to be celebrated in Seville and Barcelona. Its initial aim was to promote Granada's craft industries in line with the north African tradition of the city, and it was supported by a good number of intellectuals including the architect and historian Leopoldo Torres Balbás, the poet and Arabist Emilio García Gómez and the art historian Antonio Gallego Burín, who wrote an impressive article hailing Granada as the great Spanish centre of Africanism and the most natural point of contact between the two peoples. He described the geographical and commercial proximity of Granada to north Africa, such that in 1503 a customs post had been set up in the kingdom as the main centre of African trade. The city remained a site of melancholy nostalgia to the north Africans, he claimed, whose traditions gave sap and vigour to twentieth-century Granadan industries. The city's history resonated across the world as well as throughout Spain, as the reliquary that preserved the last Muslim presence in western Europe. The organizers of the Hispano-African exhibition hoped it would arouse cordial feelings between peoples of different cultural backgrounds and foster a climate of mutual enlightenment.

Sadly, it never took place. Granada's ambitions had run counter to the tenor of recent events, when Spain's attempts to gain control of Morocco failed disastrously in 1921 at the loss of almost 20,000 Spanish soldiers in the Moroccan Rif, forcing the Spanish army to retreat to Ceuta and Melilla. The attack on Morocco had been a source of social friction and this, combined with the dramatic fall of the monarchy in 1931 when the Republic was established, had meant a change in priorities. There was some compensation for the failure of the exhibition plans, as Granada received a great boost when the dispositions of the Royal Decree dated 9 August 1929 on the defence of national artistic treasure designated Granada as an 'artistic city'. It was a significant moment in the history of the place, which imposed a moral duty of preservation on any future urban planning.

In the first three decades of the twentieth century, Granada's population rose by 50 per cent to 100,000 inhabitants, as the urban space expanded at the expense of the *vega*. The refined public spaces, hotels, the new thoroughfares, trams, the railway, the electric lights that twinkled in the darkness, all were the visible markers of an ever-evolving, prosperous and confident city. The mindset of the inhabitants had become more outward-looking, more open to the world beyond. No one expressed this better than Lorca, when in 1927 he explained the inspiration behind his new journal, *El Gallo* (*The Cockerel*), as:

> ... loving Granada, but with our thoughts fixed on Europe. Only in this way can we draw out the most deeply hidden and subtlest local treasures. A journal about Granada for those outside it, that takes the global pulse in order to distinguish its own unique heartbeat; a happy, lively, anti-localist, anti-provincial journal of the world, like Granada, which has a name in the universe and a crown of glory. Granada is not the Café Colón, Pavaneras street, the Gran Vía etc. Granada is another more permanent, more elevated thing in the national consciousness: a place of historical and poetic frontiers, and the murmur of pure beauty.[155]

But the clash between beauty and violence so familiar in the history of the city was poised to shatter the upbeat mood, as optimism ceded to conflict in a battle not with foreign assailants but against the enemy within.

BETWEEN DEATH AND VICTORY: THE REIGN OF TERROR

On 20 July 1936 the Maison Dorée café was packed out, I was standing in the doorway as there was no room inside. We were all listening to the radio when we saw cars and lorries full of men dressed like labourers wearing military berets, armed with rifles, they came from the Gran Vía and went down Reyes Católicos

where the café was, shouting 'Long live the Republic'… and some
of them waved the Republican flag.[156]

Vicente Castillo's eye-witness account makes it plain that he, like
other citizens in the street, believed that the militants they had seen
were government supporters. Nothing could have been further
from the truth. It was five in the afternoon when the garrison of
troops stationed in republican Granada to defend it rose up against
the liberal government of President Manuel Azaña. They left their
barracks on the orders of Colonel Antonio Muñoz and headed for
the town centre, tricking the people on the street into thinking
they were supporting the republicans. The rebels stationed artillery
at key points throughout the city, in the Plaza del Carmen in front
of the town hall, in Puerta Real and in Plaza de la Trinidad just
round the corner from the civil government offices, which were
occupied without resistance. The civil governor General Campins,
along with his guards and the mayor, were all taken prisoner. An
hour earlier, Campins had been horrified to find out that his
own officials were involved in the uprising, which became clear
when they took him to the military command and forced him
at gunpoint to sign a declaration of war. Shortly after, the police
caved in to the rebels and the Radio Granada building in the Gran
Vía was occupied, enabling the declaration of war signed by the
governor to be broadcast every half-hour from 6.30 p.m. onwards.
By early evening all the official buildings of the city centre were
occupied, with the loss of just one rebel soldier.

The abrupt shift from a liberal and progressive city to a place
under military rule, where violence and terror roamed the streets,
was the consequence of what was happening on the wider Spanish
political stage, in combination with circumstances particular to
Granada and to Andalusia. Spain had remained neutral during
the First World War but for the first forty years of the twentieth
century its political landscape was refashioned by monarchy,
republic and dictatorship. When King Alfonso XIII abandoned

Spain in 1931, the Second Republic was proclaimed under Prime Minister Manuel Azaña, who instigated an ambitious programme of reform. From 1933 to 1936, the Republic came under right-wing conservative control until a left-wing coalition won the elections in February 1936, with Manuel Azaña, now a political veteran and left-wing figurehead, as its new President. He took the reform programme further by bringing in agricultural renovation. The English writer Gerald Brenan lived in the Alpujarras until 1934 and described the political mood in striking terms: 'Spain became the scene of a drama in which it seemed as if the fortunes of the civilized world were being played out in miniature.'[157] He pointed out that the rising tensions began as a straightforward class struggle between reactionary landowners and revolutionary peasants and factory workers, the latter mainly supported by small business owners and intellectuals, and the landowners by the Church, the Army and most of the middle classes. Granada proved to be a special case from the earliest days of the Republic. Social conflict was more severe in the province of Granada than in other agricultural districts because the labourers and farmers involved were often well-educated, organized socialists unlike their poorer, downtrodden counterparts elsewhere in Andalusia, and the landowners belonged to the extreme political right. These men who often owned a hundred acres of rich, irrigated *vega* were powerful, yet many peasant workers were prosperous and belonged to the UGT (*Unión General de Trabajadores*, or General Union of Workers), the socialist trade union. That did not prevent unemployment from becoming a major problem in country areas. Around 1934, Brenan recounts stories of frequent riots, nightly explosions from home-made bombs, and cars that were stopped to force their drivers to 'make a contribution' to the fund for the unemployed. It was wise to keep off the streets after dark.

The unrest of rural workers ran up against the mindset of the leaders of the rebellion against the democratic Republic. Generals Mola, Franco and Queipo de Llano regarded the Spanish working classes, like the Moroccans, as an inferior race to be tamed by violence. There was a double irony in the fact that despite this opinion, they would be happy to deploy Moroccan mercenaries from the colonial army to repress and terrorize, using Spain's ancient African enemy in a war between its citizens. The repression was brutal and was intended to be so. The orchestrator of the coup, General Mola, stated the ambition to eliminate 'those who do not think as we do'.[158] The overthrow was controlled in the south by rebel commander Queipo de Llano, who would later be dubbed the 'butcher of Seville' for the thousands of executions without trial carried out under his command by the military during the first months of the Civil War in the summer of 1936.[159] The backlash from the extreme left echoed the discourse of the rebels, and Republican areas condemned not only the military right but also bankers, industrialists, landowners and even the clergy, who were, in their view, in cahoots with the rich. Around Granada, where numbers of unemployed labourers had risen drastically into the tens of thousands, landowners claimed that lack of work was an invention, and in the area of nearby Jaén, hungry peasants who gathered acorns and windfall olives or collected firewood were denounced as kleptomaniacs and severely beaten by the Civil Guard. In 1934, mass hunger reduced workers in Guadix to eating grass.

According to the Falangist Onésimo Redondo, a virulent anti-Semite, the Spanish working class was identified with the Arabs, who had been roundly defeated by his heroine, the great Queen Isabella of Castile, and naturally Andalusia was to be condemned as the hotbed of a Jewish and Arab conspiracy against Western civilization. In an article in the fascist monthly JONS in May 1933, Redondo described the southern labourers as Marxist bandits who broke into farms to steal because they were too lazy to work. His greatest fear was 'the re-Africanization of Spain' by Jews and Moors, 'aristocrats and plebeians who have survived ethnically and spiritually in the Peninsula and in Europe'.[160] A new Reconquest was needed to fend off the African threat and it came in the form

of the most extreme kind of violence, a military coup by the
Nationalists, planned at a secret meeting of army officers in Madrid
on 8 March 1936 and led by General Mola. The day after, Granada
suffered a vicious right-wing attack, designed to provoke reprisals.
A squad of gunmen who supported the fascist political party La
Falange Española fired on a group of workers and their families,
wounding a large number of women and children. In response,
local left-wing parties called a general strike that provoked street
violence, during which two churches and the offices of the Falange
were set on fire and the premises of the right-wing newspaper *Ideal*
were destroyed. All day on 9 March, Falangist snipers fired on left-
wing demonstrators from the rooftops, and on firemen attempting
to control fires that had broken out. After this, violent incidents
took place as if by sleight of hand, often caused by mysterious
strangers who disappeared as quickly as they had materialized.
Later, serious skulduggery came to light when some of the most
radical anarchists and communists in the city were revealed to be
Falangist agents provocateurs.

When the Spanish Civil War finally broke out in July 1936,
Granada was torn in two. In the burning heat of July and August,
streets and squares bore witness to scenes of both victory and defeat,
of triumph for those who supported the coup and death for those
loyal to the Republic. The existence of two opposing realities
created an extraordinary atmosphere – balconies were decked with
flags, hymns were sung, voices calling for the death of democracy
rang clear and the Church gave its blessing to those sentiments. In
the same breath, former ways of thinking disappeared, savagery
surfaced, victims were taken for a 'walk' (the euphemism for death
by firing squad). In the same city streets where victory was raucously
celebrated, silence settled with the dust. The story of Granada
during the Civil War was quite different from that of Cordoba
and Seville, and was not told in the local or national press. The
Defensor de Granada published its final edition on 19 July with an
explicit headline: 'Citizens: Long Live the Republic!' (*Ciudadanos:*

¡Viva la República!). Just days later, the newspaper was closed down and silenced. Instead the right-wing daily *Ideal* was revived and the atrocious reality escaped its pages, which bore no mention of the violent repression unleashed at that time, merely a brief note on the back page, like the one dated 8 August, that referred to the shooting of 'twenty imprisoned individuals' by way of 'reprisal for the bombardment' by Republican planes. Generally, news was restricted to the detention of workers' leaders and Republican chiefs, and focused on the fact that they were armed and therefore dangerous. The traces of people's lives were lost and silence meant they were dead.

As it had been in the reign of Sultan Boabdil and during the Morisco rebellion in the sixteenth century, the working-class Albaicín was the main centre of resistance, with its narrow maze of small streets that lent themselves to defence. Barricades were put up along streets leading to the Albaicín, including the Carrera del Darro, the entrance to the Cuesta de Chapiz, and Calderería Vieja to prevent the rebels entering the district. Strategically placed rebel artillery battered the residents of the Albaicín, who fired back with the few pistols and shotguns they possessed, refusing to give in. They held out for several days. By the morning of 23 July, ammunition had run out and improvised surrender flags began to appear on balconies. The Nationalist forces invaded the area, at the cost of uncountable working-class casualties, while a few brave Republicans escaped, as Vicente Castillo, who described the initial coup in the city, recounts: '… that night, members of the resistance in the Albaicín withdrew to the mountains, en route to La Peza… Guadix, Colomera.'[161] Their escape gave rise to the legend of the mysterious rebels known as the Niños de la Noche (Sons of the Night), whose enigmatic nocturnal resistance activities at times saved hundreds of people and took on a mythical quality for the besieged Granadans, whose hopes were buoyed by the idea that escape might be possible. Even so, hundreds more Republicans were arrested and taken to prison, where they were interrogated and brutalized; many were shot. On 24 July, *Ideal* reported on the efficiency of modern arms, noting the marks of fire from rifles, pistols, machine-guns and canons on many of the houses of the Albaicín that remained standing. The marks are still there today.

Terror invaded the city. General Miguel Campins, having been arrested by rebel officers and forced to read the declaration of war at gunpoint on 20 July, was tried in Seville for 'rebellion' and shot two days later. The letters General Franco had sent asking for him to be shown mercy were torn up by Queipo de Llano. The newly appointed civil governor of Granada, Commander José Valdés Guzmán, reactionary and ill-tempered from the pain of his war wounds sustained in north Africa, allowed the Black Squad of the Falange to sow panic among the population. This sinister unit of about fifteen men was made up of well-known local right-wing fanatics and thugs and those desperate to hide their left-wing past, and they entered the homes of republicans at night, seized them and shot them dead against the cemetery wall near the Alhambra. There was no trial. One of the leaders, Juan Trescastro Medina, declared that he was prepared to slit the throats of any Reds,[162] including babies at their mother's breast. During the course of the war, more than 5,000 civilians were shot in Granada, many of them at the cemetery, whose caretaker went mad and was committed to an asylum on 4 August. Three weeks later, the new caretaker had to move from the lodge at the cemetery gates as the cries and screams of the dying proved unbearable. Helen Nicholson, an American supporter of the Republicans, lived near the Alhambra and described the ghastly sounds heard in the early hours: '… about two a.m. the noise of a lorry and other vehicles climbing the hill to the cemetery woke me up, and soon after I heard the noise of gunfire, followed by the vehicles returning.'[163] Then there was silence. The death toll included a great number of doctors, lawyers, writers, artists, schoolteachers and, above all, workers, many of whom were denounced by newly recruited Falangists in the city who were ruthless in the locating and seizing

30. *Alhambra and Albaicín* by David Roberts.

31. Reyes Católicos (Catholic Monarch's Street) in the city centre around 1900.

32. The Huerta de San Vicente, the summer home of the Lorca family in Granada from 1926 to 1936.

33. Federico García Lorca with his two nieces Conchita and Tica at the entrance of his house in Granada in 1935.

34. *opposite* The Dar al-Horra palace, official residence of the Sultana Aixa, wife of Abu l'Hasan and mother of Boabdil, last sultan of Granada.

35. Portrait of Mariana Pineda Muñoz.

36. A Muslim woman praying during Ramadan in Granada in 2018.

37. *opposite* Andalusia's Museum of Memory (Museo de la Memoria de Andalucía) in the Avenida de las Ciencias, which opened in 2009. Its striking contemporary building can be seen from afar.

38. *previous page*
Aerial view of Granada
in 1957 showing Calvo
Sotelo and the areas
of San Lázaro and
Cartuja from the
Pajaritos district.

39. *Albaicín* by abstract
expressionist artist
José Guerrero, born in
Granada in 1914.

40. An Easter
procession with one
of the magnificent
floats bearing a statue
of Christ.

of suspects. No one dared speak of those whose lives were lost, and fear precluded asking for explanations from the authorities. Bereaved families never mentioned their murdered loved ones in public. As historian Miguel Ángel del Arco Blanco remarks in his account of the conflict, 'this Granada of silence, absence and pain sadly contemplated the other, victorious Granada',[164] thousands of whose citizens took part in victory parades and patriotic ceremonies in the midst of the most brutal repression.

Granadan newspaper columnists took the official line in the weekly Falangist *Patria* and in the Catholic daily *Ideal* that the Reds were not true Spaniards but beings corrupted by materialism, freemasonry, Judaism and imported Marxism. Cartoons presented the Red as an inferior, ferocious, pestilent creature, lacking in morals, heroism and faith. To be a supporter of democracy and the Republic suddenly became a sign of evil and immorality, so that the dehumanized Republican antagonist entirely justified their brutal repression. In the end, Granada donned the deep blue of the Falange, and thousands of its residents swelled the ranks. Many young Granadans went to fight at the Front, including Bonifacio Soria Marco, a member of the militia who saw the war as 'a reconquest, inch by inch, of a land beleaguered by barbarism and destruction'.[165] Blue-shirted Granada embraced the New Spain with arms raised in salute, its public spaces blazoned with the symbols of the rebels. In mid-August 1936, the red and yellow flag ousted the tricoloured Republican banner, while crucifixes returned to the streets and classrooms as the city was once more made Catholic. The Albaicín, the feisty worker's bastion, was literally plastered with niches for statues and crosses, along with other, more sinister symbols that adorned the streets including emblems of Nazi Germany and fascist Italy, countries which the rebels considered worthy of their admiration. On Sunday 17 August the municipal band gave a concert in Plaza del Campillo to give the public the opportunity to sing the hymns of the Falange over and over again. In February 1937, hundreds of Falangists congregated outside the town hall and destroyed voting papers and glass urns as a symbol of their opposition to democracy.

And so the terror went on until – by early April 1939 – General Franco had all Spain under his control. Yet the war did not end there. It morphed into persecution not on the battlefield but in prisons, concentration camps, military courts and even in the seeking out of exiles. Martial law was imposed until 1948. In Granada, many citizens who fled to the east of the province were captured – 5,500 cases were tried in 1939, and even worse, in the twenty years between 1939 and 1959, 1,001 people in Granada were executed after military trial. The concentration camps, including those in the bullrings of Granada and of Baza, in the sugar factory in Guadix and the old racecourse in Armilla, were hellish places of torture, hunger, illness and death for at least 43,700 prisoners of war.[166] Over a hundred mass graves were registered in Granada alone by the Association for the Recuperation of Historical Memory, founded in 2000. It would be some forty years after the coup in Granada in July 1936 before democracy was resurrected upon the death of Franco in 1975.

On 27 July 2017 a memorial was inaugurated in the cemetery in Granada, created by the architect Carmen Moreno Álvarez to honour the victims of the Civil War murdered on that spot. The *Railings of Memory* (*Rejas de la Memoria*) stretch for 43 metres along the cemetery wall and are fashioned in iron out of the names, places of origin, dates of birth and death of those executed, and include those who have not been identified. In the sunshine their unique details are projected onto the landscape, against the earth and the olive trees, and individual names are often adorned with red carnations left by their descendants. It is a striking, poignant monument to those who shall not be forgotten and serves as a constant reminder of the darkest chapter in the history of Granada, and of Spain, since the sixteenth century. Twice before the Civil War of 1936, in the titanic struggle between Muslims and Christians that led to the surrender of the city in 1492, and in the Morisco rebellion of 1568, Spaniards from Granada had fought and killed each other in religious wars. This time it was politics, not religion, that set brother against brother, in a perceived crusade against an invader within that re-enacted the conflicts of medieval and early modern times and harnessed them as propaganda for fascism. The peerless Eden of the Muslim poets had become a hell on earth.

A LOVE BETRAYED:
FEDERICO GARCÍA LORCA
AND GRANADA

In the tragic drama of the life of Federico García Lorca, Spain's greatest modern poet and playwright, the curtain rises on a rural setting whose backdrop is a vista of sun, mountains, rivers and trees with a foreground of wild flowers, grazing horses and farmers working the land, which set the tone of his early days. Lorca was born, as he put it, 'in the heart of the *vega*', in the village of Fuente Vaqueros, on 5 June 1898, at a time when the sugar-beet trade was booming. Landowners like his father, Federico García Rodríguez, one of the wealthiest men in the village, could make a fortune. Lorca wrote: 'My whole childhood was centred on the village. Shepherds, fields, sky, solitude. Total simplicity.'[167] His boyhood in the *vega* gave him a deep, emotional association with the land, and an awareness of the ancient interdependence between the natural world and humans, which he expressed in a poetic language rooted in the memory of those natural motifs and scenery evoked at the start. His village was different from others in the *vega*, since its inhabitants were liberal-minded, bolshie, rebellious and unconcerned about religion. It was a surprisingly progressive and open place, blessed with an abundant supply of water from the underground springs that flowed beneath it from the Sierra Nevada. The main characters who appeared in Federico's earliest memories were family and friends, country folk like his father, who had also been born in Fuente Vaqueros. There, his first wife Matilde had died and he had married again, to Vicenta Lorca Romero from Granada, a primary school teacher who would be the poet's mother. There is a tradition that a long way back Lorca's family had gypsy blood, and he believed that he had also inherited Jewish blood from his mother, whose name Lorca she shared with an important town in Murcia that had a flourishing Jewish community in the Middle Ages.

Federico was very popular in the village and was invited to eat so often at other children's houses that his mother complained. Although he was flat-footed and not interested in sport, he and all his family had musical talent, and the games and songs of his childhood made a lasting impression on him. In 1906, when he was eight, a travelling puppet theatre arrived in Fuente Vaqueros. Federico was so enthralled that he refused to leave the village square or have dinner, and next day he set up his own version on the garden wall. Soon his mother bought him a real puppet theatre from the best toy shop in Granada, feeding a fascination that he expressed in later life in several puppet plays, including the extraordinary *Puppet Play of Don Cristóbal* (*El retablillo de Don Cristóbal*) which was performed in Madrid in 1935, with Lorca operating the puppets. In 1907 his family moved for two years to another village, Asquerosa (later renamed Valderrubio), but the first nine years of their son's life in the *vega* of Granada left an indelible imprint on him and found its voice in the world of nature, myth, passion and death that evolved in his poetry and plays.

The second act of Lorca's life takes place in the city of Granada itself. Visualize an exquisite patio with a tiny fountain, shaded by the leaves of vines. There are geraniums, violets and forget-me-nots in pots, and the perspective opens out onto a garden with a fine magnolia tree at its centre, complete with a stable and paddock in the background. The scene is tranquil and opulent, as befits the house of a wealthy landowner, and represents the terraced house on several floors that Federico's father rented in the Acera del Darro in Granada from 1909 until 1916. The family's move to the city marked the start of what was perhaps the future poet's greatest love affair, with Granada itself. It was a time when the city had not yet sprawled into the *vega*, whose orchards, farms and fields blended seamlessly with the last streets of the urban centre. The lower course of the Darro had not yet been silenced beneath tons of concrete and still displayed its romantic, picturesque charms. New characters peopled the stage as Federico went to secondary school, discovered his talent for music and enrolled in Granada University.

He and his brother Francisco attended a small private school, the College of the Sacred Heart of Jesus,[168] in the secluded Placeta de Castillejos near the cathedral. Despite its name, it was a school free from any Catholic influence, as his parents wanted the boys to have a liberal education. Federico did not really apply himself at school, and his brother was a more outstanding student because around that time Federico found a new passion. He began to play the piano, spending hours a day at the keyboard, stimulated and supported by his music teacher Antonio Segura, whom he revered. His parents had their hearts set on proper professional careers for their sons and insisted on Federico enrolling at the university rather than pursuing the musical path he favoured. In October 1914 he started the course to prepare him for study in the Faculties of Philosophy and Letters, and of Law, where his university record was solid but not brilliant, perhaps mainly because he hardly bothered to sit an examination in three years. In May 1916, when Federico was eighteen, Antonio Segura died suddenly. The loss of a great friend and teacher, who had supported him in his aim to study music in Paris, was a blow to Federico and it proved to be a turning point in his life. Firmly opposed to their son's plans for a career in music, Lorca's parents, who held the purse-strings, insisted he finish his degree. Finding his musical ambitions thwarted, Federico turned to writing poetry instead.

Later in the summer of 1916, the Lorcas moved to a flat in the fashionable Gran Vía, where Federico was fascinated by their neighbour opposite, a very pretty and enterprising young woman, Amelia Agustina González Blanco, known as 'La Zapatera', the Shoemakeress, because she kept a shoe shop in the Calle de Mesones. Amelia was also a feminist and suffragette, who had founded a political party, *El Entero Humanista* (The Complete Humanist), although she had no success as a candidate in the municipal elections and was later shot dead in the 1936 military coup. Federico's growing sense of his literary destiny manifested itself in his first publication, *Symbolic Fantasy* (*Fantasía simbólica*), which appeared in February 1917 in the Granada Arts Club bulletin. He had lived in the city for over seven years and it had cast a spell over him and inspired his first written work, a piece of theatrical dialogue that aimed to define the essence of Granada. Federico saw the structure of his city in terms of colours and sounds, dominated by ever-present silver water, dark green cypresses, copper and bronze stone against the intense turquoise of the Sierra, the wind playing the organ pipes in the narrow city streets, the indistinct yet passionate noises of the Albaicín, the moaning river, metallic, cello-like sounds in the Alhambra woods, in a city of fantasy and poetry. *Symbolic Fantasy* was the harbinger of a brilliant literary career that unfolded amid a group of talented authors, artists and academics that included the writer Melchor Fernández Almagro and the painter Manuel Ángeles Ortiz, who met each day in a special corner of the bar, the *Rinconcillo*, at the Café Alameda in Plaza del Campillo, between 1915 and 1922, with the aspiration of restoring Granada's cultural eminence.

These were also the years of Lorca's friendship with Manuel de Falla, when they conceived and organized the Cante Jondo festival of 1922, and the time when the poet wrote his famous *Poem on Cante Jondo* and conjured up his ever-popular *Gypsy Ballads* created between 1924 and 1927. Lorca lived and breathed the city of Granada, with which he identified completely. On his trip to New York in 1929, he wryly described himself as 'a very pure example of the most granadanly Granadan Granadanism'

('... *un purísimo ejemplo del granadinismo más granadinamente granadino*').[169] No one has understood Granada better or more profoundly, nor written about it with greater empathy and genius. In his 1927 collection of vignettes of the city, he took the title of a seventeenth-century poem by the Granadan poet Pedro Soto de Rojas, 'A paradise closed to many, gardens open to few', as the perfect definition of Granada and its *cármenes*. Lorca had confessed in 1924 that he adored the city, the whitewashed wall, the fragrant myrtle, the fountain, and thought the essence of its art lay in what he called the 'aesthetic of the diminutive', which expressed the retiring, introspective personality of the place. Its artists had always worked on a small scale, carefully wrought and embodied in the intricate arabesque patterns of its Moorish tiles, and in its marquetry, ceramics and embroidery. To him, Granada's elegiac tone reflected the clash between East and West that he saw in its two palaces, the Alhambra and that of Charles V, then solitary and full of ghosts. The poet saw the fall of Muslim Granada as a cultural calamity and was outspoken in an interview in 1931:

> It was a disastrous event, even though they may say the opposite in schools. An admirable civilization, and a poetry, astronomy, architecture and sensibility unique in the world – all were lost, to give way to an impoverished, cowed city, a land of skinflints where the worst middle classes in Spain are stirring things up.[170]

It was a remark that would come back to haunt him. Lorca loathed the repression and persecution that had been inflicted by Ferdinand and Isabella once the city was in Christian hands, and identified with the victims: 'I believe that coming from Granada... allows me to understand people who have been persecuted: the gypsy, the negro, the Jew, the Morisco, that all Granadans carry inside us.'

While the Sacromonte was home to the gypsy dancers and singers Lorca befriended, he saw the Albaicín as a stage where the fleeting shadows of the past enacted the city's ancient rites and tragedies:

... the fearful and fantastical Albaicín, of barking dogs and sorrowful guitars, of dark nights in these white-walled streets, the tragic Albaicín of superstition, of card-reading, spell-casting witches, of strange gypsy rites... of cabalistic signs and amulets, of souls in torment, of expectant mothers, the Albaicín of old prostitutes who know how to cast the evil eye, of seductresses, of bloody curses, of passions... the Albaicín of fountains, bowers, cypresses, festive railings, the full moon, the old musical ballad, the Albaicín of the convent organ's horn of plenty, of Arab patios, pianos, generous, humid living rooms smelling of lavender, of cashmere shawls, of carnations... All the tranquillity and majesty of the vega and the city are matched by the anguish and tragedy of this Moorish district.[171]

Granada in all its contradictions and complexities was the focus of the new journal *El Gallo* founded by the group of young local writers whose life and soul was Lorca. It finally appeared in 1928, and the poet enthused over its purpose, which was '... to express, to sing, to shout to the four winds this living, bleeding beauty of Granada, this irresistible beauty, which wields a sword and wounds like music'.[172] Yet that beauty was always tempered by the passion, sorrow and death that haunted Granada's past and moulded its essential character, and which lie at the heart of the *Gypsy Ballads*. Lorca pointed out that the ballads seemed to have several different protagonists but in reality had only one leading figure, Granada, though he also claimed that the principal actor was *la Pena*, deep sorrow. In his mind, clearly Granada and deep sorrow were one, a revelation that laid bare Federico's strong sense of doom and foreboding.

The final act of Federico's life begins as he looks out from his bedroom window towards the fields of the *vega* he loved, with snow-covered peaks and mountain slopes behind, overlooked by the sentinel of the Alhambra. In 1926, his father bought a handsome farmhouse on the outskirts of the city, which he renamed in honour of his wife Vicenta as the Huerta de San

Vicente. If you walk there today you pass through modern streets to reach the extensive contemporary park where the once typical white-walled villa of the *vega* stands, but when the Lorcas owned it, it was surrounded by an orchard and market garden. It was heaven to Federico, who loved to write there. He was on the point of a breakthrough in his career that would make him rich and famous, the first performance of *Mariana Pineda*, his only historical drama, in Barcelona on 24 June 1927 with the actress Margarita Xirgu playing the lead role, and the sets painted by the dramatist's new friend, Salvador Dalí. The play was a success and was put on in Madrid later that year, amid a frisson of fear that its presentation of a liberal, free-thinking tragic heroine (see Chapter 11) might be banned by the right-wing dictatorship of Primo de Rivera. As well as Dalí, Lorca became good friends with the filmmaker Luis Buñuel, along with the constellation of talented writers who became known as the *Generación del 27* (Generation of '27), which included the poets Rafael Alberti, Gerardo Diego, Dámaso Alonso and Jorge Guillén. The next year, *Gypsy Ballads* went on sale in July and was an immediate success – sales soared and Federico rose to stardom in just a few weeks, with one critic claiming that the ballads would enthrone him as the finest poet of his generation.

But his vexed and clearly passionate relationship with Salvador Dalí troubled him greatly and led him to turn unexpectedly to religion for help. The Virgin of the Sorrows is the patroness of Granada and is honoured in Holy Week with a procession that leaves the Alhambra church at midnight and descends through the Alhambra woods to the town centre. At Easter 1929, in honour of the Virgin of the Sorrows, the woods were lit by hundreds of coloured flares that transformed them into a sacred grove. Just before the procession began, someone arrived at the church imploring permission to march with the members of the Guild. It was Federico, who was allowed to replace one of the standard bearers and don the penitent's habit and its pointed hood. He walked at the head of the procession, carrying one of the Guild's three heavy crosses, as the bell of the Torre de la Vela rang out over the city. When the procession was over, he disappeared unnoticed, as he had arrived.

The poet made two long trips abroad to New York and Cuba in 1929–30, and returned to Granada in July 1930 with celebrity status. Nine months later he was in Madrid, where he was caught up in the election day riots in April 1931 that led to the founding of the Second Republic and the possibility of a new democratic Spain. But by August he was back at the Huerta de San Vicente, writing a new play, *When Five Years Pass* (*Así que pasen cinco años*), and working on his celebrated tragedy *Blood Wedding* (*Bodas de sangre*) for Margarita Xirgu, a play only finished after the first successful summer tour of his theatre company La Barraca in 1932. Lorca's brilliant initiative to take theatre to the people with his travelling troupe of players, who put on productions of classical plays from the sixteenth and seventeenth centuries for village folk, proved to be an outstandingly successful cultural experiment.

Lorca's electrifying, charismatic personality made him a favourite wherever he went. But Nazism was on the rise in Germany and the poet did not hide his views on the subject, joining the Association of Friends of the Soviet Union in 1933 and signing a protest against Hitler's fascist barbarism. His family moved to Madrid for a change of scene, renting an enormous flat in Calle Alcalá, where Federico moved in with them. There followed a long, successful trip to Argentina in 1934 but when he returned to Spain, life had changed. He visited Granada in Holy Week and discovered a city in the grip of political conflict, where the right-wing council treated the workers with disdain. Undeterred, he was back in the house in the Huerta by the summer, finishing off his next great drama, *Yerma*. In September, his friends treated him to a special dinner, among whose guests numbered the eminent Arabist Emilio García Gómez, head of the university's brand-new School of Arab Studies inaugurated by the government in 1932. In his memoirs, García

Gómez recalled the evening, describing his conversation with Lorca about his new collection of poems *Poems from the Country Estate* (*Diván del Tamarit*), whose Arabic title evoked Islamic Granada and for which Emilio wrote the introduction. He believed that Lorca's 'delirious' love of Granada and his fascination with water linked him to the tradition of Islamic poetry of Andalusia. The *Diván* conjured up his vision of the city as a place haunted by the fleeting nature of love and the relentless passing of time, overshadowed by the premonitory terror of death.

In the months preceding the Popular Front's election victory in February 1936, the unpleasant mindset of the Granadan right surfaced in their nickname for Lorca, who was known among the local bourgeoisie as 'The Queer with the Bow-tie' ('*el maricón de la pajarita*'). In a radio interview on 6 April, Federico claimed that the deep cultural divisions in Granada, symbolized by the stark contrast between the Alhambra and the palace of Charles V, were still apparent. He attacked the myth that the fall of the Moorish kingdom was a great Christian victory over paganism, a view totally opposed to the basic premises of right-wing thinking. This proved a very unwise move that did not go unremarked by the city's conservative bigwigs. In ultra-reactionary Granada, not only was the poet loathed for his homosexuality but it also transpired that the success of his father's business was deeply resented because he paid his employees well, lent his neighbours money and built homes for his workers, thereby shaming those who did not.

By the time July came, tensions were high. When his parents had returned to Granada, Lorca remained in Madrid but now decided to ignore the advice of his friends to stay in the comparative safety of the capital. He insisted on travelling to Granada, where he said he could at least work. He resolved to join his parents there on 13 July and packed with the help of his friend Rafael Martínez Nadal, who recalled Lorca's intense agitation. That night the poet left a package with Nadal, asking him ominously to destroy it if anything happened to him. It contained some personal papers – which are yet to be identified – and the manuscript of Lorca's last, highly experimental play *The Public* (*El Público*).

By next morning he was in the Huerta de San Vicente with his parents and was delighted to find that a telephone had just been installed. News of his return made the newspapers but his scathing criticism of the middle classes, which had caused a lot of trouble, had not been forgotten. Following the ousting and murder of the civil governor Campins, and the military coup in the city, panic reigned. On the first day of the uprising, Federico took a basket of food to his brother-in-law Manuel Fernández Montesinos, the young socialist doctor who was Mayor and husband of Federico's sister Concha. Federico hurried home in tears, unable to deliver the food, and retreated to bed. On 6 August, a Falangist squad arrived at the Huerta de San Vicente and searched it thoroughly, though no one knew what they were looking for, unless it was the non-existent secret radio Lorca was rumoured to keep in order to contact the Russians. The Huerta had an adjoining house where the caretaker Gabriel Perea lived. On 9 August, the squad returned, searching for Gabriel's two brothers, who had been wrongly accused of killing two people in Asquerosa. Federico witnessed their arrival and rushed out to protest Gabriel's innocence, upon which he was thrown to the ground and kicked. Before the squad left, they warned him that he was under house arrest and must not leave the premises, which put the fear of God into him. He fled to the house of his friend, the poet Luis Rosales in Calle del Ángulo 1, around the corner from the civil government building in Calle Duquesa that was the rebel headquarters.[173]

A week later, on 16 August, his brother-in-law Manuel and twenty-nine other prisoners were shot in the cemetery before sunrise. Federico was devastated. In the afternoon of that day, the rightists hunting for 'Reds' went looking for him and arrested him at the Rosales house, convinced he was a Russian spy. The whole operation was on a disproportionate scale – the block was cordoned off, surrounded by police and guards, and men were even posted on rooftops to prevent him from escaping. Trembling, weeping and near collapse, Federico appeared in the street in dark grey trousers, white shirt and loose tie, with a jacket over his arm. Once in the civil government building, he was searched and locked in a first-floor room, where he was taken food and coffee by his sister's nanny, who recalled that the room was bed-less and bare except for a table, pen and paper. The next day, Luis Rosales's brother José obtained an order for his release and rushed to Calle Duquesa but it was too late. Lorca had already been taken away.

Valdés, the governor, had asked General Queipo de Llano for advice on what to do with the poet and his reply came back: 'Give him coffee, plenty of coffee' – the euphemism used to recommend an execution. Valdés could have reprieved Lorca but tragically saw him as a communist subversive with a morally repugnant private life, who had made scurrilous attacks on Granada's middle class. In the early hours of 18 August, a friend of Lorca's, Ricardo Rodríguez Jiménez, saw him being taken out of the government building as he was leaving the police station after listening to the daily late-night broadcast:

> That night I left the station around 3.15 a.m. and suddenly heard someone call my name. I turned around. 'Federico!' He threw an arm over my shoulder. His right hand was handcuffed to that of a schoolmaster from La Zubia with white hair. 'Where are they taking you?' 'I don't know.' He was coming out of the Civil Government building, surrounded by guards and Falangists belonging to the Black Squad, among them one who had been thrown out of the Civil Guard and who joined the killers… Someone stuck a gun in my chest. I screamed: 'Murderers! You're going to kill a genius! A genius! Murderers!'[174]

A few seconds later, the two men were pushed into a car and taken to a makeshift prison outside the village of Viznar, where they were kept till early morning. Before sunrise, they were dragged out and driven along the road towards nearby Alfácar. There was no moon. The lorry stopped near an ancient spring, aptly called Aindamar, Fountain of Tears, by the Arabs. There Granada's greatest poet was shot dead at 4.45 a.m. on 18 August 1936, along with the disabled primary school teacher Dióscoro Galindo González and two bullfighters from Granada. Among his murderers was almost certainly Juan Luis Trecastro, who boasted later that morning in the city that he had just helped shoot García Lorca, for good measure firing 'two bullets into his arse for being a queer'. Federico became a Republican martyr overnight – Granada's most passionate advocate had been betrayed and killed by men from his own beloved city. But in the context of the Civil War, his murder was just one more among the many killings of town councillors, doctors, teachers, university staff and thousands more workers and trade unionists that took place in the province. Even so, the brutal extinguishing of such a remarkable and visionary talent marked one of the darkest days in Granada's annals.

Granada's history in the first fifty years of the twentieth century was dominated by upheaval, violence and war. The immense structural changes undertaken in the name of progress and modernity in order to reconfigure the new geometric city had aligned it with Europe, where similar developments were taking place. But that up-to-date European identity had been acquired at a price, which was the destruction of much that contributed to Granada's singular urban character. Architectural upheaval was matched by a political upheaval whose dominant notes were violence, betrayal and conflict. Political perspectives changed radically along with urban perspectives, and in that context Europe exerted a devastating influence on Spain, and consequently on Granada. Aided by the new technology of the radio and documentary film, fascist ideology summoned up the ancient demons of invasion and reconquest that struck at the heart of Granada's being, rehashing the old propaganda of the crusade of militant Catholicism victorious over the Arab interlopers and once again bringing about that most terrible of conflicts, the war between citizens of the same country, and of the same city. Granada was no longer a paradise on earth but became a netherworld of terror, ignorance and blind prejudice where all that was liberal, generous, free-thinking and egalitarian must be eliminated in obedience to the brave new world of the dictator. The murder of Federico García Lorca testifies to that. The key tool of the dictatorship, repression, was not only physical and psychological. It was used to suppress that part of the history of Granada and of Spain – namely its Islamic past – that was deemed unacceptable and dangerous, creating a historical narrative which all but eliminated references to those diverse cultures – Arab, Jewish, gypsy – that are an inextricable part of Granada's identity. Lorca was unequivocal in his admiration for and appreciation of the many cultures of his native city, and summed up that struggle for recognition played out in the material life of the place:

> The uninformed traveller will experience, along with the incredible variation of forms, landscape, light and scent, the sensation that Granada is the capital of a kingdom with its own art and literature, and will find a curious mixture of Jewish and Morisco Granada, apparently grown dim due to Christianity, but alive and incorruptible because they are unknown. The prodigious pile of the cathedral, the great imperial and Roman seal of Charles V, do not preclude the existence of the small shop owned by a Jew who prays before a silver image made from the seven-branched candelabrum, nor have the sepulchres of the Catholic Kings prevented the crescent moon from surfacing at times on the breast of the finest sons of Granada. The fight goes on, obscure and expressionless... expressionless, no, for on the red hill of the city are two dead palaces, the Alhambra and that of Charles V, that sustain that duel to the death that is fought in the conscience of the Granadan people today.[175]

GRANADA
THE PEOPLE III

11

VEILED VOICES

Granadan women

❖❖❖❖❖❖❖❖❖❖❖❖❖❖❖

DIVINITY, POETRY AND MAJESTY

In the time before history was recorded, a distinctive female element held sway over the lands of what is now the province of Granada. Take the Cave of Bats in the Alpujarras, where twelve eerie skeletons sat in darkness and silence for almost five thousand years, forming a half-circle that faced the corpse of a woman, her stark skeleton embellished with the grass necklace, sea-shells and boar's tusk that betoken ritual. Her position at the head of the semi-circle implies female authority, perhaps as a shaman or priestess of a goddess or fertility cult. Three thousand years later, the famous Lady of Baza, the life-size Iberian sculpture created between 400 and 350 BC and discovered in a warrior's tomb in north-eastern Granada, portrays a figure of maternal pre-eminence, a funerary goddess watching over the life and death of her soldiers. Long after, in the years just before the birth of Christ, the society of hierarchy and aristocracy that had evolved at that time also embraced the power of female divinity, enshrined in the alabaster statue of the Goddess of Galera created in the East around the seventh century BC but buried in the province of Granada with funerary goods as a prestigious sacred object. For a duration of 3,500 years, before the coming of Roman society and then of Christianity, the guardian spirits of the place where Granada would be founded were female.

The association of Granada with the female emerged again much later, in the reign of the Muslim dynasty of the Nasrids, when the fourteenth-century court poet Ibn Zamrak saw the feminine face of Granada, which he symbolized as a bride bejewelled with bright flowers and the dew. A century later, the Castilian ballad *Abenámar* recounts how the Christian king John II came with his army in sight of the city and marvelled at its beauty. To him too, it symbolized the female, again as a potential bride who might be wooed by his offer of marriage, and to be sure, the elegant grace and beauty of the interior of the Alhambra was a far cry from the severe, martial demeanour of the castles of Spain. Granada is a city where scale is crucial. Its proportions are not overwhelming, megalithic and military, like Rome's Colosseum, nor does it have vast public spaces which dwarf its inhabitants, like Moscow's Red Square. Granada is built on a human scale, which favours the domestic setting, the traditional domain of women. Even the Alhambra, on the outside a fortress, is transformed on the inside into a sequence of exquisite spaces for private living. In contemporary times, Juan Moreno Aguado's monument to Sultan Boabdil, unveiled on 2 January 1997 in the small park near the Paseo del Violón, set amid towering blocks of flats, marks the place Boabdil handed the keys of the city to King Ferdinand in 1492. It consists of two bronze statues, one of the sultan and another of a young woman handing him a rose as a symbol of love and in hope of forgiveness. This poignant female figure represents Granada and is the latest incarnation of the city as a woman. Yet that spirit of the feminine that haunts the place did not prevail in the cavalcade of communities inhabiting the city since the birth of Christ, Roman, Visigothic, Muslim and Catholic. All were patriarchal societies that tended to suppress and marginalize women, and the history of Granada is mainly the history of men, whether soldiers, rulers, intellectuals, artists, politicians or religious figures. Yet as if inspired by the early divinities of the place, an unexpected number of Granadan women have stepped out of the shadows of patriarchy to exert a memorable influence on the culture, politics and religious life of the city.

Nazhun Bini al-Qala I al-Garnatiyya was Granada's first woman poet and although we do not know the exact dates of her birth and death, we can surmise that she was born sometime in the second half of the eleventh century. There are stories that she was low-born, even a slave, but it is more likely that she came from a family of high rank and it has been suggested that she was possibly the daughter of Abu Bakr, the governor of Granada, himself a poet and man of learning. But as Abu Bakr was born in 1091, this cannot be true because we know Nazhun had met the great poet al-Mahkzumi, who died in 1070. Nazhun had a good education, possibly at court, showed special skill in Arabic rhetoric and a great flair for writing poetry. At the time, Granada had become the capital of Muslim Spain, where poets were highly respected and had a privileged place in society, and in contrast with the Christian states north of Andalusia, female poets were not unusual. Anthologies and historical works in Arabic written in the twelfth century by authors such as the Andalusian poet and historian Ibn Bassam, who died in 1147, and later accounts by the great historian al-Maqqari among others, give us information about the famous women of Andalusia in the eleventh and twelfth centuries. Al-Maqqari even includes a special section on women poets.[176]

Nazhun was a match for many male poets with her mischievous wit and inventiveness, and she often got the better of them, trading obscenities or sexual innuendo without inhibition. The Arab historian Ibn al Khatib relates an anecdote about the day the famous and forbidding blind poet al-Makhzumi visited the Almohad governor of Granada, Ibn Said, in his palace.[177] Nazhun was present at the gathering and intentionally tried to provoke the old poet by asking him in verse how a man raised among the goats and sheep of a tiny village could possibly appreciate the music and fine wine of the Granadan court. Al-Makhzumi accused her of being a whore, an insult she fielded by challenging him to decide which of them was the better poet because, she said, 'Although I am a woman by nature, my poetry is masculine.' The rhymed insults continued until the governor intervened and smoothed things over. Nazhun was brave and unabashed in her verbal attack on a man who was feared even by the governor, and her attitude contradicted expectations of female behaviour at that time. On another occasion she caused an uproar when the most celebrated poet in all Andalusia, Ibn Quzman, visited Granada and met a group of other poets including Nazhun in some local gardens in La Zubia. The great bard arrived dressed in yellow and Nazhun, clearly unimpressed by the poetic genius, at once mocked his clothes, likening him to the golden calf of the Israelites. It was a piece of banter that ended up with Ibn Quzman getting a ducking in the nearby pond, which obliged him to change into some less flashy clothes.

Another equally celebrated woman poet also lived in Granada, in the twelfth century a bit later than Nazhun. Her name was Hafsa bint al-Hayy al-Rakuniyya, who was born into a rich Berber family around 1135. Granada was in turmoil as the Almoravids fell from power and were replaced by the Almohad caliphate, but as she grew up, Hafsa seemed untouched by the upheaval all around her. She was given a special education at the new court, where she flourished and shone intellectually, becoming a teacher herself. But her success marked the start of her misfortune in a cruel transition from joy to tragedy as the ecstasies and sorrows of love expressed in her poetry came to dominate the reality of her life. Around 1154 at court she met and fell in love with another young poet, Abu Yafar, well known among the Granadans. His family were descended from the illustrious Banu Said clan and his father was pre-eminent in Almoravid Spain. The family castle was at Alcalá la Real, on the border between Granada and Castile, where Abu Yafar was taught by the foremost sages of the time and developed such a passion for poetry that he forsook an important political career in its favour. Before long he was named the Poet of al-Andalus and became private secretary to the new governor of Granada, Abu Said, son of the caliph.

Hafsa Bint and Abu Yafar were probably the most famous couple in Andalusia at that time, and their verses to each other have stood the test of time. It seems Hafsa often took the initiative in their affair, as this poem shows:

> Shall I visit you or shall you visit me? For my heart always
> bows to what you long for;
> My mouth is a source of clear, sweet water, and the hair of
> my head is a leafy shade.
> I hoped you were thirsty and struck by the sun, when the
> noon hour would bring me to you.

Yet a major problem arose when Abu Said also fell for Hafsa, creating a love triangle whose tensions she tried to contain. But in the end, Abu Yafar succumbed to his jealousy of her friendliness with the governor, and made the fatal mistake of rebelling. His personal rebellion coincided with another, greater revolt, between the Jewish and Mozarabic populations of the city, who lived on the Alhambra hill, and the Almohads, who were in the Albaicín. Abu Yafar sided with the Jews and Mozarabs against the governor of Granada's father, but he was detained and imprisoned. Abu Said never won Hafsa's love – he had Abu Yafar executed in 1163, upon which Hafsa dressed in mourning like a widow and left the court forever. She composed elegies to her dead lover and before long left for Marrakech, where she became the tutor of the Caliph's daughters. Hafsa died in Marrakech over twenty-five years later, in 1191. Around sixty lines of her verse survive, in nineteen poems that included beautiful love poetry, elegies, satires and even obscene verse, in all of which she lives on as the most celebrated woman poet of medieval Andalusia.

During the seven centuries of Muslim rule in Spain, 116 highly educated Andalusian women are recorded, not all of whom were poets, although forty-four wrote verse. Some were copyists, secretaries, lexicographers and grammarians. The wife of a fourteenth-century *qadi* from Loja in Granada province was known for her outstanding legal knowledge. The social and religious context of the lives of these women highlights their uniqueness, since the patriarchal structure of medieval Islam confined women to the family environment, and involvement in political events was against the law. Any political activity undertaken by women was labelled 'court intrigue', a dismissive phrase aimed to remove women from the political scene. Women at court usually had a decorative role, evoked vividly by the fourteenth-century vizier Ibn Khatib, who complained that Andalusian women went 'to extremes in adornment and colourful clothing, competing so much in the use of embroideries and brocades, and in the ostentation of their various garments, that it becomes licentious'.[178]

Written records of Muslim Granada refer almost exclusively to upper-class aristocratic women, the wives, concubines, mothers, daughters and other family members of the Muslim rulers, who were mentioned by name. Women of the royal court could own property, which gave them a degree of agency. In late fifteenth-century Granada, the real estate owned by female royalty came sharply into focus in the final decades of Muslim rule as a vital aspect of the power struggles within the Nasrid family itself, and between the Nasrids and their Christian conquerors. High up in the Albaicín, concealed amid a maze of winding, narrow alleys, the recently refurbished Dar al-Horra Palace, the Home of the Honest Woman, opens its doors to reveal a secluded, tranquil *carmen* with remarkable panoramic views over the west of the city and over the Alhambra itself. Built in Nasrid style, it has an intimate central patio with a fountain, and its viewing points have uplifting words like 'blessing', 'happiness' and 'health is life' carved into their plasterwork in Arabic. Originally it was part of a large estate with orchards and gardens, and the Honest Woman it is named after was the Sultana Aixa, mother of Boabdil and legitimate wife of the emir Abu l'Hasan. The palace was specially built for her to move into when she left the Alhambra to distance herself from the intolerable situation she found herself in when her husband rejected her for the Christian captive Isabel de Solís. From her vantage point opposite the Alhambra, she could act independently and also keep an eye on comings and goings in the seat of power.

These properties became important assets for Boabdil's family after the conquest of the city in 1492. Ferdinand and Isabella's royal secretary, the powerful and astute Hernando de Zafra, wrote a letter to the monarchs in September 1492, disclosing that he had used all his cunning to contrive Boabdil's departure into exile in north Africa, and that he, his mother, sister and wife were all selling their remaining inherited lands as fast as they could to provide money for their new lives. This was not a decision taken lightly but their property was soon snapped up, presumably for a good price, by purchasers who ignored the preferential right to this property of Ferdinand and Isabella agreed in the terms of surrender. In retaliation, the royal pair intervened and confiscated the property, which is how a great deal of ancient Nasrid lands came under Christian royal ownership.

Aixa owned other property as well as Dar al-Horra, including land in the regions of Beas and Huétor Santillán, now a national park zone, where her son Boabdil's wife Moraima also had estates, and some of the original documents of sale still exist. The Archive of the Royal Chancellery in Granada holds the translation into Spanish of a document of sale in Arabic by one Mohammed de Mora from the town of Santa Fe, dated 31 December 1493, two months after Boabdil and his family had sailed into exile.[179] It concerns the sale on behalf of the Sultana Aixa of one of her properties, a farmhouse in the village of Cijuela in the *vega*, along with grazing land, the tower of Mocatín and its copse, other houses and extensive areas of land including a stream, a lake and plots of arable land. It was clearly a substantial estate and was sold to the powerful aristocratic governor of Santa Fe, Francisco de Bobadilla. Today Cijuela is proud of its Nasrid heritage; it has a population of over 3,000 people, complete with its lake and tower, and its fertile land is still irrigated by the original Arab water channels. The sale was an evident case of acquiring Nasrid property to give to Christian nobles and others faithful to the Catholic monarchy, to compensate them for their part in the Granada war. The bill of sale does not mention the amount Aixa received for her land but we do know that in another transaction a local man, Juan de Haro, paid 1,000 gold doubloons as well as cloth and silk worth 150,000 maravedis for the farmstead of Huete owned by Boabdil's daughter. In the end, Juan de Haro lost his money, as Hernando de Zafra confiscated the property, which happened to end up in his own hands, by fair means or foul.

Aixa's political power and economic clout as a Nasrid princess was unprecedented in the history not only of the dynasty but also of Muslim Spain, although it did not match the supremacy and influence of her Catholic counterpart, the great Queen Isabella of Castile. Even more surprising than Aixa's authority was the rise to royal dominion of the Christian captive Isabel de Solís, who appeared in Chapter 4. Known as *la Romía,* meaning an apostate Christian, she bewitched the emir Abu l'Hasan, Boabdil's father, who abandoned Aixa and installed Isabel in the Dar al-Horra palace before Aixa took it over, until he decided to live with her in the Alhambra as his queen, when she took the Arabic name Zoraya. Archival evidence shows that her elevated status as the favourite wife of the sultan had significant repercussions on her life after the death of Abu l'Hasan. A young girl of an alien faith and modest background, Zoraya acquired a remarkable amount of property in Granada after her two sons had been born into the royal line. From an Arab document dated December 1476 we know that the sultan granted her legal ownership of an estate in the district of Godco in the Alpujarras. He made it clear that he was giving it to her 'as the mother of his son', the prince Sa'd, and when Sa'd's brother was born in 1478, his mother received more gifts from the royal treasury as her own property.

When an inquiry was held in 1506 to establish the exact whereabouts of the lands she had once owned, several elderly Islamic jurists who had previous dealings with the royal household were questioned and made it clear that she possessed a large amount of property. One witness even testified that the discord in the royal family was intensified by the fact that Abu l'Hasan gave so much of what he had inherited and owned to Zoraya. When the sultan and his brother Muhammad el Zagal acquired a large inheritance from an aunt in 1483, Abu l'Hasan immediately passed on his share to his and Zoraya's sons, instead of to his rightful heirs, the children he had with Aixa. When in 1489 Boabdil finally got the better of his uncle, who retired to be a lord in the Alpujarras before his final disappearance into exile, Zoraya and her two sons were with El Zagal, who endowed them lavishly from his new estates. After the fall of Granada in 1492, Zoraya, still a Muslim, was living in Cordoba, while Ferdinand and Isabella took her two sons under their wing and had them baptised at Santa Fe in April of that year, and carefully educated at the Christian royal court. By 1501 Zoraya, who had reverted to her original name of Isabella and to the Catholic faith, was herself living in Seville, where the Catholic Monarchs provided for her material needs in the form of an annual pension of 150,000 maravedis after her re-baptism.

But Isabella of Granada (as she was then known) had no luck in recovering the property she owned that had fallen into the hands of Queen Isabella of Castile, despite her legal efforts to do so. In the 1506 inquiry Isabella/Zoraya stated that she and her sons had lost the Dar al-Horra mansion, which the Queen converted into the Monastery of Santa Isabel la Real before it became state property in the twentieth century. She also lost another house in the Alcazaba Cadima, along with an old granary used as a pottery in the Realejo district. Yet she still had about ten rural estates of different kinds, in the *vega*, and in the area known as Quempe, as well as in the north of Granada. A legal document dated 1510 also shows that she owned a shop in the parish of Santa María (Saint Mary), close to the dye works belonging to her sons in the Zacatín.[180] Isabella would have had some rents from these properties, giving her a degree of financial independence, and supplementing the pension she already had from Christian royal coffers. Her story is an astonishing one, starting with the terrifying ordeal of her capture by Muslim troops and her unlikely rise to favour and fame as a Muslim queen and renegade Christian. She survived after the death of her husband the sultan and played an active part in the tense final days of Muslim Granada, only to turn back to Christianity and end up as a woman with substantial real estate, her two sons marrying into the Castilian aristocracy. Isabella de Solís was at the heart of a love affair that some have likened to the one between King Roderic and La Cava that was blamed for the Muslim invasion of 711.[181] Both love stories create a certain symmetry between the start and end of Muslim rule in Spain, but the extent to which Isabella of Granada could be held to account for the fall of the city to the Christians is arguable, although her presence certainly precipitated the discord in the Nasrid family that marred the last ten years of its reign. Even so, unlike her namesake, Isabella of Castile, she died on a date forgotten – no historical record of Isabella of Granada remains after 1510.

NUNS, NECROMANCERS AND PERFORMERS

The aura of female divinity that enfolded Granada from primitive times found a new manifestation in the Catholic incarnation of the city as the birthplace of devotion to the Immaculate Conception of the Virgin Mary. Holy, mysterious and equivocal, the Immaculate Conception was a highly contentious issue that had come into focus in the early 1200s, when Saint Bernard of Clairvaux and, later, Thomas Aquinas were early opponents of the idea, while the theologian Duns Scotus and the Franciscan Order supported it, to the extent that it was known as 'Franciscan' doctrine. The issue centred upon whether Mary, mother of Jesus, had been born without sin, in other words without the intervention of man, a controversy that coloured the religious life of Granada in the late sixteenth century, where the record of its vexed blend of polemics and veneration is preserved for posterity in stone. If you walk down from the Hospital Real towards the Puerta de Elvira in the city of Granada, you will see a towering monument fifty to sixty feet high in the Plaza del Triunfo, an elegant pillar standing on a plinth with two tiers sculpted by the Granadan Alonso de Mena. The pillar has an elaborately decorated capital stone upon which a statue of the Virgin Immaculate (*Virgen del Triunfo*) stands, the crescent moon at her feet and a reliquary below her hands containing a piece of the True Cross given to the Jesuits of Granada by the Vatican's Cardinal Baronius. Around the base, carved angels hold banners inscribed with the words '*Maria concebido sin pecado original*' ('Mary conceived without original sin'). The plinth above shows a coat of arms and three carved figures, and the column itself is carved and gilded and records the thirty-two attributes of the Virgin. It is splendid and imposing, a pioneer work of its kind in Spain[182] and a paradigm of the Baroque in Western Christendom, echoing the monumental commemorative columns of Classical Rome, such as the Column of Trajan. The casual viewer would never suspect that it was anything but a fine memorial to the purity of the Virgin Mary – but it was involved in an extraordinary dispute during which the inscriptions on the base invoked the wrath of members of the Inquisition, who demanded their removal.

It all began over four hundred years ago, soon after Archbishop Pedro de Castro had moved to Seville to take up the See in 1610, leaving his beloved Lead Books behind. In those remarkable documents, the Virgin Mary is the voice of prophecy and authority, and she remains a central figure in both Christianity and Islam. When the archbishop departed from Granada, the Catholic Church in Spain was involved in a heated debate over whether the Immaculate Conception could be deemed indisputable. Pedro de Castro had taken to promoting the idea that the Lead Books contained references to her Immaculate Conception, upon which authority it could be established as the belief of the apostles. If the Lead Books were genuine, he suggested, then they contained doctrinal proof of enormous theological importance throughout the Christian world. In other words, they would be essential Scriptures. There was great popular support for the official recognition of the Immaculate Conception and it was hoped that the Pope would confirm it as an article of belief. By the sixteenth century it was already forbidden to oppose the doctrine as heresy but it still had opponents in Rome.

Castro's translators told him that the Lead Books were clear on the matter and that the first book, *The Fundamentals of the Faith*, stated explicitly that Mary was created without original sin. The Archbishop, who was deeply devoted to the Virgin, made the Sacromonte the home of this theological mystery. The white marble foundation stone of the Abbey was inscribed in Arabic: 'Mary was untouched by original sin', a phrase also etched on his personal seal, along with the Seal of Solomon from the Lead Books. It appeared to be an ironic, even provocative move to present a Catholic doctrine in the language of Islam and of the lead texts, in particular when the Pope had ordered the archbishop not to publish or refer to the contents of the Lead Books in any form.

The erection of the monument to the Virgen in the Plaza del Triunfo in September 1621 went one step too far, and it was the inscriptions that caused the trouble. The one on the south side was fairly innocuous, although it commemorated Granada's clear oath of allegiance to the doctrine of the Immaculate Conception and honoured the birth of the heir to the throne, Prince Baltasar Carlos, in 1609. But the one on the north face recounted the Lead

Books' version of Saint James's life in Spain, stating that Saint James asserted in his books and preached in Spain that Mary was untainted by original sin. Above the inscription is the figure of Saint James the Moor-slayer (*Santiago matamoros*) on horseback, with the corpses of Moors at his feet. It is a telling image that the people of Granada contemplated after the final expulsion of the Moriscos in 1609, and still contemplate today.

The inscription on the east face related how the Arab Saint Thesiphon, born blind and miraculously healed by Christ, also stated that the Virgin Mary was untainted by original sin, while the fourth inscription to the west shows the history of his brother Cecilius, who likewise declared his belief in the Immaculate Conception of Mary in his books. A carving of him carrying two of those books from the Sacromonte stands above the inscription. The monument was blatantly a symbol of Baroque Granada's devotion to the mystery of the Immaculate Conception, but also to the Lead Books, and the flagrant espousal of their cause proved too much for certain members of the Holy Office. The Inquisition in Granada ordered any further work on the monument to stop at once. The ban angered its sponsors and the apologists of the Lead Books. The city finally appealed to the king, who in an act of rebellion against the Church, decreed that the inscriptions should be completed. So, the monument remains as the first ever memorial to the Immaculate Conception of the Virgin, and the Abbey of the Sacromonte stands as a shrine to the belief in her conception without sin, a cause embraced passionately by its founder Archbishop Castro, which Granada continues to celebrate each year on 8 December.

Granada's wholehearted devotion to the Virgin was a powerful element in the new Christian identity of the city adopted after 1492, when the pure air of Catholic piety had attracted so many religious orders that convent life set the tone of the place. Inspired by the very first hermits on Mount Carmel, the visionary Saint Teresa of Avila and the priest Saint John of the Cross founded the Order of the Discalced, or barefoot, Carmelites in the mid-sixteenth century, and in 1582, Teresa sent one of her nuns, Ana de Jesús, to Granada to found a Carmelite convent there, at first with just six nuns in a small dwelling house. Saint John of the Cross acquired the fine but crumbling mansion that had belonged to the family of Ferdinand and Isabella's Gran Capitán, Gonzalo Fernández de Córdoba, in the Realejo district. There, a young woman called Luisa Granada Altamirano took her vows in 1598. She was born around 1570 into an eminent family, her father a descendant of Nasrid royalty who became Christians and started the renowned Granada Venegas family line. Luisa had a clear religious vocation and took the name Luisa de San José, choosing the Discalced Carmelite order because of its harsh austerity, which matched the new spirit of the Church in Spain. She rose to become Mother Superior but while there was holiness in abundance, money proved in short supply to finish the building work needed. Trusting in God's mercy, she had the first stone laid in August 1618 but when the work was complete there were no funds to pay the bill, as the worried nuns reminded their superior. Luisa seemed unconcerned and, as if miraculously, a letter arrived from an acquaintance in Madrid donating the amount needed.

Luisa had prophetic visions that could often foretell the future accurately, and her reputation reached the Court and the remotest parts of Spain. Politicians sought her out for advice and help, both religious and worldly. She died in her late sixties, after forty days of acute pain and lying on hard planks, on 24 August 1638. It may seem a great paradox that a woman of Morisco, even Nasrid, ancestry, who grew up as the Morisco expulsion was looming on the horizon in 1609, became a devout Catholic nun but it was not a unique situation. By the time of her death, many former Muslim families had become fully assimilated into the life of Christian Granada.

Convent life was oddly a kind of liberation for certain women. While often it provided an occupation for women whose families had no dowry to enable them to marry, or offered a place of refuge from the world, some found it a haven where they could read, write, assume responsibilities and be free from patriarchal oppression. It was in the cloister that the first known Granadan woman to write her autobiography put pen to paper. María Gertrudis Martinez del Hoyo Tellado came into the world in September 1750 as a frail, sickly child with a shy, reserved nature and a vivid imagination. She disliked childhood games and was taught to read by her brother's tutor. Devotional books took her fancy early on, and a clear religious vocation, which she recalls began at the age of six, led her to enter the Franciscan convent of the Conception in the Albaicín, up a steep slope near the River Darro,[183] when she was seventeen. Three years before, her father had died, which left her inconsolable and her family with money problems, so that when María finally took the veil as María Gertrudis del Corazón de Jesús in April 1770, she was joined by her elder sister Micaela. Her widowed mother Leonor joined them shortly after in 1771 but her presence created work and suffering for María, despite her devotion to her.

María had a bad time at first – she was often ill as well as suffering psychologically, which made her feel a burden to the community. She began to have visions of Jesus, mystical experiences that were viewed sceptically by her sisters. These encounters became frequent and intense and were her only consolation amid her constant physical suffering and difficulties. She was appointed sacristan of the convent, which gave her the chance to meet the preacher Father Diego José de Cádiz during Lent 1779, who was in Granada to combat what he saw as the evils of eighteenth-century rationalism. After an intense and frequent exchange of letters, María became Father Diego's spiritual advisor.

Her own confessor, Father Alcober e Higueras, abbot of the Collegiate Church of the Saviour in the city, encouraged her to write her autobiography to ease her feelings. It is this work, the *Vida* (*Life*) that gives us direct access to María's innermost experiences.

Father Alcober also gave a clear description of her appearance, 'tall, naturally graceful and modest in bearing, with black hair, large, lively, black eyes, a straight nose and thin lips', which matches her only existing portrait (hanging in the Monastery of the Conception) in which she is wearing her nun's habit. María's spiritual communications with God became more frequent and subtle, and in her own words: 'I spoke to the Lord more easily than I do to my sister.'[184] She tells us that a wound in her side opened up, as her body began to show the stigmata, especially during Lent, and several times she was on the point of death due to the severity of her pain and mortification. But María finally foresaw the day of her demise in a vision and passed away shortly after, on 13 January 1801, aged fifty-one, after thirty years of devotion to the religious life. A copy of her autobiography, including the last notes on her final illness and death added by her confessor, is kept at the Monastery of the Conception in Granada, where she was buried in the cloister.

María was not the only woman writer of her ilk in Granada. Sister Ana de San Jerónimo, born as Ana Verdugo de Castilla in 1696, spent most of her life in the city, where she was something of a prodigy, learning Greek, Latin, Spanish and Italian from her father, a man of great humanist culture who gave her an education rare for women of her time. She was also an accomplished painter and poet but felt compelled to follow the religious life in the Convent of the Guardian Angel in Granada, against her parents' wishes. Ana died in 1771 and left a body of poems of considerable importance, as well as two theatrical works. The most exceptional female writer of eighteenth-century Granada was María Josefa de Hermida Maldonado y Marín, born in 1796 in the city. She wrote a book on how to listen to Mass with true devotion, translated from a French original. What is astonishing is that she produced this seventy-five-page translation at the age of seven years old.

As the holy women of Granada enriched and elevated the cultural life of the city with their blend of the mystic and the literary, outside the tranquil security of the convent, unholy women walked on the wild side of urban life. The Granada tribunal of the Inquisition was one of the most active in Spain and its records open a window onto a dark underworld of sorcery and witchcraft populated by women, sometimes gypsies, but often ancestors of Moriscos or Jews, impoverished women on the margins of society who learned to live by their wits. They trod a no man's land between legitimacy and transgression, where sorceresses, *hechiceras*, used white magic for healing, affairs of the heart and money, while witches, *brujas*, attended black Mass, covens and sabbaths, made a pact with the Devil and denied Christianity. In 1593 a prostitute in Granada of mixed race named Isabel de los Reyes dropped a small bag containing strange objects, including a piece of the altar stone stolen from a church, that contained the relics of two saintly martyrs. Someone denounced her to the Inquisition and she confessed that she carried the amulet to protect herself from ill-treatment by her customers.

The reputation of Mariana de Escabias y Valvivia, who was twenty-three and lived in Granada with her mother in the 1660s, was less innocuous. Nearly thirty separate witnesses accused her of casting evil spells and producing illnesses in others, and she was arrested by the Inquisition in 1664 for helping two Frenchmen to hunt for treasure. The inquisitorial account describes how she made candles using the blood of snakes and bugs, and slit the throat of a black hen over the supposed treasure site – to no avail for all they found was a saucepan containing a few old bones. More successful was María de Orta, one of the most prolific magic-makers in the district of Granada, whose trial began in 1734 for blasphemous spell-making. Like other witches and enchantresses, ritual sites such as churches, cemeteries and crossing points were the scenarios for her magic, and she ensnared her customers in the street, at inns and markets, as well as in prisons. María made out she was very repentant, as the Devil had deceived her, and she was given a caution and penances. In 1744 she was tried again for similar offences, confessed fully and was again given penances, so that her knack of evading the full wrath of the Inquisition on a number of occasions made her very powerful in the eyes of society. The most horrifying case of witchcraft in the province of Granada took place in November 1752, when Antonia Guillén murdered a child and used his blood as a sacrificial offering. The Inquisitor's account of this dreadful deed contains the most gruesome details, corroborated by several witnesses, yet bizarrely, the death was designated as the result of a superstitious spell and Antonia Guillén was merely ordered to wear the *sambenito*[185] and sent to prison for eight years. These recorded cases of sorcery and witchcraft among Granadan women spanning a period of one hundred and fifty years bear witness to the performance of the black arts as a form of female resistance to religious, social and cultural conditions, as a weapon that could be used in everyday life to override the dictates of patriarchal Catholicism and lend power and agency to its practitioners. That resistance invoked pagan, diabolical superstition, light years away from the erudition and sacred spirituality of Granada's saintly Sisters, yet together they fortified the warp and weft of the intricate tapestry of women's history in the city.

Other Granadan women claimed the limelight in a different kind of performance. In the 1600s and 1700s the region made an important contribution to the theatrical arts, with local actresses at the forefront. Heading the cast of Granadan leading ladies was Fabiana Laura, who took to the stage in the mid-seventeenth century at a time when it was hard for women to work in the theatre, which was seen as a lower-class profession akin to the medieval minstrel. The anonymous work *Dialogues on the Plays* (*Diálogos de las comedias*) of 1641 described actors as lustful and vice-ridden. In the time of the great dramatist Lope de Vega (1562–1635), theatre became the rage but women could not appear on stage until 1587, when they were authorized to dance and sing. Fabiana came from a good family – her father was a doctor in the San Matías district – but her parents turned their backs on her and she went to live with an aunt, who encouraged her fondness for classical poetry. Ignoring the wishes of her friends and family, she fled in secret to Motril, where she began acting in second-rate companies and married a Galician actor, Miguel Bermúdez de Castro.

Fabiana grew famous and played all over Spain, Italy and France. She was the first lady in the *autos sacramentales*, the dramatic religious allegories of the playwright Calderón de la Barca, and also directed her own theatre company, which put on many plays in Madrid in the 1660s to 1690s. But her private life fell apart when she discovered that her husband was having an affair with a comic actress in Seville, which ended with a duel and the annulment of her marriage. At the height of her fame, Fabiana decided to leave the theatre. She longed to return to Granada for some peace but when she arrived, her cruel relatives shut the door in her face. Applauded by kings, adored by the aristocracy, she was rejected by those closest to her. Deeply wounded, she returned to Madrid, where she died in 1698. In the modern district of Rosaleda to the north of Granada, there is a street named after this exceptional woman.

Even more novelesque was the life of María Antonia Fernández, known as 'La Caramba'. Born in Granada in 1751 into a family of actors, she performed from childhood in plays and made her debut in Cádiz, a theatre hotspot of the time. Within a decade she was one of the favourite actresses of the Madrid public, a woman whose extravagant character matched her acting. Stunningly beautiful, brazen and voluptuous, she attracted a small court of male admirers who vied for her favours and worsened her vanity. In 1781, while acting at the Prince Theatre in Madrid, she accepted the proposal of a French admirer, Augustin Sauminique, and – ignoring his parents' strong disapproval – they were married in secret. Soon Augustin realized his mistake and the marriage fell through. María Antonia was not going to relinquish all she had achieved and she was given an ecstatic welcome on her return to the boards. She became an addict of fashion, wearing garments, jewels and lace of proverbial luxury and exquisiteness. Her evening strolls in the Prado in Madrid attracted gazes of admiration, envy and disdain as women vied to imitate her style.

One evening in September 1785, as María Antonia was taking her stroll, a sudden storm forced her to run for shelter to the convent of the Capuchins in the Carrera de San Jerónimo. As she entered the shadowy, half-empty church, a priest was speaking in the pulpit and she experienced a life-changing moment. Spain's most admired actress abandoned the theatre overnight, sold her jewels and shared the proceeds among the poor. Silk and lace were swapped for a hair shirt but penitence and privation brought her life to a premature end in June 1787. 'La Caramba' lies buried in the church of San Sebastian in the capital, far from her native city.

Beneath the patriarchal gaze of Catholic society, the women of post-1492 Granada asserted themselves by means pious and pagan, through learning, literature and religious devotion, alongside public entertainment and the magical arts. In seclusion, in the public eye and on the margins, from the sixteenth to the eighteenth centuries they sought means of independent action that gave them new-found status and authority in Granada's urban life and culture.

Modern heroines: politics, tyranny and regeneration

The winds of change were blowing in Granada at the start of the nineteenth century. Liberal thinkers clashed with right-wing Conservatives against a backdrop of French occupation during the Peninsular War, and the resulting conflict and revolution led to the Spanish Constitution of 1812, a landmark in European liberalism. But when the absolutist Bourbon king Ferdinand VII returned to the throne in 1814, the constitution was revoked and all liberals were hunted down and persecuted. In this tense political climate, Eugenia de Montijo was born in a house in Calle de la Gracia in Granada in May 1826. When she was still a child, she met an old gypsy from the Sacromonte, who told her mother 'this girl will be more than a queen'. Little did her mother suspect that the prophecy would come true. As she grew older, Eugenia absorbed the liberal thinking that was normal in her family – her uncle, the Count of Montijo, whose name she inherited, was governor of Granada at the start of the century and led an important masonic lodge in the city. As a result of her inheritance when her uncle died, Eugenia enjoyed the refined education of a noblewoman in Madrid, Paris and London, returning to Paris to get over the traumatic wedding of her sister Francisca to the Duke of Alba, with whom she herself was in love. Once back in the French capital, Eugenia threw herself into social life and became the talk of the salons. Her mother wrote to Francisca that 'Eugenia was in fashion' and before long Louis Napoleon was enchanted by her too. In his youth a Romantic revolutionary, he was France's first president and its last monarch as Emperor of the French.

Their imperial wedding took place on 30 January 1853 in Notre Dame de Paris, and the Empress Eugenia was sent a congratulatory poem by the citizens of Granada. A son was born to them, despite the Emperor's philandering and Eugenia's aversion to sexual contact with her husband, and soon cracks began to appear in their marriage. War with Prussia in 1870 and the constant illnesses of the Emperor obliged Eugenia to preside over a meeting of the council of ministers in the Tuileries at dawn, where it is said she was the only man among them. Shortly after in 1873, Louis died in exile in London and Eugenia sought peace in a brief return to Granada. She died at the age of ninety-four in 1920 while on a trip to Madrid, and her final consolation was knowing France was victorious in the First World War.

Enriqueta Lozana was on the other side of the political divide from the Empress Eugenia. The daughter of an infantry officer, she was born in Granada in 1829 and by the age of eight had lost both her mother and stepmother, while her father was disabled by war wounds. At seven, like Eugenia she started her education at the Santo Domingo religious house where she learned grammar, geography, history, arithmetic and natural sciences. She had a prodigious talent and appetite for learning and published her first collection of poetry in 1846, playing the lead role in her own play *An actress for love* (*Una actriz por amor*) the following year when she was eighteen. Enriqueta had a love affair with the writer Pedro de Alarcón but his atheism and her intense Catholicism proved unreconcilable. She married Antonio Vílchez when she was thirty and bore twelve children, of whom only three survived.

Her literary fecundity was even greater. Known as the Sappho of Granada, Enriqueta wrote over 200 works, all with a religious basis or a Catholic moral, in virtually every literary form including novels, stories, legends, poetry, drama, biography, essays, letters and opera librettos. She also wrote regularly for local, regional and national periodicals, including the *Defensor de Granada*, and her complete works were published in three volumes in Granada between 1865 and 1867. Her work is inevitably limited by its moralizing dimension, and often very sentimental in true Romantic style, yet she won an extraordinary number of prizes for her writing in Granada and nationally. Enriqueta stands out as a truly exceptional Granadan woman of renowned literary stature, who held firm to her Catholic convictions amid the strong anticlericalism of her time. Despite her success, she died in 1895 aged sixty-five in dire financial straits.

Granada had about 55,000 inhabitants in the early nineteenth century and was still strongly Muslim in its structure, despite its Catholic makeover. The River Darro ran through the city, its bridges linking the honeycomb of small unhygienic streets and squares where epidemics broke out to a degree that, in 1804, the sanitary authorities enforced burials outside the city walls. Granada was rocked by the rhythmic sound of its water, the heartbeat of the city; on the outside it was a quiet, cloistered place with an acute religious spirit. History seemed to repeat itself because beneath the surface, as it had in Morisco times, the city once again hid its secret societies, free-thinking circles, masonic lodges and radical groups such as the *Confederacion de Comuneros*, the Confederation of Libertarians, which upheld Spanish liberty against the repressive monarchy. The throttling of liberalism was the crucial factor in the life of Granada's greatest heroine, Mariana Pineda, whose story is both inspiring and tragic.

Mariana was born in September 1804, the illegitimate daughter of a ship's captain of the royal fleet, Mariano Pineda, who fell in love with one of his maidservants, María Dolores Muñoz. When Mariana was two weeks old, her mother fled to marry a man who was a prisoner on bail, and her father demanded the immediate return of his daughter by the authorities, who finally placed her in his charge in November 1805. The soap opera of her infancy had only just begun, as her father died two months later and she was his sole heir. It seemed like good fortune when her uncle, José Pineda, who lived in his parents' fine house in the Carrera del Darro, with ten servants, became Mariana's guardian. But when José himself married in 1807, his new wife not only forced him to relinquish the guardianship of his niece but managed to appropriate her inheritance. Poor Mariana was given up for adoption by a couple of young prosperous traders, José de Mesa and Úrsula de Presa, who gave her a stable home at last and saw to her education.

The spectres of pain and tragedy were fated to stalk Mariana. At fourteen she was engaged to a low-ranking soldier, Manuel de Peralta y Valte from Huéscar, eleven years her senior. They married in October 1819 in the parish church of Santa Ana, when Mariana was evidently three months pregnant. A son, José María, was born in 1820, followed by a daughter, Úrsula María, named after her adoptive mother, two years later. Only months later, in April 1822, her husband died, leaving her a widow with two small children at eighteen.

Meanwhile, revolution had broken out. When the War of

Independence between Napoleon Bonaparte and Spain erupted in 1808, the uprising against the French invaders was led by a provincial council in Granada, the western headquarters. The Granadan army scored the first, most resounding victory in July of that year, keeping the French at bay in Andalusia until the occupation of the city by General Sebastiani in 1810. But the tyrant King Ferdinand VII was reinstated in 1813 and the ferocious repression of liberals began. Ramón Pedrosa y Andrade, a fanatical, intolerant royalist, was appointed criminal magistrate at the Royal Chancellery in Granada. He soon rooted out a lodge of seven Masons in a *carmen* near the Alhambra, who were arrested in the middle of an initiation ceremony. Without even time to remove their ceremonial aprons, they were marched to prison and executed.

Mariana Pineda began to play a dangerous game. A number of liberal anarchists were being held in Gibraltar, with whom she corresponded using false names. The revolutionary Romero Tejado, in jail in Malaga, let slip that she was highly thought of by the anarchists for services rendered, upon which the police put her under surveillance and caught her servant José Burel taking letters to the post office. Mariana's house was searched and evidence found of her contact with the convicts, and she was kept under house arrest for some time. Political prisoners were held in the jail inside the Chancellery, whose entrance was in Calle Cárcel Alta (Upper Prison Street). The liberal priest Pedro García, Mariana's uncle, ended up there, and as a relative she was allowed to visit him daily. She spoke in passing with other detainees, one of whom was a dangerous captive, Fernando Álvarez de Sotomayor, Mariana's cousin, linked to her romantically. Brave, enlightened, progressive, he was soon to be executed for his views. There would be no mercy and his only hope was to escape, with Mariana's help. She had a nun's outfit made as a disguise and smuggled it to Fernando, who donned it and walked straight through the main gate of the prison into freedom. Ramón Pedrosa, the magistrate, was convinced of the widow's complicity but failed to prove it.

Amidst the perilous political intrigues she was involved in, Mariana gave birth to her third child in January 1828, a girl, whom she gave away to the home for foundling babies since the father – a handsome doctor of law at the University of Granada – was engaged to a rich heiress and was not interested in the child, although he eventually acknowledged her in his will. Mariana was also hounded sexually by Ramón Pedrosa, then persecuted by him when his advances were rebuffed. The law finally caught up with her on account of a flag, which she had commissioned to be embroidered by two sisters in the Albaicín. The half-finished flag made of purple taffeta and bearing the words Freedom, Equality and Law, was delivered to Mariana's house in the Calle del Águila on the orders of Pedrosa, who had got wind of the compromising item. When his men arrived to confiscate the flag, Mariana and her mother were imprisoned in the convent of Santa María Egipcíaca. It was 27 March 1831.

No one came to save her, only Pedrosa, who offered her freedom in exchange for denouncing her accomplices but she remained obstinately loyal to her cause and kept silent. Mariana Pineda was tried behind closed doors for treason and condemned to death by garrotting on the scaffold on 26 May 1831. Three days before, she was transferred to the prison in Calle Cárcel Baja, where she remained serene. Her last concerns were for her children and she wrote a letter to her son asking him to be absolutely faithful to his political principles, look after his sister and not be ashamed of a mother who died on the scaffold. The letter never reached him, as Pedrosa confiscated it for expressing lofty ideas. An executioner arrived on the morning of 26 May and handed her the regulation black sackcloth shift and cap on a silver tray, then tied her hands with rope, after which she was led on a mule beneath black storm clouds to the Campo del Triunfo where the scaffold was mounted. Before she died, Mariana is recorded as saying: 'The memory of my execution will do more for our cause than all the flags in the world.'

Mariana Pineda's last words would be borne out, for she is

remembered in Granada and beyond for defending public liberties in exchange for her life. Public subscriptions raised the funds for her statue on a marble pedestal in the square in Granada named after her, and today the fateful purple flag is on show in the European Women's Centre opened in her old house in Calle del Águila, set up to honour her, unite women from different countries and fight for gender equality. Further afield, Mariana's name is written in gold letters in the session room of the European Parliament in Strasbourg, where there is a bust of her in the main entrance foyer that bears her name. She was immortalized in the only historical drama penned by her Granadan compatriot Federico García Lorca, entitled simply *Mariana Pineda*.

One hundred years later, violence and tragedy returned to Granada and the mere speaking of her name was banned. April 1931 had seen the proclamation of the Second Republic, a long-awaited liberal triumph which set in train cultural development and educational reform that included the liberation of women. New laws encouraged women's access to jobs in administration and State affairs, and their right to vote was approved in the 1931 Constitution. Yet in the 1930s, Granada remained ultra-conservative and resistant to change. The Civil War of 1936 turned back the clock and reinstated the repression of women, many of whom lost their lives merely for belonging to a trade union, a popular culture centre, a local socialist party or for attending a meeting or demonstration. Women threw themselves into the Civil War to fight against social regression, in fear that the laws benefitting their sex would be revoked.

In mid-August 1936, Agustina González López, the daughter of a cobbler, was taken from prison in Granada with several other women and transported in a lorry to Viznar, 10 kilometres from the city, then 'taken for a stroll', the euphemism used by Franco's Black Squad for 'death by firing squad'. Her crime was to be a writer whose subjects were feminism and liberal left-wing politics. She fought in public against hunger and poverty, attended demonstrations and even put herself forward as a socialist candidate for parliament. Before the firing squad, Agustina lifted her arms and begged the heavens for mercy, to the great amusement of her executioners. Concha Moreno Grados was a seamstress and fashion designer who taught dressmaking. As a militant socialist, she gave free sewing classes to girls at a college of the General Workers' Union in Granada, and her father, a chauffeur, fought tirelessly for workers' rights. Concha was one of a group of eight women and fifty men denounced for plotting against the new regime, and was arrested at her house in 1938. She tried to carry on her fashion business from her prison cell and wrote regularly to her parents. Her last letter was dated 21 September 1938. At dawn on 4 October 1938 she was among fifty or so men and women taken from the Provincial Prison, where they had been beaten and tortured, to be shot in the cemetery in Granada.

The female militia of the liberation front wore cartridge belts round their waists and rifles slung over their shoulders, on top of the blue dungarees that showed solidarity with the working class. They were usually women who worked in factories, shops, workshops and offices, and most of them were adolescents. Another seamstress, Lina Odena of Granada, took part in the street fighting in the city in July 1936 and met her death in an act of extraordinary courage in September of that year. Driving on a mission in Granada province, her car was stopped on the Jaén highway by a Falangist patrol. Realizing she was in enemy territory by mistake, she shot herself dead with her last bullet. It was an act of heroism that became a legend sung by soldiers at the front in ballads and poems of the Civil War.

Too many other daughters of the city suffered similar barbaric fates to those of these three heroines of Granada. While the nineteenth and early twentieth centuries showed some progress towards more enlightened views of the role of women in the world, they were also the darkest in the history of Granadan women in their brutal intolerance and subjection of all those who did not conform to patriarchal authority, whether political or religious. The suppression of women during Franco's regime up to his death in 1975 was in some ways worse than in earlier times. A woman could undertake no activity outside the home without her husband's permission – she could not start a job, a business or open a bank account, initiate legal proceedings or even go on a substantial journey without his approval. A few admirable women defiantly carved out a name for themselves, one of whom, Joaquina Eguaras (1897–1981), was not only the first female student at the University of Granada but also its first professor. On 20 September 2018, the first woman rector of the university in its five hundred-year existence, Pilar Aranda, paid homage to Joaquina by laying flowers at the monument erected in her name in the district in the north of Granada named after her. Joaquina came to the city aged two, entered the university in 1918 to study Philosophy and Letters, and later taught Arabic studies when the School of Arabic Studies was founded in 1932. She was appointed Director of the Archaeological and Ethnological Museum of Granada, a post she occupied until her retirement in 1967. Another pioneer is María del Carmen Maroto Vela, born in Granada in 1938, who has risen to eminence as a doctor specializing in microbiology. She has held a number of posts at the University of Granada, including a Chair, and is the first woman president of the Eastern Andalusia branch of the Royal National Academy of Medicine in its 267-year history. Professor Maroto was elected Doctor of the Year in 1998 and was named a Woman of Europe in 2000.

During the transition to democracy after Franco's death, women's liberation groups sprang up along with a brand of uniquely Spanish feminism that campaigned for equality of rights and fought against patriarchy and *machismo*, although not against men. The socialist government elected in Spain after the Madrid bombings of 2004, led by José Luis Rodríguez Zapatero, unveiled a cabinet in which half the ministers were women, sending a message of empowerment and encouragement to all Spanish women. It struck home in

Granada, where International Women's Day on 8 March continues to be a major event in the city calendar. When over 60,000 women took over the city centre to demonstrate against gender inequality on 8 March 2019, its spokeswoman, Paqui Fuillerat, described it as the most important women's demonstration in Granada's history. These activists are the latest in a distinctive line of Granadan women – saints, sultanas, gypsies, witches, actresses, authors and political rebels – whose words and deeds have enlivened and fashioned the life of the city since primitive times, and whose memorable presence still pervades religion, politics and culture.

GRANADA
THE PLACE IV

1950–Present

12

MEMORIES, MAPS AND MUSEUMS

Constructing the new cityscape

❖❖❖❖❖❖❖❖❖❖❖❖❖❖❖❖❖

DICTATORSHIP TO DEMOCRACY

Viewed from afar, the city seems to have a new landmark in the form of a tall, thin rectangular building that catches the sun and gleams white against the backdrop of the Sierra Nevada. It towers above the surrounding blocks of flats and red-roofed houses, the nearest thing to a skyscraper that Granada can muster. Its architects, led by Alberto Campo Baeza, built it to coincide with the main podium of the Caja Granada[186] headquarters standing parallel to it, both edifices rising to 120 metres and three storeys high, creating the impression from a distance of a new Gate to the City. Its silent, uncompromising façade belies the architectural drama that is revealed inside its central courtyard, shaped as an ellipsis from which helix-like ramps arise and intertwine in a sci-fi tangle of intersecting circles. This spectacular structure houses Andalusia's Museum of Memory (Museo de la Memoria de Andalucía), which opened its doors in 2009. Its dazzling white inner spaces and base materials of concrete, wood, steel and glass locate it firmly in the twenty-first century, at once part of the ultra-modern cityscape yet strangely dissonant with the older settlement that stretches away towards the *vega*.

Inside the museum, you find yourself in a weird, alternative and fascinating world – a massive panoramic screen dominates the ground floor area, on which are recreated the diverse land-scapes, flora and fauna of the region, as the story of Andalusia's geographical and natural development is played and replayed while we watch eras and topography change before our eyes. Beneath the screen, where the light is low, sit row upon row of lidded boxes whose contents you can touch, smell and see – soils, crops, woods, flowers and all manner of natural phenomena native to the region. On smaller screens you can choose centuries and cities by touch, as if you were in a science fiction film, or press a button to listen to historical personages from many different ages, classes and occupations who stand as if alive inside glass cases and recount their daily lives. In other areas you can feel and discover the secrets of prehistoric vases, plasterwork from the Alhambra and Baroque artworks alongside everyday tools, implements and paraphernalia of times past. All of Andalusia's history is here, with Granada playing a central role in it, as manifold geological strata and layers of cultural memory are unearthed before our eyes. Cutting-edge, hi-tech, the museum is an extraordinary fusion of the futuristic with the primordial, an interactive monument to the historical memory of Andalusia and to Granada's engagement with the contemporary world.

The glossy veneer of pioneering technology and architectural innovation embodied in Andalusia's Museum of Memory is light years away from the dire realities of life in post-war Spain and, as such, it marks the culmination of an era of extraordinary transition in the modern history of Granada that began at the end of the Civil War in 1939. At that time, all political parties had become illegal except for the Movimiento Nacional (the National Movement, the governing institution established by Franco) and Spain found itself internationally isolated after fascism had been overcome in the rest of Europe. The early dictatorship years of the 1940s were arduous and painful, as the deprivation of civil liberties was matched by a desperate lack of consumer goods. An urban map of Granada might take us on a journey far removed from the standard tourist sites, to places resonant between 1939 and 1959 that have become part of the historical memory of dictatorship in the city.[187] If you walk up the Cuesta de Escoriaza in Realejo district, you will find Joe Strummer[188] Square, a small oasis of red sand, white wall and a fountain, with spectacular views over the mountains. A huge graffito of the rock singer looks out over the iron gates of Las Palmas barracks, where the Civil Guard were stationed after the war. Silent and deserted now, in the 1940s it was a centre for the interrogation and torture of Republican soldiers and supporters, men, women and even children accused of being part of anti-Franco resistance. There, prisoners were beaten, forced to stay awake or standing for days, or subjected to electric shocks.

On the other side of town in the modern Beiro district, just round the corner from the bustling Avenida de Madrid, stands the imposing red-brick entrance gate to the old provincial prison. Nothing else remains except for a sign designating the site as a Place of Memory, in remembrance of the many hundreds of prisoners who died there in the 1940s. Built to house 500 inmates, between 1939 and 1940 it exceeded 5,000 prisoners who existed in impossibly overcrowded conditions that obliged them to sleep in corridors and outside on patios exposed to the rain and cold. Many died from illness and malnutrition, while prison officers robbed their food to sell on the black market. Some were shot at dawn. At the end of the decade, the Catholic Church, Franco's faithful ally, held its Holy Mission in the city centre for a week in October 1949, where over 120,000 citizens took communion and half the population listened to sermons aimed at re-Christianizing Spain's wayward inhabitants, who had become secularized during the democratic Second Republic and needed saving from foreign ideologies deemed to be devilish, such as socialism, freemasonry and communism. Meanwhile, the Barranco del Abogado and the Sacromonte districts held out against the fascist authorities. The census of 1950 showed 3,682 cave dwellings in an area hard for the pro-Franco military to penetrate, which became the refuge of anti-Franco rebels, including the heroic Quero family mentioned in Chapter 8, who acquired a legendary status in the city.

General Franco first visited Granada on 20 April 1939, three weeks after the official end of the war. He came down what was then Avenida Calvo Sotelo, where the road was strewn with rushes and rosemary as if he were a saint, and he was given an enthusiastic welcome. But his visit did nothing to stave off the atrocious hunger of post-war Granada, and the management of food supplies by the dictatorship was by no means motivated by altruism. Hunger was the word most repeated in oral testimonies of this time, in which some people claimed the post-war era was worse than the war itself. The symbol of their famine was the rough black bread made from rye that folk queued for with their ration cards, saving up their coupons for a measure of sugar, rice or oil to go with it. For lack of more palatable food, they ate orange peel, potato skins and cooked bean pods, a diet that caused stomach pains, fainting, illnesses such as flu, typhoid and dysentery, and many died from malnutrition. In Spain, hunger was used by the dictatorship to keep the victors onside and repress the defeated, and as a result the black market grew spectacularly. The main black-market hubs on the city map were the Plaza Bib-Rambla and the railway station, where racketeers made a fortune, while small-scale operators arrived in the city by tram or astride a donkey, bringing modest amounts of bread, eggs or potatoes to sell covertly until they were pounced on by the Civil Guard. Women played an important part in under-the-counter sales, often carrying food in hidden pockets in their clothes. On 15–16 June 1947, Argentina's First Lady Eva Perón visited Granada as part of a week's official trip to Spain, which lightened the gloom of daily life. The Argentinian government was one of Spain's few international allies and provided several tons of corn, frozen meat, maize, oil and vegetables, which helped ease the hunger for a while. In the city, she was given a splendid welcome and visited the Generalife, the cathedral and Royal Chapel, and the El Fargue gunpowder factory four kilometres north of Granada, a place where scores of workers had been killed in the past by Franco's henchmen, although this detail was not conveyed to Evita Perón.

Looking down on 1950s Granada from above, the perspective was different and perhaps deceptive. The Municipal Archive holds a series of black-and-white aerial photographs of the city taken between 1956 and 1959 from a number of different vantage points. The bird's-eye view of Granada offers one of the best vistas in the world but in monochrome footage it loses its vibrancy and luxuriance. These photos show a provincial city endowed with historical landmarks that now competed with geometric edifices of concrete and glass in districts that had lost their uniqueness. The plan to reform and widen the city layout dreamed up by pro-Franco professor and city mayor Antonio Gallego Burín, and approved in 1951, had similarities with the urban transformation plan implemented in the nineteenth century, as it was intended to impose order on a disorderly city by creating scope for urban and industrial expansion and reform. The aerial views expose the new axis of the urban centre constituted by the Gran Vía, Calle Reyes Católicos, Puerta Real and the Acera del Darro, much the same as it is today, but in the outer districts traditional houses rubbed shoulders with new rectangular blocks of flats in built-up areas that overflowed into and consumed the rural landscape of the *vega*. From above, the urban landscape spoke of prosperity and expansion, of a dense population swelling the boundaries of the developing city, but on the street, there were other modifications unseen from the air. The street map of Granada had changed significantly as a result of the new names introduced to honour the pro-Franco heroes of the Civil War. Plaza Nueva was changed to Plaza General Franco, before being changed back again to Plaza

Nueva as it is today. The current Avenida Pablo Picasso was named Avenida 18 de Julio (18 July Avenue[189]) and what is now Avenida de la Constitución, along which General Franco had travelled, was then called Avenida Calvo Sotelo in memory of an extreme right-wing leader assassinated at the start of the Civil War. Politics had reshaped the way Granadans designated city spaces by lending a fascist cadence to familiar places.

It was about this time that the English novelist Laurie Lee revisited Spain twenty years after he first explored the country on foot. He charted his experiences of Spanish post-war life in *A Rose for Winter*, published in 1955. Lee arrived in Granada one Christmas and although he never refers to politics, his colourful, romantic anecdotes capture a mood of vitality and dogged cheerfulness that rises above the painful struggle for existence in a city under fascist rule. Near the cathedral, he found a cheap café called La Casa de Paz, the House of Peace, where he could eat soup, steak and chips and fruit for a mere shilling (about £1.70p), washed down by a bottle of white wine for 4d (about 50p). On Christmas afternoon, the main entertainment was a bullfight, packed out, where six young Granadan hopefuls fought six young bulls, and all of the bullfighters were tossed, some several times, until a bull was finally killed by a sixteen-year-old called Montenegro. He had recovered from an early toss that split his trousers to the thigh to perform the final sword-thrust or *estocada* amid an avalanche of hats thrown by the admiring fans. One day Laurie Lee visited the Sacromonte, 'a crumbling city of decayed terraces',[190] scattered with tins and bottles, beggars' shacks and tents made of black tarpaulins, before moving on to the Albaicín, where he came across a group of women making lace, stitching and singing in the open air. One woman, intent upon her work, was making a bridal veil for a countess, embroidered with a mass of flowers and angels, for which she was to receive the sum of £10 (around £200 today). Perhaps his most striking encounter was with a boy of about thirteen, whom he met on his way down from the cemetery hill where he had watched mourners taking bunches of yellow and crimson chrysanthemums to honour their dead. The child was barefoot, so poor his clothes were sewn together with string, and he told Lee with great enthusiasm that he was helping his father make a cave for his family to live in. His father turned out to have no legs and his mother was lying outside in the open on a large brass bedstead, surrounded by pots and pans and cradling a child asleep on her breast. It was a surreal scene of hope mixed with desolation that exposed the way things were for the poor in 1950s Granada.

The 1960s and 1970s brought social and political improvements, perhaps as a result of the growing contact with the rest of the world set in train in 1953 by the agreement between Spain and the United States to set up US military bases on Spanish soil. Two years later, in 1955, Spain was allowed to join the United Nations and by the 1960s wealth was increasing as international firms established factories and jobs, inaugurating a period of booming growth known as the Spanish miracle (*el milagro español*), which saw Spain become the fastest-growing economy in the world behind Japan.

In Granada the key changes came in the cultural, political and social arenas. The university's Faculty of Arts and Letters became the main focus of anti-Franco opposition, and moved in the 1970s to its current building on the La Cartuja campus. The university Cine Club was one of the most important venues for cultural debate in the 1960s. The main lecture hall of the Law Faculty in Calle Oficios and other venues in the Gran Vía put on a film a week, mainly arthouse, and by 1974 there were over 300 permanent members. The paintings of the local artist José Guerrero, born in Granada in 1914, are emblematic of the new standpoints emerging from the increased growth and optimism of the 1960s. Guerrero started painting in the seventeenth-century master Alonso Cano's old studio in the bell-tower of the cathedral, from where he could see the whole city below him, which he described as smelling of chocolate, spices and fish, a place of a thousand voices and ringing bells. Conscripted at twenty-one, he served as a soldier and sketch artist in the Civil War, after which he escaped to study in Paris, Rome and finally the United States, where he lived for many years and befriended abstract expressionists Mark Rothko and Barnett Newman. Guerrero felt the strong influence of Picasso, Juan Gris and Miró, and when he finally returned to Spain and settled in Nerja, he returned to the scenes of his youth, painting strong abstract works in black, blue, red, ochre and dazzling white that portrayed his native city as it had never been painted before. His *Albaicín* (1962) and *Sacromonte* (1963–4) capture a fleeting essence in line, vivid colour and movement but perhaps his key work is *La brecha de Viznar* ('The breach at Viznar'), an abstract representation of the mass grave where Lorca was buried, with a powerful political message.[191]

In the spirit of the time, a growing number of workers' and people's groups emerged, including several new residents' associations like those in the Polígono or housing estate of La Cartuja and the district of Zaidín los Vergeles to the south-east of the city. The Communist Trade Union was founded in Granada in 1967 and took part in demonstrations and strikes. When three workers were killed by the police during the construction workers' strike of 20 July 1970, 200 men shut themselves in the cathedral on 22 July in protest at such brutal repression but were forced to abandon it two days later as the police allowed no food to enter the building. The protest was also a demonstration of support for the workers by the Church, who upheld their right to present their legitimate concerns. There were similar sit-ins in the cathedral and the church of San Isidro in April 1975, provoked by the dramatic unemployment situation and supported by the Archbishop. The protesters in the cathedral lasted over a week until lack of food won the day and resulted in thirty-five workers being handcuffed, arrested and imprisoned for three months.

Seven months later, on 20 November 1975, the dawn was grey and still, with thick fog shrouding the Spanish capital of Madrid.

At 5.20 a.m., General Francisco Franco had died there and it proved to be a watershed, ending nearly forty years of fascist rule. Overnight, the soft porn magazines hidden discreetly under the counters of newspaper kiosks went on open display to passers-by, who wandered dazed yet often secretly elated by the sombre news. In Granada, the newspaper *Ideal* issued a special edition and days of mourning and clandestine celebrations were followed by uncertainty now that Franco lay in the Valley of the Fallen out-side Madrid, and Juan Carlos I was crowned king. The next seven years saw the transition to democracy. In 1978, a new Spanish Constitution was approved by referendum, which defined Spain as a secular parliamentary monarchy. A socialist government was elected in 1982 and Spain joined the European Economic Community in 1986. It was a time of intense and rapid social change in Granada as in the rest of the country – political parties were all legalized, fundamental liberties were asserted and Andalusia received its own statute of autonomy, making it free to elect its own regional parliament. In December 1979, Granada hosted the second National Women's Day in the Isabel la Católica theatre, attended by over 1,200 participants from all over Spain as well as renowned feminists like Simone de Beauvoir. The hot feminist issues of the time were debated, including abortion, women and work, and sexuality.

By the start of the twenty-first century, parts of Granada had the appearance of many other European cities, as its cityscape evolved to accommodate modern living, although it has so far escaped high-rise tenements and skyscraper skylines. Suburbs of new flats, a fast ring-road with easy access to the airport, upmarket department stores like the Corte Inglés and Zara, all give a progressive feel to a place that has embraced consumerism and globalization to the extent that in 2012 there were five McDonald's outlets in the city. The push forward into the future looks back at a past in fragments. The new metro or light railway was opened after years of delay in September 2017 and has three underground stops in

Granada itself, one of which, Alcázar Genil, near the Science Park and Conference Centre, is next to the site of an ancient Almohad palace. The excavations revealed that the location coincided with a water reservoir that formed part of the Almohad buildings, which were preserved and incorporated into the design of the new station. Thirteenth-century stones merge with contemporary glass and steel to create a visually striking aesthetic experience rare in an underground rail station. In the town centre, the Hotel Eurostars Gran Vía (housed in a classic Renaissance building) boasts an extraordinary entrance foyer with a glass floor beneath which fragments of Almohad ruins are exposed to view literally beneath our feet. In these cases, the ultra-modern honours the ancient past of a city keen to preserve its albeit fragmented heritage while promoting its pioneering innovations. This desire to explore the past through present-day technology is borne out in Andalusia's Museum of Memory with which this chapter began, which harnesses the power of trailblazing science and media to magnetize the diverse history of the city, province and region. The museum's ultramodernity epitomizes the new European society of which Granada is a part, but at the same time sets it in a historical context of age-old continuity and custom.

RE-VISITING THE PAST:
TOURISM AND TRADITION

In April 2018 the respected travel blog Foxnomad announced that 83 per cent of its readers had voted Granada the best city in the world to visit for the second consecutive year, way ahead of the 16.9 per cent who voted for Dubrovnik as runner-up. The daily paper *Ideal* reported that this success built upon 2017, when Granada was also voted the most beautiful city in Spain. Not surprisingly, its tourist numbers have rocketed, with an increase of 7 per cent in the first half of 2019. The jewel in Granada's crown, the Alhambra is a UNESCO World Heritage site and, as such a place of outstanding universal value, is besieged by so many visitors national and international – as many as 2,766,887 in 2018 – that it is close to the maximum capacity permitted by UNESCO. From medieval wanderers to the Grand Tour, Victorian leisure travellers to today's mass tourism, Granada continues to beguile outsiders. The current free street map of Granada, tellingly headed 'Map of Granada's historical monuments', prioritizes sites of tourist interest, listing fifty-seven heritage sites in the urban area, as well as marking the Albaicín, Alhambra, Realejo and city centre in pink as tourist areas. When in 1940, in the early days of mass tourism, Antonio Gallego Burín oversaw the conversion of the old silk market, the *alcaicería,* into a 'bazaar of Hispano-Moroccan craftsmanship' with the aim of beautifying the historic city and appealing to visitors, he could not have foreseen the future flood of sightseers. 6.2 million of them spent a night in the city in 2018, bucking the trend of stagnation in the tourist sector nationally in a city even more popular than Spain's sun and sea resorts.

Such a love affair with the Andalusian Eden is in part the result of its contemporary image, for Granada is a city of the mind as much as a material entity. Its latest avatar rises up from a palimpsest of history and fiction that is deciphered through its museums, monuments and heritage sites, but also in a virtual reality. The business of recreating Granada's twenty-first-century image is increasingly conducted online by means of interactive maps, virtual tours of historic buildings, digital newspaper libraries, old maps, engravings and photos, seasoned with a dash of everyday reality in the form of the opinions and experiences of other travellers. The Alhambra official website invites readers to engage with a three-stage experience consisting of online discovery of the history of the palace and gardens, prior to visiting the monument itself in a choice of different ways and tours, and finally experiencing its past through exhibitions, activities and workshops in which visitors can take part. The creation of tourist anticipation before the visit followed by direct involvement afterwards are crucial in promoting the outstanding historical and cultural value of Granada's monuments.

In real time, we can walk down from the Muslim palace to the old silk market in the town centre, revamped after the Civil War and now part of a city tourist route on the Alhambra website, complete with YouTube videos. Once this historic enclave was an enclosed space but now forms part of the urban layout. For five centuries it has been a commercial hub, from the sale of silk in Nasrid times to the trade in contemporary souvenirs today.[192] The old silk market appeared on the 1787 map of the city by Tomás López, when it housed individual shops, as it still does. The first shop-owner after the Civil War to sell tourist goods was Miguel Mariscal, who traded in hand-made leather goods from the city, embossed and decorated in local style, and now the *alcaicería* sells all manner of exotic souvenirs, lace, leather, bags, fans, kitsch figurines, local marquetry and Moroccan lamps in its maze of narrow streets. In the 2000s the silk market was restored to an appearance of its original state, its plasterwork façades were renewed, its lighting and pavement redesigned on the basis of nineteenth-century photographs. These renovations were part of the contemporary revival of the city's Arab past, although in late 2018 the city council prohibited the traditional souk-like display of wares outside in the streets, as it hindered the flow of pedestrians through the area. Today's *alcaicería* is a vivid present-day re-creation of a part of Granada's Arab past, rooted in history but fabricated to conform to an imaginary interpretation, a theatrical representation in which tourists, shopkeepers and tour guides play their part in keeping the medieval Muslim market alive by bestowing contemporary meaning on it.

While tourism revisits the city's Moorish past, Granada's traditions and festivals point in another direction, which has a perceptibly Christian orientation. The town hall website's City Heritage pages aim to pinpoint Granada's unique identity through its material and symbolic expression in the flags, standards, shields, maces and seals that are the repositories of its historical memory, as well as through its art and the historical personages of the city, exemplified by the Catholic Monarchs, the painter Alonso Cano, Saint John of God and Mariana Pineda among others. Traditional local artefacts such as Fajalauza ceramics, ornamental glasswork from Castril, furniture, tools and religious images are brought to the fore as special markers of the customs and character of the province. A separate webpage lists the eleven main festivals of the city,[193] eight of them religious celebrations, and all of which are solemn public ceremonies described as enshrining Granada's history, which for the purposes of the website begins in 1492. On the last Sunday in May, town councillors and other dignitaries gather at noon in Mariana Pineda square before her statue, all dressed sombrely in dark suits, along with four mace-bearers in crimson velvet outfits from the nineteenth century, each carrying a silver mace. An offering of flowers is made to Granada's modern heroine, followed by a short concert by the municipal band. Later in the year, on 12 October, Columbus Day, the discovery of the Americas by Christopher Columbus on that date in 1492 is celebrated by a procession both civic and religious that takes in two emblematic places: first, the Royal Chapel where Ferdinand and Isabella lie, and then the junction of Reyes Catolicos and the Gran Vía, the location of the bronze statue of Columbus showing Queen Isabella the parchment detailing his plans for his journey, according to the capitulations agreed at Santa Fe outside Granada in November 1491, which gave the explorer permission to undertake his first famous voyage of discovery.

These secular festivals honour crucial elements of the city's history – the road to Spanish imperialism that began just outside Granada, and the secular martyrdom of a liberal thinker – yet these events are inevitably outshone by the ritual ceremonies that display Granada's deep devotion to female divinity, enacted in the festivals of the Virgin of the Sorrows and the Virgin of the Rosary. The Virgin of the Sorrows is a patron saint of the city who is believed to shelter and protect the city from harm during droughts, earthquakes and other natural disasters. Her festival comes in the autumn, on 15 September, when thousands of local people queue at the doors of the Basilica named after her to leave their offerings of flowers. The city turns into an autumn market where you can buy local specialities of the season such as barberries, jujubes, pomegranates and special Pies of the Virgin, baked in a wood oven and filled with pumpkin purée. Soon after, on 7 October, Granada, and in particular the Realejo district, begin their devotions to a co-patron saint, Our Lady of the Rosary, in a ceremony established by Fray Hernando de Talavera and the Catholic Monarchs just after their conquest of the city. A statue of the Virgen of the Rosary stands in the church of Santo Domingo, an anonymous sixteenth-century polychrome sculpted image magnificently decked out in a rich silver gown in the style of the court of King Philip II. A star is said to have miraculously appeared before the sculpture in 1679. The Virgin emerges from her shrine every 12 October to be solemnly carried through the streets at six in the afternoon.

The major Christian festival of Christmas is a milestone in the Catholic year and is celebrated in Granada, as we have seen, with traditional Nativity cribs, each one a work of art that transforms the streets into mini-theatres where the birth of Jesus is imbued with a distinctively Granadan flavour. The sense of spectacle continues with the Procession of the Three Wise Men on the night of 5 January, when the city is transformed into a magical, illuminated gathering place for residents and tourists alike. The other great Catholic celebration, Holy Week, began in Granada soon after 1492 with the founding of Christian brotherhoods and fraternities, but came into its own in the early twentieth century. At that time five new guilds of penitents were formed and Easter in Granada was designated by the Secretary of State for Tourism as a 'Festival of international tourist interest' on the basis of its antiquity, continuity and deep-rootedness, which involves the participation of Granadans in a wide variety of original and diverse public ceremonies. In 2017, it was voted the most spectacular Holy Week in the country. The *pasos* or floats carrying statues of Christ or the Virgin seated on a throne, each one presented by individual guilds and brotherhoods, are renowned for their simple beauty, set against the startling backdrop of the Alhambra or winding their way through the tortuous alleys of the Albaicín, sometimes in complete silence. In all, thirty-two processions make their way to the cathedral during Easter week, in what is known as a visit or station of penitence, culminating with the children's procession on Easter Sunday, when they carry a small float bearing the Infant Jesus on a throne, to the accompaniment of church bells and musical instruments.

Granada leads the country in the opulence and drama of its religious festivals, so it comes as a surprise to learn that Christmas and Easter have less importance to its citizens than its two most prominent public ceremonies, the festival of Saint Cecilius and the Día de la Toma, the day when Nasrid Granada surrendered to its Christian conquerors. Saint Cecilius is the main patron saint of the city and every year since 1646 his festival has taken place on the first Sunday in February in the grounds of the Abbey of the Sacromonte. Every year, come rain or shine, around 5,000 people make the pilgrimage along the winding road through the Sacromonte and up the steep hill lined with fig trees and prickly pears to the Abbey, many carrying sticks to help them climb the slope. Elderly folk in sports gear and trainers, excited children, tourists and locals who catch the packed town buses, all go to honour the first Bishop of Granada, who they believe was martyred and died on the Valparaíso hill long ago. The people of Granada treat the occasion as a grand picnic. On 3 February 2019, the town council handed out the traditional fare consisting of 1,000 kilos of broad beans, 4,500 '*salaíllas*' (a kind of salt bread) and 180 kilos of salted cod, while the pilgrims spread out over the hillside to enjoy their food. In February 2010, the statue of Saint Cecilius was presented for the first time in procession, and every year since, on the Saturday before the pilgrimage, the statue – made by Francisco Morales at the end of the nineteenth century and restored by a Granadan craftsman – is carried through the streets of the Realejo area of the city to musical accompaniment. The parish donated a pectoral cross and ring to the statue and, to the surprise of the locals, the Roman Curia returned the original pectoral cross belonging to the image, a piece of jewellery known as the Cross of Saint Cecilius, given back to adorn the saint on the day of procession.

Newspapers have reported the revitalization of the tradition of Saint Cecilius in recent years, inscribing the festival firmly within a Christian tradition whose longevity reveals just how successful the founder of the Abbey of the Sacromonte, Archbishop Pedro de Castro, was in establishing a Christian heritage for the city that pre-dated the Islamic invasion and conquest of 711. Inextricably bound up with the fabrication of the Lead Books in the sixteenth century, the relics of the Christian martyrs including Saint Cecilius were authenticated by the Granadan religious authorities in the seventeenth century and were never condemned by the Vatican, unlike the Lead Books. The new cathedral in Granada, built on the remains of the old mosque, always claimed the importance of the martyrs in the whole affair, and before the Sacromonte artefacts came to light, and on the basis of the Torre Turpiana finds, the first altarpiece erected on the cathedral site was dedicated to Saint Cecilius and to the origins of Christianity in that place. It was a cult based on the old medieval tradition in which Cecilius was considered the first evangelist of Granada before it became a Muslim city, and the cathedral altarpiece is the first cultural image of the saint. The cult persisted in the cathedral, where new sculptures and paintings were placed in significant places, blatantly flouting the decision of Rome to obliterate the texts confirming his presence in the city. As recently as the early twentieth century, a stained-glass window depicting Saint Cecilius was placed over the main entrance door, parallel to one depicting Saint Gregory.

The persistence of this traditional festival, attended by the Mayor of Granada and other dignitaries, bears witness to the power of the events that took place over four hundred years ago, when a group of brave Moriscos invented the story of the Lead Books and planted relics in the old Torre Turpiana and on the Valparaíso hillside. Today a central feature of the newly refurbished museum of the Abbey of the Sacromonte is the sacred caves, formerly underground ovens for slaking lime in Roman times, where the bodies of the martyrs including that of Saint Cecilius were allegedly burned and their bones unearthed. These subterranean grottos are presented on the Abbey's website as a magical realm, a site of spirituality and faith. The festival of Saint Cecilius and the Abbey of the Sacromonte are crucial to the Christian identity of Granada but their existence cannot fail to uncover the ambivalent history of an indelible Islamic past. The Morisco Miguel de Luna might be proud to learn of the revival of the cult of Saint Cecilius and the Sacromonte, which he and his co-fabricators brought into being.

The other most important festival of the year in Granada marks the day at the start of 1492 when the city ceased to be the Muslim state capital and became part of the Christian kingdom of Castile. On 2 January every year, the local people celebrate the moment of Sultan Boabdil's surrender in the festival commemorating the capture of their city by Ferdinand and Isabella, known as the *fiesta de la toma*. This controversial annual festivity was instigated as one of the stipulations of King Ferdinand's will, written in the town of Madrilejos and signed on 22 January 1516, just hours before he died. Each year a procession of civic dignitaries proclaims the Christian victory, hoisting the royal standard and Ferdinand's sword to the strains of the national anthem. Since the 1990s, the fiesta has been opposed by left-wing intellectuals and artists, including the violinist Yehudi Menuhin and the French-Lebanese novelist Amin Maalouf, on the grounds that it is xenophobic and inappropriate. Opposition groups clash verbally during the commemorations but Granada pays no heed. In 2016, 2,000 Granadans gathered at the town hall to hear the ceremony and see the procession that follows, in which those taking part wear fifteenth-century Christian costumes, with the exception of just one figure dressed in Moorish style. The Archbishop of Granada, Javier Martínez, officiated at a Mass in the cathedral where the tombs of the Catholic Monarchs lie, praising the humanity of Queen Isabella and describing the end of the Granadan war as 'probably the most exquisitely humane end to any war', in which, he said, the Christian monarchs sat at the same table as the vanquished. This royalist rhetoric appears to reinforce the Christian status of the city, when in fact it discloses a deep-seated and continuing anxiety about its religious and cultural identity, an anxiety encapsulated in that moment of surrender. The archbishop attributed the peaceable nature of that moment to the offices of the Christian queen, whereas the reality was markedly different. It was in fact Boabdil who chose capitulation over further violence, who worked with the Catholic Monarchs' emissaries to achieve a hard-won agreement. It was Boabdil who renounced his sovereignty and his kingdom to save his people.

To many Granadans, the *fiesta de la toma* may seem an innocuous celebration of their own local history but it has become a crucible of religious and political tensions.[194] On 2 January 2019, the use of megaphones was banned along with far-right flags and racist slogans to avert the threat of protests and demonstrations, amid the climate of national political unease that has seen a powerful surge in support for ultra-right-wing movements akin to those hitting the headlines in other European countries. The far-right political party Vox, which has been so successful in recent elections, used the Día de la Toma to tweet: 'We do not want to forget, nor should we, that 527 years ago today Granada was liberated by the Spanish troops of Ferdinand and Isabella, ending eight long centuries of reconquest against the Muslim invader.'[195] Vox's office in Granada retweeted: 'We should feel proud of our history and prevent the same invader from trying to dominate us again.' Meanwhile, the left-wing group Open Granada (Granada Abierta) denounced the festival as racially intolerant and a mouthpiece for neo-fascism. The *fiesta de la toma* today exposes the deep rift in Spanish society between nationalist views favouring an anti-immigration stance that bodes ill for Granada's significant Muslim and Moroccan population, and those who embrace and promote the city's historic multicultural and multiracial diversity. Reconnecting with Granada's past through tourism and traditional festivals reveals the schism created in a city whose Catholic identity is continually reinforced through a strong focus on Christian ceremonies and history, yet which owes its international appeal to a Muslim past that renders its identity ambivalent.

LONGING FOR GRANADA: THE RETURN OF ISLAM

As far back as the eleventh century, Granada's power to arouse deep longing and nostalgia was recorded in writing. When the Jewish poet Moses ben Ezra lived in exile in Castile after the Almoravid invasion in 1086, he described his desire to go back to his native city: 'If ever God returns me to the Glory of the Pomegranate my way will be successful.' The Nasrid sultan and poet Yusuf III, who reigned in the fifteenth century, also wrote eloquently of the anguish of his separation from Granada during his imprisonment in Salobreña castle: 'My heart was wounded by the sword of separation, the running tears are burning my cheeks. My yearning has not ceased despite my distance from you, like a body whose soul has left it.' Ibn Zamrak, star in the firmament of Andalusi poets, had waxed lyrical a century earlier when separated from his birthplace:

I was filled with wonder from the bottom of my tormented heart that yearns when the wind blows. Had the beloved been able to attain his desire, he would have flown to his homeland, for which he so yearned. When the nightingale in the trees began to sing, I stayed awake until dawn. Granada is the beloved's abode, it is the object and the wish. Its beauty is blinding, nor does the rain refrain from falling on its soil.[196]

Ten centuries later, that ardent nostalgia for a heaven lost lives on in the words, images and music of contemporary Spain, and to a greater degree, of modern Arab culture. Since the 1990s, a number of Spanish writers have revisited Granada's past in works of historical fiction, most of which are set in the medieval city and rewrite its history from the Muslim viewpoint. Among the key figures, the Castilian playwright and poet Antonio Gala found great success with the publication of *The Crimson Manuscript* (*El manuscrito carmesí*) in 1990. This marvellous novel, winner of the prestigious Premio Planeta book prize, uses the ploy of a secret manuscript written on the crimson paper of the Chancellery of Granada, which turns out to be the story of Boabdil's life set down by the sultan himself. Antonio Gala saw into Boabdil's heart, and in his imaginative exploration of the relationships of the sultan with his family, the court and with the Christians, he gave us the most eloquent possible assertion of Muhammad XI's worth and greatness of spirit. Gala wanted to show how this medieval ruler's date with destiny has resonance for us today. In 2004, the Zaragozan writer Magdalena Lasala published her novel *Boabdil, tragedy of the last king of Granada* (*Boabdil, tragedia del último rey de Granada*), the third in a trilogy whose protagonists are major figures of Muslim history in Spain, starting with the great tenth-century caliph Abd al-Rahman III, followed by the tenth-century Umayyad general Almanzor, and culminating in the life of Boabdil. Lasala's portrait of the last sultan of Granada is sympathetic if sentimental, and insistent on the role of destiny in the life of the Muslim ruler, cast as a man bearing the inescapable weight of 'the inherited disaster of history on his shoulders'.

The sensational story of the Lead Books also inspired a number of fictional recreations, including the evocative novel *The Hand of Fatima* (*La mano de Fátima*), published in 2009 by the Barcelona lawyer Ildefonso Falcones, which tells the epic story of Hernando, a young man who starts of life as a mule-driver and finds himself trapped between two religions and two love affairs. Crucially, Hernando is involved in copying the lead texts written by Alonso del Castillo and Miguel de Luna in Arabic, and his involvement in the Lead Books affair marks the secret life he leads as a crypto-Muslim desperately fighting to avoid the final expulsion of all Moriscos. In this epic re-invention of Granada's history, the Lead Books are ultimately powerless to prevent the inevitable banishment of the Morisco people from Spain. These novels and others like them express nostalgia for Granada's past not through individual yearning but in terms of a longing to reformulate that history from a non-traditional, unconventional point of view, by retelling events from the perspective of the Muslims.

Modern Arab novelists and poets have also turned to Granada as a way of reflecting on both their past and present, often using the motif of discovering lost medieval Granada in the course of a visit to Spain. Their work has created a mythology of al-Andalus as a place of high culture and learning, religious tolerance and Muslim political ascendancy. It is evoked as a utopia where religions co-existed in harmony and the arts flourished – the idea prospered of a Muslim Arab Golden Age admired by medieval Europe. In their re-creation of al-Andalus lies the memory of a grand civilization, as well as a reminder of inner conflict and of royal and political decline. The 1994 novel *Granada* (*Gharnāta*) by the Egyptian professor and novelist Radwa Ashur is part of a trilogy about a small Arab family who remain in Granada after the fall of the city in 1492. It narrates the agony of the Moriscos forced to leave their paradise, with the Albaicín at its heart, a besieged Arab enclave whose confined spaces are mapped out with detailed street names and located between the Alhambra, symbol of military and cultural loss, and the Sierra Nevada, a terrain of escape and exile. The world of the novel is one of pain, conflict and intolerance but one in which there is still hope, as Ashur likens Granada to Jerusalem, once occupied by the Romans but reclaimed by its inhabitants. The imagined world of early Granada echoes the present realities of displacement, forced exile and emigration in the Arab world, and converts Ashur's novel into a political statement about the modern Arab nation.[197]

The imaginary evocation of al-Andalus and Granada is equally compelling in the work of the Tunisian film director Nacer Khémir, in whose 1984 movie *Wanderers of the Desert* (*Les baliseurs du désert*) and its 1990 sequel *The Dove's Lost Necklace* (*Le collier perdu de la colombe*) al-Andalus and Granada form the Eden from which the Arabs were expelled, evoked variously as a lost land, a withered garden, an absent father and a dry pomegranate, each of whose seeds contains its own heaven on earth. They reflect a vision of al-Andalus as a fracture, a wound, a frustration in the Arab psyche, whose cure is to dream of return and to renew the search for the lost paradise. This is not merely a cinematic fantasy or a book-bound flight of imagination but an attitude vividly present in day-to-day life. A few years ago, someone engraved 'We will get you back, God willing' in Arabic on a windowsill in the Alhambra, an act that underlines the special power the place has in the cultural memory of many Arabs – Syrians, Egyptians, Tunisians, Moroccans – a place they associate with a zenith in Arab and Muslim culture. Syrian popular culture abounds with references to Granada and other Andalusian places of memory, not only in TV programmes and music videos but also in the names of streets, shops and neighbourhoods, as well as the Hotel Granada in Aleppo, and a village named after the city between Hama and Homs in western Syria. The connections between north African and Andalusian music are culturally significant, and the musical concerts held in the 2000s in Syria in which the musical heritage of Andalusia was performed were accompanied by promotional literature that asserted the importance of the lost paradise of al-Andalus in Arab cultural memory and expressed an impatience with the present and aspirations for equivalent achievement in the future.

Similarly, in Morocco, the inclusion of Andalusian music in that country's national musical heritage began at the time of Moroccan independence in 1956, when it became part and parcel of Moroccan nationalism. The Moroccan oud player Saïd Chraibi's CD *The Key to Granada* went on sale in August 2001, its title recalling how once a year Chraibi's Andalusian grandfather would bring out the key to the family house in Granada and weep for the place they left behind in 1592. The Tunisian craftsmen in Chapter 7 told a similar story and some Sephardic Jews also still hold the keys to their homes in the city. These old, material remnants of a past vividly remembered are the shared symbols of loss, exile and of an unquenched longing so strong it is said that older generations of Andalusians in Rabat often finish their prayers with the words: 'May God take back our lost paradise.'[198] At the same time, performing, visualizing and writing about past connections between Granada, north Africa and the Middle East embodies not just a vision of how things might have been then but also of how they might be in the future, and embraces the forging of a cultural identity that is new but has ancient roots.

In the present, the cultural texture of Granada is equivocal. The new mindscape of forward-thinking originality combined with European and global perspectives on Granada's role in the world nevertheless honours the past in local traditions and festivals, museum exhibitions and a contemporary tourism that embraces Granada's Islamic heritage, a mindscape out-pictured in the twenty-first-century cityscape. Modern living has been accommodated in rectangular apartment blocks served by department stores and a fast ring-road, yet age-old issues surface in modern graffiti, and the city's ambivalent history resounds in the tourist office's promotion of its Muslim culture. If you turn off Plaza Nueva up the side streets in the opposite direction to the Alhambra, you enter another dimension. In this other reality of winding, narrow alleyways, there are shops selling exotic Moorish spices and perfumes, bars and restaurants offering Moroccan food, and local residents who greet each other in Arabic. You might be in a north African country but you have entered the Albaicín, a UNESCO World Heritage site like the Alhambra, where slogans like 'No to Moors' and 'Moors go home' clash with a romantic mural of an Arab princess that celebrates the district's mixed cultural environment. The Albaicín is home to many of those who might be considered as the successors to Granada's medieval Arab heritage, immigrants from north Africa who have arrived in increasing numbers on Spain's southern shorelines. According to the United Nations Migration Agency, in 2018, migration from Morocco to Spain accounted for 65,400 crossings, 58,600 of those by sea, traffickers often landing their flimsy, overcrowded boats at Motril on the Granadan coast. Spain's at times Islamophobic, anti-immigrant reaction to these new arrivals has a deep and powerful resonance. The Muslim invasion of 711 has cast a long shadow and fear of the marauding, invading Moor runs deep in the Spanish psyche, aggravated nowadays by the arrival of young, penniless Muslims who embody the frequently voiced fear that the Moors have returned to claim what was theirs.

It was the memory of such a fear that struck Laurie Lee when he arrived in 'the most beautiful and haunting of all Spanish cities' sixty years ago and observed at once that Granada had never recovered from the flight of the Moors:

> When the cross-bearing Spaniards returned to their mountain city they found it transformed by alien graces and stained by a delicate voluptuousness which they could neither understand nor forgive. So they purged the contaminated inhabitants by massacre and persecution; and in the courts and palaces they stabled their

mules and horses. But the inheritors of Granada, even today, are not at home in the city; it is still dominated by the spirit of Islam. Fascinated and repelled by it, they cannot destroy it, but remain to inhabit an atmosphere which fills them with a kind of sad astonishment, a mixture of jealousy and pride.[199]

These observations gain some confirmation in the views of those white European residents of the Albaicín who find the oriental feel of the neighbourhood unsettling. The new immigrants are known as 'moros', a word with strong cultural resonance, since it was used to describe the soldiers of the Muslim armies that entered Spain in the eighth century, as well as the medieval Muslim inhabitants of al-Andalus, before it acquired its current, pejorative, anti-immigrant meaning. In the Albaicín, its use fosters fears of a north African takeover that might be seen as an inherited right. One resident, named Carlos, spoke openly of his concerns, stating that Granada had invited the immigrants to come because they are good for the economy but now there are too many: 'They are trying to take over, this is what I think. And the government allows them to do what they want, but what they don't see is that it's happening all over again and in a couple of years it will be too late; we'll be living in Morocco.'[200] Carlos is envisaging a second Muslim invasion, this time apparently by infiltration rather than by attack, and it is clear that his anxiety relates to Islam rather than to immigration. Yet many other residents welcome the Moroccan Muslims, whose visible presence gives a whiff of authenticity to the marketable Moorish image of the Albaicín. A good number have boosted Granada's trade by setting up souvenir shops selling oriental artisan items and inexpensive trinkets there, contributing to the revitalizing of the old Moorish quarter.

The story of one family of Syrian refugees reveals to what extent the former Muslim state of Granada has become a tolerant haven for the dispossessed. Ahmed Youssef, a dentist from Damascus, visited the city in 2008 and found a society in which he felt at home: 'The Andalusian way of living attracted me... we share a history going back to the Phoenicians.'[201] When rockets began to fall on the district of Damascus he lived in, as unrest in Syria became unbearable in 2012, and the prospect of returning to Syria looked slim after the arrival of ISIS, Youssef and his wife Nawal moved to Granada, a place that seemed familiar and which they feel is closest to their own culture and way of life. Youssef's two sons were born there and he believes it is a unique place in Europe, as well as a welcoming city for an Arab to live. They have made a success of things and now run a small hotel in the city centre, as well as opening the Syrian-Spanish Cultural Space, a centre that offers cookery courses and language exchanges and provides a space for locals and Syrians to interact, just 300 metres from the entrance to the Albaicín.

While the Youssef family and others like them have found acceptance and sanctuary inside the city, tolerance for Muslim converts is in short supply. The return of Islam to Granada has sparked ancient tensions between traditional Catholics and members of the *Islamic Community in Spain* (*Comunidad islámica en España*), originally known as the *Society for the Return of Islam in Spain* when it was founded in 1980. The earlier local version sprang up in the late 1970s when a group of young Spanish hippies living in the Alpujarras south of the city converted to Islam as part of a larger international group, the Murabitun World Movement, led by a Scottish convert, Ian Dallas, who took the Muslim name Shaykh Abdalqadir As-Sufi Murabit. Its main aim is to restructure global economic and political systems according to Islamic principles, and Granada was chosen as the heart of the movement on the basis of its singular Muslim history.

While Abdalqadir al-Murabit's plan to found an Islamic caliphate with an economy of gold dinars may have been a pipe-dream, Islamic converts living in Granada have taken significant steps, such as lobbying to prevent the annual celebrations of the fall of Granada into Christian hands. In 2003, Spanish Muslims were called to prayer at the new Great Mosque of Granada, the first to be opened in the city since Ferdinand and Isabella claimed it for the Christians, and it has been seen as the focal point of a new Islamic revival. It took twenty years to build and stands on a hill, looking out over groves of orange trees and cedars to the Alhambra. Its construction was initially opposed by city leaders, whose objections were overcome when it was agreed that the new minaret should be slightly shorter than the Catholic church of Saint Nicholas next door. It was funded by money from the governments of Morocco and the United Arab Emirates, who spared no luxury in its construction, and new plans are afoot to extend the building. Its gardens abound with roses and jasmine, and its fountains are embellished with exquisite cobalt blue and teal green tiles, while the inner areas display silk carpets and teak doors. The President of the mosque foundation, Malik Ruiz, who has adopted the title of Emir of Spain, has said that Granada will return to Islam after its five-hundred-year interruption, not by launching a Muslim reconquest of al-Andalus but by returning to its Islamic roots. Nowadays the city is overwhelmed by tourists eager to capture its image in the thousands of photos snapped every day on their mobile phones, each one reinforcing the notion that this is a place with a Moorish heritage, a city that embraces a religion rejected as heretical centuries ago. The return of Islam to Granada is the heart of an Islamic revival that is part and parcel of an Andalusian nationalism that seeks the cultural unity of the region. Its ambitions are embodied in the first Islamic university of Andalusia, the Universidad Internacional de Averroes de al-Andalus, established in Cordoba following the full recognition of Islam by the Spanish State in 1989, and in the numerous Andalusian websites preaching tolerance, freedom and love for the homeland. Sultan Boabdil and the Morisco Miguel de Luna would rejoice to hear the voice of the muezzin as he calls the faithful to prayer for the first time since it was banned in the city around the year 1500.

Changing lifestyles and changing architecture, both human and urban, are constructing a cityscape that is diverse and original. In less than fifty years the city has lived through a seismic shift from dictatorship to democracy, with many young people returning to work in Granada after it was left a ghost town during the financial crisis that began in 2008. The focus is on the urban at the expense of the rural, and the streets are now peopled with alternative youth, new-age artists, foreign exchange and university students, as well as north African immigrants, Muslim converts and a multitude of tourists. Street art has become a craze, spearheaded by the internationally famous Niño de las Pinturas (The Graffiti Boy), Raul Ruiz, whose funky spray-paint murals adorn the walls of the Realejo district in vibrant images depicting themes of social justice, flamenco, age and youth. Granada's answer to Banksy keeps its vibe youthful and original, and 'El Niño' has won a cult following and has created a dedicated street art route for tourists to follow. Radical new plans are afoot to reconfigure the cityscape once more. A group of left-wing intellectuals and experts headed by medieval archaeology and history professor José Martín Civantos has put forward the bold idea of uncovering the River Darro along Reyes Católicos, thereby reinstating the old bridges and reshaping the adjoining street area, re-naturalizing the river and giving it new life. It chimes with the aims of a global movement to rediscover urban rivers in cities worldwide, known as 'daylighting', and it constitutes a bid to reconnect Granada not only with its river but also with its past and its distinctive identity.

The future of the city is inescapably locked into that past, which manifests itself in the present not only in its monuments but also in annual performances, re-enactments, anniversaries and local traditions, and in the memorabilia, artisan crafts and trinkets for sale in museums, shops and markets. It is a future which could see Granada established as the cultural reference point of the Western world. In August 2019, the town hall announced that it was preparing an application and strategic plan to be awarded the

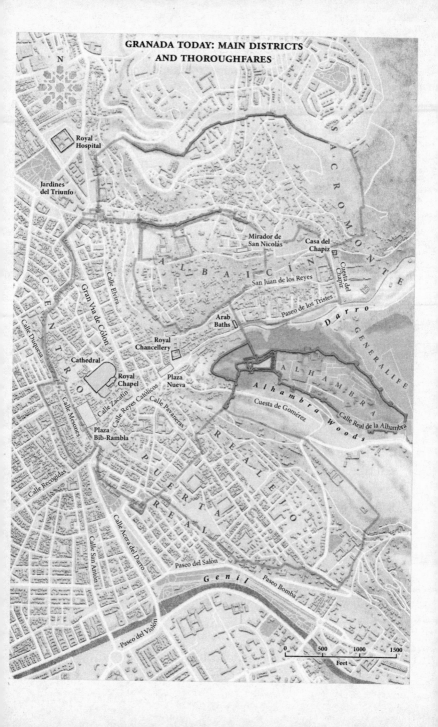

GRANADA TODAY: MAIN DISTRICTS AND THOROUGHFARES

N

Royal Hospital

Jardines del Triunfo

Mirador de San Nicolás

Casa del Chapiz

Cuesta del Chapiz

ALBAICÍN

SACROMONTE

San Juan de los Reyes

Calle Elvira

Gran Vía de Colón

CENTRO

Calle Duquesa

Paseo de los Tristes

Darro

GENERALIFE

Arab Baths

Royal Chancellery

Cathedral

Royal Chapel

Plaza Nueva

ALHAMBRA

Calle Zacatín

Calle Reyes Católicos

Calle Pavaneras

Alhambra Woods

Cuesta de Gomérez

Calle Real de la Alhambra

Calle Mesones

Plaza Bib-Rambla

PUERTA

REAL

REALEJO

Calle Recogidas

Calle Acera del Darro

Calle San Antón

Paseo del Salón

Paseo Bomba

Genil

Paseo del Violón

0   500   1000   1500

Feet

accolade of European Capital of Culture 2031. The documents were expected to take six months to prepare and would include a proposal for an international cultural programme, with its accompanying infrastructure and services, whose keynote will be the city's impressive and globally renowned artistic and historical heritage. If the bid is successful, it would be a crucial staging-post in Granada's history. But echoes of the past are never far away. In the same month, the online newspaper *El Independiente* ran an eye-catching headline: 'The emir of Qatar reconquers Granada', referring to the news that an Arab ruler has become the owner of a property in the city for the first time since Sultan Boabdil left the Alhambra more than five hundred years ago. Tamim bin Hamad al Zani, who was born in Doha in 1980 and became Emir of Qatar in June 2013, has bought the Carmen de San Agustín, a large estate now in some disrepair, which in Nasrid times was part of the *vega* but now lies inside the city boundaries, in the Albaicín. It is said that the emir, who is one of the richest men in the world and ranks ninth on the wealthy list of heads of state, paid 15.2 million euros for the property, which conceals its splendid gardens, swimming pool and tennis court behind high stone walls in the lovely Carril de las Tomasas. It is an orchard paradise in the Pearl of Islam, as the city was once known in the Muslim world, and a real treasure for the Emir, who is greatly enamoured of all things Spanish and has an excellent relationship with the Spanish royal family. The presence of an Arab Muslim ruler once more in the heart of the Albaicín might prove controversial but, meanwhile, Granada watches and waits.

13

EPILOGUE

*Vanished Eden or
Paradise regained?*

•·•·•·•·•·•·•·•·•·•·•·•·•·•·•

Stay awhile here on the terrace of the Alhambra and look
    about you.
This city is a wife, whose husband is the hill.
Girt is she by water and by flowers
Which glisten at her throat,
Ringed with streams; and, behold the groves of trees which
    are the wedding guests,
Whose thirst is assuaged by the water-channels.
The Sabika hill sits like a garland on Granada's brow,
On which the stars are entwined,
And the Alhambra (Allah preserve it!)
Is the ruby set above that garland.
Granada is the bride whose headdress is the Sabika
And whose jewels and adornments are its flowers.[202]

When the last sultan of Granada handed over the keys of his
paradise to his Catholic nemesis on 2 January 1492, it was a
moment of surpassing significance. In that instant, Spain and
Europe reach a crucial crossroads, a shift in the cultural paradigm
from European Islamic state to Christian dominion that marked
a new stage in the clash between two great world religions and

cultures. For Granada and its people, it also represented a moment of transition from possession to loss of that paradise so magnificently evoked in Ibn Zamrak's fourteenth-century poem above, and so sorrowfully relinquished by Boabdil. The poet and the sultan shared a vision of a sublime life that has haunted the human imagination throughout our known history, as long ago as the time of the Sumerians of ancient Mesopotamia, who lived around 4000 BC and believed in Dilmun, a fabulous land in the East where there was no sickness and all creatures lived in harmony. In Ibn Zamrak's vision of his native city there are echoes of another poet, the Roman Virgil, who saw a lost paradise in the Greek rural ideal of Arcadia, while the idea of a fall from paradise is shared by Judaism, Christianity and Islam. In our times, paradise has in part become an unacknowledged faith, a driving myth of consumerism and progress that manifests itself in the search for the perfect holiday location and in the glossy airbrushed beauty of fashion magazines. Yet implicit in all these concepts of paradise is the idea that something has either been lost, is unattainable or is constrained by a border, whether physical, cultural or imaginary, to the extent that it has become mythical rather than material.

The many visions of Granada as a utopia share these features but it is striking that they also depart from them. From the earliest written allusion to a rural idyll by Abd al-Malik ibn Habib in the ninth century, to the eulogies of the Nasrid poets and the astonished delight expressed by foreign travellers to the city before the sixteenth century, Granada was not just an imaginary paradise but a lived reality, in which its physical and geographical beauty, natural abundance, flowing water and ideal climate combined with the glories of Muslim architecture and gardens to create a visible, touchable Arcadia. It was not until that defining moment in Granada's history in January 1492 that the idea of a lost paradise took hold in the minds of those Muslims who remained in the city and province after its Christian conquest. Later, this notion shaped perceptions of the city in the wider Arab Muslim world, as well as providing a source of reflection for certain foreign tourists during the nineteenth and twentieth centuries. That it was also a lost paradise to Granada's Jewish population, exiled later in 1492, is clear in the words of the Sephardic ballads still sung today in north Africa. For the Catholics, it was a paradise gained by conquest but in need of transformation. Under Christian control, Granada became aligned with Rome, the seat of papal authority, and with Jerusalem as a sacred, biblical city, giving it an aura of legendary religious supremacy that countermanded its Muslim image as a new Damascus, the Andalusian simulacrum of Arabia, an analogy that persists in Arab written and visual culture.

Cities are many things but rarely utopias, and as both city and province, Granada is unusual in its nature as an urban as well as rural paradise. Its landscapes and cityscapes constitute its material, lived spaces while its mindscapes reflect its power to inspire imagination and representation. Together, they have shaped and affected the life and culture of Spain, and influenced international culture and politics. Granada is a place always ancient and always new, and each aspect has fostered the other in imaginative, but often conflicting, ways. In its ancient and medieval incarnations, Granada was self-contained, hidden behind great defensive outer walls that separated it from the surrounding *vega*, with which it had precisely defined contact via the imposing city gates that punctuate the ancient fortifications. It was a tale of two cities, its lower reaches sharing the typical layout and structure of an Arab city par excellence, turned in upon itself, a maze of intricate, winding alleys of houses on a hillside, where, secluded from the outer world, family life was conducted behind closed doors. Granada's souks were market-places for the rich foodstuffs grown in the fertile plains below and for the artisan craftwork and silk of local rural traders, yet its main lines of commerce ran to distant places, to north Africa and parts of Europe, Italy in particular. In its second city, the palatine citadel of the Alhambra, lay the centre of administration, where government and religious functions all existed apart, detached from its alter ego below.

After 1492, the Christianization of Granada brought radical changes to its cityscape and began a process of urban reconfiguration in which streets were widened and Muslim buildings repurposed for Christian use. As in many European cities, the advent of modernity extended that Renaissance configuration. A growing population and fresh ideas brought a new view of the urban structure, rectilinear, efficient, designed to create an open, healthy, orderly environment with the administrative buildings of civic authority at its centre. Ancient and medieval Muslim Granada existed in uneasy truce with its modern overlay, the veneer of Catholic art and architecture and its urban reshaping unable to erase its essential Arab and Islamic nature. In a sense, the new Christian city that stood on the threshold of the sixteenth century was a paradise betrayed for the Muslims who remained after 1492. The longed-for prize to which the Catholic Monarchs had aspired, the trophy that stirred Christian wonder and admiration in early ballads, soon fell prey to the violence of religious conflict and repression in a society whose Morisco population adopted in many cases a semblance of Christianity, a false appearance that matched the exterior architectural makeover of the place.

Granada stood apart from the rest of Europe at that time. The European domination of urban life by the Christian Church and by tradesmen's guilds had imposed both authority and repression, as well as fostering identity and security in Europe's medieval cities. That domination did not take hold in Granada until the Renaissance, as commerce and Christian culture expanded in equal measure. Then, the only paradise in mind was a spiritual one, envisaged as the heaven of the Catholic afterlife, solely attainable through virtue and asceticism. The eighteenth-century European Enlightenment had a quite different, secular view of virtue, which was embodied in the concept of what a city should be. For certain intellectuals, including Adam Smith and Voltaire, the urban contrast between rich and poor, from which Granada was by no means exempt, provided the very basis of social advancement in so far as the wealthy aristocrat created work for countless artisans, labourers and poor folk. The essence of an ideal city was a kind of civilized virtue defined through freedom, trade and art, which laid the foundations for industry and culture.

But this optimistic thinking about cities as places of progress and civilization was quickly turned on its head by the grime and destitution of the industrial age. The poverty, squalor and disease that changed the tenor of life in Granada in the nineteenth century was part of a more general urban degeneration throughout Europe, ravaged by industrialization and the dramatic expansion of populations. Slum dwellings like those along the banks of the River Darro, and outbreaks of cholera that decimated Granada's population in the 1800s, were a far cry from the view of the city as a paradise or even as enshrining virtue. Instead they mirrored the growing perception of cities as places of vice and corruption, both physical and spiritual, a kind of hell on earth. The architectural evolution of Granada in the nineteenth century aimed to solve the crisis in its urban life at that time and, according to the lights of the era, set it on an orderly, healthful path to modern existence, albeit at the irreparable loss of crucial parts of the city's material heritage. Yet the past permeates Granada's present to an unusual degree and shields it from the feeling of permanent transience and rootlessness that bedevils so many younger cities. The powerful force of tradition expressed through festivals, rituals and ceremonies, combined with the strong sense of belonging of its people, buck the trend of today's metropolises, tying people together through ancient connections and proclaiming the justifiable pride of the Granadan people in their history.

In his *Anatomy of Criticism: Four Essays,* the esteemed Canadian critic Northrop Frye made a telling observation on the relationship between the past and present: 'The culture of the past is not only the memory of mankind, but our own buried life, and study of it leads to a recognition scene, a discovery in which we see, not our past lives, but the cultural form of our present life.'[203] That recognition scene can take different forms. If we could listen to Granada's past, hear its soundscape, it might seem at once strange yet familiar. At first, the only sounds must have been bird cries and the roar of wild beasts, the wind, thunder, the music of running water and ritual chanting, the crackling of fires. Then the Romans, and later the Visigoths, brought the sound of Latin, then Germanic tongues, armies marching, horses' hooves, the clash of weapons and cries of fear, the sounds of settlement, the hewing of stone and the tapping of chisels. Then came the eerie clarion of the *shofar*, the Jewish ceremonial horn, and the soft rhythms of Hebrew; and after, the Muslims' call to prayer, the mighty bell tolling in the Watchtower of the Alhambra, the song of nightingales, the clang of swords, and an Arabic tongue that shaped the native vernacular. Centuries passed before the muezzin ceased to cry, and peals of church bells marked the hours and the days but could not silence the wild Morisco music, the *zambras* with their Arab pipes, trumpets and Moorish guitars. High above the city, the *duende* roused the frenzied accents of flamenco, an anguished lament that rose above the harsh new metallic beat of mechanization, the whinnies of horses replaced by the whistle of trains and blare of car hooters. Violence and death returned as brother fought brother, the sword superseded by the crack of gunshots, the terrifying thrum of approaching planes, screams of terror, and then silence. Now peace reigns in the rhythmic swish of traffic and the drone of passing airliners and, after five hundred years, the muezzin calls once more.

This imaginary historical soundscape of Granada highlights contrasts that are echoed in its landscape and cityscape. The complex, multiple histories embodied in those two fundamental features have moulded the opposing visions of paradise and of hell, both lived and imaginary, that have shaped Granada's image from the start. Over a period of three hundred million years, its landscape has been forged from quartzite and schist, marble and red clay, limestone and sandstone to create a place of abundance, shelter and natural defences, and its rural environment, rich in flora and fauna, has always been inseparable from the city that arose on its rocky outcrops. It is also a landscape of legend, linked to the imagined utopia of the lost civilization of Tartessos, and an earthly paradise to match its heavenly counterparts. There have been subtle changes to this landscape over the centuries, though its olive groves, vineyards and mulberry orchards have been there since earliest times. Other crops, like sugar cane and sugar beet, have changed the scenery and brought mechanized machinery to the *vega*. Soil has been eroded and the city has spread out and claimed the fertile land, but the original old Arab irrigation systems, mostly modernized now, still carry their life-giving water to the crops and pastures, and to the city itself. In its broader sweep, the Granadan landscape remains majestic, ageless and unchanging, still a sublime spectacle of colour and light.

Unlike its timeless backdrop, the cityscape of Granada charts the visual history of its changing past, whose multiple perspectives reflect its diverse peoples and cultures. The latest techniques in 3D geological modelling might show us a cross-section of the permanent strata, the underground layers that form the bedrock of the city, to reveal an extraordinary sedimentary record of Granada's many peoples. Below the city streets lies the memory of its creators compressed in stone, its foundation in the seventh-century BC Iberian oppidum in the old Albaicín, overlaid and expanded by successive Roman, Visigothic, Jewish, Zirid, Nasrid and Christian structures. This is the realm of the dead, the hidden roots of the city that are now coming to light, made visible by the latest archaeological excavations. The underground world also shelters a memory of things concealed or revealed – beneath the Alhambra runs a network of passages that betoken Nasrid intrigue and conflict, escape routes that lead outside the city bounds, as well as the dungeons that cruelly confined the Christian slaves who laboured on its construction. On the hillside of the Sacromonte, the caves of its Abbey guard the remains of its Christian martyrs, vivid reminders of the intertwined past of Granada's Moriscos and Catholics. In the town, the hidden river runs beneath our feet and silently marks the friction between progress and tradition in the nineteenth-century refashioning of the urban landscape.

Above ground it is Granada's Muslim and Christian history that dominate from all perspectives. The French poet and novelist Victor Hugo argued that architecture was man's earliest form of writing, his first fixing of cultural energy in coherent form. Viewed from above, the great red fortress stands as a testament to the military and cultural power of the Nasrid dynasty of Muslims, who finished building it on the hill of the Sabika, from where it looks down over the city and interacts with it as a dominating, forceful Islamic presence. Down in the city centre, the destruction of the ancient mosque to construct the Renaissance cathedral created by Diego de Siloé and Alonso Cano was a blatant superimposition of Catholicism upon Islam through the medium of architecture. It is a lasting monument to the power of Catholicism in Spain, and to the political might of Ferdinand of Aragon and Isabella of Castile. Their decisive choice to be buried in the pantheon of the Royal Chapel reflected their desire to give the city of Granada abiding political and religious significance as the place where their Christian Reconquest came to an end. The Abbey of the Sacromonte looks down over the city, at once a symbol of Christian dominance in Granada and also a tacit testimony to the Morisco plight that inspired the Lead Books and brought the building into being.

Viewed from a distance, the city skyline delineates its vital landmarks, ancient and modern. The outline of the Alhambra is not as it once was, before its mighty rectangular watchtowers and walls, that seem to grow organically out of the vegetation, were altered to incorporate the flat, squat shapes of Charles V's

Renaissance palace. As minarets became bell-towers after 1500, and new churches sprang up as mosques were demolished or re-purposed, the skyline took on its defining outline, half-Islamic, half-Christian, which changed little in the centuries that followed. Nowadays, modern flats and buildings like the glass and steel conference centre on the left bank of the River Genil, and the Caja Granada museum, have modified but not overwhelmed the historic urban horizon.

The inhabitants and visitors to the city experience it at ground level as a labyrinth of fragmentary or limited impressions of streets, buildings, hidden patios and gardens, an impression intensified in the old Moorish and Jewish quarters. Granada has always been a city of viewing points, of shifting perspectives that can be glimpsed from the belvederes of the Alhambra, the terraces of the Albaicín, in motion on a modern tourist bus or even from the top of the giant Ferris wheel inaugurated for Christmas 2019, with its spectacular 360-degree views of the illuminated night-time city beneath. In its streets, Granada displays its hybrid history in human form through the many statues and monuments that honour certain individuals who have in some way shaped it. The city spaces are adorned with three-dimensional effigies of Granada's Catholic heroes of the Reconquest in the form of statues of King Ferdinand II of Aragon, Queen Isabella I of Castile, Christopher Columbus and Gonzalo Fernández de Córdoba, the 'Gran Capitán' of the Catholic Monarchs, while likenesses of Fray Luis de Granada, San Juan de la Cruz and the Virgin Mary reinforce its Christian piety. Sculptures of great artistic figures of the city – the architect Alonso Cano, the composer Manuel de Falla, and the poet García Lorca among others – swell the ranks of Granada's great and good, alongside the gypsy Chorrojumo and the matador Frascuelo. Modern women too are revered in bronze, including the flamenco dancer María Cortés Heredia, Eugenia de Montijo, Empress of France, and the liberal heroine Mariana Pineda. Just two official monuments acknowledge Granada's Muslim and Jewish past, the statue of the medieval Hebrew translator Ibn Tibbon and the memorial to Sultan Boabdil on the outer edge of the city.

Today the street map has been redrawn and the *vega* is smaller, the urban sprawl larger, yet the sense of continuity in a place inhabited continuously for well over two thousand years gives strength and reassurance. Many races, tribes, faiths and languages have come within its horizons; Granada has different worlds and times within it, and has taken on many identities. The original concept of civilization, which is the society, culture and way of life of a people, was linked to towns and cities, deriving from the Latin word 'civitas' meaning a city – an entity that has no meaning without its inhabitants. In the case of Granada, its image has been fashioned not solely from its landscape and the historical density of its cityscape, but equally from its mindscape, the opinions, attitudes, perceptions, and imagination of the countless generations of people who have lived within the bounds of the city and province, as well as those who have visited it or admired it from afar. In some ways it is an unreal city, a place of myth and invention, a site of stories, founded by a ritual hero and poised between reality and fiction, appearance and truth. It is the epitome of ambivalence, an intensely Arab creation recast by a Christian history fabricated from legend. Its dominant paradigms are paradise and hell, represented in its two extremes, beauty and violence.

The violation of the vision of paradise by the intrusion of hell hovers subliminally in the mindscape of Granada, a barely acknowledged idea that silently evokes the sustained history of conflict that has bedevilled the region. Much of that conflict was born of successive waves of invasion and often of conquest, Phoenician and Carthaginian, Roman, Visigothic, and Islamic, part of the cycle of life and death of cultures that decline and fall, supplanted by a new and potent challenger. Then came the first Jewish pogrom; the warring of the Nasrid clan and street-fighting in the Albaicín as Boabdil strove to defend his city first from his family rivals, and then from the Christian armies; the cruel wars of the Alpujarras when Granadan Moriscos fought tooth and nail against their Catholic conquerors; the shocking death of Mariana Pineda, and latterly, the atrocities of the Civil War. All testify to an unusual and distressing degree of bloodthirsty brutality in the name of religion and politics in the region of Granada alone. It shows a dark side to paradise, a paradise lost that has left a palpable sadness and nostalgia in the air.

Even so, it is precisely the origins of this antagonistic combination of opposites that gives Granada its singular status. It is the stage on which an intense and long-lasting drama of clashing civilizations has been played out, and can justly stake its claim to be Spain's primary city. The uniqueness and importance of its history and culture are pre-eminent, since no other single settlement on the peninsula, or indeed in Europe, can claim such a varied multicultural heritage. It has been the scene of historical watersheds, in the transition from Roman state to Visigothic kingdom, from Visigothic to Arab territory, and then after nearly eight hundred years, the transformation into a Spanish Christian possession, and all have played a vital role in shaping the history, society and culture of Spain. Granada was the place where Islamic rule finally ceased to exist in Europe, and where Spanish Catholicism became all-powerful. The longest-lasting and predominant culture over that period of time has been the Islamic one, which galvanized Granada's distinctive fusion of Muslim and Hispanic heritages. In this respect, Granada reflects the ambivalent identity of Spain and is key to the vexed contemporary debate on just how that identity should be perceived.

The current controversy over Spanish identity that arose in the wake of 9/11 has been harnessed by today's mainstream politics. In November 2018, the ultra-right-wing political party Vox posted two tweets, one with a short film clip showing their leader Santiago Abascal disguised as the early medieval hero and Christian Visigothic nobleman, Don Pelayo of Asturias, riding alongside his soldiers to music from the *Lord of the Rings* films, to lead the new reconquest of Andalusia. At a meeting in Seville just days later, Abascal opened a Pandora's box by upholding the Andalusia of the Catholic Monarchs over and above that of the early twentieth-century politician Blas Infante, father of Andalusian nationalism.[204] Abascal's discourse of national, monarchical Catholicism, which promotes the idea of Spain united after the fall of Granada in 1492, echoes Francoist rhetoric and aligns itself largely with an equivalent ultra-right-wing ideology current in politics across Europe. But in Spain's case, the associated Islamophobic, anti-immigration stance adds an extra dimension. This topical right-wing exploitation of a crucial aspect of Spain's medieval history is an ideological tool used to reinforce the ambition to uphold a patriarchal, hierarchical, unrelievedly Catholic nation. It is closely linked to the existing and frequently vituperative polemic regarding the nature of Spain's unique character, contested by many Spanish writers, intellectuals and academics. The Spanish Middle Ages stand at the heart of this hotly debated affair, and the longstanding conflict of opinions inevitably polarizes into two opposing camps – there are no shades of grey. It is never Cataluña, or Galicia, or the Basque country that is the issue. What is always at stake is how Spain defines itself, how it measures itself, with regard to its Islamic heritage and to that feared yet desired Other whose unresolved relationship plays on the Spanish mind. Spanish identity today, and Spain's place in Europe, are at the heart of the debates and controversies arising from the concepts of invasion, conquest and reconquest that endure in historical memory as a result of seven centuries of Muslim presence in the peninsula. Granada embodies that presence and as a result is central to Spain's conception of itself. Its buildings and city structures are a palimpsest of Spain's multicultural history, from the earliest Iberians, Romans, Visigoths and Muslims to today's city with its Catholic, Muslim and Jewish population.

The city might seem a paradise lost amid nationalist Catholic rhetoric but Granada can be a beacon for the future. The word *convivencia,* meaning 'living side by side', has become popular again recently. When Franco died, Spaniards were very aware that a lack of *convivencia* had led to Civil War and it became the watchword of the Transition; it was also the theme of King Philip VI's Christmas Day speech in 2018. But its original usage was as a term to describe the living together of Christians, Muslims and Jews in medieval Spain, sometimes, but not always, in mutual tolerance. Paradoxically, there never was *convivencia* in the strict sense in Granada during the Middle Ages, nor after. From the start of Nasrid rule in the city, it was an entirely Arabic-speaking Islamic state, with a small Jewish population but no native Christians, only those who were passing traders or official visitors, although Christians and Muslims interacted daily on the frontier between Granada and Castile, and there was *convivencia* in the form of regular diplomatic and administrative exchange between Islamic state and Christian kingdom. Today, Islam has returned to the city but this time on a different footing. It is generally tolerated and accepted by Granada's non-Muslim inhabitants and *convivencia* truly reigns in the city for the first time.

In June 2018, a year before the announcement in August 2019 that Granada would bid for the award of European Capital of Culture 2031, a delegation from five EU countries – Cyprus, France, Greece, Portugal and Spain – met in the Alhambra to discuss the challenges facing the European Union in the spheres of foreign affairs and defence, in which the ever more important need for dialogue with the Islamic world was on the agenda. Granada was chosen as the city of reference for this group of politicians because of its historic multiculturalism, special relations with the Arab world and the universality of its links with other civilizations and cultures. At a meeting which led to the signing of the Declaration of Granada, whose aim is to bolster the fight against people trafficking and guarantee the rescue of migrants, the delegates reflected that few places in the world could be more inspiring than Granada in fostering cultural understanding and enabling a future of cooperation, peace and development throughout the Mediterranean. It was held up to other European parliaments as an example of *convivencia* that derives from its history as a place of confluence of many cultures, giving it a universal significance.

The Alhambra was the apt setting for such a meeting, majestic in its global power as a touristic and cultural reference point, and above all as the hallmark of Granada's true heritage, and guiding light for the multicultural values of the present and future. The great fortress is also an unshakeable reminder of the local cultural nature of al-Andalus within the Spanish Islamic artistic tradition. Some years ago, in 2008, the art historian Andrew Graham-Dixon made a TV programme on the art of Spain. His views were bold, almost startling, in the acuteness of his perception of the significance of the Moorish art of Spain. In his opinion, that art, albeit shockingly neglected, is the guardian of the secrets of all Spanish art and its unique intensity. He spoke of the explosive results of the meeting of East and West in Spanish visual art and architecture, which he felt holds the key to understanding all of Europe and its culture. Standing in the grounds of the new mosque, facing the Alhambra, Graham-Dixon remarked that Spain is almost the only place in modern Europe 'where you can still almost physically grasp the fact that the history and culture of the Islamic world is part of all our DNA'.[205]

What does it mean to be born and live in Granada today? Its supremacy among Spanish cities is heightened by its growing European and international standing, not solely as a place of outstanding cultural value but as a city of overwhelming possibility as an influence for good. In that context, the full meaning of its eight-hundred-year Islamic heritage is still being worked out. Al-Andalus is a country of the past but it lives in the present and looks toward a future in which Granada may be reformulated, restored and reconstituted in the imaginations of Spaniards and of Muslims as they honour its Arab dimension. That reimagining involves a search for cultural continuity that might transcend the political and religious fragmentation of Spain and of Europe and bring their diverse races and creeds together. In doing so, Granada's paradise may one day be regained.

BIBLIOGRAPHY

* * * * * * * * * * * * * * *

General

Delumeau, Jean, and O'Connell, Matthew (trans.), *History of Paradise: The Garden of Eden in Myth and Tradition,* trans (New York: Continuum, 1995).

Documentos de Nuestra Historia (Granada: Ayuntamiento de Granada, 2000).

Doubleday, Simon R. and Coleman, David, *In the Light of Medieval Spain: Islam, the West and the Relevance of the Past* (New York: Palgrave Macmillan, 2008).

Edwards, Gwynne, *A Cultural Journey through Andalusia* (Cardiff: University of Wales Press, 2009).

Fanjul, Serafín, *Al-Andalus contra España* (Madrid: Siglo XXI de España Editores, S.A., 2000; 2nd ed., 2001).

Fuentes, Carlos, *The Buried Mirror – Reflections on Spain and the New World* (London: Deutsch, 1992).

Gamboa, José Manuel, *Una historia del flamenco* (Barcelona: Espasa, 2011).

Girón, César, *Miscelánea de Granada. Historia. Personajes. Monumentos y sucesos singulares de Granada* (Granada: Editorial Comares, 1999).

_____, 'El símbolo de un reino', *Ideal* (21 Aug. 2017).

_____, 'Granada: Heráldica y Vexilología', *Ideal* (28 Aug. 2017).

Góngora y Martínez, Manuel, *Antigüedades prehistóricas de Andalucía, monumentos, inscripciones, armas, utensilios y otros importantes objetos pertenecientes a tiempos más remotos de su población* (Madrid: C. Moro, 1868).

González Alcantud, José Antonio, *Al-Ándalus y lo andaluz: Al-Ándalus en el imaginario y en la narración histórica española* (Cordoba: Almuzara, 2017).

Graham-Dixon, Andrew, *The Art of Spain,* DVD (BBC Worldwide Limited, 2010).

Hooper, John, *The New Spaniards* (London: Penguin, 1986; 2nd ed., 2006).

Lowenthal, David, *The Past is a Foreign Country – Revisited* (Cambridge: CUP, 2015).

Martín Salazar, Los *cantes flamencos* (Granada: Diputación Provincial de Granada, 1991).

Moffitt, John F., *The Arts in Spain* (London: Thames and Hudson, 1999).

Rawlings, Helen, *The Debate on the Decline of Spain* (Manchester: Manchester University Press, 2012).

Rollason, David W., *The Power of Place: rulers and their palaces, landscapes, cities and holy places* (Princeton/Oxford: Princeton University Press, 2016).

Stone, Damien, *Pomegranate: a global history* (London: Reaktion Books, 2017).

Urban History

Armenta García, Carmen María, 'La conservación de la imagen de la ciudad histórica: el estudio del color en la carrera del Darro' in Juan Calatrava, Francisco García Pérez and David Arredondo Garrido (eds.), *La Cultura y la Ciudad,* Granada: Universidad de Granada, 2016, pp. 595–602.

Asensio Teruel, Francisca, Ibáñez, Francisco José and Bueno, Antonio García, 'Paisajes velados: el Darro bajo la Granada actual' in Juan Calatrava, Francisco García Pérez and David Arredondo Garrido (eds.), *La Cultura y la Ciudad,* Granada: Universidad de Granada, 2016, pp. 603–9.

Calatrava, Juan, 'Ciudad histórica y eventos culturales en la era de la globalización' in Juan Calatrava, Francisco García Pérez and David Arredondo Garrido (eds.), *La Cultura y la Ciudad,* Granada: Universidad de Granada, 2016, pp. 851–61.

Calatrava, Juan, García Pérez, Francisco and Arredondo Garrido, David (eds.), *La Cultura y la Ciudad* (Granada: Universidad de Granada, 2016).

Dauro, un río en la imagen de la ciudad (Granada: Fundación Emasagra and Caja Granada, 2009).

García Bueno, Antonio and Medina Granados, Karina, 'El Sacromonte: patrimonio e imagen de una cultura' in Juan Calatrava, Francisco García Pérez and David Arredondo Garrido (eds.), *La Cultura y la Ciudad,* Granada: Universidad de Granada, 2016, pp. 633–9.

García Pérez, Francisco Antonio, 'El agua oculta. Corrientes subterráneas y sacralización territorial en la Granada del siglo XVII' in Juan Calatrava, Francisco García Pérez and David Arredondo Garrido (eds.), *La Cultura y la Ciudad,* Granada: Universidad de Granada, 2016, pp. 689–700.

Handlin, Oscar and Burchard, John (eds.), *The Historian and the City* (Cambridge/Massachusetts/London: Massachusetts Institute of Technology, 1963).

Hermes, Nizar F., *The City in Arabic Literature* (Edinburgh: Edinburgh University Press, 2018).

Jerez Mir, Carlos, 'Granada: lectura de la ciudad moderna por medio de sus panorámicas y vistas generales' in Juan Calatrava, Francisco García Pérez and David Arredondo Garrido (eds.), *La Cultura y la Ciudad,* Granada: Universidad de Granada, 2016, pp. 201–7.

Martínez de Carvajal, Ángel Isac, *Historia urbana de Granada* (Granada: Diputación de Granada, 2007).

Martínez Jiménez, Nuria, 'Granada: ciudad simbólica entre los siglos XVII y XVIII' in Juan Calatrava, Francisco García Pérez and David Arredondo Garrido (eds.), *La Cultura y la Ciudad,* Granada: Universidad de Granada, 2016, pp. 619–24.

Pike, Burton, *The Image of the City in Modern Literature* (Princeton: Princeton University Press, 1981).

Sánchez Muñoz, Juan Antonio, 'La Alcaicería de Granada. Realidad y ficción' in Juan Calatrava, Francisco García Pérez and David Arredondo Garrido (eds.), *La Cultura y la Ciudad,* Granada: Universidad de Granada, 2016, pp. 673–80.

Villa-Real, Ricardo, *Historia de Granada: acontecimientos y personajes* (Granada: Miguel Sánchez, 1991).

Viñes Millet, Cristina, *Figuras granadinas* (Granada: El Legado Andalusí, 1995).

―――――――――, *Granada y Marruecos: Arabismo y Africanismo en la cultura granadina* (Granada: El Legado Andalusí, 1995).

Early Iberian, Roman and Visigothic Granada

Bermúdez y Pedraza, Francisco, *Antigüedad y excelencias de Granada* (Madrid: Luis Sánchez, 1608; online text at www.bibliotecavirtualdeandalucia.es/catalogo/consulta/registro.cmd?id=7185)

Fernández Casado, Carlos, *Aqueductos romanos en España* (Madrid: CSIC, 2nd ed., 2008).

Fernández Castro, María Cruz, *Iberia in Prehistory* (Oxford: Blackwell, 1995).

Gill, I. R., 'The orthography of the Ashburnham Pentateuch and other Latin manuscripts of the late protoromance period – some questions of palaeography and vulgar Latin linguistics', *Bulletin of the Institute of Classical Studies* No. 23 (1976), pp. 27–44.

Molina González, Fernando and Roldán Hervás, José M., *Historia de Granada I: de las primeras culturas al Islam* (Granada: Editorial Quijote, 1983).

Pérez, Ramón L., 'La excavación arqueológica de la villa romana de los Vergeles descubre la 'carambola perfecta' que explica la historia de Granada', *Ideal de Granada*, 9 Aug. 2018.

Richardson, J. S., *The Romans in Spain* (Oxford: Blackwell, 1996, reprint 1998).

Salvador Ventura, Francisco, *Hispania meridional entre Roma y el Islam: Economía y sociedad* (Granada: Universidad de Granada, 1990).

Sánchez-Prieto Borja, P., Díaz Moreno, Rocío and Trujillo Belso, Elena, Edición de textos alfonsíes en REAL ACADEMIA ESPAÑOLA: Banco de datos (CORDE) [en línea]. Corpus diacrónico del español. <http://www.rae.es> [7 de marzo 2006]: *Estoria de España*, Ms. Escorial Y.I.2

Muslim Granada

Boloix Gallardo, Bárbara, *Ibn Al-Ahmar: vida y reinado del primer sultán de Granada* (Granada: Editorial Universidad de Granada, 2017).

Bush, Olga, *Reframing the Alhambra* (Edinburgh: Edinburgh University Press, 2018).

Coleman, David, *Creating Christian Granada: Society and Religious Culture in an Old-World Frontier City, 1492–1600* (Ithaca and London: Cornell University Press, 2003).

Dickie, James, 'Granada: a case study of Arab urbanism in Muslim Spain' in Salma Khadra Jayyusi (ed.), *The Legacy of Muslim Spain*, Vol. I (Leiden: Brill, 1992, 1994), pp. 88–111.

―――――――――, 'The Hispano-Arab Garden: Notes towards a typology' in Salma Khadra Jayyusi (ed.), *The Legacy of Muslim Spain*, Vol. I (Leiden: Brill, 1992, 1994), pp. 1016–35.

Dodds, Jerrilyn, 'The Arts of al-Andalus' in Salma Khadra Jayyusi, (ed.), *The Legacy of Muslim Spain*, Vol. I (Leiden: Brill, 1992, 1994), pp. 599–619.

Drayson, Elizabeth, *The Moor's Last Stand: How Seven Centuries of Muslim Rule in Spain Came to an End* (London: Profile Books, 2017; pbk 2018).

García Sánchez, Expiración, 'Agriculture in Muslim Spain' in Salma Khadra Jayyusi (ed.), *The Legacy of Muslim Spain*, Vol. I (Leiden, Brill, 1992, 1994), pp. 987–99.

Grabar, Oleg, *The Alhambra* (London: Allen Lane, 1978).

Handler, Andrew, *The Zirids of Granada* (Florida: University of Miami Press, 1974).

Harvey, L. P., 'The Mudejars' in Salma Khadra Jayyusi (ed.), *The Legacy of Muslim Spain*, Vol. I (Leiden: Brill, 1992, 1994), pp. 176–87.

Hurtado de Mendoza, Diego, *Historia de la Guerra de Granada* (Barcelona: Red ediciones, 2010).

_____, 'The Political, social and cultural history of the Moriscos' in Salma Khadra Jayyusi (ed.), *The Legacy of Muslim Spain*, Vol. I (Leiden: Brill, 1992, 1994), pp. 201–34.

Irwin, Robert, *The Alhambra* (London: Profile Books, 2004).

Lévi-Provencal, E. and García Gómez, Emilio (introduction and trans.), *El siglo XI en 1ª persona: las 'Memorias' de Abd Allah, último Rey Zirí de Granada, destronado por los Almorávides (1090)* (Madrid: Alianza Tres, 1981).

Mármol y Carvajal, Luis, *Historia del [sic] rebelión y castigo de los moriscos del Reino de Granada* (Edición digital: Alicante: Biblioteca Virtual Miguel de Cervantes, 2001).

Patronato de la Alhambra y Generalife (sponsoring body), *Arte y culturas de Al-Andalus : El poder de la Alhambra* (Granada, 2013).

Peinado Santaella, Rafael Gerardo and López de Coca Castañer, José Enrique, *Historia de Granada II: la época medieval. Siglos VIII–XV* (Granada: Editorial Quijote, 1987).

Puerta Vílchez, José Miguel, *Leer la Alhambra: Guía visual del monumento a través de sus inscripciones* (Granada: Patronato de la Alhambra y Generalife, 2010).

Vernet, Juan, *Lo que Europa debe al Islam de España* (Barcelona: Acantilado, 1999).

Viguera, María José, 'On the social status of Andalusi women' in Salma Khadra Jayyusi (ed.), *The Legacy of Muslim Spain*, Vol. I (Leiden, Brill, 1992, 1994), pp. 709–24.

Jewish Granada

Arié, Rachel and López Ruiz, Antonio (trans.) 'La expulsión de los judíos de España y su acogida en tierra del Islam, de la Baja Edad Media al siglo XVI' in Manuel Barrios Aguilera y Bernard Vincent, *Granada 1492–92. Del reino de Granada al futuro del Mundo Mediterráneo* (Granada: Universidad de Granada, 1995), pp. 57–76.

Ayaso Martínez, José Ramón, 'Garnata al-Yahud: Luces y sombras en la historia judía de Granada', *Historia de Granada* (Chapter 17), *Ideal* 2002 (accessed 12 March 2019).

Bel Bravo, María Antonia, 'Apuntes para el estudio de los judeoconversos granadinos en el siglo XVI', *Chronica Nova* 14, 1984–85, pp. 47–55.

Bernáldez, Andrés, *Historia de los reyes católicos D. Fernando y Doña Isabel*, Tomo I (Seville: José María Geofrin, 1870).

Cano, José A., 'Los judíos regresan a España', *El Mundo* (edición España), 25 Jan. 2014.

'Cédula real para que los nuevamente convertidos de judíos no vivan en las Alpujarras', Documento 22 in *1492–1513, La Nueva Granada. Exposición documental* (Granada: Ayuntamiento de Granada, 1992).

Diaz-Mas, Paloma, 'La mención de Granada en los romances sefardíes de Marruecos' in *Actas del Congreso Internacional sobre Lengua y Literatura en la época de los Reyes Católicos y el*

Descubrimiento (Barcelona: University of Barcelona, 1989), pp. 191–200.

García Fuentes, José María, *La inquisición en Granada en el siglo XVI* (Granada: Universidad de Granada, 1981).

García Iglesias, L., *Los judíos en la España antigua* (Madrid: Ediciones Cristiandad, 1978).

Gonzalo Maeso, David, *Garnata al-Yahud: Granada en la historia del judaísmo español* (Granada: University of Granada, 1992; 2008).

http://granadaysusreligiones.blogspot.com/p/ruta-judia.html

Kamen, Henry, *The Spanish Inquisition: An Historical Revision* (London: Phoenix Press, 1997).

Ladero Quesada, Miguel Ángel, 'De nuevo sobre los judíos granadinos al tiempo de su expulsión', *En la España medieval* 30, 2007, pp. 281–316.

www.palaciodelosolvidados.es/

Ray, Jonathan, *After Expulsion: 1492 and the making of Sephardic Jewry* (New York: New York University Press, 2013).

Scheindlin, Raymond P., 'The Jews in Muslim Spain' in Salma Khadra Jayyusi (ed.), *The Legacy of Muslim Spain*, Vol. I, (Leiden: Brill, 1992, 1994), pp. 188–200.

Spivakovsky, Erika (1976) 'The Jewish presence in Granada', *Journal of Medieval History*, 2:3, 215–237, DOI: 10.1016/0304-4181(76) 90021 – X.

Tapia, Juan Luis, 'La Granada de los judíos', *Ideal.es*, 23 Nov. 2008, accessed 12 March 2019.

Thouvenot, Raymond, 'Chrétiens et juifs à Grenade', *Hespéris*, 1943, Tome XXX, pp. 201–211.

Viñes Millet, Cristina, 'Moses ibn Ezra' in *Figuras granadinas* (Granada: El Legado Andalusí, 1995), pp. 23–5.

_____, 'Yosef Ha-Nagid ibn Nagrela' in *Figuras granadinas* (Granada: El Legado Andalusí, 1995), pp. 19–21.

Wigoder, Geoffrey (ed.), 'Moses ibn Ezra' in *The New Encyclopedia of Judaism* (New York: New York University Press, 2002).

Catholic Granada After 1492

1492–1513, La Nueva Granada. Exposición documental (Granada: Ayuntamiento de Granada, 1992).

Barrios Aguilera, Manuel and Vincent, Bernard (eds.) and López Ruiz, Antonio (trans.), *Granada 1492–1992. Del reino de Granada al futuro del Mundo Mediterráneo* (Granada: Universidad de Granada, 1995).

Brown, Jonathan, *Painting in Spain 1500–1700* (New Haven and London: Yale University Press, 1998).

de la Cal, Juan Carlos, 'Los hijos del exilio andalusí', https://identidadandalusi.wordpress.com/2007/10/21/los-hijos-del-exilio-andalusi/, accessed 21 Oct. 2017

Cortés Peña, Antonio Luis and Vincent, Bernard, *Historia de Granada III: La Época Moderna, Siglos XVI, XVII, XVIII* (Granada: Editorial Don Quijote, 1986).

Darwish, Mahmoud, *The Adam of Two Edens* (Syracuse: Syracuse University Press, 2000).

Documentos de nuestra historia (Granada: Ayuntamiento de Granada, 2000).

Drayson, Elizabeth, *The Lead Books of Granada* (Basingstoke and New York: Palgrave Macmillan, 2013, pbk 2016).

Harvey, L. P., *Muslims in Spain 1500–1614* (Chicago: University of Chicago Press, 2005).

_____, 'The political, social and cultural history of the Moriscos' in Salma Khadra Jayyusi (ed.), *The Legacy of Muslim Spain* Vol. I, ed. (Leiden: Brill, 1992, 1994), pp. 210–34.

Hurtado de Mendoza, Diego, *Historia de la guerra de Granada* (Barcelona: Red ediciones, 2010).

van Koningsveld, Pieter Sjoerd and Wiegers, Gerard, *The Sacromonte Parchment and Lead Books: Critical Edition of the Arabic Texts and Analysis of the Religious Ideas* (Presentation of a Dutch research project, Granada, 19 March 2019).

López Lorca, Miguel E. (dir.), *Expulsados 1609: La Tragedia de los Moriscos*, DVD (Sagrera Audiovisual/Divisa Home Video, 2009).

Luis de Granada, *Introducción al símbolo de la fe*, online text at www.cervantesvirtual. com/obra-visor/introduccion-del-simbolo-de-la-fe-o/html/fedb9048-82b1-11df-acc7-002185ce6064.html, accessed 30 Oct. 2018.

Martín Casares, Aurelia, *Juan Latino, talento y destino: un afroespañol en tiempos de Carlos V y Felipe II* (Granada: Universidad de Granada, 2016).

Martínez Jiménez, Nuria, 'Granada: ciudad simbólica entre los siglos XVII y XVIII' in *La Cultura y la Ciudad* (Granada: Universidad de Granada, 2016), pp. 619–24.

Martínez Medina, Francisco Javier, *Cristianos y musulmanes en la Granada del XVI, una ciudad intercultural. Invenciones de reliquias y libros plúmbeos: El Sacromonte* (Granada: Facultad de Teología, 2016).

Rivers, Susan T., 'Exiles from Andalusia' in *Saudi Aramco World*, July/August 1991, pp. 10–17.

Soria Mesa, Enrique, *Los últimos moriscos. Pervivencias de la población de origen islámico en el reino de Granada (siglos XVII–XVIII)* (Valencia: Biblioteca de Estudios Moriscos, 2014).

Urquízar Herrera, Antonio, *Admiration and Awe: Morisco Buildings and Identity Negotiations in Early Modern Spanish Historiography* (Oxford: Oxford University Press, 2017).

Gypsies and Flamenco in Granada

Alcobendas, Miguel (dir.), *Camelamos naquerar* (Mino Films S.A., 1976).

Bonachera, José María, *Granada y el flamenco: la historia que contar* (Granada: Diputación de Granada, Libros de Estrella, 2016).

Borrow, George, *The Zincali. An account of the gypsies of Spain* (London and Toronto: J. M. Dent and Sons, Ltd., 1914, repr. 1924).

'Breve historia del pueblo gitano y el barrio del Sacromonte', at http://sacromontegranada.com/museo/el-sacromonte/, accessed 22 July 2019.

Cadalso, José, *Cartas marruecas* (Barcelona: Editorial Crítica, S.L., 2008).

Cárdenas Granada, Andrés, '"Estás más negro que Chorrojumo", una expresión común en Granada con una historia detrás' at www.ideal.es/granada/20100319/local/granada/estas-negro, accessed 15 July 2019.

Charnon-Deutsch, Lou, *The Spanish Gypsy: the history of a European obsession* (University Park: Pennsylvania State University Press, 2004).

'Chorrojumo' at http://granada21.wordpress.com/2010/11/18/chorrojumo/, accessed 15 July 2019.

Dumas, Alexandre, *Impressions de voyage. De Paris à Cadix*, Vol. 3 (Brussels: Méline, Cans et Cie, Libraires Éditeurs, 1849; electronic text at: https://babel.hathitrust.org/cgi/pt?id=uiug.30112081966985&view=1up&seq=19)

'El "Cristo de los gitanos"' at http://abadiasacromonte.org/el-cristo-de-los-gitanos, accessed 11 July 2019.

García Bueno, Antonio and Medina Granados, Karina, 'El Sacromonte: patrimonio e imagen de una cultura' in Juan Calatrava, Francisco García Pérez and David Arredondo Garrido (eds.), *La Cultura y la Ciudad* (Granada: Universidad de Granada, 2016), pp. 633–9.

García Lorca, Federico, 'El cante jondo (primitive canto andaluz)' in *Obras completas, recopilación y notas de Arturo del Hoyo* (Madrid: Aguilar, 1955), pp. 1514–31.

Gautier, Théophile and McQuoid, Thomas Robert (trans.), *Wanderings in Spain* (London: Ingram Cooke, 1853).

'La cárcel de Albolote (Granada) acoge hoy la final del cante y guitarra del certamen "Flamenco en las prisiones"' at www.europapress.es/cultura/noticia-carcel-albolote-granada, accessed 22 July 2019.

'La historia de las mujeres gitanas del Sacromonte' at http://sevilla.abc.es/andalucía/granada/sevi-historia-mujeres-gitanas, accessed 21 September 2017.

Machado, Antonio, 'La saeta' from 'Campos de Castilla', available at www.poemas-del-alma.com/la-saeta.htm

Machin-Autenrieth, Matthew, *Flamenco, Regionalism and Musical Heritage in Southern Spain* (London: Routledge, 2017).

Martín Sánchez, David, *Historia del pueblo gitano en España* (Madrid: Catarata, 2018).

Pym, Richard J., *The Gypsies of Early Modern Spain, 1425–1783* (Basingstoke: Palgrave Macmillan, 2007).

Rodríguez Padilla, Eusebio and Fernández Autunite, Dolores, *Mujeres gitanas represaliadas en la provincia de Granada durante la Guerra Civil y la Posguerra: 1936–1950* (Mojácar: Arráez Editores, 2010).

Schreiner, Claus (ed.), *Flamenco: Gypsy Dance and Music from Andalusia* (Portland, Oregon: Amadeus Press, 1985).

Washabaugh, William, *Flamenco: Passion, Politics and Culture* (Oxford: Berg, 1996).

Eighteenth- and Nineteenth-Century Granada

Ford, Richard, *Granada: an account illustrated with unpublished drawings* (Granada: Patronato de la Alhambra y Generalife, 1955).

Gautier, Théophile, *Wanderings in Spain* (London: Ingram, Cooke, 1853).

Humboldt, Wilhelm von and Ángel Vega, Miguel (trans.), *Diario de viaje a España, 1799–1800* (Madrid: Cátedra, 1998).

Juvanon du Vachat, Agnès, *Les jardins de l'Alhambra sous le regard des voyageurs français* (unpublished Master's thesis in Aesthetics, supervised by Catherine Fricheau, José Tito Rojo, 2006).

Murray, Dundas R., *The Cities and Wilds of Andalucía* (London: Richard Bentley, 1853; 3rd edition).

Raquejo, Tonia, *El palacio encantado: La Alhambra en el arte británico* (Madrid: Taurus Humanidades, 1990).

Rodrigo, Antonina, *Mariana Pineda. Memoria viva* (Granada: Caja Granada, 2008).

Sanz Sampelayo, Juan, *Granada en el siglo XVIII* (Granada: Diputación Provincial, 1980).

Zorrilla, José, *Granada: un poema oriental*, online text at https://es.m.wikisource.org/wiki/Granada._Poema_oriental

Twentieth- and Twenty-First Century Granada

Aerial photos from the 1950s at www.granada.org/inet/wfot_Arc.nsf/3d5b5571fdf80126c12574c200227f71/a0d637b62824347bc1256ad80033db47!OpenDocument

Arco Blanco, Miguel Ángel del, '1936. La Granada de aquel verano. Una ciudad entre la victoria y la muerte', *Granada Hoy*, 14 August 2011, 0.6.16.

AS.com 'Granada, la mejor ciudad del mundo para visitar en 2018', at http://as.com/tikitakas/2018/04/11/portada/1523471460_388863.html, accessed 12 November 2018.

Atienza, Emilio, 'La ciudad posmoderna', *Ideal*, 27 November 2006, at www.ideal.es/granada/prensa/20061127/tribuna_granada/ciudad-posmoderna_20061127.html

Ceremonia y protocolo de la ciudad de Granada (Granada: Ayuntamiento de Granada, 2007).

EFE, 'Así es el plan de Granada para ser Capital Cultural Europea en 2031', *Ideal*, 2 August 2019, at www.ideal.es/culturas/plan-granada-capital-20190802141912-nt.html

Ganivet, Ángel, *Granada la bella* (Granada: Impredisur, 1920, 2nd ed. 1977).

García Lorca, Federico, *Mariana Pineda*, Nadal, R. M. and Perry, Janet H. (eds.), (London: George G. Harrap and Co. Ltd, 1957).

Gay Armenteros, Juan and Cristina Viñes Millet, *Historia de Granada IV: la época contemporánea, siglos XIX y XX* (Granada: Editorial El Quijote, 1982).

Gill, John, *Andalucía: a cultural history* (Oxford: Signal Books, 2008).

Granara, William, 'Nostalgia, Arabic nationalism, and the Andalusian *Chronotope* in the evolution of the modern Arabic novel', *Journal of Arabic Literature*, XXXVI, 1, pp. 57–73.

'Granada gana el título a la mejor ciudad del mundo para visitar', *Ideal*, 11 April 2018.

'Las otras Granadas del mundo', *Ideal*, 1 June 2018.

Lee, Laurie, *A Rose for Winter* (London: Hogarth Press, 1955; Harmondsworth: Penguin Books, 1971, repr. 1972).

Martín Civantos, José María, 'El Darro recuperado. Y tú, ¿cómo te lo imaginas?', *El Independiente de Granada*, 21 May 2019 at www.elindependientedegranada.es/politica/darro-recuperado-tu-como-te-lo-imaginas

Martínez Montávez, Pedro, *Al-Andalus, España, en la literatura árabe contemporánea: La casa del pasado* (Madrid: Editorial Mapfre, 1992).

Moreh, C., 'Inhabiting Heritage: Living with the Past in the Albayzín de Granada', *Open Library of the Humanities* 2(1): e8, pp. 1–33.

Sánchez Muñoz, Juan Antonio, 'La Alcaicería de Granada. Realidad y ficción' in Juan Calatrava, Francisco García Pérez and David Arredondo Garrido (eds.), *La Cultura y la Ciudad* (Granada: Universidad de Granada, 2016), pp. 673–80.

Shannon, Jonathan H., 'Performing al-Andalus, Remembering al-Andalus: Mediterranean Soundings from Mashriq to Maghrib', *Journal of American Folklore* 120 (477), pp. 308–34.

Starr, Stephen, 'Syrians find a home in the land of the Moors', *The National*, 7 June 2018.

Vicente Pascual, José *et al.*, *Granada 1936: relatos de la Guerra Civil* (Granada: El Defensor de Granada, 2006).

Youssef, Olfa, 'Al-Ándalus en el imaginario árabe-musulmán contemporáneo (ejemplo del cine tunecino)' in Manuel Barrios Aguilera and Bernard Vincent (eds.), *Granada 1492–1992. Del reino de Granada al futuro del mundo mediterráneo* (Granada: Universidad de Granada/Diputación Provincial de Granada, 1995), pp. 297–310.

Notes

❖❖❖❖❖❖❖❖❖❖❖❖❖❖❖❖❖

1. Paradise and Pomegranates

1   In Spanish: 'Dale limosna, mujer, que en la vida no hay nada/como la pena de ser ciego en Granada.'

2   Genesis Ch. 2: verses 8–17.

3   Koran Ch. 56: verses 15–25.

4   For further ideas on the image of paradise in Christian tradition, see Jean Delumeau, *History of Paradise: the garden of Eden in myth and tradition*, trans. Matthew O'Connell (New York: Continuum, 1995).

5   https://h2g2.com/edited_entry/A27975153.

6   Ibid.

7   María Rosa Menocal, *The Ornament of the World: How Muslims, Jews and Christians created a culture of tolerance in medieval Spain* (New York, Little Brown and Company, 2002), p. 32.

8   *Deuteronomy* Ch. 8: verses 7–9.

9   *Exodus* Ch. 28: verses 33–34.

10 *Kings* 1: Chapter 7, verse 20.

11 Luis de Granada, *Introducción al símbolo de la fe*, online text at www.cervantesvirtual.com/obra-visor/introduccion-del-simbolo-de-la-fe--0/html/fedb9048-82b1-11df-acc7-

002185ce6064.html, accessed on 30 October 2018).

12 The Royal College of Physicians in London also adopted the pomegranate on their coat of arms in the sixteenth century and it is still their logo today.

13 Queen Catherine of Aragon, wife of Arthur Tudor and later of Henry VIII of England, ordered pomegranates to be sculpted on the old Palace of Placentia in Greenwich to remind her of the city where she grew up and from where she departed for England.

14 César Girón, 'El símbolo de un reino', *Ideal de Granada*, 21 August 2017.

15 www.gastroandalusi.com/, accessed 21 January 2019.

2. The mists of time: from prehistory to the reign of the Visigoths

16 See Manuel Góngora y Martínez, *Antigüedades prehistóricas de Andalucía, monumentos, inscripciones, armas, utensilios y otros importantes objetos pertenecientes a tiempos más remotos de su población* (Madrid: C. Moro, 1868; repr. Forgotten Books, 2018), pp. 28–35.

17 This item is on display in the Archaeological Museum of Granada, Carrera del Darro 41–43.

18 See John F. Moffitt, *The Arts of Spain* (London: Thames and Hudson, 1999), p. 21.

19 See Strabo (trans.: H. L. Jones), *Geography*, Vol. III (Loeb Classical Library, 1932), pp. 2, 8.

20 To avoid confusion, 'Iliberri' or 'Iliberis' will be used in the remainder of this chapter to refer to the city.

21 See Carlos Fernández Casado, *Aqueductos romanos en España* (Madrid: CSIC, 2nd edition, 2008), p. 198.

22 The Lost Wax method of casting involves pouring molten metal into a mould that has been created using a wax model. Once the mould is made, the wax model is melted and drained away.

23 The man wearing a toga (*el togado de Periate*) is on display in the Archaeological Museum in Granada.

24 Inscriptions with item reference number CIL II 3272 and CIL II 2079, Archaeological Museum of Granada.

25 Inscription with item reference number CIL II 2074, Archaeological Museum of Granada.

26 His honorary inscription in Iliberis has item reference number CIL II 2071 = 5506, Archaeological Museum of Granada.

27 Inscription with item reference number CIL II 2075, Archaeological Museum of Granada.

28 Roger Collins, *Visigothic Spain 409–711* (Oxford: Blackwell Publishing Ltd, 2004), p. 24.

29 Elvira was the name of a region of al-Andalus, as well as a settlement situated 12 kilometres from Iliberis in what is now the Sierra de Elvira. It flourished and became the regional capital until the late tenth century, when the Berber leader Zawi ben Ziri moved the capital from Elvira to Granada, formerly Iliberis. Elvira became depopulated and remained a fortress until its destruction in 1486 by Fernando II of Aragon. See *Historia de Granada I*, p. 17–18.

30 *Historia de Granada I*, p. 44.

3. City of the Muslims

31 For a full account of the legend of King Roderic and his love affair with Count Julian's daughter La Cava, see Elizabeth Drayson, *The King and the Whore: King Roderick and La Cava* (New York and Basingstoke: Palgrave Macmillan, 2007).

32 The exoplanet Samh, also known as Upsilon Andromedae C, was named in his honour.

33 See B. Fernández-Capel Baños, 'Un fragmento del kitab al-Yurafiyya de al-Zuhri sobre Granada', *Cuadernos de Historia del Islam*, 3 (1971), p. 123.

34 E. Lévi-Provençal and Emilio García Gómez (trans. and introduction), *El siglo XI en primera persona: las "Memorias" de Abd Allah, ultimo rey ziri de Granada, destronado por los Almorávides (1090)* (Madrid: Alianza Tres, 1981), p. 74.

35 One hectare is equivalent to approximately one international rugby pitch.

36 Ibid., p. 269.

37 Ibid., p. 272.

38 The term 'sayyid' is a respectful Muslim form of address, and originally related to a person who claimed descent from Muhammad, especially through the Prophet's younger grandson Husayn.

39 Hobbes and Locke probably encountered Ibn Tufayl's novel in a Latin translation published in 1671.

40 B. Fernández Capel Baños, 'Un fragmento del Kitab al-Yu'rafiyya de al-Zuhri sobre Granada', *Cuadernos de la Historia del Islam*, 3, 1971, p. 123.

41 Ibn Sahib al-Sala (trans.: A. A. Huici Miranda), *Al-Mann bil-imama* (Valencia: Anubar, 1969).

42 Emilio García Gómez, *Andalucía contra Berbería* (Barcelona: University of Barcelona, 1976), p. 131.

43 Ibn al-Jatib (trans.: Bárbara Boloix), *Ihata*, II, p. 94.

44 Ibn Idhari (trans.: Qism al-muwahhidin), *Bayan*, II, p, 109.

45 Ibn al-Jatib, *Ihata*, p. 95.

46 Tributes were payments made periodically by one ruler to another, usually to show dependence.

47 *Crónica de Alfonso X*, Biblioteca de Autores Españoles, LXVI, p. 46. This fourteenth-century chronicle by Fernán Sánchez de Valladolid is the first history of the learned king Alfonso X.

48 A palatine city possessed royal privileges.

4. Paradise and Perdition

49 Pedro Correa (ed.), *Los romances fronterizos I* (Granada: University of Granada, 1999), p. 297. To hear a performance of the ballad, go to: www.youtube.com/watch?v=EqvpTWS_ths

50 Quoted from Ibn al-Khatib in James Dickie, 'The Hispano-Arab garden: notes towards a typology' in Salma Jayussi (ed.), *The Legacy of Muslim Spain*, Vol. II, (Leiden: Brill, 1992; 2nd edition 1994), p. 1026.

51 Ibid., p. 1025.

52 Quoted in Robert Irwin, *The Alhambra* (London: Profile Books, 2004), p. 52.

53 Ibid., p. 72–3.

54 White Death referred to dying peacefully while asleep; Black Death was caused by the plague. Idem., p. 73.

55 Quoted in Viñes Millet, *Figuras granadinas*, p. 47.

56 Quoted by Emilio García Gómez, *Ibn Zamrak, el poeta de la Alhambra, discurso leído el día 3 de febrero de 1943, en la recepción pública* (Madrid: Imprenta de la Viuda de Estanislao Maestre, 1943), p. 30.

57 Ibid., p. 63.

58 Ibid., p. 34.

59 Bermúdez de Pedraza, *Antigüedad y Excelencias de Granada* (Madrid: Luis Sánchez, 1608), p. 21.

60 James Dickie, 'Granada: a case study of Arab Urbanism in Muslim Spain' in Salma Khadra Jayyusi (ed.) *The Legacy of Muslim Spain*, Vol. I, (Leiden: Brill, 1992, 1994), p. 89.

61 See L. P. Harvey, *Islamic Spain, 1250–1500* (Chicago: University of Chicago Press, 1990), p. 243.

62 *Viajes de extranjeros por España y Portugal desde los tiempos más remotos hasta los fines del siglo XVI*, translation and notes by J. García Mercadal (Madrid: Aguilar, 1952), p. 248.

63 Fernando Nicolás Velázquez Basanta, 'La relación histórica sobre las postrimerías del Reino de Granada según Ahmad al-Maqqarī (s. XVII)' in Celia del Moral (ed.) *En el epílogo del Islam andalusí: La Granada del siglo XV* (Granada: Grupo de Investigación "Ciudades Andaluzas bajo el Islam", col. Al-Mudun, n° 5., 2002), p. 486.

64 For a full account of the life and reign of Boabdil, see Elizabeth Drayson, *The Moor's Last Stand: How Seven Centuries of Muslim Rule Came to an*

End (London: Profile Books, 2017, pbk 2018).

5. Garnata al-Yahud: City of the Jews

65   Although Diego Hurtado de Mendoza contradicts this in his celebrated history of the Granadan wars, in which he states that Granada fell to the invaders ten years after 711, in 721, and only after a long siege, perhaps suggesting that the predominant population was still Christian at that time. See Diego Hurtado de Mendoza, *Historia de la Guerra de Granada* (Barcelona: Red ediciones, 2010), p. 18.

66   E. García Gómez, p. 101.

67   José Ramón Ayaso Martínez, 'Garnata al-Yahud: luces y sombras en la historia judía de Granada', *Historia de Granada*, ch. 17, *Ideal 2002*, accessed 12 March 2019, p. 4.

68   Marcus, Jacob Rader, '59: Samuel Ha-Nagid, Vizier of Granada' in *The Jew in the Medieval World: A Source Book, 315–1791* (Cincinnati: Union of American Hebrew Congregations, 1938), pp. 335–8.

69   M. Carmoly, *Colección de Manuscritos de anécdotas hebraicas*, quoted by Graetz, chapter IV, p. 133.

70   Quoted by A. Sáenz-Badillos in *Los judíos en la historia y cultura de la Andalucia medieval* (Granada: Universidad de Granada, 1980), pp. 13–15. The translation is mine.

71   See the original text in R. P. Dozy, 'Poeme d'Abou-Ishac d'Elvira contre les juifs de Grenada' in *Recherches*, I, pp. 282–94.

72   Letters 262 and 263 from Šire h-hol, ed. Brody and quoted by Y. Baer, *Los judíos en la España Cristiana I*, (Madrid, 1981), pp. 48–9.

73   Moses ibn Ezra's poetic paraphrase of the *Book of Jonah* was adopted in the Avignon festival prayer book.

74   www.jewishencyclopedia.com/articles/8026-ibn-tibbon#anchor4

75   See Rachel Arié, 'La expulsion de los judíos de España y su acogida en tierra de Islam, de la Baja Edad media al siglo XVI', in M. Barrios Aguilera, Bernard Vincent and Antonio López Ruiz (eds. and trans.), *Granada 1492–1992. Del reino de Granada al futuro del mundo mediterráneo*, (Granada: Universidad de Granada, 1995), p. 65.

76   Miguel-Ángel Ladero Quesada, 'De nuevo sobre los judíos granadinos al tiempo de su expulsión', in *En la España medieval*, 30, 2007, pp. 281–316.

77   Paraphrased from Andrés Bernáldez, *Historia de los reyes católicos D. Fernando y Doña Isabel*, Tomo I (Seville: Jose María Geofrin, 1870), pp. 341–2.

78   'Cédula real para que los nuevamente convertidos de judíos no vivan en las Alpujarras' in *1492–1513, La nueva Granada. Exposición documental* (Granada: Ayuntamiento de Granada, 1992), p. 62.

79   See José María García Fuentes, *La inquisición en Granada en el siglo XVI* (Granada: Universidad de Granada, 1981), p. xxii.

80   Some of the best Sephardic ballads can be found on YouTube, performed by Begoña Olavide (sometimes with Jordi Savall and Hesperion XXI).

81   Paloma Díaz-Mas, 'La mención de Granada en los romances sefardíes de Marruecos' in *Actas del Congreso Internacional sobre Lengua y Literatura en la época de los Reyes Católicos y el Descubrimiento* (Barcelona: University of Barcelona, 1989), p. 198.

6. Sites of Power: City of the Christians

82 Old Christians were those who claimed pure Christian ancestry going back to Visigothic times.

83 For more detail, see David Coleman, *Creating Christian Granada* (London and Ithaca: Cornell University Press, 2003), pp. 13–15.

84 'Epistolario', Letter of 30 March 1492 to don Pedro Gonzalez de Mendoza, Archbishop of Toledo, translated from *Opus epistolarum*, Tome IX, J. López de Toro (ed.), *Colección de documentos inéditos para la Historia de España* [CODOIN] (Madrid, 1957), pp. 178–9.

85 Hieronymus Münzer, 'Relacion de viaje' in J. García Mercadal (ed.), *Viajes de extranjeros por España y Portugal*, Tome I, (Madrid: 1951), p. 358.

86 Quoted in Antonio Cortés Peña and Bernard Vincent, *Historia de Granada III: La Época moderna, siglos XVI, XVII, XVIII* (Granada: Editorial Don Quijote, 1986), p. 39.

87 A term used by Antonio Urquízar-Herrera in his excellent book *Admiration and Awe: Morisco Buildings and Identity Negotiation in Early Modern Spanish Historiography* (Oxford: Oxford University Press, 2017), to which I am greatly indebted.

88 Francisco Bermúdez de Pedraza, *Historia eclesiástica. Principios y progressos de la ciudad, y religion católica de Granada...* (Granada: Andrés de Santiago, 1638), p. 22 and 33ff.

89 Ibid., p. 23v.

90 Aurelia Martín Casares, *Juan Latino, talento y destino: un afroespañol en tiempos de Carlos V y Felipe II* (Granada: Universidad de Granada, 2016), p. 29.

91 *The Sacred Made Real: Spanish Painting and Sculpture 1600–1700*, The National Gallery, London, 21 October 2009–24 January 2010, National Gallery of Art, Washington, 28 February–31 May 2010.

92 Francisco de Zurbarán's great sculptural painting of Saint Francis standing in ecstasy, dated about 1640, may have inspired Pedro de Mena although there is no proof that he ever saw it.

7. Hoaxers, Heretics and Heroes: the Moriscos of Granada

93 Para desarraigarles del todo de la sobredicha su perversa y mala secta, les mandó a los dichos alfaquís tomar todos sus alcoranes y todos los otros libros particulares, cuantos se pudieron haber, los cuales fueron más de 4 ó 5 mil volúmenes, entre grandes y pequeños, y hacer muy grandes fuegos y quemarlos todos; en que había entre ellos infinitos que las encuadernaciones que tenían de plata y otras cosas moriscas, puestas en ellos, valían 8 y 10 ducados, y otros de allí abajo. Y aunque algunos hacían mancilla para los tomar y aprovecharse de los pergaminos y papel y encuadernaciones, su señoría reverendísima mandó expresamente que no se tomase ni ninguno lo hiciese. Y así se quemaron todos, sin quedar memoria, como dicho es, excepto los libros de medicina, que había muchos y se hallaron, que éstos mandó que se quedasen; de los cuales su señoría mandó traer bien 30 ó 40 volúmenes de libros, y están hoy en día puestos en la librería de su insigne colegio y universidad de Alcalá. Quoted in Luis Bernabé Pons, *Los Moriscos*, p. 27.

94 See L. P. Harvey, *Muslims in Spain 1500–1614* (Chicago and London: University of Chicago Press, 2005), p. 13.

95 See the Mancebo de Arévalo's *Tratado (Tafsira)*, ed. María Teresa Narváez Córdoba (Madrid: Editorial Trotta, 2003).

96 'Fue un miserable espectáculo ver tantos hombres de todas edades, las cabezas bajas, las manos cruzadas y los rostros bañados de lágrimas, con semblante doloroso y triste viendo que dejaban sus regaladas casas, sus familias, su patria, su naturaleza, sus haciendas y tanto bien como tenían, y aun no sabían cierto lo que se haría de sus cabezas', Luis Mármol y Carvajal, *Historia del [sic] rebelión y castigo de los moriscos del Reino de Granada*. Edición digital: Alicante: Biblioteca Virtual Miguel de Cervantes, 2001, Capitulo XXVII, p. 278.

97 David Coleman estimates that by 1571, the capital city had lost about a third of the overall population, i.e. between fifteen and twenty thousand Moriscos, leaving around three or four thousand behind. See David Coleman, *Creating Christian Granada: Society and Religious Culture in an Old-World Frontier City 1492–1600* (Ithaca and London: Cornell University Press, 2003), p. 185.

98 For a full, detailed account of the story of the Lead Books, see Elizabeth Drayson, *The Lead Books of Granada* (Basingstoke and New York: Palgrave Macmillan, 2013, 2016).

99 [negocio gravísimo…el mayor que hoy día tiene el mundo y quizá no lo haya tenido mayor en muchos siglos], Zótico Royo Campos, *Reliquias martiriales y escudo del Sacro-Monte* (Granada: Universidad de Granada, 1995), p. 5, note 1.

100 Gerard Wiegers and Pieter Sjoerd van Koningsveld, 'The Sacromonte Parchment and Lead Books: critical edition of the Arabic texts and Analysis of the religious ideas': Presentation of a Dutch research project, Granada, 19 March 2019, p. 14. I am extremely grateful to Professor Wiegers and Emeritus Professor van Koningsveld for allowing me to quote material from the presentation on their research project on the Lead Books relating to their forthcoming critical edition of the Arabic texts, given in Granada in March 2019.

101 For a full discussion of the legendary associations of mountains, caves and treasure, see Elizabeth Drayson, *The Lead Books of Granada* (London and Basingstoke: Palgrave Macmillan, 2013, 2016), p. 94–104.

102 [...vna Ciudad pequeña en el alto sitio fabricada, la cual descubria vna muy amena, y deleytosa vega à la vista, en medio de la qual atrauessaua vu muy hermoso rio caudaloso, los montes de su circuito estauan llenos de arboledas, y frescuras, que parecian vn Parayso en la tierra'], Miguel de Luna, *Historia verdadera del Rey don Rodrigo*, preliminary study by Luis Bernabé Pons, Granada: Universidad de Granada, 2001, p. 50.

103 See letter 19, Appendix 4.

104 Mahmoud Darwish, *The Adam of Two Edens* (Syracuse: Syracuse University Press, 2000), p. 149–150.

105 The Spanish Inquisition (in full the Tribunal of the Holy Office of the Inquisition) was established by Ferdinand and Isabella in 1478 and not finally abolished until 1834.

106 José Manuel Gómez-Moreno, *La arquitectura religiosa granadina en la crisis del Renacimiento (1560–1650)*, p. 250.

107 Cardaillac-Hermosilla, *La magie en Espagne*, p.154.

8. Mystery and Magic: Gypsies and Flamenco

108 See Richard J. Pym, *The Gypsies of Early Modern Spain, 1425–1783* (Basingstoke and New York: Palgrave Macmillan, 2007), p. 73.

109 Quoted in David Martín Sánchez, *Historia del pueblo gitano en España* (Madrid: Los Libros de la Catarata, 2018), p. 30–1.

110 In 1890, he was also painted by the Catalan poet and artist Miquel Carbonell y Selva.

111 George Borrow, *The Zincali. An account of the gypsies of Spain* (London and Toronto: J. M. Dent and Sons, Ltd., 1914, repr. 1924), p. 132.

112 Ibid.

113 Alexandre Dumas, *Impressions de voyage. De Paris à Cadix*, Vol. 3 (Brussels: Méline, Cans et Cie, Libraires Editeurs, 1849), p. 21–2, electronic text at: https://babel.hathitrust.org/cgi/pt?id=uiug.30112081966985&view=1up&seq=19

114 Quoted in Lou Charnon-Deutsch, *The Spanish Gypsy: The History of a European Obsession* (Pennsylvania: Pennsylvania State University Press, 2004), p. 70.

115 Théophile Gautier and Thomas Robert McQuoid (trans.), *Wanderings in Spain* (London: Ingram Cooke, 1853), pp.192–3.

116 "'¿Quién me presta una escalera/para subir al madero/y quitarle los clavos/a Jesús el Nazareno?"/ O la saeta, el cantar/al Cristo de los gitanos,/siempre con sangre en las manos,/siempre por desenclavar. /Cantar del pueblo andaluz/que todas las primaveras/ anda pidiendo escaleras/para subir a la Cruz.' Antonio Machado, *Campos de Castilla* at https://es.wikisource.org/wiki/La_saeta_(Machado). The Catalan poet and singer Joan Manuel Serrat put this poem to music in his album *Dedicado a Antonio Machado, poeta* of 1969.

117 José Cadalso, *Cartas marruecas*, p. 127.

118 See David Martín Sánchez, *Historia del pueblo gitano en España*, p. 54.

119 Manuel de Falla's *carmen* in Calle Antequeruela has been converted into a museum and is open to visitors throughout the year.

120 Federico García Lorca, "El cante jondo (primitivo canto andaluz)' in *Obras completas, recopilación y notas de Arturo del Hoyo* (Madrid: Aguilar, 1955), pp. 1514–31.

121 'Viene de las razas lejanas, atravesando el cementerio de los años y las frondas de los vientos marchitos. Viene del primer llanto y el primer beso.' Ibid., p. 1519.

122 '…una noche ancha y profundamente estrellada', Ibid., p. 1522.

123 'La guitarra ha occidentalizado el cante, y ha hecho belleza sin par, y belleza positive del drama andaluz, Oriente y Occidente, en pugna, que hacen de Bética una isla de cultura.' Ibid., p. 1541.

124 www.elsaltodiario.com/granada/acabar-con-la-leyenda-negra-de-almanjayar#

125 'Pena limpia y siempre sola./¡Oh pena de cauce oculto/y madrugada remota!', Federico García Lorca, *Obras completas*, p. 365.

126 Ibid., p. 382.

9. A Paradise of the Mind: Travellers' Tales from a Changing City

127 There is a short film biography of Frascuelo, in Spanish, on YouTube at www.youtube.com/watch?v=YAkinYXOED4.

128 Antonio Luis Cortés Peña and Bernard Vincent, *Historia de Granada, 3, La época moderna: siglos XVI, XVII, XVIII* (Granada: Editorial Don Quijote, 1986), p. 318.

129 J. M. Andueza, 'La Criada' in *Los españoles pintados por sí mismos* (Madrid: I. Boix, 1844), p. 30, quoted in Juan Gay Armenteros and Cristina Viñes Millet, *Historia de Granada IV: la época contemporánea, siglos XIX y XX* (Granada: Editorial El Quijote, 1982), p. 71.

130 Nicolás de Roda, 'Un domingo en Granada' in *La Alhambra*, III, pp. 225–7 and 234–6.

131 Arthur de Capell Brooke, *Sketches in Spain and Morocco*, Vol. II (London: H. Colburn and R. Bentley, 1831), p. 220.

132 Ibid., p. 255.

133 Thomas Roscoe, *The Tourist in Spain: Andalusia*, illustrated from drawings from David Roberts (London: Robert Jennings and Co., 1836), p. 260.

134 Richard Ford, *Granada: An account illustrated with unpublished original drawings*, text in Spanish and English, Spanish version and notes by Alfonso Gámir (Granada: Patronato de la Alhambra y Generalife, 1955), p. 182. This is the chapter on Granada taken from Ford's handbook for travellers in Spain, published in 1845.

135 Ibid., p. 196.

136 Ibid., p. 201.

137 A climbing Mediterranean plant like a vine, with very bitter fruit, often called a bitter apple.

138 Théophile Gautier, *Wanderings in Spain*, translated by Thomas Robert McQuoid (London: Ingram Cooke, 1853), p. 166.

139 Ibid., p. 178.

140 Ibid., p. 168.

141 Ibid., p. 172.

142 Quoted in Agnès Juvenon du Vachat, 'Les jardins de l'Alhambra sous le regard des voyageurs français', unpublished Master's thesis in Aesthetics, supervised by Catherine Fricheau and José Tito Rojo, 2006, p. 108.

143 Washington Irving, *Tales of the Alhambra* (Granada: Ediciones Miguel Sánchez, 1994), p. 77.

144 Ibid., p. 31.

145 José Giménez Serrano, *Manual de artista y del viajero* (Granada: J. A. Linares, 1846), p. 19–20.

146 A *duro* was worth five pesetas, originally the amount a labourer was paid for a hard day's work.

147 G. Honrsttuns, 'Recuerdos de Granada: Carta de un viejo touriste' in *La Alhambra*, I, 1884, n. 27, p. 3.

148 José Giménez Serrano, *Manual de artista y del viajero*, p. 334.

149 Quoted in Ángel Isac Martínez de Carvajal, *Historia urbana de Granada* (Granada: Diputación de Granada, 2007), p. 93.

150 Ángel Ganivet, *Granada la Bella*, 2nd edition (Madrid: Librería General de Victoriano Suárez, 1920), p. 5.

151 J. Bosque Maurel, *Geografía urbana de Granada* (Granada: Archivum, Editorial Universidad de Granada 1962), p. 244.

10. The Descent into Hell: Modern Granada and the Civil War

152 'En la torre de la Vela/dieron doce campanadas,/para que naciera Dios/a la vera de la Alhambra'. This is a traditional carol of Granada.

153 Quoted in Antonio Ceballes Guerrero, 'Granada, la Navidad entre los siglos XIX y XX', p. 780.

154   Ibid.

155   'Con el amor a Granada, pero con el pensamiento puesto en Europa. Sólo así podremos arrancar los más ocultos y finos tesoros indígenas. Revista de Granada, para fuera de Granada, revista que recoja el latido de todas partes para saber major cuál es el suyo propio; revista alegre, viva, antilocalista, anti-provinciana, del mundo, como es Granada. Granada tiene un nombre en el universe y una corona de Gloria. Granada no es el Café Colón, la calle de Pavaneras, la Gran Vía etc. Granada es otra cosa más permanente y más elevada en la conciencia nacional: términos históricos, poéticos y rumor de belleza pura.' Federico García Lorca, *Granada: paraíso cerrado y otras páginas granadinas* (Granada: Miguel Sánchez, 1989), p. 285.

156   El 20 de Julio de 1936 estaba este café de 'La Maison Doreé' hasta los topes, yo estaba en la puerta, no se cabía dentro. Todos estábamos oyendo la radio, en estos momentos vimos coches y camiones con gente de paisano y gorros militares, armados de fusiles, venían de la Gran Vía y bajaban por la calle Reyes Católicos donde estaba el café, daban gritos de viva la república, ... algunos llevaban la bandera tricolor', Vicente Castillo, *Recuerdos y vivencias*, Tomo I, p. 54–5, online text at https://granada.cntait.org/content/recuerdos-y-vivencias-vi

157   Gerald Brenan, *The Spanish Labyrinth* (Cambridge: CUP, 1943, 2nd edition 1971), p. xv.

158   Quoted in Paul Preston, *The Spanish Holocaust. Inquisition and Extermination in Twentieth-century Spain* (London: Harper Press, 2012, pbk 2013), p. xiii.

159   General Queipo de Llano was buried in the Macarena Basilica in Seville with full military honours. Protesters have currently threatened to file a lawsuit against the Andalusian regional government if his remains are not removed in the immediate future, in accordance with the Anda-lusian government's law of Historical Memory passed in 2017 making it illegal to glorify pro-Franco heroes of the Civil War in the region.

160   Quoted by Paul Preston, *The Spanish Holocaust*, p. 46.

161   'aquella noche los que resistían en el Albaicín se retiraron hacia las mon-tañas, camino a La Peza, ... Guadix, Colomera', quoted by Francisco José Fernández Andújar in 'La resistencia anarquista en el Albaicín (julio de 1936) Los inicios de la Guerra Civil en Granada', *Revista del CEHGR*, 31, 2019, p. 215.

162   The term 'Reds' or 'rojos' was used by the fascist rebels to describe the Republicans, due to their left-leaning ideology.

163   'alrededor de las dos me despertó el ruido de un camion y varios auto-móviles que subían la colina hacia el Cementerio, y poco después oí una descarga de fusilería, y luego los vehículos que regresan' quoted in Miguel Ángel del Arco Blanco, '1936. La Granada de aquel Verano. Una ciudad entre Victoria y muerte' in *Unidad cívica por la República*, 14 August 2011, available online at www.unidadcivicaporlarepublica.es/index.php/nuestra-memoria/la-guerra-civil/2252-1936-la-granada-de-aquel-verano-una-ciudad-entre-la-victoria-y-la-muerte

164   Ibid.

165   Ibid.

166   Pilar García-Trevijano, 'Los campos de concentración franquistas de Granada', *Ideal*, 28 March, 2019 at www.ideal.es/granada/trece-puntos-represion-20190328222058-nt.html

167 Interview with Lorca published in *La Voz,* Madrid, 18 February 1935, p. 3.

168 Coincidentally Lorca's baptismal name was 'Federico del Sagrado Corazón de Jesús', 'Frederick of the Sacred Heart of Jesus'.

169 Federico García Lorca, *Obras completas,* p. 1609.

170 'Fue un momento malísimo… aunque digan lo contrario en las escuelas. Se perdieron una civilización admirable, una poesía, una astronomía, una arquitectura y una delicadeza únicas en el mundo, para dar paso a una ciudad pobre, acobardada; a una tierra de chavicol donde se agita actualmente la peor burguesía de España.' An interview with the journalist Gil Benumeya in 1931, *Obras completas,* p. 1639.

171 '… el Albaicín miedoso y fantástico, el de los ladridos de perros y de guitarras dolientes, el de las noches oscuras en estas calles de tapias blancas, el Albaicín trágico de la superstición, de las brujas echadoras de cartas y nigrománticas, el de los raros ritos de gitanos, … el de los signos cabalísticos y amuletos, el de las almas en pena, el de las embarazadas, el Albaicín de las prostitutas viejas que saben del mal de ojo, el de las seductoras, el de las maldiciones sangrientas, el pasional … Todo lo que tienen de tranquilo y majestuoso la Vega y la ciudad lo tiene de angustia y de tragedia este barrio morisco'. *Obras Completas,* pp. 1475–7.

172 '… que expresara, que cantara, que gritara a los cuatro vientos esta belleza viva y sangrante de Granada, esta belleza irresistible, que tiene espada y que hiere como la música'. Ibid., p. 1550.

173 The building is now the Hotel Reina Cristina, with a main entrance in Calle Tablas, and serves excellent food.

174 Quoted in Paul Preston, *The Spanish Holocaust: Inquisition and Extermination in Twentieth-century Spain* (London: Harper Press, 2012, pbk 2013), from a radio interview with Ricardo Rodríguez Jiménez, p. 463–4.

175 'El viajero poco avisado encontrará con la variación increíble de formas, de paisaje, de luz y de olor la sensación de que Granada es capital de un reino con arte y literatura propios, y hallará una curiosa mezcla de la Granada judía y la Granada morisca, aparentemente fundidos por el cristianismo, pero vivas e insobornables en su ignorancia. La prodigiosa mole de la catedral, el gran sello imperial y romano de Carlos V, no evita la tiendecilla del judío que reza ante una imagen hecha con la plata del candelabro de los siete brazos, como los sepulcros de los Reyes Católicos no han evitado que la media luna salga a veces en el pecho de los más finos hijos de Granada. La lucha sigue oscura y sin expresión…; sin expresión, no, que en la colina roja de la ciudad hay dos palacios, muertos los dos: la Alhambra y el palacio de Carlos V, que sostienen el duelo a muerte que late en la conciencia del granadino actual.' *Obras Completas,* p. 9–10.

11. Veiled Voices: Granadan women

176 Arie Schippers, 'The role of women in medieval Andalusian storytelling' in *Verse and the Fair Sex: Studies in Arabic Poetry and in the Representation of Women in Arabic Literature,* a collection of papers presented at the Fifteenth Congress of the Union Européene des Arabisants et des Islamisants (Utrecht/Driebergen, September 13–19, 1990), ed. Frederick de Jong (Utrecht: Publications of the M. Th. Houstma Stichting, 1993), p. 141.

177 Ibid., p. 147–8.

178 Quoted in María J. Viguera, 'On the social status of Andalusi women' in

The Legacy of Muslim Spain, vol. II, p. 714.

179 Dossier 1852, item 18, referred to in E. Santiago Simon, 'Algo más sobre la sultana madre de Boabdil' in *Homenaje al profesor Darío Cabanelas Rodríguez, o.f.m. con motivo de su LXX aniversario, Tomo I, Granada,* 1997, p. 491.

180 For fuller details on Isabel de Solís, see José Enrique Lopez de Coca, 'The Making of Isabel de Solis' in *Medieval Spain: Culture, Conflict and Coexistence,* Studies in Honour of Angus Mackay, eds. Roger Collins and Anthony Goodman (Basingstoke: Palgrave Macmillan, 2002), pp. 225–41.

181 The antiquarian scholar Fernando Osorio y Altamirano compared La Cava and Zoraya, blaming the latter for the loss of the Muslim kingdom. See Miguel Lafuente Alcántara, *Historia de Granada, comprendiendo la de las cuatro provincias, Almería, Jaén, Granada y Málaga, desde remotos tiempos hasta nuestros días,* Vol. 3, (Granada: Imprenta Librería Sanz, 1843–46), p. 33–4.

182 See Francisco Javier Martínez Medina, 'La abadía del Sacromonte y su legado artístico-cultural' in *¿La historia inventada? Los libros plúmbeos y el legado sacromontano,* eds. Manuel Barrios Aguilera and Mercedes García-Arenal (Granada: Fundación El Legado Andalusí and Universidad de Granada, 2008), p. 281, note 90.

183 The Monasterio de la Concepción in the Albaicín and the Convento de San José de las Carmelitas Descalzas in the Realejo district are both open to visitors nowadays and have fine chapels and altarpieces.

184 See Amelina Correa Ramón, *Plumas femeninas en la literatura de Granada (siglos VIII-XX)* (Granada:

Universidad/Diputación de Granada, 2002), pp. 316–20.

185 The penitential garment of the Inquisition, consisting of a type of poncho with a hole for the head, adorned with different symbols depending on the status of the penitent.

12. Memories, Maps and Museums: Constructing the New Cityscape

186 Caja Granada is a foundation based in the city that maintains and disseminates Granada's cultural heritage.

187 See www.mapamemoriagranada.es/, the website created by the association Granada Republicana UCAR with the assistance of history specialists from the University of Granada and the Archive of Granada County Council and the Municipal Archive of Granada.

188 Joe Strummer (1952–2002) was a British rock musician whose band The Clash was part of the first wave of punk rock. When the band began to fall apart, he fled to Granada, where he was eventually honoured by having a square named after him.

189 The Avenida 18 de Julio was named after the day in 1936, at the start of the Civil War, when Franco led an uprising of the Spanish army based in Morocco.

190 Laurie Lee, *A Rose for Winter* (London: Penguin, 1955), p. 73.

191 The Museo José Guerrero is in Calle Oficios 8, near the Plaza Bib-Rambla, and displays his work along with exhibitions of the work of contemporary artists.

192 See Juan Antonio Sánchez Muñoz, 'La Alcaicería de Granada: Realidad y ficción' in *La Cultura y la Ciudad* (Granada: Universidad de Granada, 2016), pp. 673–80 for a fuller

discussion of the old silk market as a tourist enclave.

193   Major festivals of Granada in chronological order, starting on 2 January: el Día de la Toma (Day of Surrender), Saint Cecilius Day, Holy Week, Mariana Pineda day, Corpus Christi, Virgin of the Sorrows, Vow to the Christ of Saint Augustine, Columbus Day, Vow to the Virgin of the Rosary, Vow to the Virgen of the Sorrows (Earthquakes), Christmas.

194   See www.cam.ac.uk/musicandgranadas past for a detailed discussion of *la fiesta de la toma* in the context of music and politics.

195   https://twitter.com/vox_es/status/1080418155992940545?ref_src=twsrc%5E. The tweet also contains a clip from the popular TV series *Isabel* showing the moment of Boabdil's surrender to the Catholic Kings.

196   Quoted in Nader Masarwah and Abdallah Tarabieh, 'Longing for Granada in Medieval Arabic and Hebrew Poetry', *Al-Masaq: Journal of the Medieval Mediterranean*, 26:3, (2014), p. 304–5 and 314.

197   See William Granara, 'Nostalgia, Arab nationalism, and the Andalusian Chronotype in the evolution of the modern Arabic novel', *Journal of Arabic Literature*, XXXVI, 1, 2005, pp. 57–73.

198   Quoted in Jonathan H. Shannon, 'Performing al-Andalus, Remembering al-Andalus: Mediterranean Soundings from Mashriq to Maghrib' in *The Journal of American Folklore*, Vol. 120, no. 477 (Summer 2007), p. 327. This article provides a valuable full account of the creation of cultural identity in modern Syria and Morocco through Andalusian music and culture.

199   Laurie Lee, *A Rose for Winter*, p. 60.

200   Carlos was interviewed by Dr Chris Moreh, a specialist in migration and mobilities, in 2011.

201   See Stephen Starr, 'Syrians find a home in the land of the Moors', *The National* at www.thenational.ae/lifestyle/syrians-find-a-home-in-the-land-of-the-moors-1.737624 of 07/06/2018.

13. Epilogue: Vanished Eden or Paradise Regained?

202   Ibn Zamrak, translated by L. P. Harvey, *Islamic Spain 1250–1500* (Chicago: Chicago University Press, 1990), p. 219.

203   Northrop Frye, *Anatomy of Criticism: Four Essays* (Princeton: Princeton University Press, 1957), p. 346.

204   Blas Infante was executed by the Nationalists in Seville in 1936.

205   Andrew Graham-Dixon, *The Art of Spain*, DVD 2010, TV broadcast 2008.

IMAGE CREDITS

• •

INDEX

◆◆◆◆◆◆◆◆◆◆◆◆◆◆◆◆◆◆